UTSA DT LIBRARY RENEWALS 458-2440

DATE DUE

GAYLORD			PRINTED IN U.S.A.

RESPONDING TO TERRORISM

Responding to Terrorism
Political, Philosophical and Legal Perspectives

ROBERT IMRE
University of Newcastle, Australia

T. BRIAN MOONEY
Singapore Management University, Singapore

BENJAMIN CLARKE
University of Notre Dame, Australia

ASHGATE

Published by
Ashgate Publishing Limited
Gower House
Croft Road
Aldershot
Hampshire GU11 3HR
England

Ashgate Publishing Company
Suite 420
101 Cherry Street
Burlington, VT 05401-4405
USA

Ashgate website: http://www.ashgate.com

British Library Cataloguing in Publication Data
Responding to terrorism : political, philosophical and
    legal perspectives
    1. Terrorism 2. Terrorism - Prevention
    I. Title II. Mooney, T. Brian III. Clarke, Benjamin
    363.3'25

Library of Congress Cataloging-in-Publication Data
Responding to terrorism : political, philosophical and legal perspectives / by Robert Imre, T. Brian Mooney, and Benjamin Clarke.
        p. cm.
    Includes index.
    ISBN 978-0-7546-7277-7
    1. Terrorism. 2. Terrorism--Prevention. I. Mooney, T. Brian. II. Clarke, Benjamin. III. Title.

    HV6431.I477 2008
    363.325--dc22
                                                2007041399
ISBN 978 0 7546 7277 7

Printed and bound in Great Britain by TJ International Ltd, Padstow, Cornwall.

Contents

Acknowledgements

A book of this sort, being a collaborative effort, is the product not just of the authors but of all those influences both personal and professional that have sustained the authors throughout their academic careers. Collectively, the authors would like to acknowledge the sources of this support over many years provided particularly by our teachers and the students whom we have the privilege to run our ideas up against on a daily basis. We are also grateful to the participants in the original public seminars delivered at The University of Notre Dame, Australia, who stimulated and improved our thinking and indeed provided us with the impetus to turn the seminars into this book. In this respect Professor Greg Craven one of the original moderators of the public seminars deserves special mention as an encouraging influence. We would also like to thank the Research Assistants at Singapore Management University, Swati Chaudhary, Meera Ravindra Kanhere, Wong, Jan Ee and (Lydia) Khan, Cheng Wah, for their invaluable help in proof-reading and formatting the final text.

In addition, T. Brian Mooney would like to thank John Williams, Michael Levine, Alan Tapper, Alasdair MacIntyre, Fr. Tom Ryan SM and Pat, Fionnuala and Thomas for all their support. Versions of several of the part chapters contained in this volume were presented at The Australasian Association of Philosophy Conference, Canberra, in 2006 and at The National University of Singapore Philosophy Department in 2007, the comments and criticisms advanced at these venues by participants were invaluable in improving the content of my contributions. The Office of Research at Singapore Management University has been incredibly supportive of this research and I would gratefully like to acknowledge this, particularly to the Vice-Provost of research, Bobby Mariano, and the Dean of Social Sciences, David Chan.

Rob Imre and Ben Clarke wrote chapters under a heavy teaching load, and no research assistants to gather facts. As such, they would like to thank both their students, who suffered through their arguments, and their colleagues, who suffered through the endless discussions and rehashing of the arguments.

Ben Clarke would also like to thank Kieran Tranter of Griffith University Law School for his comments on the liberal theory of rights and justice and its relevance to a legal analysis of terrorism.

Introduction

This book has its origins in a series of public lectures delivered between August and October, 2005, at the University of Notre Dame Australia. The University of Notre Dame Australia has close links with its sister university in South Bend, Indiana, as well as with many other Catholic universities in the United States of America. Large numbers of American students attend the Australian campus in Fremantle each semester. I remember with great sadness the pain and fear that beset the American students as news started to filter through the campus of the tragic events of September the 11th. A pain that, not much later, was to echo so starkly among Australians after the Bali bombings and which reverberates throughout London, Madrid and, of course, which is tragically played out every day in the Middle East. What also remains so striking was the sort of debates that occurred in tutorials and seminars throughout the University in the aftermath of September the 11th. It must be admitted that a climate of grief and fear is not the most conducive to rational debate, and there was certainly some degree of insensitivity on the part of some students who were only too ready to blame American foreign policy as the ultimate source for the attacks. What I found most remarkable was the lack of consensus, not just about what needs to be done about terrorism but also the levels of confusion about what constitutes terrorism, its motivations and sources. Clearly, more understanding is needed and this book offers a series of reflections on some of the key issues related to contemporary terrorism. The book is by no means exhaustive – it does not pretend to address every issue or even to offer comprehensive solutions or understandings. Rather it implicitly points to the complexity of the phenomenon of contemporary terrorism and offers a series of meditations (*contemplationes*) as to how we may begin to understand and thus to act.

One of the major benefits of having delivered the original sets of talks, aside from the valuable comments made by students, fellow academics and members of the public, was the opportunity it afforded for each of the authors to evaluate the stances taken by the others and to incorporate these perspectives into the final product that now confronts the reader. In this sense the book is very much an interdisciplinary and transdisciplinary effort. The arguments presented by the authors are representative of their own positions speaking from within the context of their own disciplines – politics, philosophy and law – but nonetheless are nuanced and elaborated within the context of the original dialogues.

If there is a discernible unity of vision among the authors it may well be sought in their concern to further our understandings of the conditions of injustice, a concern that is mediated through the Catholic tradition – the Catholic tradition conceived of as a dialogue and not a set of monolithic dogmas.

Chapter 1 focuses on the causes of terrorism and offers some insights into possible means to deal with the phenomenon. Imre in 'The Socio-politics of Terror: Poverty,

Evil, Statecraft and Modernity' (Chapter 1.1), situates the problem by way of an attempt to dispel what he takes to be the myth that there are readily discoverable and simplistic cause and effect relationships between and among social phenomena. He argues that the 'vulgar social science' approach is not a great deal of use in terms of attempting to understand the motivations of terrorists as individuals or as groups. In suggesting this he employs four categories that are of interest to political theorists and social scientists. In the first part of Chapter 1.1 he analyzes the idea of poverty and claims that terrorism might develop in areas of the world stricken by poverty. Nevertheless, there needs to be a number of other socio-political factors involved before 'poor' people are radicalized enough to resort to political and/or religious violence. Secondly, he proceeds to analyze the concept of evil in our (post)modern age and claims that evil has no place in terrorist activity: neither in understanding nor in halting such political and/or religious violence since we are decades beyond the banalization of the idea. Thirdly, he claims that one of the problems with liberal democracies is that they have lost the value of statecraft. This has become increasingly prevalent in the post-World War II period, partially due to the fact that European empires have tried to aid the decolonization of the world and have found little need for the paternalism of the past, and thus we have seen successive governments attempt to retreat into isolationism and lash out with massive military force when such isolationisms are threatened. Finally, he argues that the modern nation-state and its relationship to politics from the end of the 1800s until today and probably into the near future will continue to foster and develop both religious and political terrorism. There are too many inherent contradictions to allow for a series of religious and political *disidenten* to remain peaceable.

In 'An International Law Approach' (Chapter 1.2) Clarke, as the title suggests, explores the causes and cures of terrorism from a legal perspective. His analysis takes its thrust from the growth of Islamist violence in the contemporary world. This is attributed, for the most part, to violations of international law. He highlights such breaches as: (1) sovereign rights (foreign invasion, military occupation, and economic domination); (2) peoples' rights (denial of self-determination); and (3) international humanitarian and human rights law (torture of detainees, denial of basic rights and freedoms). He goes on to suggest that the failure of international organizations to protect Muslim populations from the above violations of the rule of international law has contributed to the emergence of radical Islamist organizations, and that the militant ideologies of these groups resonate with disenfranchised populations who see no viable solution to their problems other than violence. On the positive side of the argument Clarke argues for a variety of UN Charter-based cures to terrorism. These include the implementation of the General Assembly's *Global Counter-Terrorism Strategy*. This strategy envisages states working together to dissuade disaffected groups from pursing their goals through terrorism; denying terrorists the means to carry out their attacks; deterring States from engaging in or supporting terrorism; developing state capacity to prevent the emergence of networks and organizations that promote religious violence; and defending fundamental rights and freedoms during the struggle to end terrorism. While highlighting the importance of recourse to peace dispute mechanisms to end state-sponsored terrorism, he acknowledges the inevitability of the use of force to disrupt, disband or destroy terror networks of non-state actors that refuse to surrender or submit to the international rule of law.

Chapter 2 addresses the vexed question as to whether the use of torture is justifiable or effective. It is recognized that even asking this question carries with it certain implications – it entertains what for many is beyond discussion, and the very asking of the question may seem to lend legitimacy to such considerations. Nevertheless, the failure to take seriously the fact that torture is widely used both historically and in contemporary treatment of 'terrorists' would imply a major failing in this work.

In 'Torture Works: But not on Terrorists' (Chapter 2.1), Imre examines the phenomenon of torture as it is embedded in a socio-political framework. His central claim is that torture is a highly effective means of social control, however, that this form of social control can fail with spectacular results. His analysis leads him to conclude that given the evidence of authoritarian, and other regimes around the world, it is clear that torture is an excellent way to ensure that populations are kept terrorized, in a very literal sense, and thus social order is maintained. The effect on people who are potentially violent critics of political regimes is to harden their positions against those said regimes. In this way, it matters little that the political regime is liberal democratic, a social democracy, authoritarian, or a version of Marxist–Leninist: the outcome will be the same. That is to say, radicals will be radicalized to act on their principles, and this radicalization will be furthered by their followers at least partially due to the torture of their newly developed group. Further, he argues that torture always works to solidify a victim mentality or world view so that individuals and groups of all kinds, radical, radicalized, or none of the above, will reject the legitimacy of the state. Only socio/psychopathic individuals will accept state legitimacy after experiencing torture. It is thus that torture works, but not on terrorists.

In 'Torture, Tragedy and Natural Law' (Chapter 2.2), I argue that the question of the justifiability of torture must be viewed within the broader moral problem of 'dirty hands' and that contemporary *act* evaluative theories of ethics such as consequentialism and deontology fail to attend to crucial dimensions of *agent* evaluation in the ethical assessment of torture. I present the 'mixed' act/agent accounts of moral evaluation in the Natural Law tradition as presented particularly in St Thomas Aquinas as more coherent in dealing with the nature of tragedy and tragic choice in ethics. I then turn to contemporary Catholic teaching as formulated in *Veritatis Spendor* and *Evangelium Vitae* and their absolutist prohibitions on torture as *intrinsece malum*. I argue that Augustine's and Aquinas's accounts of the private/public distinction may help focus our thinking on the justifiability of torture in extreme circumstances while still acknowledging the intrinsic evil of torture. I end with an argument by analogy suggesting that while St Thomas has an absolutist prohibition on lying nevertheless are occasions when what appears to be a lie is in fact not and that a similar casuistical argument can be outlined for the tragic use of torture.

In 'Terrorism, Torture and the Rule of Law' (Chapter 2.3), Clarke explores the effectiveness, legality, and strategic consequences of the use of torture as a counter-terrorism tool. He does so by assessing the practice of certain states that have used coercive interrogation methods on terror suspects; critically appraising whether such conduct can be reconciled with fundamental human rights/norms, and at a deeper level, with the rule of law itself; and, analyzing the damage that torture does to efforts to win the 'hearts and minds' of local populations and others whose support is crucial to the success of counter-terrorism operations. Throughout he highlights rule of law-based 'lessons learned' from military and policing operations where torture was used against terror suspects and others.

Chapter 3 addresses issues related to the impact of globalization on terrorism. In 'Legal Aspects of Globalization' (Chapter 3.1), Clarke explores the relationship between processes of globalization and the proliferation of terror organizations. He highlights the role diaspora communities have played in the export and financing of ethnic and religious conflict, including terrorist campaigns from Northern Ireland to Sri Lanka. The use of global communication and media technology by terrorist organizations to disseminate ideological and propaganda messages are noted. The impact of colonialism and nationalist struggles in contested territory are also explored. The Zionist struggle for a Jewish state in Palestine and the corresponding question of an Arab state in Palestine are examined in some detail. The consequent escalation of extremism in the Middle East is traced, and the connection between the rise of Islamist terror and the failure of the international legal order to offer dispossessed Palestinians a just resolution is highlighted. The catastrophic growth of sectarian violence in Iraq since 2003 is also critiqued. Having assessed these trends, a range of responses to ethnic and religious terrorism are posited.

In 'Terrorism, Story-Telling and Existential Communication' (Chapter 3.2), I argue that our inability to fully understand terrorism is directly attributable to broader failures in our understanding of moral philosophy and ultimately to failures in grounding a universal concept of rationality. The range of fundamental disagreements in respect to issues of deeply held beliefs in philosophy and everyday life is extraordinary. Clearly the domain of the religious is one central arena of deeply cherished but fundamental beliefs which radically diverge. Here we may think of the disputes that often violently divide the Muslim from the Jew, the Hindu from the Buddhist and all of the religious traditions from the atheist. This is true not just between religions but within religious traditions as is so painfully witnessed in the internecine conflict between various Christian denominations as too the tensions between the Sunni and Shia factions of Islam. Such religious disagreements are often enough supervened by political dimensions. In philosophy too, whole departments in the academies have fallen apart on deeply held beliefs. The sheer amount and intensity of contested beliefs surely forces us to ask whether there is a position or positions (beliefs) that are incontestably true. The battlefield of warring beliefs apparently suggests a negative response. The late philosopher David Lewis wrote that: 'Whether or not it would be nice to knock disagreeing philosophers down by sheer force of argument, it cannot be done ... . Once the menu of well-worked out theories is before us, philosophy is a matter of opinion.' But should the discussion end as perilously as so many contemporary writers think? Does it all come down to the shrill clamor of assertion and counter assertion as Alasdair MacIntyre thinks? Here I argue that there are strategies to continue conversations at an even more meaningful level than on the basis of competing conceptions of reason. I propose 'story-telling' and an account of emotional relatedness as two such strategies before presenting an account of the *pathemata* (the experiences we fatefully undergo) that underlies such strategies.

In 'The Politics of Religious Violence' (Chapter 3.3), Imre asks two main questions, firstly, is religious violence different from terrorism in general, and secondly, is religious violence, and by implication, political violence under the general rubric of 'terrorism', anathema to liberal democracy? He claims that all kinds of political violence are intimately linked to democracy and democratic change. Religious symbols and religious organizations have been linked to change towards and away from democracies in the modern period. As proof he points to the shifts in political legitimation in Poland from the 1950s to the 1980s, and the cooptation of Orthodox Christian symbols in Russia by the Bolsheviks. He also claims that there is, and will continue to be in the near future, a clear *modus operandi* for groups seeking, and eventually gaining political and social change, by the use of force, in all kinds of societies. He claims further that we are probably witnessing the change of said violence into a generalized kind of religious violence. This means that the danger of the 'new' version of a religious terrorist is that they are performing for God and not for the international media. Thus, by the time we have realized that all we need to do to shut down the PLO in the 1970s is to not publicize anything they do, the world has passed us all by. Today, it is immaterial whether or not the global media sees Bin Laden, or other similar manifestations, the terrorism will continue in the eyes of God. If religious terrorism becomes the dominant mode of violent political change, then there is no real way to stop the phenomenon, except by divine intervention.

The final chapter addresses a variety of public-policy, social theory and moral questions associated with contemporary terrorism. In 'Bungle in, Bungle out, Muddle through' (Chapter 4.1), Imre provides an assessment of some administrative, public policy, and social policy approaches that are designed to deal with terrorists and terror organizations. He utilizes some key examples such as the FLQ and Sikh terrorist organizations in Canada, the RAF in West Germany, the Red Brigades in Italy, and the Weather Underground in the USA. His main thesis is that modern and post-modern bureaucracies are very limited in their capacity to deal with the terrorist phenomenon. He claims that the move from the banalization of human experience (characterized by the post-World War II period) to the 'governmentality' of the late modern period (characterized by the post-Cold War era), has provided us with both limitations and opportunities in how we deal with terrorism. Underlying this part chapter is at least one central claim that modern bureaucracies have only the capacity to bungle these major problems, and that muddling through will be democracy's saving grace.

In 'Effective Counter-Terrorism: Sound Foreign Policy, Intelligence Gathering, Policing, Social Engineering, and Necessary Use of Force' (Chapter 4.2), Clarke posits a policy framework to help defeat rather than ferment international terrorism. Counter-terrorism law and policy in Australia is critiqued in this context. Particular attention is paid to the role of intelligence agencies and their relationship with government. This discussion links into consideration of how foreign policy can help or hurt counter-terrorism initiatives. He also examines the importance of regional cooperation, and capacity building, particularly in regions where developing states may be vulnerable to infiltration by terrorist groups. The effectiveness of counter-terrorism policies is also considered by reference to a range of operational factors including the need for adequate resources, training, and community support to enable counter-terrorism activities to be conducted successfully over the short, medium and long term.

In 'Just War and Terrorism' (Chapter 4.3), I argue that the tragic unfolding of world events since 11 September 2001 has added great urgency to practical and theoretical issues arising from the phenomenon of international terrorism. I apply a traditional concept of just war theory drawing largely on Aquinas and Augustine to legitimate violent action against groups who are not (or need not be) themselves representatives of states. Traditional just war theory is couched largely in terms of the legitimacy of defensive war directed at polities. I argue that new applications of the theory are required to deal with contemporary international terrorism. In presenting a new application of the theory I argue that the purely defensive conception of just war advocated in recent Catholic Church documents and taken up by some contemporary theologians and philosophers is problematic. In dialogue, particularly with Joseph Boyle, I maintain that traditional just war theory provides the salient criteria for a polity's violent actions against groups that are not themselves, or at least need not be, polities – including actions that may be characterized as punitive rather than purely defensive in nature. The traditional concept of just war is in this respect more coherent.

T. Brian Mooney
Singapore Management University

Chapter 1

Terrorism: Causes and Cures

1.1   The Socio-politics of Terror: Poverty, Evil, Statecraft and Modernity

Rob Imre

In this part of the chapter I challenge the notion that we can discover simplistic cause and effect relationships between and among socio-political phenomenon. This means that the 'vulgar social science' approach is not a great deal of use in terms of attempting to understand the motivations of terrorists as individuals or as groups. I have done this by using four categories that are of interest to political theorists and social scientists. In the first section I analyze the idea of poverty and claim that terrorism might develop in areas of the world stricken by poverty, but there needs to be a number of other socio-political factors involved before 'poor' people are radicalised enough to resort to political and/or religious violence. I then analyze the concept of evil in our (post)modern age and claim that evil has no place in terrorist activity: neither in understanding nor in halting such political and/or religious violence since we are decades beyond the banalization of the idea. Thirdly, I also claim that one of the problems with liberal democracies is that they have lost the value of statecraft. Statecraft has been replaced by 'spin', cynical diplomacy, and has little to do with visionary solutions to some of the grave problems facing the globe. Finally, I argue that the modern nation-state and its relationship to politics from the end of the 1800s until today and probably into the near future will continue to foster and develop both religious and political terrorism. The homogeneous sets of categories social scientists sometimes use leave us with a kind of 'groupism' according to Rogers Brubaker (2004) in which the multi-layered identities of individuals are placed into groups and are thus claimed to operate with degrees of exclusionism. It is with this part of this chapter that I frame later more specific treatments of terrorism and it is thus that I claim that looking for systematic cause and effect might not be altogether enough to do away with the violence.

In this part, I examine the social and political context of the phenomenon of terrorism. My contribution to this chapter is concerned with treating terrorism as a dynamic and constantly shifting phenomenon that can be contextualized, that can be examined as a phenomenon with countervailing social forces, and as a political problem that we can situate in the midst of the politics of particular nation-states and (non-exclusive) groups within those nation-states. In doing so, it leads us to a number of analytical questions about terrorism including, but not limited to, the following set of problems. Can terrorism be grounded in a particular set of cause and effect relationships? If we examine political and sociological contexts, will we somehow end up with a series of causes that show specific linkages and then take us through to specific end-points? This is a broad topic and could lead to any number of things about terrorism. For example, one of the major issues is the so-called Islamic fundamentalist phenomenon.[1] There are also political problems such as the failure of the United States and its major European allies to understand the implications of the Iranian Revolution and the politics leading up to the 1979 revolution. First, the United States' Central Intelligence Agency (CIA) aiding in the demise of the Iranian leader Mossadeq in 1953 and bringing back the 'Shah' and then looking the other way when the Shah begins to treat his people so poorly; and secondly the Carter administration being forced out of office largely due to the failure to gain the release of hostages held in Iran immediately following the revolution. The first example offers a kind of demonstration of the demise of statecraft thesis: placing short-term economic and strategic concerns above long-term strategies. The second example about Carter shows the change in the nature of terrorism and terrorist forces by offering a new kind of approach beyond the typical bomb-lobbing campaigns that dominated the landscape from the Russian anarchists of the turn of the 20th century to the IRA bombers in the post-World War II period. It makes hostage-taking and negotiation the way forward for terrorist organizations and it delivers the Reagan administration the reasons for secretly dealing in arms trading with right-wing groups in Latin America and other parts of the world.[2] This is one of the indications of the change in terrorist tactics at this particular time.

However I should like to discuss causes and cures of terrorism as a socio-political phenomenon in broad terms in order to discover any potential links with the big causes and possible effects. As mentioned above I shall discuss the effects of poverty, the question of evil, address the demise of statecraft as a problem for recent governments, and examine the problem of the modern nation-state.

Poverty

This is a socio-political problem that has been with us throughout the ages, but in the modern period we see a different kind of character develop with poverty. What I mean by this is to say that poverty is not the result of regions of the world that are somehow disconnected or separated from the rest of the world. In fact, as we see modernity develop, we also see greater and greater connections with varieties of people from around the world. Poverty might be considered as a part of the emerging global social order in the post-Cold War world.[3] We see multinational corporations with the capacity to spread their products everywhere, we see televisions with the capacity to spread their messages of prosperity and consumerism, and we also see the closing of national borders and the attempts to limit and demonize the movement

---

1 A number of analysts have questioned the notion of 'fundamentalism' as a phenomenon and two excellent sources are Olivier Roy (2004) and Jeroen Gunning (2007).

2 The idea about never negotiating with terrorists is simply false and this 'negotiation' has in fact always occurred in one form or another. The notion of negotiation as a particular relationship between terrorists and nation-states deserves greater attention in the analyses of terrorism as a phenomenon.

3 See Bauman's *Wasted Lives* (2004) for a treatment of this issue.

of migrants. Poverty then inherits the liberal notion of individual responsibility in a kind of warped way in which liberal democracies now have the capacity to reinforce divisions among nation-states to such an extent that we can actually blame the poor and get away with it! In a kind of neo-Dickensian version of our understanding of poverty, globalization delivers the ultimate tautology for poverty. People are poor because they are poor.

What I mean by this is that if we are all operating within some version of a globalized liberal democratic/capitalist paradigm, then it becomes easy to claim that people living in the Global South are poor in terms of their gross incomes compared to the Global North, their lower wages buy more, and their lives are also less complicated. This is incorrect on at least three fronts. First, purchasing power parity indices tell us something else: the poor in the Global South are still quite badly off.[4] Secondly, the 'lives less complicated' argument, or in more colloquial terms those living in the Global South are often referred to by tourists as being 'poor but happy', is clearly an argument about the powerless delivered by the powerful in the contemporary global world. And thirdly, being poor in the Global South, or anywhere else, is most often not a matter of choice. As such the only pathway out of this problem for a large number of the global population is through migration which is made increasingly more difficult in the post-Cold War period.

In today's globalized context we are left with a situation in which people are poor, they know they are poor because the global media outlets tell them so, and they seek to change their circumstances and move in to non-poverty. This leads to all kinds of conflicts in which the struggle for power in nation-states in the Global South can be directly related to their attempts to climb out of poverty. But the question here is: does this directly cause terrorism? Do various groups, mired in grinding poverty, seek political violence that will overthrow a given political order? And will these various groups couple this protest with religion thus adding a spiritual dimension to their struggle and as a result complicating possible responses? Would we have the types of madrasses that we do, which are very different from similar South Asian institutions of pre-partition India, if this grinding poverty did not exist in South Asia and if various Arab groups from Saudi Arabia and Egypt, among others, were not exploiting this misery? Would we have the continual cycle of genocidal violence that exists around the world if we did not have the huge amount of arms shipments from the producers in the Global North to consumers in the Global South, who are trying to shore up their scarce resources against perceived local threats? And if the citizens and the denizens of those nation-states in the Global South were able to meet their basic needs of food, clean water, shelter, clothing, freedom from disease, freedom from oppression and so on, then would we have political problems with violence, terrorism, and religious terrorism/violence that we do today?

These linkages certainly do exist but this does not necessarily mean that there is a direct cause and effect relationship between poverty and the contemporary problem of terrorism. It does mean that it provides an important ideological justification for terrorism if terrorist groups can identify themselves as victims of the modern

---

4 The United Nations, World Bank, and *The Economist* magazine, as three different sources, will all confirm this in some detail.

globalization process that is driven by wealthy Global North nation-states. This means, of course, that terrorists need not be living in poverty themselves, but need only identify with the victimization. Some of the most intractable conflicts in the contemporary world, and the modern period, have little to do with a situation in which groups of people are kept poor relative to their co-nationals or co-religionists. But if we look at this as a human security issue, we can see a somewhat different problem emerging (Thomas 2000). There is also an all too obvious ethical dimension to this problem that I am deliberately steering away from: the claim that there should be a normative challenge to getting rid of poverty. My examination here is somewhat different in that I am asking about direct links to political violence.

In treating this as a human security issue and examining a set of concerns that link poverty to a greater global security concern, human security has become one of the leading paradigms in political science. According to this view, there are a set number of types of 'non-traditional' security problems that are usually also transnational problems (Terriff *et al.* 2003). The typical sorts of problems are grouped into categories that involve the environment, access to education, health care, clean water, and a regular food supply. And most human security analysts agree that we need to ensure human security of all kinds. We have the means and the capacity to do so, and yet we do not. There is easily enough food on the planet in this globalized era, easily enough money around to cure major Global South diseases like malaria but we'd rather spend it on Viagra, and we'd rather accept the corporate argument that we need to patent seeds that can only be used in one growing season and need massive amounts of chemicals to support their growth because 'the world needs cheaper food'. This is not the case. The world has plenty of food. We just don't let everyone eat. We can argue about who gets which cars and who gets the big TV screens after everyone gets fed and has access to drinking water and the basic necessities of life. All of which is completely possible under current objective world conditions. Poverty continues to be the great breeding ground of terrorism and provides justification for some terrorist movements around the world but we still cannot make an objective link between the two. Most especially displaced groups living in refugee camps such as the Palestinians in Jordan, who were exiled again as the new king of Jordan pressed them out of that territory so the double scattering of peoples has moved already radicalized Palestinians to Lebanon, Syria and Iran, and eventually some significant numbers to participate in the violence in Iraq. Eliminating poverty, ensuring that human security at all levels exist – that is to say: we have clean water, proper sanitation, and indeed equal life-chances for everyone – will go a long way to eliminate specific terrorist threats around the globe. But this is not *proof* nor is it a necessary, nor a sufficient condition for the development of terrorism and terrorist groups. Poverty cannot guarantee radicalisation, nor must it be present in order to see radicalization occur.

There is another underlying problem here when we talk about poverty. There is an assumption that greater poverty equates with less political power. With the spread of globalization, the definition of power itself changes in a number of ways (Haugaard 2002). Competing ideas about the role of the nation-state in the increasingly transnational world are dealt with later on in this part of the chapter and here I am concerned with this notion of links between radicalizing people who are relatively poor to the point where they are ready to use violent means to change their circumstances. An interesting way to conceptualize this part of the poverty problem is to examine the political circumstances of Indigenous peoples around the world. For example, if we compare the Canadian context with New Zealand and Australia, we see that there are relatively higher levels of political protest in New Zealand from Maori groups, principally about land issues, and from specific First Nations peoples in Canada. Some groups in Canada, such as the Inuit in the Nunavut territory, have a version of self-government and as such no longer participate in protests against the government: they *are* the government and have the same status as any other provincial/territorial government in the federal system of Canada. Other First Nations/Indigenous groups in Canada do not enjoy the same level of autonomy and some have engaged in violent stand-offs with various levels of government in Canada and have taken their protests further than the Maori in New Zealand. The Mohawks at Kahnasatake, for example have blockaded territory, fired guns to warn police away from their territory, and have given demands to the provincial government. Other groups in Canada have done similar things in recent years in Caledonia, Ontario, Oka, Quebec, and other parts of the country.

By contrast, there are very few organized protests, little political rebellion and certainly no violent resistance that might be considered 'terrorist' coming from Indigenous/Aboriginal groups in two other nation-states that serve to illustrate this point. In Norway and in Australia, we see Indigenous groups who are at the opposite ends of the poverty scale in terms of basic social indicators used by sociologists as well as any political science category we might choose to employ. For example, education levels (as an end result), access to education at all levels (in terms of state provisions), health care as in institutional access, general health levels, formalized dispute settling mechanisms, self-government and autonomy, constitutionally guaranteed group rights, and equalized life chances. The list goes on. As a kind of summary indicator, Sami in Norway have similar life expectancy as the average Norwegian, and have a constitutional amendment in place to protect group rights and a 'way of life' for the Sami. Most Canadian First Nations peoples, but not all, have some similar versions of self-government and/or autonomy, some have a history of treaties going back to first clashes/contact with colonizers, and have a current legal status in terms of group rights enshrined in the Canadian Bill of Rights. The New Zealand Maori have an original treaty document in the Treaty of Waitangi which guarantees their status as custodians of the land in New Zealand. In both the case of Canada and New Zealand, First Nations and Indigenous groups usually lag behind the average comparable Canadian and New Zealand citizen in most social indicators, but the lag is not nearly as severe as in the Australian Aboriginal/Indigenous/Torres Strait Islander Peoples cases. There are certainly problems in the Canadian and New Zealand context, as the life expectancy lag is roughly five years, personal income is lower than average, social and family problems exist at higher than average levels and so on. So New Zealand Maori and Canadian First Nations groups have some significant catching up to do and if we seek to bring all of this under a general rubric of 'poverty' there is some slight gap coupled with a number of political guarantees of rights. Neither is it the case that the various forms of treaties and rights built into the legal systems of New Zealand and Canada are settled cases. There is a good deal of dispute about them. But this is fundamentally different to what occurs in Australia.

The Australian case is shamefully the worst of all those mentioned previously and might be characterized among the worst treated of all Aboriginal/Indigenous groups in the developed world. Above mentioned social indicators have gaps of 17 to 20 years in terms of average life span, death in childbirth for both mothers and babies are nowhere near the Australian average and are much closer to some of the poorest parts of the developing world, there are no constitutional guarantees of group rights of any kind, no movements legal, political, juridical, social, or otherwise towards some of the many options of political autonomy or self-government by Indigenous groups from other countries and the rate of poverty is far and away highest among Australian Aboriginal groups in comparison to circumpolar northern groups such as Inuit in Canada or Sami in Scandinavia as well as the Maori in New Zealand. As such, Australian Aboriginal people ought to be the most militant, indeed even verging on terrorist, in terms of reclaiming their legitimate right to be custodians of the land, demanding guarantees of specific rights as other aggrieved minority groups, including first settler minority, around the world. In comparison, however, there is barely a whimper. Certainly no armed stand-offs, some legal action on land claims, but nothing in the way of what has happened in Canada, Scandinavia, and New Zealand. The thesis that poverty and terrorism are directly linked in terms of cause and effect cannot be the case when we examine Indigenous people around the world nor can it be the case when we see how large portions of the globe are suffering.

Evil

Evil exists and becomes banal in modern societies (Arendt 1964). This is because evil is a social product, socially constituted, and since all of modern life is subject to this banalization, so is the idea of what constitutes 'evil.' Torture, genocide, mass murder, are often the results of people 'just doing their jobs' signing the right forms, and ensuring that people remain in their rationally determined categories. This also means that, like all human relationships in the modern period, they become both commodified and institutionalized. Resistance to domination is very difficult outside of the iron cage of bureaucracy and/or capitalist modes of production. Evil is made banal just as all aspects of modern life are made banal. And here we are left with at least two problems: one is a modern problem and the other post-modern. The modern problem is the problem of the (liberal) incapacity of the social sciences to deal with the issue of evil. The best it can hope to offer is a *post facto* legal challenge to evil but only if it has been codified and placed into a liberal-constitutional legal system. For example, war crimes tribunals and tribunals dealing with genocide and crimes against humanity are increasingly more effective as a measure to prosecute individuals. But they remain after-the-fact prosecutions. Their victims are already dead. We have seen this most recently with the crimes committed during the dismantling of Yugoslavia, the genocide in Rwanda, and the genocide in Darfur.

On the other hand, the post-modern problem is one in which we see liberalism superseded by a Foucauldian 'governmentality' in which individuals now 'choose' this banalized evil as a mode of self-fulfillment that is completely unreflexive. For example, the illusion of choice permeates everything we do in contemporary society, and if we see modern (liberal) practices create a type of choice in which we do not participate in the creation of options, rather like surfing TV channels, then we are stuck with the implications of those choices even if they lead to the destruction of human lives. This means that there is a rational structure of the bureaucracy, it permeates all that we do, we can neither resist nor escape, but the problem for the neo/post-Weberians who might agree with both Foucault and Rose, is to point out that modern human beings may not *want* to resist or escape. They have made a 'choice' and the 'choice' is good (even though it might well be evil). Perhaps this is where the cosmic struggle of the religious terrorist comes in to reject these 'choices' and as such create a different kind of struggle. Terrorism then, especially when it takes the form of religious violence, might be seen to be led by philosophers, rather than 'evil' individuals.

Let us elaborate on this point for a moment. Is it evil to take human beings from their parents, homes and communities, brutalize them, and purposefully make them think they are not worth the same as others in society? It certainly is and this should be identified as such. We should be able to say that the process of colonization that occurred around the world was not merely the result of people doing their jobs and trying to get on with their daily lives, but also the result of a kind of cooperation that supported such a process. While this may not result in a legal culpability, it certainly points to a process of evil, like other modern processes that result in disenfranchisement, displacement, and in some cases murder. This seems to require a kind of Hegelian courage in that there are fewer and fewer instances in which we see people acting as political actors with choices exercising their human agency to deliver a political verdict based on 'right' politics. This is not 'right-wing' politics of the various kinds of political conservatism, but a kind of politics based on the 'right and just' decision.

Political leaders and people of all kinds must participate in order to make evil a reality experienced by perpetrators rather than a banality of modern life. The existence of evil in modern society needs all of us for it to work properly, not just the evil genius, evil dictator, or evil twin so often portrayed in place of an explanation of complex socio-political change. While political leaders in the West talk of evil-doers, so too do their terrorist opponents until it becomes a relativized slanging match with each calling the other bad people. A major cause of terrorism is our acceptance of violence and brutality and our capacity to ignore the violence and brutality that creeps into our everyday lives. We need to name this for what it is and reject it. A direct cause of terrorism in the modern era is the capacity of terrorist organizations to deliver their message through the media and deliver their message of violence to the world. This can only be done if we accept this deliverance as part of our everyday lives. A direct cause of the rise of terrorist organizations is the willingness of news outlets and popular movies to publicize and deliver a constant barrage of terrorist scenarios. Evil and evil acts of brutality and violence then become part of the background to all our lives. And once again, it is not a question of simple cause and effect used by so many 'vulgar social scientists': that is to say, this is not a debate about whether or not exposure to television violence has a detrimental, and/or desensitizing effect on viewers. And here one can substitute films, video games, news reports and the like, for television. My claim is a deeper one. That this version of banal evil permeates our lives to the extent that it is virtually ignored as it forms a kind of background noise to everything we do, or when it is made conscious, it is so deeply embedded that the relativized 'choice' of self-fulfillment can be actualized. One chooses to sign the death warrants because it happens to be a job one is good at, thus self-fulfilling, and above all, a matter of 'choice'. In a way, we could claim that we all live in a kind of Kafkaesque dystopia with no real alternative. Some have rejected this banalization in various ways and perhaps the terrorist in the contemporary world is doing this as well. Both performing for God and thinking as a philosopher, thus neither evil nor banal.

I suggest here that we reject the modern concept of the banality of evil as a way to combat terrorism. Do not allow administrative structures to dictate what we do. Demand that there be a humanization of all relations. Do not allow torture and brutality to become commonplace and an accepted mode of conduct. Do not allow war and violence to remain as accepted modes of social action. We all have the capacity to be good people and this must be encouraged. Modern societies have ensured that this banality is built into all of us. We have lived in social structures that create socio-political divisions, in many cases random ones, and then dehumanize people on the basis of some random physical characteristic. We must reject this and demand that these institutions accept human beings rather than force human beings to conform to a particular model of behaviour and attitude. The banality of evil thesis means that terrorist campaigns can be relativized and then polarized as being just as right and good as all other claims. We must end this in order to effectively do away with problems of terrorism, but we must also do so in our own societies. We must name killing as such where people are being killed. But this would also mean that some difficult realities would need to be discussed in some detail in our own polities. We would need to examine the records of our own governments first and foremost. We would need to question the various political decisions that have led to some terrible consequences in recent times as well as a real examination of the 20th century which some have characterized as the 'century of genocide.' There have been some courageous and tragic examples of this in recent years ranging from the Tiananmen Square protests, the Sarajevo marches demanding an end to the war, the North Korean dissidents who have attempted to leave their regimes behind and have been rejected by embassies in China and sent back, through to entire governments in Germany and Canada admitting to genocide and working towards reparations. These are examples of people who stood up to both tyranny as well as the banalization of evil in their lives. We must demonstrate that we have an understanding of war by demanding its end as so many people did before the outbreak of the most recent invasion of Iraq. When we incrementally increase the levels of acceptable violence in society we are doomed to experience it ourselves. A direct cure for terrorism and terrorist activities is to reject participation of terrorism at any level. This means rejecting violence at any level. This means that we categorically reject torture, we reject public officials that seek to divide us based on superficial physical attributes and we reject people's claims to the justification of the use of force for political ends.

Modern societies have shown a great capacity to shift responsibility in directions away from individuals and towards systems of blame. Modern societies have a great capacity to develop the administrative shrug of the shoulders where rules are not questioned only implemented. It is through this so-called 'proper procedures' that evil becomes banal and that terrorist ideologies can fester.

The Demise of (Great Power) Statecraft

The problem of terrorism in a globalized and unipolar world changes its meaning and function in some interesting ways. Perhaps using the terminology 'death of statecraft' is premature and somewhat sensationalist. After all diplomats still talk to each other and nation-states still make attempts at communicative action, so I shall employ the term 'demise' as referring to a process and will use this with some degree of specificity. Also, there might be cause for optimism. Perhaps statecraft can still survive in the 'middle powers', perhaps with some political actors, and perhaps much of the demise is fuelled by an uncaring and apathetic public unwilling to take politics seriously. But my concern here is that we are stuck in a situation in which negotiation and mediation takes on a pejorative meaning. The general public and their political leaders see this as a weakness rather than strength. And even something beyond the dichotomy would do: perhaps the 'cleverness of negotiation' rather than the sleaziness of 'getting what you want.' There are too many ready-made solutions that present themselves as givens, foregone conclusions, rather than as worst-case scenario options. For example, since in the developed world, or 'West', we have a massive military potential we are called to use it and since we have a situation in which we are stuck with terrorists we are asked to accept torture and brutality as an everyday occurrence. By not using the traditional methods of statecraft and negotiation we are throwing away some of our best chances at dealing with terrorism. A direct cause of terrorism and terrorist activity is that disgruntled and aggrieved political groups will feel their only resort to change can be political violence. Since the assumption is that negotiation is not possible, violence and brutality must be used in order to achieve their aims. A direct cause of terrorism is the fact that people who are living in the most dire of circumstances cannot talk to embassy officials and ask for help. A direct cause of terrorism is that people cannot air their grievances in public forums and meetings designed to discuss massive problems of ethnic rivalries, famines destructions caused by war and so on. Traditional statecraft would go a long way to mitigate the forces of terror.

And what of this 'traditional statecraft'? Here I am referring to a kind of knowledge vacuum that is created during decolonization. It is not a knowledge vacuum of statecraft *per se*, but rather a seemingly complete inability to understand what the decolonizers want out of the post-World War II global order. With the decline of the European empires, and the 'Tragedy of Great Power Politics' playing out its last vestiges, as Mearsheimer claimed, the paternalistic claims over territories around the world had rapidly begun to disappear. Conflicts began to spring up for a variety of complex reasons. In some cases it was the result of humiliations by colonial powers, in some cases it was the result of power shifts among newly forming states, and in many cases the conflicts came about due to the retreating great powers' attempt to maintain a hold on the economic exploitation of various former territories through a Cold War ideological justification. The United States sought to maintain dominance in the Latin American and South American nation-states, the British had a difficult time in the former Malay and Singapore colonies not to mention the Palestinian lands. Indonesia, the partitioning of the British Raj-held territory in South Asia, and all the various retreats by the colonial powers from Sub-Saharan Africa demonstrated that the world was rapidly changing its political alignments. In this case, global politics became one of almost complete misunderstanding of the needs of various groups emerging as political forces during the Cold War period.

All of this is accelerated and exacerbated by the wave of globalization and democratization in the 1990s. It would seem that this is the time for the kind of statecraft in which political leaders attempt to develop a set of negotiations beyond the zero-sum game of global great power politics. It has been disappointing to see that we are approaching the two-decade point from the end of the Cold War and the optimism at the end of the 1980s and beginning of the 1990s has ended in greater conflict. Perhaps part of this disappointment is the realization that the entrenchment of our problems with political violence are grounded in our very conceptions of the 19th-century version of the nation-state. If this is the case, then overcoming the problem of terrorism might mean that we need to fundamentally change our understanding of the key political organization of the modern period.

Development of the Modern Nation-State

The development of the modern nation-state presents us with a set of problems that we have not dealt with in the era of globalization.[5] We are in a situation in which the modern nation-state is now intimately linked with terror and terrorism. Disgruntled groups with historical grievances have legitimate cause for complaints as modern nation-states have worked to homogenize populations and attempted to ensure that any political resistance is quelled. Modern nation-states, the political leaders, and much of their populations work to construct ethnicities so as to claim they share ancestry, and thus people outside of the shared ancestry will have difficulty sharing the territory of the nation-state. It is a clear way to make divisions and ensure that there are people defined as 'other' who cannot claim a kind of belonging in a new or emerging socio-political order. Terrorism and terrorist groups for the past 150 years of political history of the modern nation-state have developed from this position. Did we need a genocide of the Armenians to ensure that the Turkish nation-state was modernized? Did we need a purge of Muslims from the southern portions of the Russian empire to ensure that Russia modernized? Did we need a crackdown on Basques in Franco's Spain to ensure the Spanish people were 'united as one'?

---

5 In this section I introduce this theme and deal with some of the specifics later on in the book. There are a goodly number of works examining this problem of the development of the nation-state in general and the linkages with terrorism in particular. There is still scope to examine how nations and nationalism can be linked to the problem of terror.

Why did we leave the Palestinians 'defined out' of legitimate holders of their own territory? Terrorism is a direct cause of the development of the modern nation-state.

One way to deal with this problem of being stuck in the 19th-century version of the homogenizing nation-state is to fully embrace the possibilities of globalization and move towards a cosmopolitan ethic. I postulate here that the best way to end the current wave of terrorist activity is to open borders as fully as possible. Whether we look at globalization as a process that evolves over the *longue durée* and includes the development of the European empires from the 1500s, through to the giant trading companies such as the British East India Company, or we claim that globalization is restricted to comparatively recent events with the rise of the United States and the new version of a kind of global dominance (hegemony), we are still left with the problem of the movement of large groups of people. Unfortunately it seems that we have left much of the decision-making about the new globalization, whether it is a continuation of European empires or not, in the hands of a few wealthy and powerful people. In a democracy, this means that we have abrogated our responsibilities to ourselves and our communities by allowing things to get this far. We haven't demanded that our governments do anything beyond keeping mortgage rates and consumer goods prices low. Australia has been criticized as the 'mortgage nation' for prioritizing this aspect over other political concerns. We should demand the freedoms that we innately have, in a liberal sense, and we must shoulder the responsibilities to our communities by going beyond the nation-state. Open borders would achieve the great promises of the pre-World War I period in which we saw the spread of ideas about human liberty that were destroyed in the Great War. The response to this destruction was to retreat into fascism and we are seeing elements of this again since the end of the Cold War. We should support the multinational NGOs working to bring global cooperation to the world and support initiatives that seek to make the capacity to build terrorist organizations greatly reduced. We should reject all the homogenizing effects of the modern nation-state, demand the acceptance of diversity and when we are told that we must do things to 'build the great nation', or to uphold 'national values' that we are told are exclusively our own, or to accept decisions made in the national interest we should be deeply suspicious of what we are told. A clear example of conflict and war avoidance is that specific 'cosmopolitan' attempt embedded in various versions of multiculturalist societies around the world. It is extraordinary that nation-states such as the United States, Canada, Mexico, Australia, New Zealand and others have managed to embrace people from all parts of the world and have avoided major internal conflicts. These migrant societies, each with their own brand of multiculturalism and/or pluralism, have seen people from around the world, at various points in their political histories, join these nation-states enthusiastically. It is this kind of radical pluralism, indeed even cosmopolitanism (although sometimes unwittingly), that flies in the face of attempts by political leaders to act on this homogenization principle and to move beyond the (serious) limitations of this national concept.

Conclusion

I have looked at some of the causes and cures of terrorism through a kind of general social science lens and have made an attempt to take some steps back from much of the media spin surrounding these issues. I have deliberately not looked at religion in this case as that will be dealt with in a later chapter. I have also deliberately avoided counter-terror measures that are specific policy issues as that too will be treated in a later chapter. I have looked at terrorism in its broadest sense and have asked that people think about terrorism as a phenomenon with a political history grounded in human societies around the world. This means that we are all linked to the big problems of the world globally. It is a difficult conclusion in that it is similar to the kind of conclusion that so many environmentalists make about large problems of climate change, water usage, energy efficiency and the like. It is difficult to see the connections without either claiming an individual guilt for actions taken, or on the other hand rejecting the notion that one can claim such intimate associations to these seemingly distant problems. The next logical step is to examine some of the international legal perspectives on this phenomenon, as Ben Clarke does in the next part of the chapter, after which the book goes on to examine various other aspects of socio-political, legal, and philosophical aspects of responses to terrorism.

References

Abeyratne, S. (2004), 'Economic Roots of Political Conflict: The Case of Sri Lanka', *The World Economy*, Vol. 27, No. 8.

Arendt, H. (1964), *Eichmann in Jerusalem* (New York: Viking Penguin).

Bauman, Z. (2004), *Wasted Lives* (Polity Press: London).

Bloom, M. (2005), *Dying to Kill: The Allure of Suicide Terror* (New York: Columbia University of Princeton).

Brubaker, R. (2004), *Ethnicity Without Groups* (Cambridge: Massachusetts: Harvard University Press).

Combs, C. (2006), *Terrorism in the Twenty-First Century* (New Jersey: Pearson).

Crenshaw, M. (1998), 'The Logic of Terrorism: Terrorist Behaviour as a Product of Strategic Choice' in Walter Reich (ed.), *Origins of Terrorism* (Woodrow Wilson Center Press).

Dalby, S. (2002), *Environmental Security* (Minneapolis: University of Minnesota Press).

Gambetta, D. (2005), *Making Sense of Suicide Missions* (Oxford: Oxford University Press).

Goodin, R. (2006), *What's Wrong With Terrorism?* (Cambridge: Polity Press).

Gunning, J. (2007), 'A Case for Critical Terrorism Studies', *Government and Opposition*, Vol. 42, No. 3, pp. 363–93.

Haugaard, M. (2002), *Power: A Reader* (Manchester: Manchester University Press).

Hoffman, B. (2006), *Inside Terrorism* (New York: Columbia University Press).

Jurgensmeyer, M. (2000), *Terror in the Mind of God* (Berkeley: University of California Press).

Kymlicka, W. and He Baogang (eds) (2005), *Multiculturalism in Asia* (Oxford: Oxford University Press).

Laquer, W. (2004), *No End To War: Terrorism in the Twenty-First Century* (New York: Continuum).

Mearsheimer, J. (2001), *The Tragedy of Great Power Politics* (New York: Norton Publishers).

Roy, O. (2004), *Globalised Islam* (London: Hurst).

Sagemen, M. (2004), *Understanding Terror Networks* (University of Pennsylvania Press).

Simms, M. and Warhurst, J. (eds) (2005), *Mortgage Nation: The 2004 Australian Election* (Bentley: API Network).

Terriff, T., Croft, S., James, L. and Morgan, P. (2003), *Security Studies Today* (Cambridge: Polity Press).

Thomas, C. (2000), *Global Governance, Development and Human Security* (London: Pluto Press).

1.2   An International Law Approach

Ben Clarke

Introduction

Since the terrorist attacks of 11 September 2001, discourse on the 'causes and cures' of terrorism has been voluminous.[6] It has emerged from within a variety of academic

---

6 An extensive 'Terrorism Bibliography' is available at the National Memorial Institute for the Prevention of Terrorism. <http://www.mipt.org/>. The following is a small selection of the available literature on the causes and cures of terrorism: Alexander, Yonah (2002), *Combating Terrorism: Strategies of Ten Countries* (Ann Arbor, MI: University of Michigan Press); Adams, Simon (2004), *All the Troubles: Terrorism, War and the World After 9/11* (North Fremantle, Australia: Fremantle Arts Centre Press); Addicott, Jeffrey F. (2003), *Winning the War on Terror: Legal and Policy Lessons From the Past* (Tucson, AZ: Lawyers & Judges Publishing Company); Ahmed, Rafiuddin (2001), *Terrorism* (IPRI paper; no. RP 1/01. Islamabad: Islamabad Policy Research Institute); Alexander, John B. (2003), *Winning the War: Advanced Weapons, Strategies and Concepts for the Post-9/11 World* (New York: St Martin's Press); Alexander, T.J. (2003), *The Battle for the Hearts and Minds: Using Soft Power to Undermine Terrorists Networks* (Cambridge, MA: MIT Press); Rehman, Javaid (2005) *Islamic State Practices, International Law and the Threat from Terrorism* (Oregan, US, Oxford and Portland). Useful literature published prior to 11 September 2001 includes: Ansari, Masud (1988), *International Terrorism: Its Causes and How to Control It* (Washington, DC: Mas-Press); Alexander, Yonah (1979), *Control of Terrorism: International Documents* (New York: Crane Russak); Acquaviva, Mike (1989), *Terrorism: Special Studies* (Bethesda, MD: University Publications of America); Alali, A. Odasuo (1991), *Media Coverage of Terrorism:*

disciplines. This is unsurprising. The topic lends itself to multi-disciplinary analysis.[7] Sociologists, moral philosophers, political economists, historians, theologians, and legal scholars can offer useful and distinct perspectives on the issue. The importance of multi-disciplinary analysis of these issues has long been recognized by the United Nations (United Nations Sub-Commission on the Promotion and Protection of Human Rights 2004).[8]

This exposé offers a contribution to scholarship in this field by examining the causes and cures of terrorism from a legal perspective and more specifically, from within the paradigms of the rule of law and human rights. While the causes and cures of terrorism are many and varied, this part of the chapter focuses upon the link between the growth of terrorist violence and violations of human rights and the rule of law. For this writer, notions of 'law', 'justice' and 'rights' are understood within the framework of liberalism. The Universal Declaration of Human Rights (1948) and other key international human rights instruments are endorsed, and construed within the liberal tradition. This part commences with a critique of Islamist terror, and a normative and historical assessment of terrorism in general. Thereafter the focus is upon three points which are made and defended:

1. Terrorism is often a by-product of violations of human rights and the rule of law.
2. The failure of states and international organizations to work together to achieve a just resolution of local and international conflicts has provided fertile conditions for the proliferation of terrorist organizations.
3. Terrorism is likely to be reduced or extinguished through general compliance with the international rule of law and international human rights norms. In the present

---

Methods of Diffusion (Terrorism and the Mass Media. Newbury Park, CA: Sage Publications); Alon, Hanan (1980), *Countering Palestinian Terrorism in Israel: Toward a Policy Analysis of Countermeasures* (A Series in International Security and Arms Control. Santa Monica, CA: RAND); Alterman, Jon B. (1999), *How Terrorism Ends* (Washington, DC: United States Institute of Peace).

7 See for example the International Association for Philosophy of Law and Social Philosophy (IVR). Its membership includes political scientists, law professors and political philosophers. The American Section of IVR recently produced a volume in a series entitled AMINTAPHIL: The Philosophical Foundations of Law and Justice. See also Steven P. Lee (ed.) (2007), Intervention, Terrorism and Torture.

8 In 1997, the United Nations Sub-Commission on the Promotion and Protection of Human Rights, a body established by the Commission on Human Rights Sub-Commission, appointed Kalliopi K. Koufa as a Special Rapporteur to conduct a comprehensive study on terrorism and human rights. In her final report the Special Rapporteur commented on 'the complexity of the issue of terrorism and human rights and the need to draw on disciplines other than international law for fuller understanding of terrorism and to fashion responses to terrorism and how to reduce acts or threat of acts of terrorism.'

Koufa noted that 'two of the most important essential topics falling into this category are (i) examination of the many root causes of terrorism and (ii) review of strategies to reduce or prevent terrorism in all its manifestations.' Paragraph 67 'Specific Human Rights Issues: New Priorities, In Particular Terrorism And Counter-Terrorism' (Final Report of the Special Rapporteur) E/CN.4/Sub.2/2004/40 GE.04-14677 (E) 160704 25 June 2004.

international legal environment, this requires, *inter alia,* international cooperation in the implementation of Security Council resolutions on counter-terrorism.

It is necessary from the outset to highlight a significant caveat on the discussion that follows. Clearly there are a myriad of social conditions that have in the past, and will in the future, give rise to terrorism. This renders the goal of compiling a definitive list of causes and cures unattainable. It is only by detailed study of specific contexts that qualified conclusions can be drawn. With this is mind, the conclusions drawn here are limited to the most prevalent form of contemporary international terrorism: attacks by radical Islamists upon civilian populations. Islamist terror networks such as al Qaeda engage in terrorism in order to further an ideological struggle against 'apostate' regimes and peoples (known collectively as *kafur*). Their attacks are designed not only to intimidate the public but also to ignite an armed struggle that will lead to Islamic rule according to their politico-religious ideology. As events in Iraq have shown, the path to 'restoration of the Caliphate' is a bloody sectarian war. To date most of the victims of religious violence have been Muslim civilians. The ideology being promoted reflects the terrorists' conception of what Islam requires of the believer. Sometimes war is waged between two or more rival radical Islamist factions of Arab fighters who each brand the other(s) apostates. At other times Mujahideen factions have united in armed struggles to depose regimes that are considered un-Islamic. These groups share the Islamic belief that militant jihad involving fighting and killing (*qital*) is justified to expel non-Muslim invaders, depose 'apostate' rulers and defend Muslim populations from oppression and injustice (*zulm*) (Ali Khan 2004, 172–191). In Iraq, persons deemed to be 'collaborators' with the Coalition occupation were targeted for summary execution by a range of radical Islamist factions.

At this juncture it is necessary to define the terms 'Islamist' and 'radical Islamist.' Islamist is a term used to describe those who believe in Islam as both a religion and a political ideology (Husein 2007). Trevor Stanley has observed that '[T]he most useful definition of Islamism is encapsulated in the synonym "Political Islam", which refers to those political movements that treat Islam as their political ideology' (Stanley 2005). Sunni Islamists include the Muslim Brotherhood, al Qaeda, Hizb ut-Tahrir, the Taliban and Saudi Wahhabis, whereas the revolutionary doctrine of the Iranian government is a Shi'ite Islamist ideology (Stanley 2005). Islamists generally reject the drift towards 'western' (as opposed to 'Islamic') values as well as any transition from Islamic to secular governance. While not all Islamists are willing to resort to terrorism to impose or defend their ideology, those who do so are described here as 'radical Islamists.'

Radical Islamists have engaged in terrorist attacks both in Muslim states and countries where Muslims are in the minority. In the case of the former, a call may be issued for the general population to join their struggle, or rival sectarian groups may be immediately targeted as pagans or *kafr*. In states where Muslims are in the minority, radical Islamists may resort to terrorism for a range of reasons including revenge (in response to attacks upon Muslims at home or abroad), protest (against some perceived injustice or insult to Islam), to win new territory or re-claim territory once governed by Muslims, or to try to force a shift in the foreign policy of the targeted state. For radical Islamists, civilian victims of Islamist terror attacks may fall into one of two categories: Muslim martyrs who will go to heaven; and those condemned as infidels, heretics or apostates (*kafur*). A detailed analysis of the historical and political circumstances that have given rise to radical Islamist ideologies is beyond the scope of this part of the chapter.

PART I: TERRORISM: A HISTORICAL AND NORMATIVE ASSESSMENT

The Nature of Terrorism

It is trite to recall that war is a blunt instrument. Even wars waged between conventional armed forces that adhere to international humanitarian law produce civilian casualties (Lacina and Gleditsch 2005).[9] However terrorism is an even blunter instrument than conventional warfare. It is designed to kill the innocent. It is a tool used since antiquity by the militarily weak to pursue outcomes unattainable on the battlefield in a conventional war between standing armies.

Terrorist violence is a common by-product of wars of aggression.[10] When one state invades and occupies another in violation of international law, resistance by the local population to the invading army is a time-honored tradition (Nabulsi 1999; Clarke 2005).[11] When an invading force engages in brutality towards the local population, the latter are often inclined to engage in guerrilla resistance. This may involve attacks on enemy soldiers as well as the use of terror tactics against those who collaborate with occupying forces. It is not surprising that war ravaged populations have resorted to such extreme measures, particularly during a brutal occupation. Such measures are (from the occupied population's perspective) often viewed as acts of patriotic resistance in the face of foreign aggression. History is replete with examples.

---

9 This situation has persisted despite improvements in the accuracy of weapon delivery systems and stricter humanitarian norms on who may be targeting during war. The main reason for the high civilian death rate is the failure of belligerents in many armed conflicts to respect the rules of international humanitarian law.

10 Waging a war of aggression is a crime against international law. High ranking German and Japanese officers were convicted of this crime against peace at War Crimes Tribunals convened in Nuremberg and Tokyo after World War II: Case No. 72 *The German High Command Trial, Trial of Wilhelm Von Leeb and Thirteen Others,* United States Military Tribunal, Nuremberg, 30 December 1947–28 October 1948. The crime of aggression is also listed among those crimes over which the International Criminal Court (ICC) has jurisdiction: See Article 5 Rome Statute of the International Criminal Court (UN Doc. A/CONF.183/9). However the ICC may not prosecute such crimes until states parties to the Rome Statute have agreed upon a definition of the term 'aggression.'

11 See Nabulsi, K. (1999) *Traditions of War: Occupation, Resistance and the Law*; Clarke, B. (2005) 'The juridical status of civilian resistance to foreign occupation under the law of nations and contemporary international law', *University of Notre Dame Australia Law Review* 7, 1.

A Glance at the History of Warfare and Terrorism

Resistance by local inhabitants to enemy occupation can be traced back to Roman times. In 9 CE, the might of the Roman Empire was challenged from within. Germanic tribes launched guerrilla attacks on passing Roman brigades. In that year, Germanic 'freedom fighter' Hermann the Cheruscan ('Arminius') defected from the Roman army and put together 'the great revolt of Germania' (Gundarsson). In an unprecedented display of barbarian resistance to Roman occupation, Arminius's forces attacked Roman legions as they passed through the heavily wooded territory of Teutoberger Wald. Three Roman legions were utterly destroyed in the Battle of Teutoberger Wald, and the Romans were soon cast out of Germania and back past the Rhine (Lendering 2006). Around 15,000 legionnaires were killed and hundreds more executed after being taken prisoner. For the Romans, barbarian resistance of this kind would have been regarded as terrorism.

In the 19th century the tables were turned. Germany, then an expansionist military power, faced stiff resistance from local inhabitants in foreign lands it occupied. French and Russian peasants defending their homeland against the German army were known by their countrymen as patriots and partisans. To the German occupiers they were terrorists or *franc-tireurs* (Nabulsi 1999, 47).[12] German soldiers had orders to shoot them on sight.

During the Napoleonic era, military juntas in Spain engaged in partisan war against French occupying troops (Nabulsi 1999, 49). Russian partisan units sought to replicate the success of the Spanish resistance. An organized strategy of partisan warfare was employed against the French who were occupying large parts of Russia (Nabulsi 1999, 49). Meanwhile the Prussian assembly at Konigsberg authorized resistance to French occupation. It issued an edict on how the population were to respond to French forces. Both the *Landsturm* (militia forces which formed part of the Prussian army) and *Landwehr* (meaning 'defence of the country' but referring to irregular militias) were authorized to engage French forces (Nabulsi 1999, 49). The Prussian edicts emphasized the duty of all citizens to resist the invasion force with whatever means at their disposal (the so-called *levée en masse*). There was also support among Poles for the notion of 'people's war' and the legality of insurrectionist movements under Polish constitutional law and international law (Bierzanek 1977, 128, 129).[13] However military powers such as France took ruthless measures[14] to put down resistance in occupied territory.[15] This approach reflected

---

12 The use of the generic term *franc-tireurs* by Germany, to describe local citizens who resisted Prussian invasion, is itself a powerful example of how those who engaged in the defence of their homeland were viewed by military powers.

13 At the end of the 18th century Polish territory was divided between Prussia, Russia and Austria.

14 Reprisals (including burning villages) and hostage taking were the method of maintaining the distinction between legal and illegal combatants, as well as discouraging the local population from supporting the resistance (Nabulsi 1999, 33). Although it could be counter productive (Nabulsi 1999, 33).

15 French General Marbot noted that 'All means are permissible against those who revolt', *General Marbot Memoires* (Paris: E Plon Nourrit et Cie 1880) iii, 382 (cited in Nabulsi 1999, 31).

their belief that military necessity of an occupying army legitimized such action, and their utter rejection of partisan resistance to occupation as a legitimate method of warfare.[16] The threat that such resistance may pose to occupying troops was recognised by a 19th century commentator on the Peninsular Campaign (1807–14) who characterized insurrection of armed peasants as military anarchy and noted that in such circumstances 'men cannot be restricted in the customs of regular war' (Napier 1889).[17]

What is evident from this discussion is that the modern concept of terrorism has been defined by military powers. Their conception of legitimate warfare shaped the customary and treaty law of war. By branding all *francs-tireurs* as unprivileged belligerents, military powers excluded partisans from the benefits and protections of combatant immunity under the laws of war. To great powers it mattered not that smaller nations could not expect to defeat military powers in a conventional war fought between regular armies on the battlefield. Nations that relied for their national defence upon guerrilla or partisan methods of warfare suffered greatly. *Francs-tireurs* were frequently shot upon capture or surrender. Summary execution was justified by military powers on the grounds that these militants did not meet the qualifications of belligerency and were therefore unprivileged fighters. When the opportunity arose at peace conferences held at Brussels (1874), The Hague (1899 and 1907) and Geneva (1949), a number of smaller nations argued that treaty law should offer protection to partisans. However the issue was never fully resolved. Militias and volunteer corps (including organized resistance movements) forming part of the armed forces of a party to a conflict were eventually recognized as lawful belligerents – an acknowledgment of their important role in the Allied struggle during World War II.[18] Nonetheless, guerrilla *methods* of warfare were not specifically addressed under the 1949 Geneva Conventions.

Between 1974 and 1977 attempts were made at Geneva to regulate guerrilla warfare. After much debate a protocol emerged which recognized the right to struggle against 'alien occupation, racist regimes and colonial rule.'[19] Under this instrument irregular forces that participate in such struggles must belong to the armed forces of a party to the conflict. Those who do not, are deprived of the protections of combatant immunity.[20] Under this legal regime, non-state actors who wage war without a state ally cannot expect to be recognized as combatants. Consequently patriotic resistance by isolated bands of fighters, even against foreign occupation won through a war of aggression, remains punishable under the laws of war. Unprivileged fighters may

---

16 All military occupiers defended their actions against civilians by reference to 'the protection of their troops' (Nabulsi 1999, 30).

17 Napier, W. (1889), *A narrative of the Peninsular Campaign 1807–1814* (London: Bickers & Son), ii 205 as quoted in Nabulsi (1999, 30). See also Mougenot, R. (1903), *Des pratiques de la guerre continentale*, 377.

18 See Article 4, Paragraph 2, Geneva Convention III (1949) and Additional Protocol I (1977).

19 See Article 1, Paragraph 4, Additional Protocol I (1977).

20 See Article 4, Paragraph 2, 1949 Geneva Convention III, and Articles 43 and 44, Additional Protocol I (1977).

be punished for their participation in the fight *per se*.[21] They may be treated like common criminals or terrorists and prosecuted under domestic law.

From the early days of the Coalition occupation of Iraq, US military spokesmen regularly branded all who opposed Coalition forces (whether Iraqi military personnel, foreign jihadists, local sectarian militiamen, or Ba'ath loyalists) as terrorists. This broad brush approach oversimplified the legal situation. It excluded the possibility that, in the early stages of the occupation at least, Iraqi soldiers who continued the fight were in fact combatants and therefore entitled to POW status upon capture. Not all of Iraq's military commanders had surrendered or been captured or killed by the time President Bush declared victory in Iraq. Some remained at large and loyal to clandestine remnants of the Ba'ath leadership. Indeed Iraq's Commander in Chief Saddam Hussein continued to call for resistance until silenced by his captors in late 2003. US statements branding all resistance fighters as terrorists must therefore be viewed as political comment rather than objective legal analysis. The same may be said of Saddam's video and audio messages released during the occupation. Saddam repeatedly called upon all Iraqis to resist the Coalition forces. One must look elsewhere for a persuasive and impartial assessment of the legal status of Iraqi resistance forces.

Terrorism or Heroic Resistance? The Role of *Real Politick* in Reactions to Militant Jihad

The contrast between the US reaction to jihadist struggles in Afghanistan (1979–89) and Iraq (2003–04) could not be starker. In both cases isolated bands of foreign and local jihadists waged armed struggles against foreign occupation. Both occupations were regarded by the bulk of the international community as the birth child of an illegal invasion. Mujahideen forces in Afghanistan fought Soviet occupation for a decade. They were regarded by a succession of US presidents as heroic and patriotic freedom fighters. Whether they qualified as combatant forces under the laws of armed conflict was, for the US and its Cold War allies, beside the point. By contrast the legal status of local and foreign jihadists who fought the occupiers in Iraq was very much the point. They were condemned by the 'Coalition of the Willing' as terrorists. Their right to enter the battlefield was strongly contested. This is of course unsurprising. Iraq was to the US what Afghanistan had been to Russia.

In the 1980s Russia labelled the disparate resistance forces arrayed against its occupying army as 'terrorists.' Meanwhile the 'terrorists' were being generously funded by US Congress. Thirty million US dollars was allocated for supplies to the Afghan resistance in 1980.[22] President Carter claimed that the US had 'a moral obligation' to help the resistance in Afghanistan.[23] The US worked with a number

---

21 See Articles 64–68, Geneva Convention IV (1949).

22 Kakar, M. Hassan (1995), *Afghanistan: The Soviet Invasion and the Afghan Response, 1979–1982* (University of California Press), 148.

23 Bernstein, 'Arms for Afghanistan'; FBIS Trends, 19 March 1980; *Boston Globe*, 5 January 1980 cited in Henry S. Bradsher (1983), *Afghanistan and the Soviet Union* (Durham, NC: Duke University Press), p. 223 note 97.

of states to do just that (Bradsher 1983, 223). Camps to train Afghans in guerrilla warfare were established in Carter's home state of Georgia (Bradsher 1983, 223). In December 1982 the Reagan administration reportedly ordered the CIA to provide the Afghan insurgents with bazookas, mortars, grenade launchers, mines, and later shoulder-fired anti-aircraft missiles (Kakar 1995, 148). Reagan increased funding for weapons to the mujahideen from $280 million in 1985 to $470 million in 1986, and $639 million in 1987. The Saudis eventually matched US contributions dollar for dollar, while other states including Israel and Pakistan also aided the resistance in various ways.

This brief historical review demonstrates that when it comes to distinguishing terrorist violence from a legitimate armed struggle, the positions adopted by states often reflects their political agenda. Law becomes a malleable instrument of statecraft rather than an objective standard that is consistently followed by states over time. When occupying powers face militant opposition, they have often adopted a narrow view of what constitutes legitimate resistance. When 'the shoe is on the other foot' – so to speak – they are willing to adopt a broader view. This reflects an age-old tendency of 'great powers' to place their own political interests above the international rule of law when the two collide (Simpson 2004).

To some extent, this tendency is the product of continuing ambiguity surrounding (1) the legal status of armed struggles against foreign occupation and (2) the qualifications of belligerency. This uncertainty is the legacy of difficulties experienced by states at conferences held at The Hague (1899 and 1907) and Geneva (1949 and 1977). States have been unwilling to codify a prohibition on resistance by local inhabitants to foreign occupation. They have declined to define lawful belligerency in such broad terms as to allow a general right of civilian participation in war (other than during a *levee en masse*). This contradictory state of affairs has not been, and may never be, resolved. Clearly a general right of civilians to attack occupying troops at will would expose the civilian population to grave danger. Armed forces would then claim the right to launch attacks on towns and villages from which civilian fighters emanate. This result would be unacceptable. International humanitarian law seeks to limit war to a context between combatant armies and exclude civilians from the battlefield. If civilians were legitimate targets of occupying forces, the central thrust of international humanitarian law, namely the protection of civilians during war, would be undermined. The contradictions outlined here, and others besides, underscore the challenges that confront states as they struggle to reach agreement on the text of a comprehensive treaty on terrorism.[24]

Having briefly noted the legal, historical and political complexities of terrorism in the context of war, attention now turns to the issue at the heart of the negotiations over a comprehensive treaty on terrorism – defining 'terrorism.'

---

24 See *Draft Comprehensive Convention on International Terrorism* (annexed to the report of the ad hoc committee established by the UNGA resolution 51/210 of 17 December 1996 – Sixth session 28 January–1 February 2002).

PART II: DEFINING TERRORISM

Before analyzing the causes and cures of terrorism, the concept must be defined. Much ink has been spilled in the struggle to reaching international agreement on a common definition of terrorism (see United Nations Office on Drugs and Crime 2005). There are a number of reasons why this task has been so difficult. One problem is the pejorative nature of the term (Sorel 2003; Quenivet 2005). Another is the willingness of some states to exempt violence by actors with 'legitimate motives.'[25] These difficulties have been addressed in a recent binding resolution of the UN Security Council which rejects the 'legitimate motive' rationale and creates an 'objective' definition of terrorism. Resolution 1566 (2004) for example declares that:

> [Terrorist acts] ... are under no circumstances justifiable by consideration of a political, philosophical, ideological, racial, ethnic, religious or other similar nature ...[26]

The General Assembly has done the same. In October 2005 the member states of the UN unanimously declared:

> We strongly condemn terrorism in all its forms and manifestations, committed by whomever, wherever and for whatever purposes, as it constitutes one of the most serious threats to international peace and security.[27]

As Cassese has observed, insurgents can no longer resort to terrorism and still be considered freedom fighters.[28] The UN General Assembly made this clear as far back as 9 December 1994 when it defined terrorism as:

> Criminal acts intended or calculated to provoke a state of terror in the general public, a group of persons or particular persons for political purposes are in any circumstance unjustifiable, whatever the considerations of a political, philosophical, ideological, racial, ethnic, religious or any other nature that may be invoked to justify them.[29]

Under this formulation, terrorism includes the deliberate targeting of civilians for political or religious purposes in attacks designed to incite terror in a general population. As noted, the international community has recently reaffirmed that such action can

---

25 Sorel, Jean-Marc (2003), 'Some Questions About the Definition of Terrorism and the Fight against Its Financing', *14 The European Journal of International Law 365*, 3; Cassese, A. (2005), *International Law*, 2nd Edition (Oxford: Oxford University Press), p. 467.

26 SC Res. 1566 (2004) UN Doc. S/RES/1566 (2004), 8 October 2004, Operative Paragraph 3. See Sam Blay, Ryszard Piotrowicz, and Martin Tsamenyi (2004), *Public International Law: An Australian Perspective* (Melbourne: Oxford University Press).

27 *Final Outcomes Document*, General Assembly, World Summit, September 2005, Paragraph 81.

28 Cassese, above note 25, 480.

29 UN Doc A/RES/49/60, Paragraph 3 'Measures to eliminate international terrorism'. Note: this resolution has since been reaffirmed, having been annexed to General Assembly Resolution 52/165 (Measures to eliminate international terrorism) of 15 December 1997. Resolution 52/165 condemns all forms of terrorism and was adopted without a vote.

never be justified legally, morally, or ethically.[30] While states are in agreement on this principle, there remains a lack of uniformity of practice. Some states lack the resolve to rein-in certain groups that engage in terror. There are also concerns that some of the terrorism is state-sponsored. Terror attacks upon civilian populations are a frequent occurrence in the Middle East. Whilst most are blamed on non-state actors such as al Qaeda, there is from time to time compelling evidence of state-sponsored terrorism. A lack of will among some states to curb these activities has been one of the principal barriers to conclusion of a comprehensive treaty on terrorism.[31] The causes and potential cures of terrorism are explored in the following sections.

PART III: CAUSES OF TERRORISM

Debate over the causes of terrorism has intensified since the attacks of 11 September 2001. The quest to identify a definitive list of causes of 'terrorism' has been impeded by the amorphous nature of the concept. To focus on general explanations is largely unsatisfactory. If meaningful causes are to be isolated, the parameters of the discussion needs to be narrowed. Analysis of particular terrorist attacks or campaigns of terror are more likely to produce useful answers than a study of terrorism as a broad phenomenon. A detailed analysis of the context in which terror attacks occur would require an examination of religious, political, historical, cultural, nationalist and ideological undercurrents. This part of this chapter will focus on the most significant terrorist threat of the early 21st century – Islamist terror. This is itself a complex field of enquiry. The brief observations which follow offer only a partial critique of the causes of Islamist terror.

Islamist Terror

Western and Muslim majority states alike have identified Islamist terror as a significant security challenge.[32] The former have responded by curbing civil liberties to protect their citizens. In some cases they have limited freedom of speech in an effort to halt anti-religious expression. This approach is justified, in part, on the assumption that suppressing criticism of Islam will limit the possibility of religious extremists being offended and engaging in religious violence. (Defamation of Islam is punishable

---

30 See notes 26 and 27 above.

31 Syria has been accused by UN investigators of involvement in the assassination of former Lebanese Prime Minister Hariri in 2005: 'New Hariri report "blames Syria" '(11 December 2005), <http://news.bbc.co.uk/2/hi/middle_east/4519346.stm>, accessed 2 January 2006; Lederer, Edith M. and Wadhams, Nick, 'U.N.: Syria, Lebanon Involved in Slaying', *Associated Press* <http://abcnews.go.com/International/wireStory?id=1235565>, accessed 2 January 2006. Another example of state-sponsored terrorism is the Ba'ath regime in Iraq. Former Iraqi president Saddam Hussein made payments to the families of Palestinian suicide bombers who launched terror attacks against Israeli citizens. See also: Alexander, Yonah (1986), *State Sponsored Terrorism* (Washington, DC: Center for Contemporary Studies).

32 See for example: 'Jordan and the Global War on Terrorism', Official Statement Foreign Ministry, The Hashemite Kingdom of Jordan (2004), <http://www.mfa.gov.jo/pages. php?menu_id=118#j2 >, accessed 16 April 2007.

under Shariah law.) Meanwhile Arab regimes have been warning their Western allies for years that full democracy in Muslim majority states will deliver Islamist parties government and install in power those whose ideology is inherently anti-democratic and hostile to Western influences. However the repression of Islamist parties by autocratic Arab regimes has itself to be identified as a cause of terrorism (A. Khan 2004). Adding to this complex mix is the fact that concerns about Islamist violence are shared by Muslim and non-Muslim populations.[33] Clearly the phenomenon of Islamist terror and its ideological foundations are complex. They are the product of an array of factors including:

1. Longstanding divisions – whether religious, tribal or ideological – between Muslim and non-Muslim sects in the Arab world and beyond;
2. Shifting allegiances and alliances in countries like Afghanistan, Lebanon and Iraq;
3. State sponsorship or patronage of terrorist organizations, militias and cells;
4. The failure of states to halt the activities of terrorist groups operating within their borders;
5. The presence of US military forces at various times in Arab states – such as Kuwait, Lebanon, Qatar, Saudi Arabia and Iraq. Some Muslims regard this as a direct violation of their religion;
6. The invasion and occupation of Iraq by a US-led coalition of forces in violation of the Charter of the United Nations. This was viewed by some Muslims as a trigger for militant jihad against the occupiers;[34]
7. The disastrous impact that a series of Middle East wars have had upon the lives of millions of Muslims; and
8. The willingness of state and non-state actors to exploit the Iraq war to further their ideological objectives. The pre-eminent example is the militant campaign launched by Musab al-Zaqawi and his supporters (discussed below). The Coalition war provided radical Islamists with the vital ingredient they needed to recruit large numbers of volunteers to undertake suicide bombing missions as part of a deliberate strategy to ignite sectarian war.[35]

---

33 See 17-Nation Pew Global Attitudes Survey (14 July 2005), *Islamic Extremism: Common Concern For Muslim And Western Publics*.

34 The concept of 'jihad' (or struggle) is enshrined in the text of the Koran and has spawned a significant body of Islamic jurisprudence: See Bostom, Andrew G. (ed.) (2005), *The Legacy of Jihad: Islamic Holy War and the Fate of non-Muslims*. Sayyid Qutb advocated global jihad so that all peoples could be freed of destructive Western influences and a universal Islamic order established. Qubt's theory was derived from the text of the Koran and scholarship derived from the Koran. His thoughts underpin the ideology of global jihad advocated by al Qaeda's second in command Ayman Zawahiri, himself a student of Qubt in Egypt. See Qutb, Sayyid (1964), *Ma'alim fi'l-Tariq* (*Signposts on the Road,* or *Milestones*) pp. 48, 61, cited in Loboda, Luke (2004, Thesis) 'The Thought of Sayyid Qutb: Radical Islam's Philosophical Foundations', <http://www.ashbrook.org/publicat/thesis/loboda/home.html#64>, accessed 18 April 2007. See also Qutb, Sayyid, 'Jihad in the Cause of God', in Bostom, Andrew G. (ed.), *op. cit.*, p. 238.

35 A bipartisan US committee has accepted that the invasion of Iraq causes an escalation in terrorism. See *The Iraq Study Group Report: The Way Forward – A New Approach* (2006),

Other causes of Islamist terror have their origins in Palestine. They include:

1. The failure of Britain to safeguard the rights of Palestinians following the Balfour Declaration (1917) – a document which made contradictory promises to Jewish and non-Jewish inhabitants of Palestine;[36]
2. The failure of the Paris Peace Conference to deliver Arab autonomy under the Treaty of Sèvres (1920);
3. The seizure of Palestinian territory by Zionist extremists in the 1940s and the expulsion of thousands of Palestinians from their homes;
4. Decades of intermittent violence between Arabs and Jews fuelled by extremists on both sides. Jewish extremists included the Haganah who authorized the attack by Irgun and The Stern Gang (Lehi) on Deir Yassin on 9 April 1948 (over 100 Palestinians were massacred).[37] Survivors were forced into exile at gun-point. Like hundreds of other Palestinian villages, Deir Yassin no longer exists.[38] Arab extremists included Muhammed Amin al-Husseini (grand mufti of Jerusalem, supporter of anti-Jewish policies of Hitler's Nazi regime in Germany, and Yassar Arafat's mentor), who attacked Jews in a campaign of terror dating back to the 1920s (Lewis (1999);
5. The assassinations by the Lehi of Lord Moyne (the Britain Minister Resident in the Middle East in 1944)[39] and Count Folke Bernadette (the UN appointed mediator on the question of Palestine in 1948),[40] together with the bombing of the King David Hotel by Irgun in 1946 (91 people were killed). These

---

<http://permanent.access.gpo.gov/lps76748/iraq_study_group_report.pdf>, accessed 17 April 2007; 'Trends in Global terrorism: Implications for the United States' (Declassified Extract from the US *National Intelligence Estimate* (2006)), <http://www.globalsecurity.org/intell/library/reports/2006/nie_global-terror-trends_apr2006.htm>, accessed 17 April 2007.

36 The promise to protect Palestinian rights was reaffirmed in the Palestine Mandate (1920): His Majesty's Government view with favour the establishment in Palestine of a national home for the Jewish people, and will use their best endeavours to facilitate the achievement of this object, it being clearly understood that nothing shall be done which may prejudice the civil and religious rights of existing non-Jewish communities in Palestine, or the rights and political status enjoyed by Jews in any other country.

37 See Eric Silver (1984), *Begin*, pp. 88–99; Joseph Heller, *The Stern Gang: Ideology, Politics and Terror 1940–1949* (1995), p. 208; Yitzhak Shamir, *Summing Up* (1994), p. 71. These events must be seen in the context of Arab–Jewish violence dating back to 1920. This includes the Arab attack on Tel Hai (1920), the Arab–Jewish violence in Jerusalem of 1921, the Arab revolt of 1929, the Arab rebellion of 1936–39: See Philip Mattar (1988), *The Mufti of Jerusalem: Al-Hajj Amin Al-Husayni and the Palestinian National Movement*, pp. 33–72; Ahron Bregman (2002), *A History of Israel*, pp. 21–37; Yitzak Shamir, *op. cit.*, pp. 8–9.

38 The site where the village of Deir Yassin once stood is now a Jewish neighborhood called Har Nof. It is in northwest Jerusalem.

39 Moyne shared his government's policy that an Arab federation should be established in the Middle East. This prospect was a threat to the Lehi's vision of a Jewish homeland: Joseph Heller, *op. cit.*, pp. 137–8, p. 138.

40 Bernadette's proposals (which included the partitioning of Palestine and the designation of Jerusalem as an international city) were also unacceptable to the Lehi. They regarded the draft UN plan as a threat to their Zionist designs for a Jewish state that included Jerusalem.

operations set a precedent for modern terrorism in the Middle East. They also paved the way for Britain's withdrawal from Palestine and the unilateral declaration of the State of Israel in 1948. The latter act triggered war between Israel and its Arab neighbours and has been the source of intermittent terrorist activity by Arab opponents of Israel ever since;

6. The denial of Israeli citizenship to exiled Palestinians. (This was a key reason why Israel's neighbors rejected Israel's right to exist and contended that Israel had no right of self-defence and could be attacked at any time – even decades after Israel's creation (Walzer 1992, 82));

7. The Basic Law of Jerusalem (1980) in which Israel claims Jerusalem to be the eternal capital of Israel. (This purported annexation of Jerusalem was in direct defiance of binding UN resolutions and has been condemned by the Security Council);

8. The prolonged occupation of Palestinian territory (the West Bank and Gaza Strip) by Israel;

9. Decades of military, economic and political support by the US for the State of Israel whilst hundreds of thousands of Palestinian exiles have remained impoverished, stateless and dispossessed in the occupied territories and neighboring states;

10. The contrast between the conditions of Palestinians in refugee camps and that of Jews living in settlements located in former Palestinian villages that are now part of Israel;

11. The willingness of state and non-state actors who oppose the existence of Israel to resort to resistance methods that are prohibited under international law. Aware that their objectives are unlikely to be met by conventional warfare (due to Israel's military strength and its close relationship with the US) many of these actors have embraced extreme ideologies that justify and encourage the killing of Israeli civilians;

12. The emergence of non-state actors such as Islamic Jihad, al Qaeda, Hamas and a plethora of other groups that adhere to such ideologies and put them into practice.

Having highlighted a number of causes of Islamist terror, attention now turns to the writer's general theory on the causes of terrorism. Put simply, the theory is that most forms of terrorism have a common antecedence – actual or perceived injustice arising from violations of human rights and the rule of law. In the following part this theory is applied as 'universal causes of terrorism' are examined.

Universal Causes of Terrorism

Violations of international law   The primary source of terrorism is the perception by the terrorist that some wrong has been done to justify a violent response. This 'wrong' involves the violation of some basic right that is cherished by the terrorist. The right may have been breached by a historical event, such as a war of aggression, or multiple violations of international law such as genocide and wrongful dispossession of local inhabitants. Ongoing conduct such as prolonged military occupation or foreign domination in violation of UN resolutions may also be the trigger. Terrorist organizations are sometimes formed to vent frustration at prolonged or persistent violations of UN resolutions. Their aim may be to bring about a 'violent cure' to these wrongs. As with the initial wrong, the terrorists' response also violates human rights and the rule of law. The international rule of law is the principle that all states are subject to and bound by international legal obligations. For those who adhere to human rights and the rule of law, crimes against international law that fuel terrorism, and terrorism itself, are equally repugnant. If terrorism is to be reduced, efforts must be made to address the violations of international law that trigger terrorist activity.

International norms that bind all states form part of a body of law known as 'public international law.' Its main sources are customary and treaty law. Customary law is comprised of rules that have, over time, been accepted by states as legally binding upon them. State practice provides evidence of the existence of customary rules. A number of principles of state responsibility form part of customary law. Under these principles states attract responsibility for international wrongs. However where great powers are the perpetrators of the wrong (or protect the wrongdoers), those responsible for violations of international law are unlikely to be held accountable. In these situations the wronged party may be left without a remedy. Palestinians sought but did not receive justice through the UN and other legal channels. Not everyone is willing to put up with such an outcome, particularly where their sacred religious texts authorize armed opposition to occupation, oppression and injustice. The resurgence of Islamic militancy in the Middle East and Afghanistan, and the fermentation of radical ideologies that sanction terrorism were not surprising (A Khan 2004). These were a predicable outcome of the above conditions, echoing uprisings against foreign occupation of both Muslim and non-Muslim lands dating back centuries.

Historical grievances   Terrorists often regard themselves, and those whose interests they claim to be defending, as victims rather than perpetrators. They target states and communities whom they regard as responsible for injustices. Chechen terrorists have justified their actions by reference to: (1) Russian repression of Chechen aspirations for independence, and (2) the long and brutal history of Russian occupation and oppression of Chechnya dating back to the 17th century. The Basque separatist movement ETA, the Tamil Tigers in Sri Lanka, Sikh extremists in India, the IRA in the United Kingdom, the ANC in South Africa, and Pro-Palestinian militant organizations in various parts of the Middle East all shared a common desire to end actual or perceived violations of rights recognized and protected under international law. They have all sought to reverse the impact of ongoing or historical grievances. (Grievances which, in most cases, arise from conduct amounting to crimes under current international law.) Many of these crimes have now been codified in the Rome Statute of the International Criminal Court.[41]

---

41 These include the crime of aggression, war crimes, crimes against humanity and genocide.

As has been noted, where the international community has been unwilling or unable to take action to prevent crimes against international law (such as wars of aggression, genocide, brutal occupation, war crimes and crimes against humanity) victims of such crimes have often taken matters into their own hands. They do so in pursuit of justice, retribution, and an end to dispossession (see Pape 2005). Self help measures aimed at securing an end to violations of fundamental rights, can however escalate beyond what the founders of resistance struggles intended or planned. PLO terrorism in Jordan in 1970 is one example. It led to the expulsion of the PLO from Jordan the following year.

International law and the rise in global terror Developments in international law may also have contributed to the rise in global terrorism. Treaty recognition of the right to struggle for self-determination gave a number of non-state actors (and their struggles) a level of international recognition they had hitherto lacked. Some chose to pursue self-determination by recourse to terrorism. The question of whether international law recognizes the right of non-state actors to use force to win self-determination is now examined.

Struggles waged to win self-determination By the 1970s there was significant pressure, particularly from members of the Non-Aligned Movement of States, for formal recognition of the right of peoples subject to colonial rule, foreign occupation and racist regimes to resist the same. The opportunity for the codification of this right under treaty law arose at the Diplomatic Conference of Geneva of 1974–77. After much negotiation the conference adopted Article 1(4) which confirmed that the Protocol applies to 'armed conflicts in which peoples are fighting against colonial domination and alien occupation and against racist régimes in the exercise of their right of self-determination.'[42] There are now 167 states party to this Protocol. Nonetheless, Article 1(4) remains one of the most controversial provisions of Geneva law. This is evident from the reservations and declarations of many states upon ratification of the Protocol. The article has been strongly criticized by Western states and commentators. Many have claimed that it offers a justification for guerrilla warfare and terrorism. A careful reading of the Protocol as a whole reveals that it neither promotes terrorism nor offers protection to perpetrators. The combined effect of Articles 1 (General principles and scope of application), 43 (armed forces), 44 (combatants and prisoners of war), 48 (the basic rule that civilians are protected persons and may not be deliberately targeted during armed conflict) and 56 (protection of the civilian population) is that terror attacks are never permissible. Only *combatants* enjoy immunity from punishment for the act of taking part in an international armed conflict. As noted above, in order to qualify as combatants, those participating in hostilities (including those waging struggles against alien occupation)

---

42 Article 1(4), Protocol Additional to the Geneva Conventions of 12 August 1949, and relating to the Protection of Victims of International Armed Conflicts (Protocol 1) Adopted on 8 June 1977 by the Diplomatic Conference on the Reaffirmation and Development of International Humanitarian Law applicable in Armed Conflicts.

must belong to or form part of the armed forces of a party to an international armed conflict. Moreover:

> In order to ensure respect for and protection of the civilian population and civilian objects, the Parties to the conflict shall at all times distinguish between the civilian population and combatants and between civilian objects and military objectives and accordingly shall direct their operations only against military objectives. (Article 48)

This rule applies to all participations, from members of 'organized resistance movements' to soldiers in regular army battalions. Further requirements that must be met by those wishing to struggle against alien occupation include command responsibility.[43] All armed units participating in hostilities 'shall be subject to an internal disciplinary system which, *inter alia*, shall enforce compliance with the rules of international law applicable in armed conflict.' These rules must be strictly observed. It is clear that many clandestine resistance groups operating in Iraq during the recent occupation did not comply with all of these requirements. The targeting of markets, police stations and government buildings demonstrated a disregard for the ban on indiscriminate attacks on civilians. Other breaches of international humanitarian law (IHL), including hostage taking and the summary execution of captives, were also widespread. The same can be said of Mujahideen forces that resisted Soviet occupation of Afghanistan in the 1980s. Russian soldiers were routinely tortured and killed by Mujahideen. Russian forces also resorted to grave violations of IHL in their treatment of the enemy.

It may be argued that international recognition of the right of peoples to struggle for self-determination has fueled international terrorism. It has, for example, lent a degree of legitimacy to non-state actors who deliberately target civilian 'collaborators' as part of their campaign to bring an end to foreign occupation. However the Protocol condemns terrorism and denies immunity from punishment for those who engage in it. By prohibiting attacks on civilians, and requiring parties to a conflict to place their troops under responsible command, the Protocol reinforces the illegality of conduct (such as terrorism) that breaches these norms.

Terrorism as a response to brutal occupation   Brutal occupation has been another source of terrorism. Such occupations have occurred at various points throughout human history. If the occupier engages in genocide against local inhabitants, attacks by civilians on occupying troops and those who collaborate with them will be excused under the local law. Of course the perpetrators of genocide are unlikely to afford those who forcibly resist the same a fair trial upon capture. However if prosecuted they would have a defence: either the personal right of self-defence or the right of self-defence in aid of another. A classic example of where this defence would have been recognized by a competent tribunal is armed resistance by Jewish

---

43 Article 43, Protocol Additional to the Geneva Conventions of 12 August 1949, and relating to the Protection of Victims of International Armed Conflicts (Protocol 1) Adopted on 8 June 1977 by the Diplomatic Conference on the Reaffirmation and Development of International Humanitarian Law applicable in Armed Conflicts *entry into force* 7 December 1979, in accordance with Article 95.

partisans in the Warsaw Ghetto during World War II. In the midst of the Holocaust Jews in Warsaw and elsewhere were destined for the gas chambers. Theirs was a desperate struggle to avoid annihilation. The summary execution of local civilians for collaborating with the Germans would under normal circumstances be murder or terrorism. However given the circumstances such actions were excusable as force used in self-defence or defence of others.

Resistance movements that are unable to expel an occupying army through conventional warfare have often engaged in terrorism in an attempt to: render the occupied territory ungovernable; turn public opinion against the occupation; and persuade the occupying army to leave. However it is only in extreme cases, such as genocide, that recourse to terror tactics against civilian collaborators could be justified.

Foreign policy Bad foreign policy choices may also trigger terrorism. One example is the illegal invasion and subsequent occupation of Iraq. This conduct violated Article 2(4) of the UN Charter. Military adventurism of this type can rapidly inspire acts of terror. Indeed, in states where sectarian divisions are rife, the descent into civil war and widespread terrorist violence may be difficult to halt. The 2003 invasion and subsequent occupation of Iraq without prior Security Council approval has provoked a ferocious and sustained terrorist campaign.

Israel's prolonged occupation of Palestinian territory has also inspired waves of terrorist violence. In recent decades two intifadas have been waged against Israel and hundreds of terror attacks launched against the Israeli public. Israel's response has cost hundreds of Palestinians lives and led to the prolonged detention of thousands more.

Sometimes the full impact of foreign policy decisions may not be realized for many years. The indiscriminate arming of Mujahideen in Afghanistan during the Soviet occupation is a good example. As noted above, hundred of millions of dollars worth of weapons and training were provided to Mujahideen, including an Islamist warlord named Gulbuddin Hekmatyar. He received more support from the US and Pakistani agents than any other resistance leader (Kaplan 2006). Former US congressman Charlie Wilson noted that Hekmatyar was regarded in the early 1980s as a 'dangerous fundamentalist' who had engaged in the assassination of moderate Afghans (Crile 2003, 212–13). He went on to rule Afghanistan twice as prime minister, after the Soviet withdrawal. Hekmatyar was infamous for his use of fear, intimidation and terror to assert control. While in power, he used the weapons and resources provided by foreign states during the Soviet occupation to crush potential rivals. During this period Islamist extremism prevailed over voices of moderation in Afghanistan. The trend continued after Hekmatyar fled Kabul on the approach of the Taliban. After gaining power, the Taliban gave sanctuary to al Qaeda, which trained volunteers for Islamist terror operations. Since 11 September 2001, Hekmatyar has endorsed al Qaeda, called for attacks on the US, and threatened to fight the Kazai government (Jamali 2005).[44] Recently he claimed that his fighters

---

44 Al Jazeera airs Hekmatyar video, 6 May 2006, <http://english.aljazeera.net/English/archive/archive?ArchiveId=22504>; A. Jamali (27 January 2005), 'Gulbuddin Hekmatyar: The Rise and Fall of an Afghan Warlord', *Terrorism Monitor*, Volume 3, Issue 2.

helped Osama bin Laden escape from the mountains of Tora Bora in 2001. CIA efforts to assassinate Hekmatyar were unsuccessful (Crile 2003, 213). The current government of Afghanistan regards Hekmatyar as one of the most significant threats to the stability of the country, and a source of ongoing Islamist terror.[45]

Hekmatyar and his followers were but one of a number of Islamist factions that were supported by the US, Saudi Arabia and other states during the 1980s. Tens of millions of dollars worth of weapons, training and supplies were given to various jihadis who have gone on to organize and execute terrorist attacks against both Muslim and non-Muslim governments. Volunteers from across the Arab and Islamic world flocked to Afghanistan to join the jihad against Soviet occupation. They included many Arab extremists whose governments were often happy to be rid of them. Some went on to form terrorist organizations of their own. One such organization is al Qaeda. It has used Afghanistan and Pakistan as training grounds and bases from which international terrorist activities were planned and launched.

Al Qaeda's success in inspiring a global campaign of Islamist terror can be traced back to the foreign assistance provided to Osama bin Laden and other jihadis during the Soviet occupation of Afghanistan. Abu Musab al-Zarqawi, who went on to lead Al Qaeda in the Land between Two Rivers during the US-led occupation of Iraq, traveled to Afghanistan in 1989 to join the jihad against the Soviet occupation. It was there that he met and befriended Osama bin Laden. Ayman al-Zawahiri also travelled to Afghanistan in the 1980s and met Osama bin Laden. These three men have been implicated in some of the most serious acts of terrorism committed in the 21st century. Bin Laden was then running a base in Afghanistan for Mujahideen. It was called *Maktab al-Khadamat* (MAK). Al Qaeda evolved from MAK. The MAK was funded by wealthy Muslims and the governments of Saudi Arabia and the United States. Covert assistance was also provided by Pakistan. The US funneled much of its support for the MAK through the Pakistani Inter-Services Intelligence Directorate (ISI) (Crile 2003).

In summary, it is clear that the decision to finance and arm Hekmatyar, Osama bin Laden and other Islamist extremists, and the failure to recover funds and weapons from them after the Soviet withdrawal, were costly mistakes. These mistakes contributed to the emergence of the Taliban, al Qaeda and Abu Musab al-Zarqawi's terror network in Iraq.

The multiplier effect   The impact of bad foreign policy choices may be compounded over decades, rendering the 'repair job' even more complicated and expensive. Multiple generations may be effected. Take foreign occupation and dispossession for example. Where territory is forcibly annexed and families dispossessed, the impact of the loss of homes, businesses, property and family members may be keenly felt for decades. A multiplier effect may be created. Where stateless descendants of the

---

45 In August 2006 five accused terrorists linked to Gulbuddin Hekmatyar were arrested by officials in the northern Afghan province of Kapisa: Marzban, Omid (21 September 2006), 'Gulbuddin Hekmatyar: From Holy Warrior to Wanted Terrorist', *Terrorism Monitor* Volume 4, Issue 18, <http://www.jamestown.org/terrorism/news/article.php?articleid=2370138>, accessed 17 April 2007.

dispossessed grow up in refugee camps, historical grievances are lived out every day. For many Palestinians in refugee camps in Lebanon, the occupied territories, and elsewhere, their daily plight reinforces the sense of injustice. Forced exile; dispossession; limited opportunities; statelessness; economic hardship – it is unsurprising that some members of these populations become radicalized. Feeling they have nothing to lose, some are willing to conduct suicide attacks against the civilian population of the occupying state. Over time occupying states may find that there is no military solution to such violent resistance. It is not easy to suppress militants who have nothing to lose and something to gain from engaging in acts of terror. Violent repression of occupied people does not solve the problem. It is likely to aggravate the situation by breeding more potential terrorists and fermenting extremist ideologies. Such ideologies may evolve in ways that undermine respect for the laws of armed conflict. New forms of terror may be used – methods that go far beyond what most would regard as acceptable methods of resistance. The prolonged occupation of Palestine has fermented ideologies that encourage small children to be groomed for 'martyrdom' operations. Terror attacks on Israeli civilians are glorified as a legitimate response to oppression, rather than condemned as violations of IHL. In December 2006 the Iraqi Study Group[46] underscored the centrality of the Palestine question in the growth of international terrorism.

The tragedies of contemporary Palestine and Iraq suggest that it is preferable for military powers to comply with the international rule of law in the first place. That is, to avoid military occupation of territory without prior UN approval. The intergenerational effects of such military operations may last many decades and have a profound role in fueling future terrorism.

Political Islam Not all Islamists advocate or engage in violence. However attacks by radical Islamists upon civilian targets from Glasgow to Jakarta (not to mention the multitude of suicide bombings in Iraq) demonstrate that many Islamists are ideologically driven to engage in terrorism. Consequently radical Islamist ideologies must themselves be recognized as a root cause of terrorism. This is not a new problem. Islamist organizations have been resorting to political violence in a bid to overthrow established governments for decades. As early as the 1950s Hizb ut-Tahrir (The Liberation Party) called for the toppling of Arab regimes and the establishment of an Islamic state (Husein 2007). In 1952 it applied to be formally recognized and established as a political party in Jordan. The Interior Ministry rejected its application and banned the party. So did every other Arab state where this group operated. By contrast, some European states such as Britain have allowed Islamist parties to 'lay down ideological roots.' Ex-Islamist Ed Husein posits that this policy was a mistake and the evidence is the 2005 London Bombings carried out by British Islamists (Husein 2007). Clearly the belief that both: (a) the violent removal of 'apostate' regimes, and (b) the killing of *kafr* (including innocent civilians from rival sects), are justified in the cause of militant jihad, have inspired non-state actors such as al Qaeda to commit heinous crimes. An effective response to such terrorist

---

46 Baker, James A. III *et al.* (2005), *The Iraq Study Group Report*, <http://www.usip. org>, accessed 10 December 2006.

organizations requires, *inter alia*, the deconstruction of their ideological foundations. One way of doing so is to subject the spiritual and political leaders of such groups to fair and public trials. In this way witnesses to these crimes are able to lay before the accused and their supporters the inhumanity of their actions. Another is the closure or reform of maddrasses that promote hatred, intolerance and violence.

Repression, Corruption and Autocracy in the Arab World

Democracy is yet to flourish in the Middle East. In most states political reform has been gradual. Sometimes the democratic project takes a backward step. This has occurred in many Arab states in the years since 11 September 2001. Security threats, whether real or exaggerated, have provided governments with the excuse to consolidate their grip on power. Political assassinations, military coups and attempted coups are not uncommon events in the Arab world. The same is true of state-sponsored terror against local and foreign targets, much of it in the form of government repression of political dissent. In such a climate 'state of emergency' decrees are common. They provide legal cover for suspension of the constitution and with it a range of basic rights and freedoms. Freedom of the press and the right of political protest against government decisions are often the first casualties.

In some nations the pendulum has swung back and forth between military rule and democracy. The general population is sometimes complicit in the process. They may believe that surrendering basic rights and freedoms to government will make them safer. They will be protected by a 'strong president.' Their nation will become more powerful. Their religion and culture will be defended. However with autocracy comes a range of unpleasant consequences. When citizens cannot openly criticize the government, transparency and accountability from politicians cannot be guaranteed. Nor can high ethical standards be demanded of public officials. Without the checks and balances required for responsible government, corruption and organized crime can flourish and prospects for a vibrant, democratic and human rights-based society recede.

This has been a common theme across the Middle East for decades. Only in Israel, Turkey, Lebanon and now Afghanistan and Iraq are the ruling elite elected. In Lebanon, democracy is undermined by the influence of sectarian militias, foreign interference and regional tensions. In a number of Arab states there is a limited form of democracy. Jordan for example, is a constitutional monarchy where political parties may contest elections and participate in government. However the King retains ultimate power. In 2007 a Muslim Brotherhood party the 'Islamic Action Front' had 15 deputies in the 110-seat Jordanian House of Parliament. However upper house members are appointed by the King, political parties are closely monitored and the political process as a whole is overseen by the monarchy.

Whether such tight control over the electoral process is justified is a matter of debate. One fear is that Islamist parties will gain the majority of seats in parliament, seize control of the state, and bring the democracy process to an abrupt end. Another is that, as has occurred in Gaza, the ruling Islamist party may contain such extreme elements – and thereby attract such opposition from abroad – that it cannot form a stable government.

Both Jordan and Egypt have recognized that where dissent is repressed it will go underground. They have encouraged radical Islamist groups to renounce violence as a precursor to participation in the political process. Egyptian President Hosni Mubarek, the consummate Arab autocratic, walks both sides of the 'political reform street.' Reform is both welcomed and suppressed. Mubarek accepts US funds designated for liberal reform, made gestures in this direction, and all the while gaoling his critics. A ban on religious parties is not currently enforced. The Muslim Brotherhood now commands around 20 per cent of the seats in parliament. Meanwhile members of the Brotherhood have been arrested in the lead-up to the 2007 elections. Cairo's numerous state-run security prisons are overflowing. In Egypt everyone knows that real power resides in the hands of Mubarek and his security apparatus and not the parliament. While terrorist attacks are not unknown nor are they common. This appears to be due to the effectiveness of the security apparatus in suppressing religious and political dissent, rather than effective policy measures aimed at eliminating such causes of terrorism as poverty, unemployment, corruption and intolerance.

Globalization and technology   Globalization has contributed to the escalation of terrorism in a variety of ways. Technological advances have provided significant opportunities for terrorist organizations. Instantaneous electronic communication can be utilized to recruit members, coordinate attacks and build alliances with other organizations and criminal networks. The internet has been used to market and promote terrorist struggles to a global audience. It can also be used to access information, weapons technology, and other resources required to conduct sophisticated terrorist operations. Media and internet tools may also be exploited by states to heighten fear of terrorism for political purposes. These themes were explored in a documentary written and produced by Adam Curtis entitled the *The Power of Nightmares*.[47] A year later, Peter Taylor responded with a documentary which challenged many of Curtis's claims.[48] Taylor highlights the fact that it is not only extremist ideologies that are spread through the internet, but also detailed instructions on how to make bombs and engage in suicide attacks. These sites are regularly updated, and when blocked, new ones are created. Taylor demonstrates the role such websites have played in the promotion of terrorism and the radicalization of young Muslims. He highlights cases where information loaded onto websites in one state has inspired terrorist attacks in another. A more detailed analysis of the role of globalization in the rise of international terrorism is offered in Chapter 3.

Use of force in violation of UN Charter norms   The use of military force in violation of UN Charter norms deserves separate mention. Its consequences in the Palestinian context have been noted. In summary, when unlawful force is used with impunity it can create a climate of outrage. This outrage may be expressed through terrorist attacks. The 2003 invasion of Iraq triggered outrage across the Arab world. The vast

---

47 *The Power of Nightmares* was first aired on BBC 2 in Britain on 3 November 2004.

48 Peter Taylor's documentary, *The New Al-Qaeda: Jihad.com*, originally broadcast on BBC 2 on 25 July 2005.

majority of people across the Middle East opposed the invasion.[49] Unsurprisingly, no Arab nations committed ground troops, although a few close allies of the US provided logical support and allowed foreign troops to mass on their territory in the lead-up to the war. The bulk of Arab financial and material support for Iraq appears to have gone to the resistance, Iraqi families and locally based organizations, rather than the Coalition-backed initiatives.

The devastation visited upon Iraq, a Muslim nation, by non-Muslim armies, provoked sympathy and support for those willing to fight US troops. It also gave radical Islamists (some of whom went on to target each other) a territorial base and training ground from which to organize and launch attacks against a vast array of targets both within and beyond Iraq.

The consequences of large scale use of military force, particularly air strikes, cannot be predetermined or controlled. Air strikes upon targets within towns and villages almost inevitably lead to civilian casualties and unintended property damage. Armed resistance is to be expected when such force is used and damage inflicted without the approval of the international community. Where military targets prove impregnable, some resistance groups may be willing to resort to attacks upon civilians who are deemed to be collaborators. Retaliation against those who wage such wars may not be immediate. It may take time for resistance fighters to organize and launch attacks on the enemy. Indeed retribution may be sought long after the 'war' has ended, far from the battlefield, and against non-military targets. For Israelis, the 'original sin' of 1948 has been visited on subsequent generations through terrorist attacks carried out in many places, over many decades.

PART IV: CURES

Compliance by states with the rule of law and human rights

Within a rule of law paradigm, the cure for terrorism is the opposite of its cause. To quell terrorism states must act in accordance with the rule of law and human rights. They should attempt to resolve disputes through peaceful resolution methods, such as diplomacy, mediation, arbitration, and the use of the good offices of international statesmen. If they are to work there will usually need to be willingness by all or most sides to compromise. If these methods fail and use of force is deemed necessary, it should be used within the UN Charter framework (that is, in self-defence or with Security Council authorization). Where states act outside the international rule of law (for example by waging war outside the Charter framework), sooner or later those whose rights they have violated may try to respond through illegal and repugnant means, such as terrorism.

It is easier and quicker to destroy the social fabric of a community that to try to rebuild it. Halting or preventing terrorism in states that have been subject to

---

49 In Jordan 90 per cent of the population opposed the war. While King Abdullah repeatedly warned the US not to invade, he had little option but to side with the US, allowing Coalition Special Forces to enter Iraq from Jordan. See generally <www.worldpublicopinion. org> and <pewglobal.org>.

unlawful invasion and military occupation may be exceedingly difficult. Events in Palestine and Iraq attest to this fact. A range of policy responses are required after states have engaged in occupations of this nature. They include: bringing an end to occupation; compensation for economic loss, personal injury and wrongful death; return of seized lands and property; and the prosecution of the perpetrators of violations of international law. Moreover, substantial and long-term assistance may be required to ensure viable institutions are established in states and territories that have experienced such occupation. Sustained international cooperation – perhaps over decades – may be needed to prevent them becoming 'failed states' and possible terrorist havens. Significant investment in education, infrastructure, industry, technology and development may be required. This is also true of countries like Afghanistan, where for generations the local inhabitants have known nothing but war and the state has only recently been liberated from tyrannical rule.

Dialogue

Throughout history, military commanders have recognized that there is often no military solution to guerrilla struggles waged by people willing to employ methods of terror. Bringing warring parties together for serious dialogue is often difficult. States generally refuse to 'negotiate with terrorists.' The reason usually given is that negotiation is a sign of weakness and may encourage further acts of terrorism. Yet if the root cause of such violence is actual or perceived oppression, resistance forces that engage in terrorism (to bring oppression to an end) are unlikely to be deterred by the characterization of their behavior as inherently evil. They are instead likely to believe that theirs is a righteous struggle.[50] Rather than seeing themselves as 'terrorists' they are likely to regard themselves as brave and heroic fighters whose actions are justified under their ideology until their objectives are achieved.

At some point, states that have been unable to end terrorist attacks may decide that the political costs of maintaining the *status quo* outweigh the risks of compromise and commencing dialogue. Concessions by both sides may be necessary to reach this point. Dialogue with terrorists creates the opportunity to talk down those who would take innocent life. It offers the chance to broker cease-fires and work towards the peaceful resolution of armed conflicts. Grievances on both sides must be heard and legitimate concerns addressed. This is not 'giving in to terrorism.' Ongoing dialogue is a proactive mode of reducing the prospect of future acts of terror. Dialogue may involve diplomatic, political, military and religious figures. The prominent role of Islamist groups in contemporary international terrorism has heightened the need for dialogue between – and within – faiths and religious sects. Efforts to increase

---

50 Not all campaigns of terrorist violence are inspired by past injustice. Some perpetrators of terrorism may be motivated by base motives such as greed, the desire to cause suffering and deep seated racial or ethnic hatred that cannot be traced to any past injustice. However such cases are rare. The killing of civilians is universally condemned. People are unlikely to engage in such barbarism without a strong sense of grievance. Those who follow extremist ideologies are invariably driven by some deep sense of injustice, something powerful enough inspire the anger and hatred that motivates individuals to engage in acts of terror.

awareness of other faiths, and promote tolerance and cooperation, can encourage moderation in religion and help eradicate religious sources of terrorism. Pope John Paul II saw the importance of dialogue in efforts to resolve disputes. He went to great lengths to promote and engage in dialogue between the Church and Islamic leaders (see 'Pope Urges Muslims to Help Defeat Terrorism'). Moreover, the Vatican has repeatedly repudiated the use of force to resolve disputes ('Pope condemns war in Iraq' 2003).[51] A number of influential Islamic scholars have done the same. Their role has been significant. It includes discouraging Muslim youth from adopting Islamist ideologies that lead to terrorism, and 'talking down' extremists who advocate the use of terror. By recourse to the Koran, the Hadith,[52] the Sunnah[53] and other sources of Islamic jurisprudence such as the writings of eminent scholars, the flaws in extremist Islamist ideologies may be identified and communicated (Brandon 2005).[54] This may be done by highlighting prohibitions on such conduct found in text of the Koran, verses of Sunnah, and *fatwas* issued by various Islamic leaders and scholars (see 'UK Muslims issue bombings fatwa').[55] This methodology has the potential to dissuade individual extremists from: (a) engaging in violence against the state; (b) subverting

---

51 For a contrary view see: Willey, David (10 February 2003), 'Catholic theologian says Iraq "just war" ', <http://news.bbc.co.uk/2/hi/europe/2747199.stm>.

52 M.M. Azami's *Studies in Hadith Methodology and Literature*, offers the following definition of a hadith:

According to Muhaddithiin [scholars of hadith – ed.] it stands for 'what was transmitted on the authority of the Prophet, his deeds, sayings, tacit approval, or description of his sifaat (features) meaning his physical appearance. However, physical appearance of the Prophet is not included in the definition used by the jurists.'

Thus hadith literature means the literature which consists of the narrations of the life of the Prophet and the things approved by him. However, the term was used sometimes in much broader sense to cover the narrations about the Companions [of the Prophet – ed.] and Successors [to the Companions – ed.] as well.

(University of Southern California, Compendium of Muslim Texts) <http://www.usc.edu/dept/MSA/fundamentals/hadithsunnah>, accessed 5 December 2005.

53 The Arabic word '*sunnah*' has come to denote the way Prophet Mohammed lived his life. The Sunnah is the second source of Islamic jurisprudence, the first being the Koran. University of Southern California, Compendium of Muslim Texts, <http://www.usc.edu/dept/MSA/fundamentals/hadithsunnah>, accessed 5 December 2005.

54 Yemeni Judge Hamoud al-Hitar uses a simple system during dialogue with prisoners. Brandon notes that Hitar 'invites militants to use the Koran to justify attacks on innocent civilians and when they cannot, he shows them numerous passages commanding Muslims not to attack civilians, to respect other religions, and fight only in self-defense.' Hitar claims that 'Three hundred and sixty-four young men have been released after going through the dialogues and none of these have left Yemen to fight anywhere else.'

55 On 19 July 2005 more than 500 British Muslim religious leaders and scholars have issued a *fatwa* condemning the London Bombings of 7 July 2005. They noted that Islam condemns violence against innocent people and declared that suicide bombings are 'vehemently prohibited.' Dozens of similar *fatwas* have been issued since 11 September 2001 by Muslims organizations, conferences and scholars across the world.

the role of courts by engaging in extra-judicial killings; (c) killing civilians; and (d) engaging in other forms of conduct that is *haram* or forbidden in Islam.[56]

Talking down 'evil'

Aside from theological persuasion, other methods may be employed to encourage Islamists to follow the path of non-violence. Legal, philosophical and ideological objections to the taking of innocent life can be emphasized. Prohibitions on the killing unarmed civilians – under customary laws of war, the Geneva Conventions (that codify norms of humanitarian law) and human rights law can be highlighted. The role that Islamic nations have played in the development of this body of international law can be emphasized (see Cockayne 2002). Moreover the futility of terrorism as a tactic for overthrowing established regimes can be noted by reference to historical examples. Powerful arguments can be presented that terrorist organizations have rarely achieved their objectives but instead taken innocent life in a futile struggle. Islamists may also be persuaded that their concerns are best addressed through the political process and with due respect for human rights. Allowing Islamist parties to participate in elections may assist in such efforts. So too will efforts by governments to bring their laws and practices into conformity with human rights law. By contrast, where government policies create or perpetuate injustice or oppression, members of terrorist organizations will be more resolute and less likely to be depart from the path of violence.

Addressing the injustices that fuel radical Islam

Islamist ideologies that encourage followers to use violence to gain political power have emerged from time to time throughout the history of Islam. The doctrine of militant jihad is deeply rooted in the Koran and Hadith, the writings of eminent Islamic scholars, and the main schools of Islamic jurisprudence. Militant jihad against invasion and oppression is regarded by many Muslims as a sacred duty. It is upon these theological foundations that radical Islamists have built their politico-

---

56 The circumstances in which violent jihad is justified in Islam have been debated over many centuries. A detailed discussion of this issue exceeds the scope of this study. Rich and diverse legal traditions have emerged on the Islamic law of war. The principle sources of Islamic law inform this debate. They include the Koran, the Sunnah (traditions of the Prophet Mohammed) and the opinion of celebrated Muslim jurists. The focus of debate about violent jihad and its limits invariably revolves around: (a) interpretations of the sources of Islamic law; (b) the contemporary relevance of Islamic practices from earlier times; (c) assigning priority to conflicting verses by application of the doctrine of abrogation; and (d) application of principles of itjihad (independent legal reasoning). For a useful English language collection of Islamic jurisprudence on this topic see Bostom, Andrew G. (ed.) (2005), *The Legacy of Jihad: Islamic Holy War and the Fate of non-Muslims.* For competing Islamic interpretations of jihad see Rehman, Javaid (2005), 'The Concept of Jihad in Islamic International Law', 10(4), *Journal of Conflict and Security Law*, 1, 6–13. For the militant jihadist ideology that inspired al Qaeda and its affiliates see Musallam, Adnan A. (2005), *From Secularism to Jihad: Sayyid Qutb and the Foundations of Radical Islamism.*

religious ideologies. Whenever Muslim lands are invaded or Muslim populations are oppressed, there is the possibility of militant jihad. Where states fail to act to halt such injustices, non-state actors may feel compelled to take up arms to defend Islam and the *umma*. For these reasons it is unlikely that radical Islamist ideologies will ever be completely and permanently eradicated.

Where Arab governments are weak and riddled with sectarian divisions (for example, Lebanon and the Palestinian Authority) radical Islamist organizations have often arisen to fill the political vacuum. In 1988 Osama bin Laden and Ayman al-Zawahiri co-signed their 1998 'fatwa' calling upon '… every Muslim … to kill the Americans and plunder their money wherever and whenever they find it.' They did so in response to, *inter alia*, conditions in Saudi Arabia (including the presence of US troops in that country). In the decade since, most Muslims have *not* answered al Qaeda's call. While support among Muslims for al Qaeda's *goals* remains high, most reject its *methods* (terrorism).[57] This suggests that most Muslims want: corruption; injustices against Muslims, oppression by Arab and foreign regimes to be brought to an end – but not through the indiscriminate killing of civilians. This view has been propounded by innumerable Muslim scholars and leaders since 11 September 2001.

Democracy in the Middle East

Opinions vary on whether vibrant democracies can emerge across the Middle East. There are a number of obstacles to be overcome. Lasting peace between Israel and its neighbors is the main one. The occupation of Palestinian territory provides a platform for radical Islamists to recruit followers and wage a terrorist campaign against both the Israelis and '*kafrs*' (Muslims who seek to rein in non-state actors and make peace with Israel). Another problem is the culture of violence as a means of resolving problems. Political assassinations of Arab leaders and attempts at the same have been part of the political landscape for a long time. In the post-colonial era such activities have been carried out by an assortment of actors including agents of the West, political or faction rivals, and radical Islamists seeking to overthrow the existing political order. A lesson learned by Arab leaders, whether brutal or benevolent, is that a powerful *maktaba* (intelligence and security service) is essential for survival. Nonetheless there is a widespread belief that these problems are exploited by Arab regimes to justify the denial of democracy and human rights. Most Arab states have had a measure of democracy at some stage since gaining independence from colonial rule. Today most have a limited form of democracy, as has been noted above. In some, like Syria and until recently Iraq, there is only one presidential candidate on the ballot paper. Disenchantment at the absence of the democracy and ongoing religious and political violence is reflected in satellite TV programs. Governments are criticized and solutions to the democratic deficit are debated.

---

57 'Large and Growing Numbers of Muslims Reject Terrorism, Bin Laden: Negative Views of West and US Unabated', 12 June 2007 <http://worldpublicopinion.org> accessed 12 June 2007; 'Muslims Believe US Seeks to Undermine Islam: Majorities Want US Forces Out of Islamic Countries And Approve of Attacks on US Troops', 12 June 2007 <http://www.worldpublicopinion.org> accessed 12 June 2007.

In the wake of the terrorist attacks on 11 September 2001, the democratic project has been set back in Muslim states. Wars in Afghanistan and Iraq have delivered weak elected governments and a rise in terrorism by radical Islamists (Al Qaeda in Iraq, and the Taliban and Al Qaeda in Afghanistan). US patronage is vital to the survival of both regimes. Insurgents in both states have employed terror tactics as they strive to topple what they regard as 'apostate' governments. Meanwhile, Turkey, a secular state with a pro-Islamist government, continues to battle a sustained terrorist campaign/insurgency by the Kurdistan Workers' Party (PKK) in south east Turkey.

It remains to be seen whether Islamist parties in the Middle East will be able to preside over stable and enduring democracies. The Islamic revolution in Iran delivered clerical rule and only modest democratic gains have been achieved since. Elections in Algeria in 1991 were annulled after an Islamist party won the contest. The victorious party was subsequently banned. In other Muslim states in the region democracy is limited. Turkey is the most democratic, although this secular state is undergoing a slow political and constitutional crisis over the contest between secularist and Islamist polity. Massive opposition rallies in 2007 in defence of the nation's secular constitution are a reminder to the ruling party that Islamist reforms that undermine the secular state will not go unchallenged.

This brief survey reveals that, where it does exist, democracy in the Middle East is a fragile affair. It is unclear what impact democracy will have on religious extremism in the region and vice versa. So long as Islamist parties face restrictions, full democracy cannot be achieved. Moreover terrorism by radical Islamists is unlikely to be abated until Islamists are allowed to participate fully in government. What is certain is that the vision of political Islam offered by rival sects who are sometimes willing to fight each other to gain power does not offer a peaceful, stable or attractive solution. For these reason human rights-based approaches to democracy should be nurtured and encouraged rather than Islamist ideologies. This may require the exclusion from national elections of Islamist parties that do not support democracy and human rights, and fail to renounce violence.

Strengthening internal and external security

Respect for the rule of law and human rights will not necessarily guarantee that states are immune from international or domestic terrorism. Other measures are needed to bolster national security. These include effective border security, surveillance and monitoring of those suspected of involvement in extremist organizations, infiltration and disruption of terrorist organizations and cells, monitoring of the sale of explosive substances and weapons, and the vetting of persons entering and leaving the country. In order for these measures to be carried out with optimal efficiency, states must build strong relationships with each other so that trust may be built up, intelligence shared and joint operations undertaken to apprehend, extradite and prosecute members of terrorist organizations. These matters are looked at in more detail in Chapter 4.

Counter-Terrorism Law and Policy

An effective response to terrorism requires an effective legal and institutional apparatus at state, regional and international levels. Law enforcement officials must have the power to detain, interrogate and prosecute those who commit, incite, finance or conspire to commit acts of terror. Extradition laws must also be in place to enable the deportation of visitors and other non-citizens who engage in such activities, or otherwise pose a demonstrable threat to national security.[58] Law enforcement and intelligence agencies must be adequately funded to effectively carry out their duties. Counter-terrorism squads must be professionally trained and properly resourced. There must be appropriate cooperation between federal, provincial and local authorities and agencies to facilitate effective counter-terrorism policies and practices.[59]

Identification of high risk groups

An important element of effective counter-terrorism is the capacity of law enforcement, intelligence and security agencies to identify those who pose a genuine danger to society. They must be able to distinguish such persons from those who may espouse the rhetoric of terror, or associate with terror suspects, but in fact pose no demonstrable threat. Identification of those falling into the first category can be aided by an understanding of 'the power of group dynamics.' Social psychologists have long understood the desire of people to belong to a social group, to belong somewhere in society. They also understand that 'group dynamics' can shape individual behavior. In 1955, Solomon Asch published a series of studies that demonstrated the power of *conformity* in groups (see Asch 1955; 1956). Asch demonstrated the impact of group pressure upon the modification and distortion of judgment. These studies were followed by research conducted by one of Asch's doctoral students, Stanley Milgram. In 1963, Milgram set out the findings of his *Obedience to Authority* study. It measured the willingness of participants to follow commands that may conflict with their conscience. The results were disturbing. Group members inflicted significant amounts of pain on individuals in order to be 'one of the guys.' This became one

---

58 The threat of deportation or imprisonment may deter others from involving themselves in terrorist activity. States must however be mindful that some countries of origin may refuse to receive such persons (for example, for national security). States must also ensure that they do not send terror suspects to countries where they are likely to be tortured. (A process known as rendition.)

59 In Australia, intelligence gathering and assessment is undertaken by the Australian Security and Intelligence Organization (ASIO) and the Office of National Assessment (ONA). Counter-terrorism teams include the SAS (Special Air Service Regiment, Australian Defence Forces) as well as state and Territory Tactical Response Groups. The latter include: Australian Federal Police Special Operations Team (SOT), Victorian Police Special Operations Group (SOG), Tasmanian Police Special Operations Group (SOG), Queensland Police Special Emergency Response Team (SERT), Northern Territory Police Territory Response Group (TRG), Western Australian Police Tactical Response Group (TRG), South Australian Police Special Tasks and Rescue Division (STAR) and the New South Wales Police Tactical Operations Unit (TOU).

of the most famous scientific experiments in the field of psychology (see Milgram 1963; 1974).

This 'band of brothers' dynamic, has been exploited by armed forces for centuries. It is used to motivate soldiers to participate in high risk military operations. It may also explain why individuals with no psychological abnormality have been willing to undertake suicide bombing missions. Where close bonds are formed between group members, these members become more alike in their behavior and attitudes. As the group dynamic evolves, members may feel that they have more in common with each other (and a closer attachment and sense of belonging) than with their own biological relatives. These factors may be accentuated where the group is comprised of young people who feel alienated from mainstream society. Research conducted in the wake of the London bombings of 7 July 2005 has identified a number of common characteristics of the perpetrators of these crimes. They were all members of a tightly knit group of young Muslim men who shared an intense interest in politics, a common religious tradition, and a strong ideological commitment that rendered them susceptible to radicalization to the point where they would take part in suicide bombing operations.[60]

The identification and infiltration of Islamist terror cells has become a priority for British intelligence agencies. So too have been efforts to locate and monitor radical Islamist organizations or 'lone wolves' who are trying to persuade young Muslims to adopt their violent notions of jihad. A disturbing aspect of *The Report of the Official Account of the Bombings in London on 7th July 2005*[61] is the fact that a number of the London bombers were well integrated into British society. Another concern is that al Qaeda's message alone may be enough to trigger the self-radicalization of Muslim youth. The report offers vague and general motivations for the attacks – 'Fierce antagonism to perceived injustices by the West against Muslims and a desire for martyrdom.' Yet this is entirely consistent with the video message left by one of the suicide bombers.[62] Interestingly, and in contrast to the 'martyrdom videos', the report avoids an obvious conclusion: the bombings were motivated in large part by Britain's involvement in the war in Iraq, a war which most of the British public – whether Muslim or non-Muslim – opposed.

Protection of minorities

It is clearly in the interests of Western countries to ensure that migrant populations, and local minorities, develop a sense of belonging within mainstream society, and attachment to the state. While cultural differences should be celebrated and enjoyed, minorities should be given every opportunity to integrate into the mainstream

---

60 The 7/7 Bombers – A Psychological Investigation <http://www.bbc.co.uk/sn/tvradio/ programmes/horizon/bombers.shtml>.

61 Ordered by the House of Commons to be printed 11 May 2006.

62 London bomber video aired on TV, 2 September 2005, <http://news.bbc.co.uk/2/hi/ uk_news/4206708.stm>, accessed 17 April 2007.

society.[63] This may require proactive measures including strict enforcement of laws to combat racism and discrimination in the workplace, schools and public places. Without these measures, some minority groups may become marginalized and impoverished, and their youth may become vulnerable to radicalization by extremists. Effective counter-terrorism requires protection of civil, political, social, economic and cultural rights of citizens. To alienate Muslim communities on the basis of their ethnicity or religion is morally unacceptable and strategically counter-productive for states. It may cause social divisions with a society and add legitimacy to the claims of radical Islamists. It may also undermine efforts by officials to gather intelligence on extremists operating within minority communities. This is true not only of countries like Britain but also Iraq. One of the reasons for ongoing terrorist violence in Iraq – long after the collapse of the Ba'ath regime in 2003 and the formation of a democratically elected government in 2006 – has been the failure of the Shi'ite-dominated government to protect and guarantee the safety of Arab Sunnis. Radical Sunni elements are unlikely to desist from terrorist violence until Shi'ite militias affiliated with the government and the Iraqi security forces themselves desist from engaging in similar conduct. There are signs of progress in this area, including greater cooperation between Sunnis and Shi'ite both inside and outside of government. It is significant that Sunni tribes in Anbar province are now fighting al Qaeda. However al Qaeda has struck back killing Sunni tribal leaders loyal to the Coalition and the central government in a series of suicide bomb attacks.

Balancing national security and civil rights

In pursuing counter-terrorism objectives, a balance must be struck between national security and civil rights. If fundamental rights are to be limited by counter-terrorism laws, such measures should be thoroughly scrutinized and debated by elected law makers prior to implementation. These laws should be consistent with international best practice. This issue is canvassed below in the discussion of the report of the Special Rapporteur on Human Rights and Terrorism.

State compliance with counter- terrorism obligations under Security Council resolutions

If the counter-terrorism policies of states are to be based on the international rule of law, then states must adhere to, and implement, relevant binding resolutions of the Security Council. In 1998 the Security Council responded to the growth of Islamist terror by passing resolution 1189. It requires states to take effective and practical measures in the areas of: security cooperation; the prevention of acts of terrorism;

---

63 Ayaan Hirsi Ali's experiences in Holland provide compelling reasons for states to promote integration of migrant populations and avoidance of policies that promote separation: See Ayaan Hirsi Ali (2007), *Infidel: My Journey to Enlightenment* (Free Press). See also Bruce Bawer (2006), *While Europe Slept: How Radical Islam Is Destroying the West from Within* (Doubleday). Note these books have created controversy, being both praised for their insights and condemned for inciting racism and Islamophobia.

and the prosecution and punishment of perpetrators. Three years later the Security Council expanded upon these basic state responsibilities. Shortly after the terrorist attacks of 11 September 2001, the Security Council passed Resolution 1373. It sets out a comprehensive list of state obligations. The resolution was passed under Chapter VII of the UN Charter and is therefore binding upon states. They are required to:

- Prevent and suppress the financing of terrorist acts;
- Criminalize the willful provision or collection of funds to carry out terrorist acts;
- Freeze funds and other financial assets or economic resources of persons involved in terrorism;
- Refrain from providing any form of support, active or passive, to entities or persons involved in terrorist acts, including suppressing recruitment of members of terrorist groups and eliminating the supply of weapons to terrorists;
- Take the necessary steps to prevent the commission of terrorist acts, including the provision of early warning to other states by exchange of information;
- Deny safe haven to those who finance, plan, support, or commit terrorist acts, or provide safe havens;
- Afford one another the greatest measure of assistance in connection with criminal investigations or criminal proceedings relating to the financing or support of terrorist acts;
- Prevent the movement of terrorists or terrorist groups by effective border controls and controls on issuance of identity papers and travel documents, and through measures for preventing counterfeiting, forgery or fraudulent use of identity papers and travel documents.

Full implementation of these responsibilities is beyond the resources of some nations. Wealthier states must therefore provide assistance to those that need help. Without this cooperation and assistance the global effort to counter terrorism is compromised. These issues are discussed further in Chapter 4.

Implementation of the UN Global Counter-Terrorism Strategy

In September 2006 member states of the United Nations adopted a Global Counter-Terrorism Strategy. The core elements of this 'Plan of Action' are critiqued in Chapter 4. This UN document draws upon numerous UN reports and investigations (including those of the UN Special Rapporteur on Human Rights and Terrorism). Its recommendations, if implemented, could significantly reduce terrorism.[64] In 1997 the Special Rapporteur recommended that states take a range of measures, many of which are yet to be fully implemented:

1. Avoid exaggerating the threat of terrorism and instilling fear in the community for political ends, as abuse or manipulation of the threat posed by terrorist

---

64 See note 8 above.

organizations can undermine resolve to take necessary and proportionate measures;[65]

2. Use appropriate language when defining terrorist activity;[66]
3. Keep efforts to combat terrorism focused on actual terrorism rather than other forms of violence (such as drug trafficking, organized crime, and conventional armed conflict). These offenses should not be defined as terrorist acts. Crimes not directly or indirectly related to terrorism should not be included in national counter-terrorism legislation or treated by investigative authorities as being under that legislation;[67]
4. Ensure that the perpetrators of terrorism are described in treaties and legislation in a comprehensive way. The description should include both state and non-state actors. If terrorism is to be comprehensively addressed, state-sponsored terrorism needs to be included;
5. Work together to establish international guidelines on whether states may derogate from any universally accepted human rights norms in the event of terrorist activity;[68]
6. Ensure that fundamental human rights are not abandoned in counter-terrorism legislation or treaties. A comprehensive treaty on international terrorism, should not sacrifice the principle of non-refoulement. Extradition arrangements should not be abused through the return of persons to states that engage in torture, summary execution or other forms of extra-judicial punishment of suspected terrorists.[69]
7. Review national practices that 'effectively result in impunity for terrorist acts and barriers for victims seeking remedies.'
8. International or regional tribunals should be vested with jurisdiction to prosecute state terrorism.[70]

States are still a long way from meeting these goals, all of which are important. Agreement on a final draft of the comprehensive international treaty on terrorism is still illusive. A regional court where it is needed most (the Middle East), with jurisdiction to try terrorists, is nowhere in sight.

---

65 See Paragraph 71.

66 'The rhetorical use of the expression "war on terrorism", labeling wars as terrorism, and combatants in wars as terrorists, has an extremely undesirable effect of nullifying application of and compliance with humanitarian law in those situations, while at the same time providing no positive results in combating actual terrorism.' (Paragraph 72).

67 Paragraph 74.

68 '[T]hese guidelines take into account determination of actual or perceived threat, the degree to which the threat constitutes a threat to the existence of the state, the degree to which responses to the acts or risks of acts meet strict exigency requirements, the time frame for derogations, and reporting and periodic review of any derogations.' (Paragraph 77).

69 Paragraph 75.

70 Paragraph 69.

Military force should only be used within the bounds of international law

Military operations against Islamist terror organizations (such as al Qaeda) are sometimes necessary. However such operations will only be lawful where they can be justified under Article 51 of the UN Charter (the inherent right of self-defence) or have been approved in advance by the Security Council. Situations that would warrant a military response can be easily imagined. One example is where a terrorist organization gains a foothold in a failed (or failing) state and uses it as a base from which to launch international terrorist operations. This occurred in Afghanistan during the Taliban era. Al Qaeda planned and carried out the September the 11th terrorist attacks with the support or acquiescence of the Taliban. The UN Charter provides the machinery for the international community to deal with international terrorism. Where sovereign states come under armed attack, they are justified under Article 51 of the UN Charter in using force to halt such aggression. Where the attack is launched by an international terrorist organization, force may be used to capture or kill its members and destroy the apparatus of the organization. Any other conclusion renders the sovereign right of self-defence vacuous. Alternatively a military response may be carried out under the authority of the Security Council. Either way, the military response must be carried out in accordance with international law on the use of force. Applicable norms include the principles of necessity, proportionality and the *jus in bello*. The consequences that may flow from the failure to comply with these rules are evident from the situation in Iraq. In waging what many states regarded as an illegitimate intervention – if not a war of aggression – the US and its allies triggered, *inter alia*, a wave of terrorism. This adverse outcome has threatened to outweigh the benefits gained by ordinary Iraqis from their liberation in 2003 from a brutal era of dictatorship.

Conclusion

'Curing terrorism' is a multifaceted task. Bringing religious violence by radical Islamists to an end will require close cooperation between states in the pursuit of agreed strategies. In a nutshell, states must work together to resolve the international and domestic problems that drive terrorism. Specifically they must:

1. Actively support the two-state solution to the Palestine question, which the Arab League has collectively endorsed[71] but both the Palestinian Authority and Israeli governments have prevaricated over in recent years;
2. Continue to exert real pressure on the Israelis and the Palestinians to accept such a plan and enter into a lasting peace. With this conflict resolved, the heat

---

71 It involves an independent Palestinian that lives 'in peaceful coexistence alongside a secure and recognised Israel, within the 1967 frontiers' and 'full normalisation between the Arab countries and Israel.' Under this framework 'A Palestinian capital in Eastern Jerusalem would be matched by an Israeli capital in Western Jerusalem.' See 'Address by His Majesty King Abdullah II at the 49th Munich Conference on Security Policy', 8 February 2004 <http://www.jordanembassyus.org/hmka02082004.htm> accessed 12 June 2007.

may be taken out of many of the radical Islamist ideologies that were its birth child;

3. Support UN-approved strategies in states such as Afghanistan and Iraq that have been infiltrated by terrorist organizations. Where necessary, generous assistance must be provided to facilitate development, national reconstruction, human rights, and democratic governance;

4. Work together to isolate terrorist organizations and suppress the financing and support for such groups; and

5. Recognize that a majority of people in Muslim nations want human rights and democracy but in an Islamic context. This requires an acceptance that moderate Islamist parties must be accommodated if vibrant Arab democracies are to emerge. If this indeed occurs, a cornerstone of al Qaeda's politico-religious ideology will be undermined. If governments across the region are elected, and development, education, poverty eradication, and other social and economic factors are addressed, corruption is tackled, human rights and human security are protected, the sovereignty of Muslim states is respected by foreign states, and foreign troops only enter or remain in Muslim lands with the consent of elected governments, it will no longer be credible for radical Islamists to assert that Muslims are being oppressed by 'apostate' governments.

In summary, Arab and Islamic states across the world – with the assistance of the international community – must work hard to reverse the prevailing mood on the Arab street. This mood is one of disenchantment, scepticism and anger at the hypocrisy of local and foreign governments that speak the language of democracy and human rights but deny it to people across the Middle East. In the battle for the hearts and minds of Muslims, genuine democracy and human rights guarantees must be delivered. If not, ideologies of terror propagated by radical Islamists will continue to disrupt societies in the Muslim world and beyond.

References

17-Nation Pew Global Attitudes Survey (14 July 2005), *Islamic Extremism: Common Concern for Muslim And Western Publics*.

Additional Protocol I (1977), Articles 43 and 44.

Alexander, Yonah (1986), *State Sponsored Terrorism* (Washington, DC: Center for Contemporary Studies).

Article 1(4), Protocol Additional to the Geneva Conventions of 12 August 1949, and relating to the Protection of Victims of International Armed Conflicts (Protocol 1) Adopted on 8 June 1977 by the Diplomatic Conference on the Reaffirmation and Development of International Humanitarian Law applicable in Armed Conflicts.

Article 43, Protocol Additional to the Geneva Conventions of 12 August 1949, and relating to the Protection of Victims of International Armed Conflicts (Protocol 1) Adopted on 8 June 1977 by the Diplomatic Conference on the Reaffirmation and Development of International Humanitarian Law applicable in Armed Conflicts entry into force 7 December 1979, in accordance with Article 95.

Asch, S.E. (1955), 'Opinions and social pressure', *Scientific American*, 31.

—— (1956), 'Studies of independence and conformity: A minority of one against a unanimous majority', *Psychological Monographs*, 70.

Azami, M.M. (2002), *Studies in Hadith Methodology and Literature* (University of Southern California Compendium of Muslim Texts), <http://www.usc.edu/dept/MSA/fundamentals/hadithsunnah/>, accessed 5 December 2005.

Baker, James A, III, and Hamilton, Lee H. (Co-Chairs), *et al.* (2006) *The Iraq Study Group Report*, <http://www.usip.org>, accessed 10 December 2006.

Basler, R.P. (ed.), *The Collected Works of Abraham Lincoln*, Vol. III, 'Letter To Henry L. Pierce and Others' (6 April 1859).

Bierzanek, R. (1977), 'Humanitarian Law in Armed Conflicts: The Doctrine and Practise of Polish Insurgents in the 19th century', *International Review of the Red Cross*.

Blay, S., Piotrowicz, R. and Tsamenyi, M. (2005), *Public International law: An Australian Perspective*, 2nd Edition (Melbourne: Oxford University Press).

Bostom, A.G. (ed.) (2005), *The Legacy of Jihad: Islamic Holy War and the Fate of non-Muslims* (New York: Prometheus Books).

Bradsher, H.S. (1983), *Afghanistan and the Soviet Union* (Durham, NC: Duke University Press).

Brandon, J. (2005), 'Koranic duels ease terror', *The Christian Science Monitor* (website), <http://www.csmonitor.com/2005/0204/p01s04-wome.html>, accessed 20 December 2005.

Bregman, A. (2002), *A History of Israel* (NY: Palgrave Macmillan).

Cassese, A. (2005), *International Law*, 2nd Edition (Oxford: Oxford University Press).

Charter of the United Nations (1945).

Clarke, B. (2005), 'The juridical status of civilian resistance to foreign occupation under the law of nations and contemporary international law', 7 *University of Notre Dame Australia Law Review*, 1.

Cockayne, J. (2002), 'Islam and international humanitarian law: from a clash to a conversation between civilizations', *International Review of the Red Cross*, 84, 597.

Crile, G. (2003), *My Enemy's Enemy: The Story of the Largest Covert Operation in History: The Arming of the Mujahideen by the CIA* (Atlantic Books).

General Assembly World Summit (2005, September), Paragraph 81, Final Outcomes Document.

Geneva Convention III (1949), Article 4, Paragraph 2.

Geneva Convention IV (1949), Articles 64–68.

Gundarsson, K., *Hermann the Cheruscan*, <http://www.webcom.com/~lstead/March94/Hermann.html>, accessed 20 October 2004.

Heller, J. (1995), *The Stern Gang: Ideology, Politics and Terror 1940–1949* (Portland: Frank Cass).

Hekmatyar video (Television broadcast, Al Jazeera, 6 May 2006), <http://english.aljazeera.net/English/archive/archive?ArchiveId=22504>.

Husein, E. (2007), *The Islamist: Why I Joined Radical Islam in Britain, What I Saw Inside and Why I Left* (UK: Penguin Books).

'Iraq allies reject terror link report' (2005), <http://www.abc.net.au/news/ newsitems/200507/s1417111.htm>, accessed 3 December 2005.

Iraq Body Count is a website that provides an update of reported civilian deaths in the Iraq war and occupation (http://www.iraqbodycount.org/).

Jamali, A. (2005), 'Gulbuddin Hekmatyar: The Rise and Fall of an Afghan Warlord', *Terrorism Monitor*, Volume 3, Issue 2.

Kakar, M. Hassan (1995), *Afghanistan: The Soviet Invasion and the Afghan Response*, 1979–1982 (University of California Press).

Kaplan, E. (2006), 'The Taliban Resurgence in Afghanistan', <http://www.cfr.org/ publication/10551/>, accessed 17 April 2007.

Khan, L. Ali (2004), *A Theory of International Terrorism: Understanding Islamic Militancy* (Leiden: M. Nijhoff).

King Abdullah II (2004), 'Address by His Majesty King Abdullah II at the 49th Munich Conference on Security Policy' <http://www.jordanembassyus.org/ hmka02082004.htm> accessed 12 June 2007.

Koufa, K.K. (2004), Paragraph 67, *Specific Human Rights Issues: New Priorities, in Particular Terrorism and Counter-Terrorism, Terrorism and Human Rights*, Final Report of the Special Rapporteur on Human Rights and Terrorism of the Sub-Commission on the Promotion and Protection of Human Rights (E/CN.4/ Sub.2/2004/40. Commission on Human Rights, UN Economic and Social Council, 2004).

Lacina, B. and Gleditsch, N. (2005), 'Monitoring Trends in Global Combat: A New Dataset of Battle Deaths', *European Journal of Population/ Revue Européenne de Démographie*, Vol. 21, Nos 2–3, pp. 145–66 (22).

'Large and Growing Numbers of Muslims Reject Terrorism, Bin Laden: Negative Views of West and US Unabated', 12 June 2007 <http://worldpublicopinion.org> accessed 12 June 2007.

Lendering, Jona (2006), 'The battle in the Teutoburg Forest' <http://www.livius.org/ te-tg/teutoburg/teutoburg01.htm> accessed 10 June 2007.

Lederer, E.M. and Wadhams, N., 'U.N.: Syria, Lebanon Involved in Slaying', *Associated Press*, <http://abcnews.go.com/International/wireStory?id=1235565>, accessed 2 January 2006.

Lewis, B. (1999), *Semites and Anti-Semites: An Inquiry into Conflict and Prejudice* (New York: W.W. Norton & Company).

Loboda, L. (2004) Thesis, *The Thought of Sayyid Qutb: Radical Islam's Philosophical Foundations*, <http://www.ashbrook.org/publicat/thesis/loboda/home.html#64>, accessed 18 April 2007.

London bomber video (Television broadcast, 2 September 2005), <http://news.bbc. co.uk/2/hi/uk_news/4206708.stm>, accessed 17 April 2007.

Marzban, O. (21 September 2006), 'Gulbuddin Hekmatyar: From Holy Warrior to Wanted Terrorist', *Terrorism Monitor* Vol. 4, Issue 18, <http://www.jamestown. org/terrorism/news/article.php?articleid=2370138>, accessed 17 April 2007.

Mattar, P. (1988), *The Mufti of Jerusalem: Al-Hajj Amin Al-Husayni and the Palestinian National Movement* (New York: Columbia University Press).

'Measures to eliminate international terrorism', UN Doc A/RES/49/60, Paragraph 3.

Mendes, P. (1998), 'A Historical Controversy: The Mufti of Jerusalem, The Palestinians and the Holocaust', 12 *Australian Journal of Jewish Studies*, 81–102.

Milgram, S. (1963) 'Behavioral Study of Obedience', *Journal of Abnormal and Social Psychology*, Vol. 67, 371–8.

—— (1974), *Obedience to Authority: An Experimental View* (London: Tavistock).

Morgan, A. (11 February 2003), 'Australians targeted, says Bali bomber', *Sydney Morning Herald* (website), <http://www.smh.com.au/articles/2003/02/11/1044725746886.html>.

Mougenot, R. (1903), *Des pratiques de la guerre continentale durant le Premier Empire* (Paris: Librairie Militaire R. Chapelot et Cie), p. 377.

Musallam, A.A. (2005), *From secularism to Jihad: Sayyid Qutb and the foundations of radical Islamism* (Westport: Praeger Publishers).

'Muslims Believe US Seeks to Undermine Islam: Majorities Want US Forces Out of Islamic Countries And Approve of Attacks on US Troops', 12 June 2007 <http://www.worldpublicopinion.org> accessed 12 June 2007.

Nabulsi (1999), *Traditions of War: Occupation, Resistance and the Law* (Oxford: Oxford University Press).

Napier, W. (1889), *A narrative of the Peninsular Campaign 1807–1814* (London: Bickers & Son).

'New Hariri report "blames Syria" ', 11 December 2005, <http://news.bbc.co.uk/2/hi/middle_east/4519346.stm>, accessed 2 January 2006.

Palestine Mandate (1920).

Pape, R.A. (2005), *Dying to Win: The Strategic Logic of Suicide Terrorism* (Random House).

'Pope condemns war in Iraq', 13 January 2003 <http://news.bbc.co.uk/2/hi/europe/2654109.stm>, accessed 3 December 2005.

'Pope Urges Muslims to Help Defeat Terrorism', <http://www.islamonline.net/English/News/2005-08/21/article01.shtml>, accessed 3 December 2005.

Quenivet, N. (2005), 'The World after September 11: Has It Really Changed?' 16 *European Journal of International Law*, 562, 564.

Qutb, S. (1964), *M"alim fi'l-Tariq* (*Signposts on the Road*, or *Milestones*).

Rehman, J. (2005), 'The Concept of Jihad in Islamic International Law', 10(4), *Journal of Conflict and Security Law*, 1, 6–13.

Rome Statute of the International Criminal Court, Article 5. (UN Doc. A/CONF.183/9*).

SC Res. 1566 (2004) UN Doc. S/RES/1566 (2004), 8 October 2004, Operative Paragraph 3.

Secretary-General's lecture at the 35th National Conference of Trinity Institute 2 May 2004 – New York, <http://www.un.org/apps/sg/sgstats.asp?nid=905>, accessed 3 December 2005.

Security Council Resolution 1373, UN Doc. S/RES/1373 (2001), operative paragraphs 1–3.

Shamir, Y. (1994), *Summing Up* (London: Weidenfeld & Nicholson).

Silver, E. (1984), *Begin* (London: Weidenfeld & Nicholson).

Simpson, G. (2004), *Great Powers and Outlaw Nations* (Cambridge: Cambridge University Press).

Smith, J. (19 July 2005), 'Official report 'linked terror risk to Iraq', <http://news.independent.co.uk/uk/crime/article300193.ece>, accessed 3 December 2005.

Sorel, J.-M. (2003), 'Some Questions About the Definition of Terrorism and the Fight against Its Financing', 14 *The European Journal of International Law*, 365, 366.

Stanley, T. (2005, July). 'Definition: Islamism, Islamist, Islamiste, Islamicist', *Perspectives on World History and Current Events* (website), <http://www.pwhce.org/islamism.html>, downloaded 30 March 2007.

Taylor, P. (25 July 2005), 'The New Al-Qaeda: Jihad.com' (Television broadcast) Britain: BBC 2.

'The 7/7 Bombers – A Psychological Investigation', <http://www.bbc.co.uk/sn/tvradio/programmes/horizon/bombers.shtml>.

The Hashemite Kingdom of Jordan Foreign Ministry (2004), Jordan and the Global War on Terrorism Official Statement, <http://www.mfa.gov.jo/pages.php?menu_id=118#j2>, accessed 16 April 2007.

The International Covenant on Civil and Political Rights (1966).

The Power of Nightmares (Television broadcast, 3 November 2004), Britain: BBC 2.

Trends in Global Terrorism: Implications for the United States (Declassified Extract from the *US National Intelligence Estimate* (2006)), <http://www.globalsecurity.org/intell/library/reports/2006/nie_global-terror-trends_apr2006.htm>, accessed 17 April 2007.

'UK Muslims issue bombings fatwa', 19 July 2005, <http://news.bbc.co.uk/2/hi/uk_news/politics/4694441.stm>

United Nations Office on Drugs and Crime (1 December 2005), *Definitions of Terrorism*, <http://www.unodc.org/unodc/terrorism_definitions.html>, accessed 1 December 2005.

Walters, P. (12 November 2005), 'Terror turns into growth industry: Jihadists have evolved into start-ups independent of al-Qa'ida and they are winning', *The Australian* (website), <http://www.theaustralian.news.com.au/common/story_page/0,5744,17218908%255E601,00.html>, accessed 3 December 2005.

Walzer, M. (1992), *Just and Unjust Wars: a moral argument with historical illustrations*, 2nd Edition (Basic Books, a division of HarperCollins).

Willey, D. (10 February 2003), 'Catholic theologian says Iraq "just war" ', <http://news.bbc.co.uk/2/hi/europe/2747199.stm>.

Chapter 2

Is Torture an Effective Response to Terrorism?

2.1 Torture Works: But not on Terrorists

Rob Imre

In this part of the chapter I examine the phenomenon of torture as it is embedded in a socio-political framework. I claim here that torture can be a highly effective means of social control. I also claim that this social control can fail with spectacular results. My analysis leads me to conclude that given the evidence of authoritarian, and other regimes around the world, it is clear that torture is an excellent way to ensure that populations are kept terrorized, in a very literal sense, and thus social order is maintained. The effect on people who are potentially violent critics of political regimes, is to harden their positions against those said regimes. In this way, it matters little that the political regime is liberal-democratic, a social democracy, authoritarian, or a version of Marxist–Leninist: the outcome will be the same. That is to say, radicals will be radicalized to act on their principles, and this radicalization will be furthered by their followers at least partially due to the effects of torture on members of their newly developed group. Further, torture always works to solidify a victim mentality or world view so that individuals and groups of all kinds, radical, radicalized, or none of the above, will reject the legitimacy of the state. Only socio/psychopathic individuals will accept state legitimacy after experiencing torture.[1] Torture becomes the pre-eminent example of state terror, sanctioned by nation-states with large militaries that exert influence domestically and internationally. It is thus that torture works, but not to stop terrorists and terrorist organizations.

Information Gathering

Torture works. Torture can be an effective means of extracting information from people. There has been a good deal of discussion about torture and its re-emerging place in modern democracies willing to go to great lengths to protect themselves against invasion and incursion. This discussion has centered on the idea of legitimating torture. Social scientists need to ask several kinds of questions about this. One of the

---

1 Of course, in order to accept my thesis, one would need to also accept that terrorists are not initially socio/psychopathic. If they were, then torture would appear to be justified in at least two ways. First, to ensure that actual/potential terrorists (who are in this case socio/psychopathic) are tortured into accepting the legitimacy of the state. And secondly, that ordinary citizens are kept in fear of the state through torture.

main questions needs to be formulated somewhat like this: what kind of information is extracted in a typical torture session? Then we can ask about reliability of that information, what kinds of things are going to be said in such a session, and how will the people conducting the torture be able to return to other duties prescribed by the institutions for which they work.

There are two opposing views here about the efficacy of torture in extracting information. One view claims that the people involved will be under such duress that they will say anything to have the torture stop. Another view says that under such threats, the individual will deliver semi-reliable information in order to save themselves and others from similar experiences. Both of these can be true, but if we are asking questions about terrorists, and how all of this might affect both individual terrorists as well as groups that have organized to challenge the state and/or the culture in which they live, then the information itself is not the sticking point. Intelligence organizations have long held the view that unless they are able to devise a method that can somehow (medically) extract information, it will always be somewhat unreliable. That is to say, intelligence organizations do not use torture to extract information. Torture is used for other purposes.

How Does it Work?

First, and most important, torture works on civilian populations to keep them in line. For example, if there are people living their everyday lives in a variety of modern and/or contemporary societies, torture will operate as an effective threat and control mechanism. People who have something to lose, people who are linked to families and social groups of all kinds, people who find meaning in their work and resist authorities telling them how to conduct their lives, and people who are not trained to engage in varieties of combat, and people who are not accustomed to experiencing high levels of violence in their everyday lives, will have great difficulty dealing with torture.

Dictators throughout the world in the modern period have managed to use this method to keep their civilian populations in line. From Saddam Hussein in Iraq to Stalin in Russia, to Pinochet in Chile, and many others, we have seen that torture works.[2] To paraphrase Zygmunt Bauman: dictators will need far fewer police on the streets than in a democracy. Part of this equation is the constant threat of random violence to the individual person at any given moment by state authorities. Torture as an institution is part of that phenomenon and this is how a modern-nation can use torture as an effective means to create social order. There are a variety of ways to maintain the threat: random house searches, ensuring that there is no recourse to legal protection, vilification of specific groups targeted as scapegoats for social disorder, looking the other way as authorities round people up and make them disappear, and so on. Basically torture works on those who live ordinary everyday lives. If any of these people contemplate getting involved in some kind of social

---

2 Especially when coupled with the murder of dissidents and internal challengers to state authority.

disorder, then torture, or the threat of torture, can act as a powerful disincentive. By this I mean to say that torture can effectively stop people from taking that first step towards being a terrorist: things like criticizing the government, skateboarding on sidewalks, discussing radical political ideas, hanging around shopping malls and not buying anything, and all such socially disruptive behavior. Torture enacted upon civilian populations can stop or at least reduce all of this behavior. But the problem for us, that is people who dwell in liberal-democracies and are used to certain kinds of both positive and negative liberties, is that the increasingly ubiquitous character of torture as an accepted way in which the powerful act towards the powerless, has the capacity to make our own worlds unrecognizable.

Secondly, torture works on terrorist organizations as well. It works to solidify a supposed victim ideology. One of the key commonalities for all terrorist organizations is to establish themselves as a collective victim of some part of a modern process. It might be the modern process of colonisation as with the ANC, it might be the encroachment of radical and alien value systems as with Islamist groups, it might be accusations of forced assimilation by dominant cultures as with the FLQ, it might be threats of religious and cultural assimilation by dominant cultures such as the Basque separatists conflict with the Spanish government, or the Tamil Tigers in Sri Lanka. One of the greatest tactics that can operate to destroy terrorist organizations is to take away this argument from their ideological position. It runs counter to some of the political debate that has gone on recently but in this context one might say 'concede to all reasonable demands' in order to take away the ideological force of the terrorists arguments. On the other hand, one powerful way to strengthen the terrorist ideological position is to subject members of these various groups to torture. And this is usually linked to other forms of violence such as forced evacuations and resettlements, destroying their homes, forcing them to adopt ways of life not of their choosing, forcing them to speak another language and ensuring they are educated in the pidgin/Creole form of that language, and so on. It has been demonstrated that terrorist organizations will have decreasing levels of recruitment, will be incapable of organising themselves into disgruntled groups of people if they are not able to say they are victims. Without this resentment of the majority, terrorist organizations lose steam and momentum very quickly. So torture is an effective way to provide an immediate empirical example of this victimhood which is far more effective than experiencing collective material conditions that are objectively poor.[3] This victimhood operates as the foundation upon which to build violent responses directed towards the perceived majority. In essence, if we want to support and encourage terrorist organizations we should use torture. There is no greater coalescence for the radicalization of individuals and groups than the use of torture, especially by state authorities. If we want to take away one of the strongest common arguments used by terrorist organizations around the world we should not use torture as a means of extracting information because it delivers one of the key foundations upon which terrorist organizations can build (McCoy 2006; Baer 2003).

There are two further problems associated with torture and allowing it to become a pervasive technique. Beyond the moral and legal arguments, there is a political

---

3 As I argue in Chapter 1.1 of this book.

reality that has been demonstrated time and again. And in the context of torture in the 20th century and beyond has shown us that once begun, it becomes very difficult to stop. In Cambodia, we saw how once begun, the act itself quickly developed in to a culture of terror with a momentum all its own, overtaking all aspects of Khmer societal reorganization. We saw that once a specific category of people were socially and politically identified, as those who can be placed under torture legitimately, that is an 'acceptable' level of torture, we saw those categories expanded. These categories quickly expanded to include professions of all kinds, educated people of any kind, until we were dealing with circumstances in which members of the populace who had any such qualifications were wandering around pretending to be intellectually handicapped so that they wouldn't be tortured or killed. The information extracted was useless as people simply shouted names so they would be left alone, those people named were also rounded up and tortured and so on endlessly until we had a full blown genocide on our hands in the torture centers and killing fields (Hinton 2002a).

We saw the same things happening in the Armenian genocide, the Holocaust perpetrated by the Nazis, the same things happening in the torture chambers of Saddam Hussein, Nicolae Ceaucescu's Romania, Augusto Pinochet's Chile, the French in Algeria, and so on. Torture operated as a form of social control over a civilian populace and in some cases led to full-blown genocides. This is a phenomenon that in many cases cannot be halted by legal forces and cannot be stopped in mid-flight by pressing people to consider the moral and legal implications. In this context then, we are more worried about institutionalized torture being one step away from genocide, as most genocide scholars would agree (Hinton 2002a, 2002b; Bauman 1990). This renders the argument for controlling and legislating for limited aspects of torture effectively useless, since we then institutionalize the legitimate means to begin the first steps of genocide. This is not a necessary nor sufficient condition for genocide and genocidal acts, but modern genocides, beginning with the Armenians during and immediately following the World War I, all have in common the capacity for authorities to regulate torture with the claim that it will be limited and only performed 'where and when necessary.'

Further, genocide scholars have grounded much of their work in the structural analyzes that grew out of an attempt to try to understand the Holocaust in Europe during the World War II. Stanley Milgram's famous experiments began as a kind of test of the 'national culture' thesis that was prevalent in the 1950s and 1960s. The argument was that there was a particular national cultural conflagration that set the preconditions for genocides and specific kinds of hatred to occur. National Socialism in Germany could occur due to specific material conditions such as massive unemployment, national humiliation in a previous large conflict, creeping poverty, domination by foreign rule through financial reparations, and so on. This set of material conditions needed to be coupled with a national preoccupation with self-aggrandizing their own culture, scapegoating a specific group within their nation-state, deference to authority, all of which led to an acceptance of authoritarianism. Milgram's test of all this was to create these conditions in a laboratory. The idea was to randomly select people who were 'average Americans' on the assumption that a 'national character' would protect them from the excesses of authoritarianism.

This of course did not occur and we saw the results of Milgram's experiments demonstrating that 'modern people' had an ingrained capacity to defer responsibility to authority figures while torturing people directly under their control. The later Zimbardo experiments confirmed similar things about human social interaction that modern people were capable of. Zimbardo's famous experiment was situated in a mock prison cell and the idea was similar to Milgram in that people would be randomly selected and the group was to be divided in two making one group all powerful and the other group completely under the control of the first. Like the Milgram experiment, Zimbardo's showed us that seemingly ordinary people can quickly change into brutalizers of other human beings given the right set of circumstances. This should be our greatest concern with torture and this is where the work of genocide scholars is so important. Browning's (1998) detailed work on just such a process in which middle-aged, middle-class, Germans can actively participate in genocide, demonstrates this phenomenon. Abu Ghraib prison shows us this yet again, in that a given set of circumstances in which people assume that their superiors in an authoritarian system has given them tacit approval to exercise their control over dehumanized prisoners as they see fit. Torture, then, can be performed quite easily by at least a few of the guards since they assume that they are neither responsible, nor doing anything more than having a little fun with sub-humans. Introducing torture as part of the lexicon of the confessional, will certainly present a variety of new dangers to our liberal-democratic societies.

While torture can work to control a given populace, and while in some circumstances torture becomes institutionalized and therefore in the hands of the powerful to be used at their whim, there is a further problem about what to do with the information that is extracted from the victims. In keeping with my social science approach, I am not looking at the moral question of whether or not it is right and/or good to use this information. Nor am I examining he legality of using information extracted under duress. I am claiming here that there is a great deal of unreliability associated with this kind of information for a number of reasons. Walter Laquer's books on the psychology of terrorism show us that while the confessional has become a ubiquitous part of modern life, as police serials on television demonstrate, the confession itself is unreliable in terms of specific bits of information that anti-terrorist squads are looking for. If we are dealing with people who are suicide bombers, people who have such a deep commitment to death and destruction that they are wreaking on the various societies against which they have their gripes, and they have disentangled themselves from their 'previous' lives and allowed another worldview to encompass them, then the information they provide is useless. The kind of terrorist that we are hoping to stop when we are sanctioning torture does not have the sorts of problems with being tortured that most ordinary people might have.

Ticking Time Bombs

This is a 'scenario' that has come about in public discussions about terrorism in the post-September 11th era of dealing with terrorism. The discussion is in no way a discussion about a new dilemma, however, and regardless of how this is being framed in debates over the last few years, the legal, philosophical, and social science questions about the use of torture in a set of conditions in which there are people in custody who 'know where and when the bomb is to go off' and the authorities are to decide about the use of illicit torture in order to gain the information, is a dilemma faced by military occupations around the world in the modern period. The same dilemmas faced the French in Algeria, the British in Palestine, the Americans in Iraq and many other historical conflicts over the past few hundred years. It is also a dilemma faced by local authorities in nation-states with established domestic challenges to their rule. This can be any number of things from criminal gangs to religious zealots to political terrorist groups. The idea of the 'ticking time bomb scenario' is a good way to examine our current modern issues with social and political dissidents so I will treat it in some detail here.

First, it is comparatively rare to see these sorts of things occur. Terrorists are not interested in prior warnings and negotiations unless it becomes a hostage taking scenario in which case the rules of engagement are quite different. This is why it is always good to negotiate with terrorists as it dilutes the shock value of their actions. But terrorist activity in the public arena is usually done for a specific purpose of shocking the audience with massive violence. Without this, there is no terror. Most of these 'ticking time bomb' scenarios are pop culture inventions that we see on various television programs or sensational movies. Most terrorist groups that look to perpetrate such violent acts are looking to complete the act. This act in itself, the suicide bombing, bombs placed in cars in public spaces, and so on, are not really in the business of negotiation. In most cases terrorist groups have a commonality in that they do no wish to negotiate with their 'enemies'. This kind of terrorism, religious and/or political, is bound up in the 'performativity' of the act. There is no 'ticking time bomb' for them, only the audience of God, or the audience of the society they seek to destroy (or at the very least destroy some of the members of that society they seek to destroy). Time limits become meaningless and using torture to extract possible information becomes just as meaningless.

Secondly, kidnappings and holding people for ransom have different boundaries around how to deal with them. This might indeed be a real 'ticking time bomb' that authorities of various kinds need to deal with. But in this case the goals are quite different. The goal of the terrorist in these cases is to seek legitimation. Before the PLO began to follow the various religious organizations in the 1990s, they were an organization that based its rhetoric around liberation and territorial security framed in a leftist/Marxist rhetoric. Their style of communication had more in common with the liberation theologists in Latin America of the same time period. PLO kidnappings and holding people for ransom was certainly a media stunt, quite shocking at the time, but it was also a way to seek publicity for what they saw as a just cause. When these organizations take the 'religious turn' in the 1990s, the justice is to be found in God, not a 'global community' or a 'global citizenry.' In this case, torturing an individual known to have information might indeed garner some facts, with all of the associated problems mentioned above, but this is not the character of terrorism today and is not the kind of 'ticking time bomb' we are currently worried about. Kidnappings cause limited harm and limited damage to society as a whole and we are worried about large scale bombing attacks. As such, torture is still unhelpful.

There is one great (and obvious) advantage that any potential terrorist or person who might know about such a 'ticking time bomb' has over their interrogators. The interrogators do not know when the bomb is set to go off. For the person being interrogated, they can in some ways 'control' the process by responding in various ways to the interrogation. It is not an obvious master–slave relationship. For a committed terrorist, one committed to dying, and one that has relinquished ties to friends and family, this is a meaningless exercise. They are already in a situation in which they have accepted death and the final consequences of their deeds.

Conclusion

Using torture to extract information has consequences for the person being tortured as well as the person doing the torturing. From a structural sociological perspective, genocide scholars have long held the view that instituting these kinds of power relationships has a social slippery-slope affect in which powerful groups and individuals can both dehumanize their victims as well as abrogate responsibility for the people in their custody. In this context, torture begins to have deleterious effects on all of the people involved and cannot be contained to the victims. The consequences of engaging in this form of activity have very limited positive gains and it might be argued that these positive gains simply do not outweigh the problems.

References

Anderson, J. (ed.) (2002), *Transnational Democracy* (London: Routledge).

Baer, R. (2003), *See No Evil: the True Story of a Ground Soldier in the CIA's War on Terrorism* (Three Rivers Press).

Bauman, Z. (1990), *Modernity and the Holocaust* (Cambridge: Polity Press).

Brettell, C. and J.F. Hollifield (2000), *Migration Theory* (London: Routledge).

Browning, C. (1998), *Ordinary Men* (New York: Harper).

Chesterman, J. and B. Galligan (1999), *Defining Australian Citizenship* (Melbourne: Melbourne University Press).

Cohen, R. (1999), *Global Diasporas* (London: Routledge).

Connolly, W. (1993), *The Terms of Political Discourse* (London: Blackwell).

Dixson, M. (2000), *The Imaginary Australian* (Sydney: University of New South Wales Press).

Gunew, S. (2004), *Haunted Nations* (London: Routledge).

Hinton, A. (2002a), *Annihilating Difference: The Anthropology of Genocide* (Berkeley: University of California Press).

—— (2002b), *Genocide: An Anthropological Reader* (London: Blackwell).

Holmes, D.R. (2000), *Integral Europe* (Princeton: Princeton University Press).

Isin, E.F. and P.K. Wood (1999), *Citizenship and Identity* (London: Sage).

Kelly, N. and M. Trebilcock (2000), *The Making of the Mosaic* (Toronto: University of Toronto Press).

Kymlicka, W. (1995), *Multicultural Citizenship* (Oxford: Oxford University Press).

—— (1998), *Finding Our Way* (Oxford: Oxford University Press).

—— and W. Norman (ed.) (2000), *Citizenship in Diverse Societies* (Oxford: Oxford University Press).

—— and M. Opalski (ed.) (2000), *Can Liberal Pluralism be Exported?* (Oxford: Oxford University Press).

Lopez, M. (2000), *The Origins of Multiculturalism in Australian Politics* (Melbourne: Melbourne University Press).

Mackey, E. (2002), *The House of Difference* (Toronto: University of Toronto Press).

McCoy, A. (2006), *A Question of Torture: CIA Interrogation From the Cold War to the War on Terror* (Manhattan: Henry Holt).

Soysal, Y.N. (1994), *Limits of Citizenship* (Chicago: Chicago University Press).

Vandenberg, A. (ed.) (2000), *Citizenship in a Global Era* (London: Macmillan).

Van Hear, N. (1998), *New Diasporas* (London: University College London Press).

Vertovec, S. and R. Cohen (eds) (2002), *Conceiving Cosmopolitianism* (Oxford: Oxford University Press).

Watson, C.W. (2000), *Multiculturalism* (Manchester: Open University Press).

2.2   Torture, Tragedy and Natural Law

T. Brian Mooney

The question as to whether torture is effective or not is one that I am wholly unable to deal with and presumably very few people are other than torturers and victims of torture, along with those who have studied the history and perhaps psychology of torture. Nor here do I propose to define torture for reasons that will become apparent a little later. I would like to begin by subverting the issue under discussion by looking at the question as to whether torture is morally or legally permissible. In particular I would like to focus on one possible line of argument which provides a very powerful position in favor of torture under strictly defined conditions rendered broadly as 'ticking-bomb' scenarios.[4]

In section one of this part of this chapter I sketch and defend an account of torture when viewed as a species of dirty hands. I argue that contemporary moral theory has emphasized act rather than agent evaluation and in doing so has inadequately dealt with the crucial dimensions of agent evaluation, motivation, emotion and tragedy in ordinary life.

I also argue, that despite the 'mixed' account of ethics, which invokes both act and agent perspectives in the natural law tradition, when it comes to the issue of torture, the natural law's tradition of employing the principle of double effect also fails to deal with the nature of tragedy and dirty hands, particularly in respect to absolutist prohibitions on torture.

---

4 The *locus classicus* for the discussion of 'ticking bomb' scenarios in the philosophical literature is Walzer M. (1973).

In section two I attempt to show that there are authoritative figures within the natural law tradition who will countenance the use of torture, by analyzing the public/private distinction within a discussion of judicial punishment. This involves an argument by analogy to show that if on the grounds argued, natural law can justify certain forms of punishment, including the death penalty and 'just war', then the tradition can also justify torture in certain very limited circumstances. In section three I employ another argument by analogy showing that there are two traditions on lying within the natural law tradition and that St Thomas Aquinas's account of lying *in exceptional circumstances* (though not termed lying) provides further grounds for the moral justification of torture *in exceptional circumstances*.

Section One

Broadly construed the issue of the justifiability of torture can be looked at as a species of a larger issue in moral philosophy, namely, is it morally permissible for a good person or a good government to have dirty hands?[5] In other words can a good person or good government choose to act in a way that is morally wrong and knowingly morally wrong but nonetheless perhaps obligatory? Stated bluntly the question is can there be acts that are justified, even obligatory, but which remain wrong and shameful? (Stocker 1990, 9ff). I cannot here set this issue out in detail[6] but it is nonetheless important to note in passing that contemporary moral philosophy has largely dealt with issues from the perspective of action. Both deontologists and consequentialists are united on this front and both are the major moral philosophies of our age. Deontologists are interested in acts because they (at least in the Kantian version) are committed to the idea that the goodness or badness of any act is not grounded in an account of inclinations or desires and thus focussed on agents but rather on the conformity of the will to an *a priori* dictate of reason – the Categorical Imperative. Consequentialists are even less interested in the nature of agents since whether an act counts as good or bad is independent of a moral assessment of an agent's character but resides in the consequences produced by acts and summed up in the early Utilitarian aphorism – 'the greatest good for the greatest number.'[7] It is precisely these kinds of ways of thinking about moral issues that are severely tested by issues of dirty hands and torture. In cases of dirty hands and torture the assessment

---

5 For a good bibliography of the extensive literature on 'dirty hands' see Rynard P. and Shugarman D.P. (eds) (2000).

6 There are, for example, different understandings of what constitutes dirty hands. Some writers situate the problem as a means-ends issue in politics, others within the private/public dimensions of moral values. Still others deny that there is any such thing, see Brandt R. (1972). For broader discussions see, Gowans C. (1994); Sinnott-Armstrong W. (1988).

7 The characterizations of deontology and consequentialism here are somewhat schematic. Recently there have been concerted efforts expended on how both deontology and consequentialism require robust accounts of character and thus a crucial focus on agents. See, for example, Baron M. (1995); Herman B. (1993); Crisp R. (1992). Although I cannot argue for it here, I think these attempts are unsuccessful.

of action cannot be separated from the moral evaluation of agents whether it involves individuals or governments.

Discussions of dirty hands have been historically found more in literature than in moral philosophy. Much of Greek Tragedy is concerned with the issues provoked by dirty hands (Aeschylus). And indeed, it is plausible to read the conflicts of desires, duties and morality in Shakespeare within this context. More recently the works of writers such as Brecht, Sartre and Camus have fully engaged with the problematic as too Styron in *Sophie's Choice* (Brecht B.; Camus A.; Sartre J-P.; Styron W.). Ancient philosophical literature is fully aware of the problem and discussions occur particularly in Plato and Aristotle but are present also in St Augustine and more generally in mediaeval literature on just war.[8] Philosophical justifications of *Realpolitik* such as those found in Machiavelli depend upon an understanding of dirty hands.

The argument I will develop in this part of the chapter runs counter to the major currents of thinking represented in the Catholic natural law tradition, and in particular to the Thomistic principle of double effect. The Principle of double effect is elaborated by St Thomas Aquinas at *Summa Theologica* II-II, Q. 64, Art. 7, in a discussion of self-defence which is itself couched and must be read in the wider framework of his rich and perceptively sensitive account of moral determinants – the act, intention/motive and circumstances (*Summa Theologica*, I-II, Q. 18, aa. 2–7). Essentially the principle of double effect argues that it is morally permissible to perform an act that has a bad (evil) effect if four central conditions are fulfilled:

1. The act to be done must be good in itself or at least indifferent – the act cannot be evil in itself.
2. The good intended must not be obtained by means of the evil effect.
3. The evil effect must not be intended for itself but only permitted.
4. There must be a proportionately grave reason for permitting the evil effect.[9]

It is from this source that contemporary Catholic criticisms of torture as an intrinsically immoral act flow. Torture it would seem breaches at least conditions (1) to (3) of the principle of double effect and perhaps also condition (4).

Indeed, torture has been clearly condemned as an intrinsically evil act in recent encyclicals particularly in *Veritatis Splendor* and *Evangelium Vitae*. In *Veritatis Splendor* a very careful and skilled level of argument is marshalled against certain kinds of teleological ethical theories, specifically consequentialism and proportionalism. Such theories are deemed to hold:

---

8 St Augustine interestingly comments that prostitution may well be tolerated in civil society as a lesser of two evils. See St Augustine, '… executioners are horrible but necessary, as are pimps and prostitutes …' (*On Order*, 2.4.12). Rist J.M. commenting on this quotation from St Augustine notes that 'Society would be worse off if they were eliminated.' See Rist J.M., 1994, 209. This will be important later in this part of the chapter.

9 Here I have closely followed the locution of Fagothey A., 1957, 97–8. See also the discussion of double effect in Oderberg D.S., 2000, 86–96.

...that it is impossible to qualify as morally evil according to its species – its 'object' – the deliberate choice of certain kinds of behaviour or specific acts, apart from a consideration of the intention for which the choice is made or the totality of the foreseeable consequences of that act for all persons concerned.

Without in any way wanting to be an apologist for proportionalism and even less so consequentialism, I will be arguing that this kind of thinking fails to see the tragic dimensions sometimes forced on good people in their moral decision-making. *Veritatis Splendor* goes on to focus on the nature of certain acts which are thought to be evil in themselves apart from the intentions from which the acts flow. It is worthwhile to quote the document in some detail here.

Reason attests that there are objects of the human act which are by their nature 'incapable of being ordered' to God, because they radically contradict the good of the person made in his image. These are acts which, in the Church's moral tradition, have been termed 'intrinsically evil' (*intrinsece malum*): they are *always* and *per se*, in other words, on account of their very object, and quite apart from the ulterior intentions of the one acting and the circumstances. Consequently, without in the least denying the influence on morality exercised by circumstances and especially by intentions, the Church teaches that 'there exist acts which per se and in themselves, independently of circumstances, are always seriously wrong by reason of their object'. The Second Vatican Council itself, in discussing the respect due to the human person, gives a number of examples of such acts: 'Whatever is hostile to life itself, such as any kind of homicide, genocide, abortion, euthanasia and voluntary suicide; whatever violates the integrity of the human person, such as mutilation, physical and mental torture and attempts to coerce the spirit; whatever is offensive to human dignity, such as subhuman living conditions, arbitrary imprisonment, deportation, slavery, prostitution and trafficking in women and children; degrading conditions of work which treat labourers as mere instruments of profit, and not as free responsible persons: all these and the like are a disgrace, and so long as they infect human civilisation they contaminate those who inflict them more than those who suffer injustice, and they are a negation of the honour due to the Creator'. ... Pope Paul VI teaches: 'Though it is true that sometimes it is lawful to tolerate a lesser moral evil in order to avoid a greater evil or in order to promote a greater good, it is never lawful, even for the gravest reasons, to do evil that good may come of it (cf. *Rom* 3:8) – in other words, to intend directly something which of its very nature contradicts the moral order, and which must therefore be judged unworthy of man, even though the intention is to protect or promote the welfare of an individual, of a family or of society in general'. ... If acts are intrinsically evil, a good intention or particular circumstances can diminish their evil, but they cannot remove it. They remain 'irremediably' evil acts; *per se* and in themselves they are not capable of being ordered to God and the good of the person. 'As for acts which are themselves sins (*cum iam opera ipsa peccata sunt*), Saint Augustine writes, like theft, fornication, blasphemy, who would dare affirm that, by doing them for good motives (*causis bonis*), they would no longer be sins, or, what is even more absurd, that they would be sins that are justified?' Consequently, circumstances or intentions can never transform an act intrinsically evil by virtue of its object into an act 'subjectively' good or defensible by choice.

I have quoted *Veritatis Splendor* here at length partly because of the nobility of vision and subtlety of argument contained in it but also because it is so lucid on the nature of intrinsically evil acts, including torture. Nevertheless, it is my contention that the issue of torture, while we may see it as an intrinsically evil act, this does not by itself exhaust the moral features associated with torture. In other words I am willing to accept the notion that torture is intrinsically evil but I want to add that it might still be justifiable and even, in certain circumstances, obligatory.

As I have suggested contemporary moral philosophy has, in its overweening emphasis on the evaluation of acts, distorted many of the tragic features associated with moral deliberation. Torture in certain circumstances can be seen as a case of dirty hands when even a good agent will act in an immoral manner, recognizing fully the immorality of the action but nonetheless conceiving of the act as justifiable and obligatory. Moreover, I think that dirty hands scenarios, far from being uncommon, are quite often normal features of morally complex lives – lives that most of us live.

Michael Stocker presents us with a series of ordinary situations which give rise to dirty hands conflicts. There is no need to rehearse them fully here but it is worth indicating just how prevalent such scenarios are in ordinary complex lives. As Stocker notes '… among the dirty features of dirty hands are people being wronged, they and their trust being violated, dishonoured, and betrayed: innocents are killed, tortured, lied to, deceived' (Stocker 1990, 17). The more dramatic examples include the impossible choice imposed upon Sophie in Styron's novel as to which of her two children she should save from the Nazis; violating a principle as the lesser of two evils; betraying an innocent person to save one's country in war; deceiving the enemy into thinking that one's loyalties have changed by publicly insulting one's old teacher (Stocker 1990, 18). Nevertheless while these do not amount to everyday cases of dirty hands analogous examples from the more quotidian aspects of life may be drawn. Stocker usefully presents the case of a rocky marriage between two loved relatives.

> Suppose that the marriage of relatives has been seriously troubled, but is now on the mend. Pleased for them, I offer to do whatever I can. Drawing me aside, my cousin says there is something I can do. As her husband suspects, she had been having an affair. Unless his suspicions are allayed, there will be no chance of a reconciliation. For both her sake and his, she asks me to help convince him that she had not been having the affair. She asks me to help her keep the truth from him, perhaps even to deceive or lie to him. This, I suggest, can involve dirty hands. (Stocker 1990, 18–19)

My own suspicion is that the field of personal and professional relationships are significantly prone to dirty hands. One might think of an example whereby one has joined several colleagues in good faith to put forward a proposal but subsequently comes to the view that the proposal is flawed perhaps because it undermines another colleague. One then rejects the proposal and in doing so breaks rank with one's colleagues causing rancor and division. Dirty hands are common because we often enough do not reflect carefully enough or because we lack sufficient foresight. In other words dirty hands show to us dimensions of human frailty, vulnerability and fallibility, and highlight that even the best of lives may be struck with tragedy.

Michael Walzer argues that it is justified and even obligatory for an official to torture someone to force the person to tell where fellow 'terrorists' have hidden a ticking bomb among the innocent populace. The scenario, of course, can be expanded.

The official has excellent grounds to implicate the person in the prospective bombing; the person has knowledge of where the bomb is planted, and time constraints leave no softer options open than torture.[10] Recently there have been attempts to argue that 'ticking bomb' scenarios are so bizarre and fantastic that they should not be taken as normative for moral discussion (Sussman). Others have suggested that the very idea of countenancing 'academic' talk of torture so fundamentally undermines the democratic ethos that even talk of its legitimacy is morally problematic (Zizek, 2002; Lukes 2005). I have some sympathy with the second complaint and I am concerned that a discussion of this sort might be used unscrupulously to lead towards a slippery slope. Nevertheless to both objections I think that the world has for a very long time been a dangerous place and that while 'ticking bomb' scenarios may be thought of by some as extraordinary they have been everyday considerations for many people living in the North of Ireland, Lebanon, Israel, Iraq, Afghanistan and a host of other historical and contemporary situations.

It is important to note that Walzer accepts that the decision to torture is not to be discounted in a consequentialist fashion. It, he argues, is not to be thought of as a good because on traditional consequentialist grounds it produces an overall better outcome.[11] On the contrary the dirty feature, in the overall assessment of the justifiable decision to torture retains its full moral significance. If one refused to torture the deaths of innocents must also be weighed and hold full moral significance. Torture in Walzer's case is justified and morally obligatory but for all that it remains a disvalue – an evil. In Bernard William's language '… moral conflicts are neither systematically avoidable, nor all soluble without remainder' (Williams 1973, 179).

A key feature of the importance of not discounting the act of torture is that it brings with it an emphasis on the role of emotions in a moral life (a feature of the good life that is often lacking in consequentialist and deontological thinking). Indeed it seems to accord with our ordinary moral intuitions that even if we are to make a dirty hands choice that we will feel bad about the choice or the circumstances that lead to the choice. This 'feeling bad' is morally significant because it in some way marks a significant aspect of self, of the agent in a world that is less than perfect. Stocker thinks the appropriate emotions in dirty hands cases are shame, regret and guilt, often followed by desire for atonement and cleansing (Stocker 1990, 29–32). Bernard Williams thinks there is room for a specific notion of regret – what he calls 'agent-regret' and this is to be distinguished from ordinary feelings of regret or remorse (Williams 1981, 20–39). I suspect Williams has in mind here a more ontological dimension in that 'agent-regret' is deeply embedded in the psyche than is yielded by expressions such as 'I wish things had been different' or 'I feel remorseful over missing your birthday celebrations.' I am inclined, however, to agree with De Wijze that there is room for a new conception of 'tragic-remorse' to capture further the role that tragedy can play in dirty hands and thus in life (De Wijze 2004).

---

10 I assume here that extreme physical and/or mental torture would be effective in getting the person to reveal information about the bomb; moreover, I assume that no other options are available given the time constraints. Both assumptions are, of course, open to rebuttal. See, for example, Arrigo J.M., 2004.

11 For a consequentialist defence of torture see Levin M. (1982).

Certainly there is an ontological dimension to such tragic-remorse and it captures but deepens the insights of Stocker and Williams. As De Wijze expresses it:

> The meta-ethical point to stress here is that the feeling of agent-regret properly recognizes the fact that our agency in the world depends only partly on our will. Consequently, our identity, character sense of integrity, is intimately tied to states of affairs that we (even if only partially) helped to bring about, and even when despite our best efforts, these outcomes turn out to be bad or undesired. The feelings of regret and remorse (the pair of feelings that are taken to exhaust all possibilities) simply do not adequately capture the nuances and richness of our moral lives conditioned by the problems of agency in a world where much of great importance is beyond our control. (De Wijze 2004, 462–3)[12]

Up to this point I have tried to show that in 'ticking bomb' scenarios torture is morally justifiable, even obligatory and in doing so have argued that torture is to be viewed under the broader moral discussion of dirty hands. I have also shown that dirty hands scenarios are more common than one might first think. I have distinguished between act-orientated moral theories and character-based moral theories and argued that act-oriented moral theories are incapable of understanding (or dealing) with the dimensions of tragedy associated with dirty hands and thus fail as moral theories for ordinary complex moral beings. However, one central platform of my critique is also the 'mixed' character and act focus of the natural law tradition. Here I have outlined the basis for criticisms of the principle of double effect for the case of torture and more broadly dirty hands. I would like now to highlight one way in which natural law theory may be able to incorporate the critiques levelled earlier in this part of the chapter and modify the absoluteness of the traditional view of torture as intrinsically morally evil.

Section Two

St Thomas Aquinas, perhaps the central figure in the elaboration of the natural law tradition, does not provide us with any specific arguments *pro* or *contra* the use of torture. In his *Exposito super Iob* he mentions in passing the case of judges who advocate torture (*tormentum*) in order to arrive at truth, but implicitly, seems to condone torture when the judges are 'acting in accordance with justice' (Aquinas, *Exposito super Iob*, 10 ad. vv. 4, 7). Moreover, since the time of St Augustine and earlier under Constantine there had been a widespread acceptance of the *practice* of torture, an acceptance that was fully institutionalized in Aquinas's own times. Pope Innocent IV in his Bull *Ad extirpanda* of 1252, ratified and reiterated by Pope Alexander IV in 1259, had legislated for the ecclesiastical use of torture.

Moreover, it would seem that an argument by analogy could well be marshalled on traditional Thomistic grounds that, since Aquinas was prepared to accept a polity's use of the death penalty, on similar grounds it should also accept the use of torture. In what follows I will examine these issues on two different platforms. In this section

---

12 De Wijze goes much further than this in his explication of tragic-remorse, unfortunately I cannot elaborate further here.

I will (too briefly) discuss St Thomas's account of the role of coercion in a polity, linking this discussion to Aquinas's distinction between private (personal) and public morality. In section three I will explore Aquinas's account of lying, focussing on his exclusions of what constitutes lies, and in both this section and section three (despite certain differences) I will present his conclusions as analogically compatible with the moral justifiability of torture in exceptional circumstances.

Above I employed the term 'polity' rather than state to connote a particular nuance of Aquinas's discussion. Aquinas, reflecting earlier Roman and Greek thinking, is more interested in political community[13] than the specific modalities of government or organization of particular states. The distinction is important because it helps us to see the situation-specific, historical and practical difficulties effecting political community when removed from specific forms of political organization. The questions that lie behind Aquinas's formulation of the problem of political community are over the nature and role of law and how, and in what contexts, political communities work best, given that human beings are considered to be social beings.

The central feature of a polity's legitimacy is its capacity to protect and enhance the people under its care to participate in the fundamental goods of human life when viewed under the desiderata of the common good. Nevertheless, there is no one-to-one correspondence between the flourishing of each individual and the broader public policy considerations required of rulers seeking the common good. Thus, Aquinas argues against legislation which prohibits all vices (*Summa Theologica*, I-II, q. 91a. 4.c) exhibiting a profound awareness of the historical exigencies and psychological variations of individuals in various polities. Instead he advocates a gradual, step-by-step, process of the institution of legislation in the role of law as teacher in reference to public and private morality: 'Those things …which neither advance nor damage the common good are neither prohibited nor commanded by human laws.'

Of key importance in respect to the common good or the public good (*bonum publicum*) are justice and peace. Justice and peace in Aquinas's view are intimately connected to friendship and love (*dilectio*) (*Opera*, 14.43). However the fullest flourishing of justice and peace depend on an attunement of the soul (the love of the good in a Platonic sense), and while the goals of a polity embraces these (particularly in its pedagogic role) its concern must be located more pragmatically. So conflicts may occur between justice and peace, as Finnis points out:

> Legislatures, *in the interests of peace*, provide that adverse possession for a length of time gives a good title even to squatters who took possession in bad faith – but a squatter who has so acted never becomes morally entitled, in good conscience, to rely on his title. (Finnis J., 1998, 288)[14]

Aquinas clearly sees the role of a polity and its government as promoting the fullest levels of human flourishing while at the same time recognizing that there are inherent imperfections built into the nature of the world. Some of these imperfections are the

---

13 This tradition is most clearly brought out in the very title of Plato's *Politeia* and echoed in Cicero's *Laelius: De Amicitia*.

14 Also see Aquinas, *Quodlibet*, XII, 9.15.

result of the imperfect 'fit' between private and public good. Once again as Finnis puts it:

> The objective of inculcating virtue for the sake of peace and just conduct is coherent with Aquinas's constant teaching that government or law, while rightly demanding of its subjects that they do what is just and abstain from doing what is unjust, cannot rightly demand of them that they do so with a just mind and will, cannot require that they be just in the central character-related sense of 'be a just person'. (Finnis 1998, 232)

But it is precisely because the pragmatic functions of government aim at justice and peace but cannot guarantee perfect virtue in citizens that government may at times be required, in the interests of the public good, to act in ways that preserves that good, but which in themselves may not be instances of justice. One area where this imperfect 'fit' is important is in regard to judicial (and ecclesiastical) punishment and coercion which leads us by analogy back to the issue of torture.

Clearly one arena in which the private/public dimensions come apart is related to the primacy Aquinas accords to conscience. Just as good government, as we have seen, cannot require more than external conformity, so too, it ought not to interfere in the private role of conscience, which must ultimately be submitted before the divine bar. It is conscience that trumps governmental interference and a conscientious citizen will be one who can discern whether or not a government or law promotes participation in central human values and goods, or whether a government or law is morally evil (or indifferent) and thus not binding on conscience.

Nevertheless, the asymmetry between the private and public good is very complex. Given a good government, that is, one that genuinely seeks to protect and enhance participation in central human goods among its citizens Aquinas still thinks that 'it is contrary to the proper character of a state's governance to impede people from acting according to their responsibilities – *except in emergencies*' (Aquinas, *Summa contra Gentiles*, III c. 71, no. 4, emphasis added). So what might constitute the nature of such emergencies whereby a government (it must be remembered that here we are dealing with the paradigm case of good government) may usurp the private roles, obligations and duties of private citizens? Aquinas's answer is only when '[P]ublic good prevails over private good' (Aquinas, *Summa Theologica*, II-II, 117, a).

One clearly demarcated area where public good is judged to outweigh private good is discussed by Aquinas under the rubric of the 'power of the sword.' As Aquinas understands it a polity's leaders have public authority in judicial and military matters, and in particular over the execution of criminals and the capacity to wage war (Aquinas, *Summa Theologica*, II-II, q. 40. a. 1; q. 64. a). Distinctions are drawn between what is legitimate for public authority and set over and against what is legitimate for private individuals. In the absence of appropriate delegated authority an individual is never morally entitled to kill someone, or act with the intention of killing someone, even when threatened by death (Aquinas, *Summa Theologica*, II-II, q. 64. a. 7 c).

An individual has a right to resist an assailant's attack in order to preserve life by use of all reasonable means. However, such means, in order to be morally legitimate, must never involve a desire or intention to deliberately kill the assailant even though the means so used to repel the assailant may have the probability (as a side-effect) of causing the death of the assailant (Aquinas, *Summa Theologica*, II-II, q. 108 a; q. 60 a; q. 64 a; q. 65 a). Indeed, for Aquinas this holds not just for attacks against the self but also anyone undeserving of being attacked. He even goes so far as to point out that passivity in the face of unwarranted attack to others is a vice (Aquinas, *Summa Theologica*, II-II, q. 188 a. 3 ad 1).

This is a classic application of the principle of double effect – the intention or set of intentions in the case under discussion is the preservation of life and the effect of repelling the assailant causing death is a side-effect of the intention. The moral requisites are divided according to Thomistic lines as the act itself, the circumstances and the motivations/intentions. In this case the act itself is defined partially under the motivation – the act of resisting unwarranted threat of life, having the foreseen but non-intended side-effect of causing the death of the assailant; the circumstances are precisely the unwarranted attack together with the physical, emotional and psychological effects produced by the attack; and, the intention is (in order to be morally licit) the desire (*finis, intentionem*) to repel the attack (Aquinas, *Summa Theologica*, II-II, q. 41 a; q. 64 a). Thus, the role that double effect plays in the Thomistic formulation is to highlight the centrality of intention in respect to morally mixed actions. So far as individuals are concerned there must be no direct intention to act counter to fundamental human goods and values, though evil side-effects may indeed be entertained and even *known* with reasonable certainty. 'The acting person's certainty – or foreseeability – that side-effects of a certain type will result does not make them intended …' (Aquinas, *Summa Theologica,* II-II, q. 64 a. 7 and 4).

However, Aquinas arrives at very different conclusions when he discusses public authority that is uncontaminated with private passions:

> … to intend to kill another in self-defence is immoral for any human being unless, having public authority, someone who is intending to kill someone in self-defence refers this to the common good, as is exemplified by the soldier fighting the enemy or the judicial officer fighting against bandits. (Aquinas, *Summa Theologica*, II-II, q. 67 a)

The public authority's right to execute a criminal or to wage a just war involve a clear intention to kill. Similarly the imposition of any form of punishment or coercion, whether to reform or deter or to educate involves an intended choice of a means to achieve a desired end. The intentional choice of these means are assessable as a 'package' in respect to the end, and this is true for Aquinas even when punishment or coercion is used simply as retribution. As Finnis puts it:

> In punishment precisely as retribution, the restriction, pain, or other loss is chosen as the suppression of the offender's will (which was indulged in the offence), and that suppression is not a mere means to some future good but rather is itself a good: the restoring of the order of justice disturbed in the offence. The choice to impose punishment

is, then, 'referred to' the common good of justice, and as such is the choice of a good (and not of a bad as a means to that good). (Finnis J., 1998, 279)[15]

It is perhaps difficult to assess whether this sort of justification of judicial punishment, including retributive punishment up to and including the death penalty can be analogically applied to the case of torture. It might be thought for example that Aquinas's appeal to justice is anachronistic. On these lines it might be argued that Aquinas's account relies on a conception of society and public good which sees persons as socially unified in a way in which contemporary societies are not. On this view it would be wrong to think of the 'ticking bomb' perpetrator as a kind of cancer at the heart of a (relatively) homogenous social group. Nevertheless from the perspective of a good government with care for the community it would be simply wrong to suppose that duties of care to the public good can be discounted. The deaths of many citizens and thereby their capacity to participate in the central goods of human life do, I suggest, merit an appeal to a broad conception of justice and peace, and the foundations of such justice and peace, which legitimates dirtying one's public hands. From Aquinas's perspective the 'ticking bomb' perpetrator in intentionally setting out to kill innocents has deviated from the order of reason and is thus excluded from the privileges attached to human beings in society. He has lapsed into the servitude of subhuman animals.[16] It is precisely this line of reasoning – a principle of forfeiture – that justifies Aquinas's espousal of capital punishment and which also provides grounds subject to justice and peace for the waging of war. And it is for these reasons that I think the analogical correspondences are strong with the judicial use of torture to preserve justice and peace 'in emergencies' (*Summa contra Gentiles*, III, c. 71).

Section Three

I will now begin to develop another analogical argument drawing out the implications of Aquinas's account of lying and showing how it is brought to bear on the issue of torture. The analogy to be drawn will propose that since Aquinas allows for cases of lying (though not termed as such) in particular circumstances, so too torture (though not termed as such) may be morally acceptable in particular circumstances. I will begin by contextualizing St Thomas's considerations on lying within the broader tradition of Christian thinking that influences Aquinas.

Boniface Ramsey has persuasively argued for the existence of two incompatible traditions of thought within Christianity over the moral status of lying and deception (Ramsey B., 1985). On the one hand there is an absolutist or quasi-absolutist

---

15 I will be arguing later that this is not quite the way to conceive of the use of torture. Moreover, it is not clear that even in the instance under discussion that Finnis's interpretation is correct. Certainly the imposition of penalties may be conceived of as good when the accent of punishment is the improvement of the offender but when punishment is retributive even though it may further a public good it nonetheless involves an intentional harm against the offender.

16 ...*in servitutem bestiarum*'. *ST*. II-II, q. 64 a. 2 ad 3.

prohibition on lying which has its articulation particularly in St Augustine but reiterated by Gregory the Great and (with some reservations I will argue for) Aquinas. On the other hand, there is another tradition, widely established, by authoritative church figures including Pseudo-Maximus (d. between 408 and 423), Clement of Alexandria (d. after 202), Origen (d. 254), Hilary of Poitiers (d. c. 367), John Chrysostom (d. 407), John Cassian (d. 432), Dorotheus of Gaza (d. c. 560–80) and John Climacus (d. c. 650), which countenances and even approves of lying in particular circumstances.

The Augustinian absolute prohibition on lying is fully argued for (and largely accepted by Aquinas) in two treatises – the *De Mendacio* (c. 395) and *Contra Mendacium* (c. 420).[17] Augustine defines the person who lies as one '…who has one thing in his mind and expresses something else in words or in any other way whatever' (*De Mendacio*, 3). Augustine's prohibition on lying goes even so far as to exclude lying in order to save another's life or to preserve corporal purity in rape, on the grounds that purity of soul is always more important than life or corporeal integrity.

Augustine nonetheless is sensitive to the degrees or hierarchy of 'sinning' involved in lies. In the *De Mendacio* he provides an eight-fold taxonomy of the degrees of immorality involved in categories of lying. In a descending scale of gravity he distinguishes:

1. the lie that is introduced into religious teaching, which under no circumstances is to be told;
2. the lie that harms another person and is of no profit to anyone;
3. the lie that is useful to one person but harmful to another, although it does not subject the one harmed to bodily uncleanness;
4. the lie that is told merely for the pleasure of lying and deceiving; and
5. the lie that is told for the sake of being pleasing in speech.
6. All of these for Augustine are to be rejected entirely. The final three categories of lie would seem to place the liar in less serious modes of moral failure, in theological terms, the lies amount to venial sins:[18]
7. the lie that is useful to someone from a material point of view and harmful to no one;
8. the lie that is useful to someone from a spiritual point of view and harmful to no one; and
9. the lie that is not harmful to anyone and preserves someone from bodily defilement.

The fact that from a subjective point of view categories of lies admit of degrees of moral seriousness (given that a person who unknowingly utters a lie is not morally

---

17 The only exceptions to Augustine's blanket condemnation of lying are the cases of artistic deceptions and jokes which he considers not to be instances of lying at all. The *De Mendacio* distinguishes between the *mendax* and the *fallax*. Only the former counts as an instance of lying. See *De Mendacio*, 2. St Thomas agrees with Augustine on both these accounts.

18 For an interesting discussion of venial and mortal sins of lying in St Thomas, see Dewan L., 1977.

blameworthy, except perhaps for the state of ignorance) in no way effects the absolute prohibition on lying – all cases of lying, even the least serious and most readily excusable are morally condemned. It is worth noting however that the theological notion of venial sin is what separates the Augustinian (and Thomistic) prohibitions on lying from the even stricter understanding of Kant. A venial sin, while still a sin, does not cut off the sinner from God's grace nor block the sinner from spiritual growth. Only a mortal sin, one of the first five categories of lies, directly rejects the inclination towards eternal ends. Kant, on the other hand, seems to think of any lie whatsoever as what Augustine and Aquinas would refer to as a mortal sin. Thus, Kant writes:

> Truthfulness in statements which cannot be avoided is the formal duty of an individual to everyone, however great may be the disadvantage accruing to himself or to another. If, by telling an untruth, I do not wrong him who unjustly compels me to make a statement, nevertheless by this falsification, which must be called a lie (though not in the legal sense), I commit a wrong against duty generally in a most essential point. That is, so far as in me lies I cause that declarations should in general find no credence, and hence all rights based on contracts should be void and lose their force, and this is a wrong done to mankind generally. Thus the definition of a lie as merely an intentional untruthful declaration to another person does not require the additional condition that it must harm another, as jurists think proper in their definition (*mendacium est falsiloquium in praeiudicium alterius*). For a lie always harms another, if not some other particular man, still it harms mankind generally, for it vitiates the source of law itself. (Kant 1949)

Augustine's *Contra Mendacium* written some 25 years after the *De Mendacio* is remarkably consistent in its condemnation of lying. Interestingly, however, further philosophical justification is given through the introduction of the notions of *causa*, *finis* and *intentio*. All of these elements must be good for an act to be good, and a good cause, end or intention cannot make a lie not a lie (Augustine, *Contra Mendacium*, 42–3). Augustine is thus the key figure in the tradition which condemns lying in all its forms and this tradition is embraced by other thinkers such as Gregory the Great and St Thomas who cites St Augustine 20 times in his discussion on lying at *ST* II-II, Q. 110.

Nevertheless, as has been pointed out an alternative tradition exists which advocates the use of lying for a greater good. In a sermon falsely thought to be penned by Maximus, Bishop of Turin, an anonymous writer (Pseudo-Maximus) draws on St Paul's first letter to the Corinthians (9:20): 'I became like a Jew to the Jews in order to win the Jews' to justify Eusebius's deception in feigning to be a heretic in order to free from capture St Dionysius who had been enchained by the Arians (Pseudo-Maximus, *Sermon*, 7.3).[19] Similarly Clement of Alexandria while praising the Christian who would not lie even in the face of torture or death makes an exception for 'therapeutic' lies, alluding to St. Paul's dissimulations in Acts 16.3 and 1 Corinthians 9.20 (Clement of Alexandria, *Stromata*, 7.9.53).

Origen directly advocates permissible deception quoting approvingly from Plato's *Republic* (Plato, *Republic*, 389) and adding:

---

19 Also see Augustine's interpretation of the same passage in *Letter* 82.

the person on whom the necessity of lying occasionally falls must be very careful to use a lie in the manner of a seasoning or a medicine, so as not to exceed the proper measure or go beyond the limits observed by Judith with respect to Holofernes. ... Hence it is clear that, unless we have lied in such a way as to seek some great good, we shall be judged as the enemies of the one who said: 'I am the Truth.'[20]

Hilary of Poitiers is particularly forthright in advocating lying for beneficial outcomes:

... there is a lie that is most necessary and sometimes falsehood is useful, when we lie to a murderer about someone's hiding place or falsify testimony for a person in danger or deceive a sick person with respect to his chances for recovery. According to the teaching of the Apostle, our speech should be seasoned (cf. Col. 4.6). For this reason the Holy Spirit tempered what is meant by falsehood by imposing conditions on lying when he said: 'Who has not lied with his tongue nor done evil to his neighbour', so that a criminal act of lying would be committed when another person was adversely affected. (*Tractatus super Psalmos*, 14.10)

John Chrysostum notes that the prohibition cannot be absolute because it depends on the intention and the good that may result from a lie. He refers to the examples of military strategists, therapeutic lying in families, lies told by physicians for the good of patients, and draws on examples from both the Old and New Testaments (*De Sacerdote.*, 1.3; 1.6).

However the fullest argument for lying is to be found in John Cassian's *Conferences*. Here I follow Ramsey's account (Ramsey, 1985, 521–3):

Cassian and his fellow monk Germanus had gone to the Egyptian dessert with the intention of growing in a more perfect life through meeting and speaking with the great Egyptian ascetics, but they had promised to return to their own monastery in Palestine at a given time. When the time came, however, they were torn on the one hand by the promise they had made ... and on the other by the strong conviction that their growth and spiritual perfection would be hindered by an immediate return to the more mediocre life of the Palestinian monastery whence they had come. Thus they agree to place their dilemma before the abba Joseph. He tells them that they should not have made a promise in the first place, but having done so, they should consider whether or not to keep it by judging what would do them less harm or be more easily expiated by making amends. Germanus quotes Christ's words in Mt.5.37 ('Say "yes" when you mean "yes"...') by way of objection, to which Joseph replies that the intention of the agent is determinative of the value of the act. ... He then gives scriptural examples of a good end being accomplished with a bad intention (Judas betraying the Lord for the salvation of the world) which is still excusable, and of a deceitful act being done with a good intention (Jacob's deception of Isaac). A few lines later the specific subject of lying is introduced by Germanus. Would breaking the promise not offer an opportunity for lying to certain weaker souls, and is not lying forbidden by express scriptural prohibition? Joseph replies by saying that those who are ill-disposed will always find harmful things in the scriptures, even when they are allegorically interpreted; the *oikonomia* of the Old Testament cannot be ignored, however, which presents numerous examples of lying used to accomplish a good end. Lying should

---

20 This is Jerome's report of the no longer extant Origen text in *Contra Rufinum*, 1.18.

be regarded as a medicine of last resort, like hellebore, which if taken in danger of death if beneficial, but if taken otherwise can cause death. When grave need arises, 'then the refuge of lying is to be sought, but in such a fashion that we are bitten by the guilt of a humbled conscience in a salutary way.' When Germanus responds to this by saying that the Old Testament permitted many things that the New forbids, Joseph concedes that even lying itself was prohibited in the Old Testament except when it was decreed by the will of God or was employed for the prefiguration of spiritual mysteries or for the saving of some holy persons. To lie in such cases is to seek the good of the other, in the words of Paul (cf. 1. Cor. 10.24, 33; 13.5), rather than one's own good, i.e. the spiritual perfection that one might attain by not lying. ... Finally the question arises as to whether one should, by telling a lie, conceal one's virtuousness or, by telling the truth, reveal it. This is an issue specifically with regard to fasting, concerning which Christ had said that it should be done in secret (cf. Mt. 6.18), but it also bespeaks the profound monastic love of humility. Even Germanus admits unhesitatingly that a lie is called for here. The discussion on lying concludes with a catalogue of lies from both Testaments, some of them falling under the rubric of broken promises.

With Cassian and later Dorotheus of Gaza and John Climacus (Dorotheus of Gaza, *Apophtlegmata Patrum, de abate Alonco*, 4; John Climacus, *Scala Paradisi*, 12) we are presented with an alternative tradition on the permissibility of lying in certain circumstances but also with an account of the 'badness' involved in lying. A 'badness' that despite the circumstances that justify lying nevertheless point to the requirement for careful deliberation and the taking up of certain affective and emotional responses. Lying is justified but not without remainder.[21] I have included this too brief survey of two moral traditions on lying within Christianity to provide the background to Aquinas's discussion and to offer a manner of thinking about lying which may help bring out the analogy I will presently draw between cases of lying and cases of judicial torture.

St Thomas's discussion of lying occurs in the *Summa Theologica* II-II, q.110. Here he takes up St Augustine's definition of a lie as 'a false statement uttered with intent to deceive' (St Augustine, *De Mendacio*, 4; *Contra Mendacium*, 12. Aquinas, *ST*. II-II, q. 110, a. 1) and breaks it up analytically into three components:

1. The falsity of the statement;
2. The will to tell the falsity, and
3. The intention to deceive.

(1) provides the material for a lie since, as he points out, it is not a lie to say what is factually false while thinking it to be true, while it is a lie to say what it is true thinking it to be false. However, Aquinas focuses mainly on (2) the wilful disconformity between one's thought and one's speech. (3) provides the motivation for lying rather than the essence of the lie itself.[22]

---

21 After Aquinas considerable effort is expended on the casuistry of lying mainly in discussions of 'mental reservation', which I believe captures quite closely some of the Thomistic thrust. See Boyle J., 1999.

22 See the discussion in Fagothey A. (1957), 250–259. In the following I am indebted to Fagothey's insights.

However Aquinas adds a very interesting dimension to the discussion of lying by locating it within the broader prospective of communication. Aquinas holds that language is conventional, it is the use of symbols developed by human reason and deeply influenced by custom and culture. As a result there are few words that have a single univocal meaning, and therefore context and convention are of crucial importance in distinguishing meanings. Communication then is the use of signs (not just words but gestures, facial expressions and so on) used to convey thought and meaning. We can lie using words, facial gestures, nods and winks. But whatever sign is employed it must be intended by the performer to convey a meaning since involuntary looks, gestures, nervous ticks need not contain meanings. Moreover for Aquinas the sign must be directed to another person or persons and the sign must express the speaker's judgement on what he/she believes to be true. So fiction which is an expression of the creative imagination and not factual judgement is not a case of lying, nor are jokes or exaggerations, but of course, context here is crucial just as it is in the use of figures of speech and in polite expressions and stereotyped formulas.

A further important dimension of Aquinas's position is discussed in terms of circumstances, and this will be crucial to drawing my analogy between lying and torture. Certain circumstances exist whereby no formal speech occurs because no communication is intended. A captured soldier, for example, may tell tall stories to his captors, but the circumstances need to be understood as such to dispel any formal seriousness to the use of the signs. So the conventionality of speech as a means of communication can yield an ambiguous account of what constitutes lying. For Aquinas in order to count as a lie it is necessary:

1. that the speaker indicate and the hearer understand that communication is being made;
2. that it is being made in all seriousness and meant to be accepted as the truth;
3. that to all outward appearances it is understood in the same sense and taken as the truth by both parties;
4. and yet it is known by the speaker to be false (Fagothey A., 1957, 253).

Aquinas's discussion is sufficiently nuanced I believe to allow for exceptions related to circumstances and context. Indeed several commentators have, by focusing on an example of a group of Jews hidden in a basement during World War II, persuasively argued that Aquinas's position is malleable enough on the grounds of 'speaking your interlocutor's language' and 'context' to allow for lying. Alexander Pruss has argued that the use of language is context specific. After using several examples of context based misinterpretation (both licit and illicit, unintended and intended) he presents the case of Helga and the Jews:

> Helga is hiding Jews in her basement. The Gestapo comes to her door. The Gestapo officer knows Helga is an upright and very honest person, and Helga knows that he knows this. The officer asks 'Are there any Jews in your house?' Helga knows that the officer knows that she knows that if she answers in the affirmative or is ambiguous or remains silent then her house will be searched and all Jews found therein will be killed. Helga thinks for a

moment. The she looks the officer straight in the eye and answers clearly, distinctly, and with an air of sincerity; 'No, there are no Jews in my house.' (Pruss 1999, 444)

Having outlined the scenario Pruss argues that Helga is not lying, and more startlingly, that if she admitted that there were indeed Jews in her basement, she would be guilty of lying. His argument rests on the notion, drawn from Aquinas, that language is not defined by dictionaries but by usage together with the idea that a lie involves deceitfully uttering something which in one's interlocutor's language is false. Here the casuistry involved hinges on the definition of 'Jew'. Pruss takes Hitler's definition in *Mein Kampf* to extend to the Gestapo officer where the Jew is described: 'When thus for the first time I recognized the Jew as the cold-hearted, shameless, and calculating director of this revolting vice traffic in the scum of the big city ...' (Pruss 1999, 445–7). Helga does not share this understanding of 'Jew' with her interlocutor and hence, for Pruss, is being truthful to the Gestapo officer, for she does not from her standpoint have 'any subhuman, cold-hearted, shameless, calculating traffickers in vices' in her basement.

Benedict Guevin takes up Pruss's argument and extends it beyond the notion of never saying 'what is false in your interlocutor's language' to include the relevance of ethical context more generally. Guevin correctly points out that truthfulness in Aquinas is embedded in his discussion of the virtue of justice (Guevin 2002, 270–71). As he puts it:

> To qualify an action such as lying, as intrinsically evil (i.e., as disordered in and of itself) is a moral judgement. Such a qualification must relate necessarily to the genus moris rather than to the genus naturae, that is, an action as determined at the physical-ontic level, where it cannot be subject to a moral qualification. To arrive at the genus moris, where a moral judgement can be made regarding an action, entails taking into account the ethical context of the action. (Guevin 2002, 270)

He illustrates this point by providing an example of entering a room to find a couple naked *in dilectio flagrente*. The *genus naturae*, the act itself is one of copulation, but in order to understand the *genus moris* of the act one has to know the context. Is it an act of conjugal union (with the purpose of producing offspring) or an instance of assault, adultery, prostitution or rape? It is only when conceived of in terms of the ethical context that a judgement can be arrived at. In the case of Helga the overarching context is the concern to protect innocent human life, and given that human communication serves the purposes of human fulfillment as an aspect of justice for social beings, the 'lie' though perhaps regrettable is, one might say, morally obligatory.

If what I have been arguing for – that Aquinas's conception of lying is subjected to an analysis of the *tele* of communication and governed by the virtue of justice – is correct, then, it does not seem unreasonable to draw the analogy with the case of torture in the 'ticking-bomb' scenario. The lives of the innocents in the latter case cannot be discounted and it is the concern with moral context and the fact that no genuine communication is possible between the captured terrorist and the authorities that justifies torture. Just as it is possible to interpret Aquinas on lying as holding that certain 'lies' are not really lies but still wrong, so too torture in the case we are discussing may be deemed not to be torture, let us call it physical and mental coercion, or just punishment with the intention of bringing the offender back to the moral realm. Nevertheless, it will still be wrong, a grave instance of dirty hands, which presents the world in a tragic light, and is accompanied by shame, regret and 'tragic-remorse.'

References

Aeschylus, *Oresteia.*

Aquinas, *Summa Theologica.*

——— *Exposito super Iob.*

——— *Opera.*

——— *Quodlibet.*

——— *Summa contra Gentiles.*

Arrigo, J.M. (2004), 'A Utilitarian Argument Against Torture Interrogation of Terrorists', *Science and Engineering Ethics*, 10, 3, 543–72.

Augustine, *Contra Mendacium.*

——— *De Mendacio.*

——— *On Order.*

Baron, M. (1995), *Kantian Ethics Almost Without Apology* (Ithaca: Cornell University).

Boyle, J. (1999), 'The Absolute Prohibition on Lying and the Origins of the Casuistry of Mental Reservation', *The American Journal of Jurisprudence*, 81, 43–101.

Brandt, R. (1972), 'Utilitarianism and the Rules of War', *Philosophy and Public Affairs*, 1, 145–65.

Brecht, B. (1930), *The Measures Taken.*

Camus, A. (1947), *La peste.*

Cassian, J., *Conferences.*

Chrysostum, J., *De Sacerdote.*

Clement of Alexandria, *Stromata.*

Climacus, J., *Scala Paradisi.*

Crisp, R. (1992), 'Utilitarianism and the Life of Virtue', *Philosophical Quarterly*, 42, 139–60.

De Wijze, S. (2004), 'Tragic-Remorse: The Anguish of Dirty Hands', *Ethical Theory and Moral Practice*, 7, 453–71.

Dewan, L. (1977), 'St. Thomas, Lying and Venial Sin', *The Thomist*, 61, 279–300.

Dorotheus of Gaza, *Apophtlegmata Patrum, de abate Alonco.*

Fagothey, A. (1957), *Right and Reason: Ethics in Theory and Practice*, 4th Edition (St Louis: C.V. Mosby Company).

Finnis, J. (1998), *Aquinas: Moral Political and Legal Theory* (Oxford: Oxford University Press).

Gowans, C. (1994), *Innocence Lost: An Examination of Inescapable Wrongdoing* (Oxford: Oxford University Press).

Guevin, B. (2002), 'When a Lie is not a Lie: The Importance of Ethical Context', *The Thomist*, 66, 267–74.

Herman, B. (1993), *The Practice of Moral Judgement* (Harvard University Press).

Hilary of Poitiers, *Tractatus super Psalmos*.

Jerome, *Contra Rufinum*.

Kant, I. (1949), 'On a Supposed Right to Lie from Altruistic Motives', in Beck L.W. (ed. and trans.), *Critique of Practical Reason and Other Writings in Moral Philosophy* (Chicago: Chicago University Press).

Levin, M. (1982), 'The Case for Torture', *Newsweek*, 7 June.

Lukes, L. (2005), 'Liberal Democratic Torture', *British Journal of Political Science*, 36, 1–16.

Oderberg, D.S. (2000), *Moral Theory: A Non-Consequentialist Approach* (Oxford: Blackwell).

Plato, *Republic*.

Pruss, A.R. (1999), 'Lying and Speaking your Interlocutor's Language', *The Thomist*, 63, 439–53.

Pseudo-Maximus, *Sermon*.

Ramsey, B. (1985), 'Two Traditions on Lying and Deception in the Ancient Church', *The Thomist*, 49, 504–33.

Rist, J.M. (1994), *Augustine: Ancient Thought Baptized* (Cambridge: Cambridge University Press).

Rynard, P. and Shugarman, D.P. (eds) (2000), *Cruelty and Deception: The Controversy over Dirty Hands in Politics* (Ontario: Broadview Press).

Sartre, J-P., *Les mains sales*.

Sinnott-Armstrong, W. (1988), *Moral Dilemmas* (Oxford: Blackwell).

Sophocles, *Theban Plays*.

Stocker, M. (1990), *Plural and Conflicting Values* (Oxford: Clarendon Press).

Styron, W. (1979), *Sophie's Choice*.

Sussman, D. (1995), 'What's Wrong with Torture?' *Philosophy and Public Affairs*, 33, 1, 1–33.

Walzer, M. (1973), 'Political Action: The Problem of Dirty Hands', *Philosophy and Public Affairs* 2, 160–80.

Williams, B. (1973), *Problems of the Self* (Cambridge: Cambridge University Press).

—— (1981), *Moral Luck* (Cambridge: Cambridge University Press).

Zizek, S. (2002), *Welcome to the Desert of the Real* (London: Verso).

2.3   Terrorism, Torture and the Rule of Law

Ben Clarke

Torture is a delicate, dangerous and deceptive thing ... The strong will resist and the weak will say anything to end the pain. (Ulpian, *Roman Jurist* AD 221–22)

Introduction

This part of the chapter explores legal issues arising from the use of torture as a counter-terrorism tool. It asks whether such conduct can be reconciled with human rights norms, the rule of law and democratic values. A variety of sources of law are examined including multilateral treaties, customary law, the writings of eminent jurists, state practice, domestic law and general principles of international law. The direct and indirect consequences of the use of torture upon terror suspects are also critiqued. Particular attention is paid to the escalation of international terrorism after revelations of detainee abuse in Afghanistan, Cuba and Iraq.

The Torture Debates

Much ink has been spilled, over many years, by lawyers (Greenberg 2006), philosophers (Crozier 1975; Walzer 1992), political scientists (Stover and Nightingale 1985), psychologists (Suedfeld 1990) and others, on the validity of the use of torture as an interrogation tactic. Allegations of serious mistreatment by US officials of detainees held at Abu Ghraib prison (Iraq), Guantánamo Bay (Cuba) and elsewhere since 11 September 2001 has rekindled the debate. A number of questions have dominated recent discourse on the use of torture. They include:

1. Does the torture of detainees yield useful intelligence?
2. Do the adverse consequences of resorting to torture outweigh the benefits?
3. Is torture an effective and perhaps necessary means of social control?
4. Can the use of torture by democratic states and other members of the UN ever be justified?
5. Is the torture of terror suspects legal?

Debate over the first question is by no means over (Greenberg 2006). While there is some evidence that coercive interrogation has thwarted terror attacks,[23] credible evidence is sparse. There is also a significant body of literature which suggests that torture is not a useful interrogation tactic if reliable intelligence is sought (Applebaum

---

23 Athey, S. (2007), 'The Terrorist We Torture: The Tale of Abdul Hakim Murad', *South Central Review*, 24:1, 73–90; Dershowitz, A.M. (2002), *Why Terrorism Works: Understanding the Threat, Responding to the Challenge* (Yale University Press). See also Israeli state practice on terror at pp. 100–103 below.

2005; Klein 2005). The second question is addressed at various stages in this part of the chapter. The third question is addressed in Chapter 1.2 and in Rob Imre's contribution in Chapter 2.1. While repression of this kind has enabled autocrats to hold onto power for long periods of time (Egypt, Syria, Iraq), *coups d'état* and assassinations to oust such regimes are common (Nigeria, Iraq, Egypt). Popular resistance struggles to oust such regimes are particularly common in the following contexts: colonial rule (Algeria, Kenya) racist regimes (South Africa, Rhodesia (now Zimbabwe)) and occupation (Palestine, Soviet-occupied Afghanistan). Whether the use of torture is an effective means of social control is therefore conditional upon a range of factors. The answers to questions (4) and (5) are the core elements of this part of the chapter. The main focus is upon the legal parameters of torture. Here the following questions are addressed:

- What is the difference between torture and lesser forms of physical and mental abuse?
- Are all forms of coercion prohibited during interrogation? Or only those methods that reach the threshold of 'torture'?
- Have any democratic states involved in the 'war on terror' crossed the threshold? Or is the torture of radical Islamists who are committed to the path of terrorism acceptable in the post-9/11 world?
- Is the 'outsourcing' of torture a violation of international law?

As will become evident, the answer to some of these questions depends upon the definition of torture adopted. A brief example illustrates the problem. Is mental coercion through sensory deprivation and the issuing of threats of violence torture? Or must there be some form of physical violence? Is sleep deprivation, prolonged exposure to cold temperatures, regular blasts of loud music torture? What about threats to harm to family members? (The latter methods are regarded by some interrogators as more effective than the infliction of physical pain.) These questions will be answered by recourse to international law, municipal law, and general comments of the UN Human Rights Committee.

Law, Democracy and Torture

A growing number of legal scholars point to the right to democratic governance as an emerging norm of international law (Fox and Roth 2000). Article 23 of the Universal Declaration of Human Rights (1948) expressly recognizes this right. While it is a non-binding resolution of the General Assembly, this resolution has been unanimously accepted by states on numerous occasions and its contents are widely recognized as being norms of customary law. Most states now regard democracy as fundamental to a well-ordered society and have some form of democratic polity. Autocratic regimes usually allow limited elections. However laws passed by parliamentary bodies in such countries are usually closely vetted by the regime and subject to veto. By contrast, states that enjoy 'full democracy' usually have stronger parliaments. Enacted laws broadly reflect the will of the majority. Where these laws prove unpopular they may be repealed (subject to any constitutional protections including non-derogable human rights norms and minority rights).

International human rights instruments that prohibit torture

When assessing whether torture is permissible in a democratic state, it is necessary to ascertain its human rights obligations under domestic and international law. As will be noted, all states are now bound by the Geneva Conventions (1949) which prohibit torture during times of armed conflict and military occupation. Most states are also parties to the International Covenant on Civil and Political Rights (1966) (ICCPR)[24] and/or the Convention against Torture and Other Cruel, Inhuman or Degrading Treatment or Punishment (1984) (*Torture Convention*)[25] – both of which ban torture at all times and in all circumstances. Enforcement of these treaty prohibitions is primarily the responsibility of states, although international enforcement is growing. For EU member states torture is banned in all circumstances and this prohibition is enforceable under the Convention for the Protection of Human Rights and Fundamental Freedoms (as amended by Protocol No. 11 Rome, 4.XI.1950).[26] (Article 3 states that 'No one shall be subjected to torture or to inhuman or degrading treatment or punishment'.) Likewise the ban is now enforceable for African states party to the Protocol to the African Charter on Human and Peoples' Rights on the Establishment of an African Court on Human and Peoples' Rights (1998) which entered into force in 2004. Torture is banned in all circumstances under Article 5 of the African Charter on Human and Peoples' Rights (ACHPR). This treaty was unanimously approved by members of the Organization of African Unity (now the African Union (AU)) in 1981. All 53 member states of the AU have now ratified the ACHPR. By contrast the Middle East and Asia lack regional accountability mechanism for human rights violations such as torture. The Arab Charter on Human Rights adopted by the League of Arab States in 1994, and the Cairo Declaration of Human Rights in Islam (CDHRI) adopted by the Organization of the Islamic Conference in 1990, both ban torture in all circumstances. There is no enforcement machinery built into these instruments other than the undertaking of states to honor the ban. A perusal of annual reports by Human Rights Watch and Amnesty International on torture in the Middle East demonstrates that this method of enforcement has been an abject failure in many states in this region. Article 5 of the American Convention on Human Rights (1969) also bans torture. However, to date, only 24 of the 35 member states of the Organization of American States (OAS) are parties to this convention. The Inter-American Court of Human Rights (1979) has a role in the promotion and protection – but not the enforcement – of human rights in this region.

---

24 It is one of three instruments – the others being the Universal Declaration of Human Rights (1948) and the International Covenant on Social and Economic Rights (1966) – that collectively form an 'International Bill of Rights.'

25 The Torture Convention was adopted by the General Assembly of the UN on 10 December 1984, and entered into force on 26 June 1987 for the first 20 states which ratified it.

26 Protocol No. 11 (ETS No. 155), entered into force on 1 November 1998. There were 46 contracting states to the Convention in September 2006.

The International Criminal Court also lacks jurisdiction over the crime of torture *per se*. Such conduct is only punishable if the perpetrator has committed torture in circumstances that constitute a war crime, crime against humanity, or genocide. This survey of international instruments reveals that the overwhelming majority of states have either ratified or adopted treaties that ban torture in all circumstances.

Restrictions on Torture under Municipal Law

A prohibition on torture may be enshrined in municipal law in a variety of ways. It may be contained in: the national constitution; a bill of rights (if any); penal law; or human rights legislation. States may be tempted to carve out exceptions (under military, national security, or counter-terrorism laws). Importantly, any attempt by states parties to the Torture Convention to override the prohibition (for example, by authorization of coercive interrogation techniques that are tantamount to torture), would breach their treaty obligations.

While recourse to torture by agents of the state is incompatible with the obligations of states parties to the Torture Convention, it also offends basic principles enshrined in the ICCPR. Having ratified this treaty, most states must now uphold its norms on the domestic plane. The torture of terror suspects cannot be reconciled with the right not to be punished before conviction (ICCPR, Article 9(3)) the presumption of innocence (ICCPR, Article 14(2)), and the right to due process (ICCPR, Article 14(2)). All are universal rights available irrespective of the reasons for detention and interrogation.[27] The torture of terror suspects renders these norms illusionary. It also undermines the rule of law in states party to the ICCPR that engage in this practice.

Torture, the Rule of Law, and Counter-Terrorism Policy

The importance of strict adherence to the rule of law in counter-terrorism policy (including the ban on torture) is widely acknowledged by jurists:

> As terrorist networks operate internationally and scorn national borders, the only way to defeat them is through concerted action at the international level. In the long term, such action can succeed only if it is firmly rooted in the international legal order, of which humanitarian law is, in a sense, the last bastion. (Bugnion 2002, 529)

> The struggle against terrorism will be won by meticulous and time-honoured police work, not by cutting corners through torture. Terrorism does not demand that we torture to defend ourselves. To the contrary, the threat of terrorism is a reminder of the importance of protecting human dignity, even of terrorists. (Smith 2005)

---

27 Justice Stephen echoes this view in the recent US Supreme Court decision in Hamdan v Rumsfeld. In denouncing the military commission process devised to try terror suspects held at Guantánamo Bay, His Honour observed that 'Even assuming that Hamdan is a dangerous individual who would cause great harm or death to innocent civilians given the opportunity, the Executive nevertheless must comply with the prevailing rule of law in undertaking to try him and subject him to criminal punishment' (Hamdan v Rumsfeld (No. 05-184) 415 F. 3d 33 P. 72).

Some ten days after the terrorist attacks of 11 September 2001, Justice Michael Kirby of the High Court of Australia observed:

> The countries that have done best against terrorism are those that have kept their cool ... Keeping proportion. Adhering to the ways of democracies. Upholding constitutionalism and the rule of law. Defending, even under assault, the rights of legal suspects. These are the ways to maintain the love and confidence of the people over the long haul. We should never forget these lessons.[28]

Moreover, given that the vast majority of states have now ratified or adopted one or more instrument banning torture, it is unlikely that any state could legislate to explicitly authorize the torture of terror suspects without breaching an international obligation. Nonetheless the practice of torture by state actors remains widespread. Much of it is carried out against political dissidents including those suspected of involvement in political violence. These factors raise broader questions: Would the 'legalization' of torture actually deter radical Islamists who engage in terrorism? (The abundance of terrorism in the Middle East notwithstanding the widespread use of torture in the region suggests a negative answer.) Does this practice simply reinforce the ideological beliefs of radical Islamists and strengthen their resolve? If the use of torture is widespread – even among states that are treaty bound to end the practice – isn't it better to legalize and regulate the practice? What impact would the 'lawful' use of torture by democratic states have upon the universal struggle to guarantee all peoples basic human rights, democratic government, and fundamental principles of justice? These questions are analyzed below.

Terrorism, Torture and Utilitarianism

The balancing of competing rights is an essential part of the process of democratic law making. However in a climate of terrorism difficult questions arise. Should the right to life of the majority override the rights of a minority (terror suspects) not to be tortured? Can an exception to the prohibition on torture be justified where the lives of thousands of citizens are imperilled by a terrorist plot? If so, should that exception be codified in law? Or should such factors be presented in court in support of a defence of necessity during the trial of the alleged torturer? Another alternative is legislation to allow for 'torture warrants' to be issued by judges who are satisfied that a terror attack is imminent and an uncooperative suspect may have information that would enable authorities to prevent the attack. If this option is pursued, what should be the scope of such laws? Should all persons who *may* have useful information be subjected to torture? Where is the line to be drawn? What of uncooperative spouses, children, neighbors and friends of the terror suspect? Before exploring these issues the status of torture under international law is assessed in more detail.

---

28 The Hon Justice Michael Kirby AC CMG, 'Australian Law – After September 11, 2001', Law Council of Australia, 32nd Australian Legal Convention, Canberra, 11 October 2001 <http://www.hcourt.gov.au/speeches/kirbyj/kirbyj_after11sep01.htm>, accessed 28 November 2005. These views were subsequently adopted by The Law Council of Australia.

International Law and Jurisprudence on Torture

Various UN organs have repeatedly recognized that torture is absolutely prohibited under international law.[29] As noted above, the paramount treaty in this area is the Torture Convention itself. It is important to highlight the fact that this is one of the most widely ratified international treaties. Almost three-quarters of the member states of the UN are bound by the treaty (144 states at the time of writing). Significantly, *no state objected to the adoption of this instrument in the General Assembly* (GA Res. 26/49 2, 1984). The ICJ,[30] the House of Lords[31] and the European Court of Human Rights[32] have all recognized that the prohibition on torture is *jus cogens* (that is, binding in all circumstances and without exception). This conclusion reflects the language of Article 2(2) of the Torture Convention:

> No exceptional circumstances whatsoever, whether a state of war or threat of war, international political instability or any other public emergency, may be invoked as a justification for torture.

Numerous other international instruments ban the use of torture, including the ICCPR. Article 7 states that 'No one shall be subjected to torture or to cruel, inhuman or degrading treatment or punishment.' Under Article 4 no derogation from the prohibition is permitted – even in times of war or national emergency. By March 2007, 156 states had bound themselves to this treaty, while the remainder are now arguably bound under custom. In 'General Comment 20' of the UN Human Rights Committee, a very broad view of what constitutes a breach of the prohibition on torture is adopted.[33] It applies '… not only to acts that cause physical pain but also to acts that cause mental suffering to the victim …' (Paragraph 5). Other forms of

---

29 On 26 June 2005 United Nations Secretary-General Kofi Annan noted in a message on the International Day in Support for Victims of Torture, that 'the prohibition on torture is non-negotiable and that includes an absolute ban on transferring anybody to another jurisdiction where there are reasonable grounds to believe that the person is at risk of torture': 'Annan stresses treaty ban on sending suspects to countries where they risk torture', Press Release, UN News Service, 27 June 2005. On the same day similar sentiments were expressed by Manfred Nowak (the Special Rapporteur of the Commission on Human Rights on the question of torture) and Louise Arbour (United Nations High Commissioner for Human Rights) in a *Joint Statement on the Occasion of The United Nations International Day in Support of Victims of Torture.* <www.ohchr.org/Documents/Issues/JointStatement26.06.06EN.pdf> accessed 28 January 2008.

30 *Arrest Warrant of 11 April 2000 Case (Democratic Republic of the Congo v Belgium)*, ICJ Rep. 2002.

31 *Regina v Evans and Another and the Commissioner of Police for the Metropolis and Others Ex Parte Pinochet (On Appeal from a Divisional Court of the Queen's Bench Division)* House of Lords (24 March 1999); See also *Al-Adsani v United Kingdom*, HRLJ 23 (2002), 39.

32 *Al-Adsani v United Kingdom* HRLJ 23 (2002), 39

33 See Human Rights Committee, General Comment 20, Article 7 (44th session, 1992), Compilation of General Comments and General Recommendations Adopted by Human Rights Treaty Bodies, UN Doc. HRI/GEN/1/Rev.1 at 30 (1994).

conduct that may constitute torture are '… prolonged solitary confinement of the detained or imprisonment …' (Paragraph 6).

It reaffirmed that:

> … no justification or extenuating circumstances may be invoked to excuse a violation of article 7 for any reasons, including those based on an order from a superior officer or public authority. (Paragraph 3)

The Universal Declaration of Human Rights[34]

'No one shall be subjected to torture or to cruel, inhuman or degrading treatment or punishment.' This declaration was adopted by the UN General Assembly in 1948. Although initially non-binding in character,[35] it has been repeatedly reaffirmed ever since, suggesting that it may now have entered into custom. If so, the prohibition on torture has universal coverage under international law.

It should also be noted that the Rome Statute of the International Criminal Court (RSICC) (1998) includes torture among the formulations of 'crimes against humanity' (RSICC, Article 7(1)(f)) and 'war crimes' (RSICC, Article 8(2)(a)(ii)). Torture is defined under Article 7(2)(e) as:

> … the intentional infliction of severe pain or suffering, whether physical or mental, upon a person in the custody or under the control of the accused; except that torture shall not include pain or suffering arising only from, inherent in or incidental to, lawful sanctions; …

Moreover, Article 55 declares that no person shall be subjected to 'any form of coercion, duress or threat, to torture or to any other form of cruel, inhuman or degrading treatment or punishment' during an investigation under the RSICC. Nor shall they be 'compelled to incriminate himself or herself or to confess guilt.' As the vast majority of states participated in the drafting of these provisions, they may be accepted as general principles of international law. At the time of writing the RSICC had been ratified by 104 states.

International humanitarian law

Torture is also banned under international humanitarian law (IHL). All four of the 1949 Geneva Conventions[36] prohibit the use of torture during times of armed conflict and military occupation. Common Article 3 expressly prohibits 'violence to life and

---

34 Adopted and proclaimed by General Assembly resolution 217 A (III) of 10 December 1948.

35 See *Filartiga v Pena-Irala*, 630 F.2d 876 (2nd Cir., No. 79-6090, 30 June 1980).

36 The four conventions of 1949 are: Geneva Convention for the Amelioration of the Condition of the Wounded and Sick in Armed Forces in the Field; Geneva Convention (II) for the Amelioration of the Condition of Wounded, Sick and Shipwrecked Members of Armed Forces at Sea. Geneva Convention (III) relative to the Treatment of Prisoners of War; Geneva Convention (IV) relative to the Protection of Civilian Persons in Time of War.

person, in particular murder of all kinds, mutilation, cruel treatment and torture.'[37] A recent Advisory Opinion of the ICJ confirmed that the prohibition applies during military occupation (*Legal Consequences of the Construction of A Wall in the Occupied Palestinian Territory*, Paras 106–114). Consequently, occupying forces are absolutely prohibited from resorting to the torture of insurgents or terrorists in an effort to glean intelligence. As noted above, the 1949 Geneva Conventions share a unique status. They are the most widely ratified international treaties in existence. With 192 states party they have universal coverage. (A record they share with the UN Charter.) All member states of the UN are therefore bound by the Geneva prohibition on torture as a matter of treaty law. The ICRC has noted that 'the great majority of the provisions of the Geneva Conventions of 1949, including Common Article 3, are considered to be customary law' (Henckaerts and Doswald-Beck *et al.* 2005). Given that all member states of the UN have now ratified these instruments, they are binding on all states under both treaty and custom, subject to any valid reservations entered by states party.

In summary, the ban on torture is universal under IHL and almost universal under international human rights law. It has now been recognized as a norm of *jus cogens* character.[38] *Jus cogens* are norms of international law recognized by the international community as being peremptory in character (de Wet 2004). No derogation is permitted from *jus cogens* (United Nations 1969, 331). States that permit torture violate *jus cogens* and therefore breach international law. Moreover Article 2 of the Torture Convention makes clear that an order from a superior or public authority may not be invoked as justification for torture. Consequently, municipal laws authorizing state officials to torture terror suspects during interrogation violate international law and should not be followed. Whether authorized by statute, the judiciary, or the president during war time, state-approved torture is never permissible under international law.

Defining Torture

Under Article 1 of the Torture Convention, terrorism is defined as:

> ... act by which severe pain and suffering, whether physical or mental, is intentionally inflicted on a person for such purposes as obtaining from him or a third person information or a confession, punishing him for an act he or a third person has committed or is suspected of having committed, or intimidating or coercing him or a third person, or for any reason based on discrimination of any kind, when such pain or suffering is inflicted by or at the instigation of or with the consent or acquiescence of a public official or other person acting in an official capacity. It does not include pain or suffering arising only from, inherent or incidental to lawful sanctions.

---

37 Note: The Geneva Conventions do not define the term but outlaw the torture of captives during armed conflict and military occupation: See Article 3(1)(a), Article 17, and Article 87. Torture is classified under Article 130 as a grave breach of the Geneva Conventions.

38 See for example *Prosecutor v Anto Furundzija*, Case No. IT-95-17/1-T10, Trial Chamber Judgment, 10 December 1998, paras 155–7.

2. This article is without prejudice to any international instrument or national legislation which does or may contain provisions of wider application.

This is the definition of torture adopted in this chapter for the following reasons. Firstly, it is authoritative (having been adopted unanimously by the General Assembly). Secondly a commanding majority of states (141 at April 2007 – including the US, the UK and Australia) are bound by the definition under treaty law. Thirdly, this definition may now have entered into customary law and thereby be binding on *all* states whether they are parties to the Torture Convention or not. Fourthly, with the exception of the RSICC,[39] none of the other major international treaties and instruments that ban torture defines the term.[40]

The Optional Protocol to the Convention Against Torture

The Subcommittee on Prevention of Torture and Other Cruel, Inhuman or Degrading Treatment or Punishment of the Committee against Torture was established under the Optional Protocol to the Convention Against Torture and Other Cruel, Inhuman or Degrading Treatment or Punishment (OPTC).[41] The Committee may visit 'any place under its jurisdiction and control where persons are or may be deprived of their liberty, either by virtue of an order given by a public authority or at its instigation or with its consent or acquiescence (hereinafter referred to as places of detention)' (OPTC, Article 4). Article 11 sets out the purposes of such visits:

> These visits shall be undertaken with a view to strengthening, if necessary, the protection of these persons against torture and other cruel, inhuman or degrading treatment or punishment.

After the visit the Committee may make recommendations to states parties concerning 'the protection of persons deprived of their liberty against torture and other cruel, inhuman or degrading treatment or punishment' (OPTC, Article 11). Most states involved in the 'war on terror' and the detention of terror suspects (including the US, Australia, Iraq, Pakistan, Afghanistan) have not ratified the OPTC and are not obligated to make its detention facilities available to investigation by the Committee. An exception is the UK. Where British forces involved in joint operations with other states carry out arrests and detentions, the Protocol inspection regime applies to such detainees.

---

39 The definition of torture in the Rome Statute is complimentary to the one contained in the Torture Convention.

40 The European Convention on Human Rights and Fundamental Freedoms prohibits torture but does not define it.

41 Adopted on 18 December 2002 by General Assembly Resolution A/RES/57/199. There were 54 Signatories and only 32 states parties to the Torture Protocol in February 2007. The Protocol entered into force on 22 June 2006.

State Responsibility: The Duty to Prevent Torture and Punish its Perpetrators

States have obligations to prevent and punish torture irrespective of whether or not they are party to the Torture Convention and its Protocol. These obligations flow from the *jus cogens* character of the prohibition against torture, which carries with it certain obligations. They include the obligation *erga omnes* to prevent and punish violations of *jus cogens*. This obligation has been recognized by the International Court of Justice.[42] Torture is considered by the international community to be so reprehensible that all states must take measures to prevent and punish it. States are therefore obliged under international law to apprehend and prosecute the instigators and perpetrators of torture. This should give caution to individuals who authorize, carry out, or assist in various ways in the use of coercive interrogation methods that involve torture.

The breach of the prohibition on torture constitutes an international wrong.[43] States have an obligation to halt such conduct immediately. They also have a responsibility to pay reparations to victims.[44]

Judicial Torture Warrants

Unperturbed by these legal norms, Harvard Law Professor Alan Dershowitz has proposed that the torture of terror suspects be placed on a legal footing. He justifies this approach by highlighting the widespread use of torture and the need to regulate such practices. Since 9/11 Dershowitz has argued in favor of the introduction of laws that empower judges to issue warrants that authorize the torture of terror suspects (Dershowitz 2004). If torture is to take place then it should occur within the framework of the rule of law. The passage of laws allowing for judicially sanctioned torture would achieve this objective. While perhaps attractive to those not versed in international law, the Dershowitz thesis can be easily disassembled upon a quick

---

42 In *Barcelona Traction* case, the ICJ stated:

[A]n essential distinction should be drawn between the obligations of a State towards the international community as a whole, and those arising *vis-à-vis* another State in the field of diplomatic protection. By their very nature the former are the concern of all States. In view of the importance of the rights involved, all States can be held to have a legal interest in their protection; they are obligations *erga omnes*. (*Barcelona Traction, Light and Power Co. Ltd.* (Belg. v. Spain), 1970 ICJ 3, 32 (5 February).)

43 'Draft articles on Responsibility of States for internationally wrongful acts', adopted by the International Law Commission at its fifty-third session (2001), Article 2 states:

There is an internationally wrongful act of a state when conduct consisting of an action or omission: (a) Is attributable to the State under international law; and   (b) Constitutes a breach of an international obligation of the State.

44 See International Law Commission Articles on State Responsibility 2001. Article 31 states:

1. The responsible State is under an obligation to make full reparation for the injury caused by the internationally wrongful act. 2. Injury includes any damage, whether material or moral, caused by the internationally wrongful act of a State.

perusal of a basic textbook in public international law. The thesis requires a narrow view of the rule of law, namely one that excludes the obligation of states under international human rights law. The rule of law is the exercise of governmental authority in accordance with previously established and properly promulgated written laws and the exercise of the law in accordance with recognized procedures (Dicey 1914). It must be conceded that the doctrine of the rule of law is silent on matters of justice, democracy or human rights. Indeed the rule of law has been embraced by democracies (the USA, India and South Africa), autocratic regimes that repress basic rights (China and Iran) and dictators (Hitler). However in the UN era states are obliged to uphold the international rule of law, including the prohibition on torture.

Legislative measures designed to validate torture would not only breach the international obligations of states parties to the Torture Convention, they would also undermine the values that underpin a democratic state. However Dershowitz's proposal faces an even greater obstacle – the *jus cogens* character of the prohibition on torture. Peremptory norm allows for no exceptions. Torture authorized by law would be in breach of the *jus cogens* prohibition. If Dershowitz's proposal was implemented, judges who issued 'torture warrants' could be treated as accomplices to the crime of torture. Not so in Dershowitz's world. There judges are unconstrained by absolute prohibitions under international law. This judicial role is eerily reminiscent of the one ascribed to judges in Nazi Germany. A number of German jurists who upheld and enforced Nazi laws (including those authorising the deportation and extermination of Poles and Jews) were convicted at Nuremberg in the 'Justices Trial.' They had given judicial approval to some of the worst atrocities of World War II. The very concept of judicially sanctioned torture smacks of 'legal process gone mad.' While a judge's primary function is to uphold laws passed by parliament, the legacy of the Nuremberg tribunal is that there is a higher duty owed by all individuals – of whatever station and rank – to disobey manifestly unlawful orders.[45] Judges have a duty under international law *not* to uphold manifestly unlawful laws, including those that violate *jus cogens*. Judges ignore this rule at their peril. In 2001 the United Nations Committee against Torture rejected the use of physical pressure by Israeli Security Agency interrogators in extreme circumstances (ticking bomb cases).[46] It

---

45 See: The Justice Trial, United States of America v. Alstötter *et al.* ("The Justice Case"), 6 *Law Reports of the Trials of War Criminals* 1 (1948); 'Trial of Wilhelm von Leeb and Thirteen Others' ('The High Command Case') (1949) 12 *Law Reports of Trials of War Criminals* 1 (Nuremberg Tribunal). See also Article 33 Rome Statute of the International Criminal Court 1998.

46 Conclusions and Recommendations of the Committee against Torture: Israel. CAT/C/XXVII/Concl.5. The Committee considered the third periodic report of Israel (CAT/C/54/Add.1) at its 495th and 498th meetings, on 20 and 21 November 2001 (CAT/C/SR.495 and 498) and adopted a number of conclusions and recommendations <http://www.unhchr.ch/tbs/doc.nsf/(Symbol)/60df85db0169438ac1256b110052aac5?Opendocument>. See also David Luban 'Liberalism, Torture, and the Ticking Bomb', in Stephen P. Lee (2007), *Intervention, Terrorism and Torture: Contemporary Challenges to Just War Theory*, 249, 254; and Eitan Felner (2005), 'Torture and Terrorism: Painful Lessons from Israel' in Kenneth Roth, Minky Worden, Amy D. Bernstein (eds), *Torture: Does it Make Us Safer? Is it Ever OK?*, 29, 32–5.

also denounced reliance upon a 'defense of necessity' to evade criminally liability.[47] Dershowitz's thesis cannot be reconciled with international law. Moreover, this writer has not been persuaded that states would be better off if they adopted his approach to counter-terrorism. It is telling that no state has been willing to implement Dershowitz's proposal.

A Brief History of State-Sponsored Torture

Prima facie, states may in the exercise of their sovereign powers, enact whatever laws they please – however ridiculous or repugnant to fundamental norms of international law. Constraints on the exercise of sovereign power include treaty obligations, customary norms, constitutional constraints and fear of international sanctions. Subject to these limits a sovereign state may pass any laws it likes. At various times throughout history sovereigns have authorized the use of torture. Law and practice in this area can be traced back to the birthplace of democracy: ancient Greece (duBois 1991, 37–8). It is also be found in the legal traditions of medieval England (Heath 1982), Spain (Kamen 1965) and modern USA (Greenberg 2006). Today torture is banned throughout Western Europe, as all 27 member states of the EU are parties to the ECHR. While the ban is enforceable in Europe through both domestic and regional human rights mechanisms, the same is not true in many other parts of the world. While most UN Member states have now ratified the Torture Convention, domestic enforcement is often poor – particularly in those states struggling against terrorism and insurgencies. Extra-judicial torture has long been, and remains, a common method of extracting confessions in many states.[48]

Until recently, few would have imagined that Western democracies, except perhaps Israel, would openly entertain the thought of passing laws permitting the torture of suspected criminals. Since 9/11 the situation has changed. While the US has engaged in the covert use of coercive interrogation methods since the Vietnam War, official acknowledgement of these practices and attempts to legitimize the same is now a matter of public record (Greenberg 2005). Moreover, a number of democratic states (including EU members) have become complicit in these practices through their involvement in the rendition of terror suspects (the outsourcing of torture to countries such as Egypt). By allowing terror suspects to be sent to countries known for systematic torture, a number of EU members have breached their obligation *erga omnes* to prevent violations of *jus cogens*. It seems that some EU member states no longer regard the international prohibition on torture as sacrosanct.

Under the Torture Convention any form of interrogation that involves the infliction of 'severe pain and suffering, whether physical or mental', in order to obtain

---

47 'Necessity as a possible justification to the crime of torture should be removed from the domestic law.' Conclusions and Recommendations of the Committee against Torture: Israel. 23 November 2001. CAT/C/XXVII/Concl. 5 (Concluding Observations/Comments).

48 See Human Rights Watch, 'Torture Worldwide', <http://hrw.org/english/docs/2005/04/27/china10549.htm>. Accessed 24 November 2005. China, Egypt, Indonesia, Iran, Iraq, Israel, Malaysia, Morocco, Nepal, North Korea, Pakistan, Russia, Syria, Turkey, Uganda and Uzbekistan are signalled out for particular criticism.

'information' or 'a confession' is torture. Moreover, interrogation involving 'cruel and unusual punishment' but not 'torture' is also a breach of the Torture Convention. Consequently, conduct of this nature by US agents during interrogations conducted in the 'war on terror' violated US treaty obligations (and the US Constitution). However seeking redress for terror suspects in US courts has presented significant challenges. Persons subjected to coercive interrogation at the US detention facilities in Guantánamo Bay, Cuba, have met with limited success in legal action against the US government. The US Supreme Court has recognized that the Geneva Conventions (and hence the prohibitions on 'cruel treatment and torture') apply to those detained by the US in Cuba. However *habeus corpus* applications for the release of those subjected to prolonged detention without charge (and coercive interrogation practices) have been refused.[49]

State Practice

While US practice has attracted intense media scrutiny, the US is by no means the worst offender when it comes to the torture and mistreatment of detainees. A brief survey of reports by UN Special Rapporteurs, NGOs such as Amnesty International and Human Rights Watch and the US State Department confirm the widespread use of torture in many countries.[50] These reports highlight the frequent use of torture by state officials to terrorize political dissidents and ethnic and religious minorities. State-sanctioned torture is endemic a various parts of South America, Africa, Asia, Eastern Europe and the Middle East. The Ba'ath regime headed by Saddam Hussein was arguably the most brutal of its era. Hundreds of thousands of Iraqis were tortured and killed by Ba'ath officials. Upon the collapse of the regime in 2003, grisly torture chambers were found in government buildings throughout the country. Even the headquarters of Iraq's National Olympic Centre was used by Uday Hussein as a torture chamber.[51] While there were great hopes that human rights would be protected in the post-Saddam era, Iraq is now a far more dangerous place for ordinary citizens than it was before the occupation. Moreover, the Iraqi government which was formed after elections in 2005 has been linked to torture and extra-judicial killings.[52] In 2006 US soldiers found detainees who had been tortured during a search of a secret bunker in an Interior Ministry compound in central Baghdad.[53] A more detailed assessment of US and Iraqi practice appears later in this part of the chapter. In the meantime, the practice of a handful of other states is briefly surveyed. This serves to highlight the

---

49 See *Rasul v Bush*, 124 S.Ct. 2686 (2004) and *Hamdan v Rumsfeld*, 126 S.Ct. 2749 (2006).

50 See note 48 above.

51 Duncan Mackay, 'Torture of Iraq's athletes', *The Observer*. 2 February 2003 <http://sport.guardian.co.uk/athletics/theobserver/story/0,10541,887103,00.html>.

52 'Human Rights Watch Report (2005), 'The New Iraq? Torture and ill-treatment of detainees in Iraqi custody' < http://hrw.org/reports/2005/iraq0105/> accessed 17 April 2007.

53 E. Knickmeyer, 'Inspectors Find More Torture at Iraqi Jails: Top General's Pledge To Protect Prisoners "Not Being Followed" ', *Washington Post*, Foreign Service, 24 April 2006; Page A01.

prevalence of state-sanctioned torture both before and after 11 September 2001. The use of torture by states as an instrument of repression is highlighted, and linkages between this practice and terrorism are considered.

Iran

Torture has long been an instrument of the state security apparatus in Iran. This is true of other states in the region including but not limited to Kuwait,[54] Egypt,[55] Syria,[56] Turkey,[57] Iraq[58] and Saudi Arabia.[59] State-sanctioned torture is routinely employed on Iranian dissidents as a method of intimidation.[60] In Iran the regime enlists both state officials (including religious police) as well as persons working for 'parallel institutions' to carry out repression. These agents of the state are known to terrorize citizens for holding religious or political beliefs that offend the state ideology. One example is persecution of the pacifist Baha'i community. They have been subjected to significant human rights abuses since the Islamic Revolution of 1979. Their crime is a religious one. They do not consider Mohammed to be the final prophet. Failure to renounce such beliefs has resulted in the torture and execution of Baha'is for apostasy.[61] Thousands of Baha'i have fled the country since 1979, while those who remain face discrimination or worse by state officials.[62] In 2002 a parliamentary bill designed to discourage torture was vetoed by Iran's Council of Guardians.[63]

---

54 See *Al-Adsani v United Kingdom*, HRLJ 23 (2002), 39; *Amnesty International Report* (2006), Page 163.

55 *Amnesty International Report* (2007), *Egypt – Systematic abuses in the name of security* 11 April <http://www.amnesty.org/en/news-and-updates/feature-stories/egypt-planned-anti-terror-law-could-intensify-abuses-20070411> accessed 27 January 2008; *Amnesty International Report* (2006), pp. 108–09.

56 *Amnesty International Report* (2006), Syria, p. 250.

57 Ibid., Turkey, pp. 261–2.

58 Ibid., Iraq, pp. 145–6.

59 Ibid., Saudi Arabia, <http://www.amnesty.org/en/region/middle-east-and-north-africa/west-gulf/saudi-arabia> accessed 17 April 2007.

60 See Human Rights Watch (June 2004) ' "Like the Dead in Their Coffins" Torture, Detention, and the Crushing of Dissent in Iran', Vol. 16, No. 2(E); See Human Rights Watch (May 2001), 'Stifling Dissent', *A Human Rights Watch Report*, Vol. 13, No. 4(E); Bahman Aghai Diba, 'Tazir: the Islamic Torture in Iran', 17 January 2006, *Persian Journal* <http://www.iranian.ws/cgi-bin/iran_news/exec/view.cgi/5/12346 > accessed 17 April 2007.

61 Helen Chapin Metz (ed.) (1987), *Iran: A Country Study* (Washington: GPO for the Library of Congress); 'Iran Hangs Bahai In Religion Case', *New York Times*, 24 July 1998, p. A-4.

62 See Amnesty International Report (2003) <web.amnesty.org/report2003/irn-summary-eng> accessed 21 April 2007.

63 'Iran: Veto on Torture Bill Condemned' <http://hrw.org/english/docs/2002/06/12/iran4038.htm> accessed 17 April 2007.

China

China's brutal repression of dissidents is widely documented.[64] An extreme case is the treatment of members of the Falun Gong religious sect. Confronted by evidence of the organized torture and murder of Falun Gong practitioners by China, the US Congress voted unanimously (420 votes to 0) that the Chinese Government should cease the persecution of Falun Gong practitioners.[65] The UN Special Rapporteur on Torture has noted reports of some 314 episodes of alleged torture. They involve over 1,160 individuals since 2000.[66] The UN report indicated that 66 per cent of the victims of these instances of alleged torture were Falun Gong practitioners.[67] In 2005 a different UN Special Rapporteur highlighted further reports of torture by state officials. The Special Rapporteur stated that the torture was carried out in a bid to force believers to renounce their belief in Falun Gong.[68] In the same year such practices were cited in the US Department of State's 2005 *Country Report on Human Rights Practices* (China).[69]

Vietnam

The Montagnard Peoples of the Central Highlands of Vietnam have been the victims of decades of torture and other forms of brutality at the hands of the central government. This ethnic minority has paid a heavy price for supporting the US during the Vietnam War. The International Commission of Jurists,[70] Amnesty International (Amnesty International Report 2005) and Human Rights Watch[71] have

---

64 See for example: 'People's Republic of China: The crackdown on Falun Gong and other so-called "heretical organizations" ', AI Index: ASA 17/011/2000, 23 March 2000; United Nations Reports on China's Persecution of Falun Gong (2004), The Falun Gong Human Rights Working Group.

65 US Congress House Concurrent Resolution 188, 24 July 2002.

66 UN Commission on Human Rights: Report of the Special Rapporteur on torture and other cruel, inhuman or degrading treatment or punishment, Manfred Nowak, on his mission to China from 20 November to 2 December 2005 (E/CN/.4/2006/6Add.6) 10 March 2006, Para 301. In comparing Chinese persecution of Falun Gong practitioners and Iranian persecution of Baha'is, it is clear that regimes driven by an atheist ideology can be as willing as their theocratic counterparts to sanction the torture of citizens whose religious beliefs conflict with state ideology.

67 Ibid.

68 UN Commission on Human Rights: Report of the Special Rapporteur on the independence of judges and lawyers, Leandro Despouy. (E/CN.4/2005/60Add. 1, 18 March 2005).

69 23 February, Section 1 (c) & (d).

70 International Commission of Jurists, *Report by the Western Australian Branch of the International Commission of Jurists concerning Sterilisations of Ethnic Montagnards in the Central Highlands of Vietnam: October 2000.*

71 Human Rights Watch, 'Vietnam: Independent Investigation of Easter Week Atrocities Needed Now', *A Human Rights Watch Briefing Paper*, 28 May 2004; Ibid.,'No Sanctuary Ongoing Threats to Indigenous Montagnards in Vietnam's Central Highlands', June 2006, Vol. 18, No. 4 (C).

all condemned torture, rape and other forms of abuse against Montagnard Peoples by agents of the state.

The United States of America

US officials have employed coercive methods of interrogation since the Vietnam War.[72] The US signed the Torture Convention (1984) in 1988 and ratified it in 1994. However upon ratification of this instrument (and subsequently) both the US Congress and a number of presidents have significantly limited the operation of the treaty with respect to the USA. In doing so they effectively altered the treaty definition of torture for the USA. For example, the US definition includes a requirement that the perpetrator have the specific intent to inflict torture. This definition has been utilized by successive US administrations as justification for conduct that is inconsistent with the spirit and letter of the Torture Convention.[73]

Before assessing the legality of interrogation methods used by the US during the 'war on terror' some preliminary observations are offered. First, standard US interrogation methods are certainly less brutal than those employed by many other states (particularly some of those who have not ratified the Torture Convention). However a number of factors have placed US interrogation and rendition practices at center stage of the international debate on the torture of detainees. These factors include:

(a) the USA's superpower status;
(b) the focus of global media outlets on the conduct of US forces in Iraq;
(c) the disconnect between prisoner abuse by US personnel
      and US demands that other nations comply with
      human rights norms and democratic principles;
(d) conflicting views that have emanated from America's
      political, military and legal institutions on whether
      prisoner abuse is an acceptable interrogation tool;[74]
(e) widespread publicity of the conviction of US personnel for involvement
      in the torture and killing of detainees at Abu Ghraib and beyond;
(f) the failure of US authorities to bring to trial other
      (higher level) perpetrators of such crimes;
(g) the fact that many of those detained (and abused) in
      Abu Ghraib were innocent civilians; and
(h) confirmation that illegal interrogation techniques used
      in Iraq were authorized by senior US officials.[75]

---

72 Michael Otterman (2007), *American Torture From the Cold War to Abu Ghraib and Beyond*; William Pfaff, 'What We've Lost: George Bush and the Price of Torture', *Harper's Magazine*, November 2005, 50.

73 Michael Otterman (2007), *American Torture From the Cold War to Abu Ghraib and Beyond*.

74 Evan Thomas and Michael Hirch, 'The Debate over Torture', *The Bulletin/Newsweek*, 22 November 2005, pp. 25–33 at 33.

75 'Many interrogation techniques authorized for use by the CIA amount to torture. Their authorization by higher-ranking officials is illegal and potentially criminal' (Kenneth

Such factors have been a set back to US attempts to promote freedom, human rights, democracy and the rule of law around the world. So too have revelations that the US has, since 2001, engaged in the rendition of detainees to third states where some have been tortured.[76] Concerns that innocent people may have been caught up in the torture/rendition dragnet were heightened when Britain and Australian nationals were detained in Afghanistan and subjected to these practices before being released without charge.[77] Secret CIA-run detention camps in Eastern Europe has raised further concerns. Precise details including the identity and number of person held in these camps and their conditions of confinement and interrogation have not been made public. The ICRC has been denied access to these camps and cannot independently assess these issues. Not all such detainees were captured on the 'battlefield' or handed over to the US by Pakistani officials. Some were abducted in European cities.[78] Amidst growing criticism,[79] US President Bush eventually admitted to the existence of secret CIA camps but rejected the claim that detainees are tortured.[80]

It is important to note that the consistent breach of an existing customary norm by a powerful state is not in and of itself sufficient to generate a new customary

---

Roth, Executive Director Human Rights Watch); Human Rights Watch, 'CIA Whitewashing Torture: Statements by Goss Contradict US Law and Practice', <http://www.hrw.org/english/docs/2005/11/21/usdom12069.htm> accessed 27 January 2008.

76 For a comprehensive analysis of US involvement in torture and rendition during the 'war on terror' see: 'United States of America: Below the radar: Secret flights to torture and "disappearance"', Amnesty International, 5 April 2006 <http://web.amnesty.org/library/index/ENGAMR510512006> accessed 27 January 2008. On 17 March 2005, the *Washington Post* reported that more than 100 people have been rendered by the US to foreign countries without legal process or access to the International Committee of the Red Cross: See Pfaff, p.52 (Note 72 above).

77 See Human Rights Watch, 'Renditions and Diplomatic Assurances: "Outsourcing" Torture', <http://www.hrw.org/campaigns/torture/renditions.htm> accessed 28 November 2005.

78 Dana Priest (2005), 'CIA Holds Terror Suspects in Secret Prisons: Debate Is Growing Within Agency About Legality and Morality of Overseas System Set Up After 9/11', *The Washington Post*, Staff Writer, 2 November. p. A01.

79 Polling conducted in late 2005 suggested that a majority of Americans regard the torture of detainees as damaging to US interests. A *Newsweek* poll taken in November 2005 found that 73 per cent of Americans agreed that America's image abroad had been hurt by the torture allegations: Evan Thomas and Michael Hirch, 'The Debate over Torture', *The Bulletin/Newsweek*, 22 November 2005, pp. 25–33 at p. 29. But see BBC opinion poll (2006) 'One-third support "some torture"', available at <http://news.bbc.co.uk/2/hi/in_depth/6063386.stm>. This poll of 27,000 people in 25 countries found that 59 per cent of those surveyed opposed torture, 29 per cent thought some degree of torture was acceptable to combat terrorism. Support was highest in Israel and Iraq with 43 per cent and 42 per cent in favor respectively (in counter-terrorism cases). The US had 36 per cent support and the UK 24 per cent.

80 'Bush: Terror suspects not tortured', 8 November 2005; Grier, P. and Chaddock, G.R. (2005), 'Leaks about CIA prisons overseas spark fury', The Christian Science Monitor, 10 November 2005 <http://www.csmonitor.com/2005/1110/p01s02-uspo.html>.

norm in favor of such a practice.[81] Without overwhelming uniformity of practice by states and the widespread belief among them that the practice is lawful, it does not form part of customary international law. Consequently the US practice of coercive interrogation of terror suspects has not given rise to a new customary norm permitting the same. Instead such conduct has been strongly condemned by the international community in general.[82] Even close allies of the US like Australia and the UK have declined to endorse the practice. This is not surprising. The practice offends both their international treaty obligations and their domestic law.

Israel

Israeli civilians have endured decades of terrorist attacks carried out by a variety of non-state actors. These organizations have a range of objectives. Their common goals include bringing an end to Israeli occupation of Palestinian territory and securing the right of return for Palestinians who were forced out of their homes and villages by Zionist guerrillas in the late 1930s and 1940s.[83] Some are committed to the destruction of the State of Israel. Zionist extremists have also engaged in terrorism. The Lehi (the Stern Gang) and the Irgun were involved in acts of terror in the course of their struggle in the 1940s to bring about a Jewish state. Examples include the 1948 assassination of the UN representative in Palestine Folke Bernadotte by Lehi operatives. (Bernadotte was about to release a report proposing the partition of Palestine and the creation of a Palestinian state.[84]) Terrorism by Zionist extremists is critiqued in more detail in Chapter 1.2. The tragic irony is that Israel (now a member state of the UN) was brought into existence through, *inter alia,* acts of terrorism, only to itself become the victim of decades of retaliatory terrorist attacks.

'Torture lite'

Coercive interrogation of captured Palestinian militants has been a routine method of Israeli intelligence gathering for decades. For a time the use of 'torture-lite' during interrogation was regarded by that state as justified. Whether this was an effective method, in the medium to long term, of halting or reducing terrorist attacks is unclear. While there are documented cases where torture has produced reliable intelligence on the whereabouts of terrorists,[85] other factors have also contributed to a reduction in terrorist attacks against Israeli civilians. One is the construction of a

---

81 See *Military and Paramilitary Activities in and Against Nicaragua (Nicaragua v United States of America)*, Judgment of 27 June 1986 – Merits, ICJ Reports 1986.

82 See *Human Rights Watch's Submission to the Committee Against Torture in Response to United States Positions Expressed During the Committee's Consideration of the Second Periodic Report of the United States on May 5 and May 8, 2006.* <http://hrw.org/us/hrw_ response_051706.pdf> accessed on 14 June 2006.

83 See Yitzhak Shamir (1994), *Summing Up: An Autobiography* (Little Brown and Company), p. 71.

84 See Chapter 1.2 above.

85 See Eitan Felner, 'Torture and Terrorism: Painful Lessons from Israel' in Kenneth Roth, Minky Worden, Amy D. Bernstein (eds) (2006), *Torture: Does it Make Us Safer? Is*

physical barrier sealing off Palestinians communities in the West Bank from Israel. Palestinians living behind the wall cannot enter Israel without first passing through security checkpoints. Since its construction there has been a significant decline in the number of attacks by suicide bombers inside Israel.

The use of torture during interrogations is formally prohibited under Israeli law. Under the Israeli Penal Code (1977) the use force or violence against a person for the purpose of extorting from him a confession to an offense or information relating to an offense is not permitted. Israel is also a state party to the Torture Convention. It ratified the treaty in 1991, subject to reservations which need not concern us. Three years later the Committee against Torture expressed its concern at 'the large number of heavily documented cases of ill-treatment in custody that appear to amount to breaches of the Convention, including several cases resulting in death.'[86] It also regarded as unacceptable the Landau Commission Report's finding that 'moderate physical pressure' was a lawful mode of interrogation. The committee concluded that such methods created 'conditions leading to the risk of torture or cruel, or inhuman or degrading treatment or punishment.' It also criticized secret standards of interrogation. These remarks are prescient given current concerns about US-sponsored rendition and torture of detainees. The Committee said:

> By retaining in secret the crucial standards of interrogation to be applied in any case, such secrecy being a further condition leading inevitably to some cases of ill-treatment contrary to the Convention against Torture.[87]

In 1997 Israel defended its use of coercive interrogation methods in a Special Report to the Committee Against Torture:

> To prevent terrorism effectively while ensuring that the basic human rights of even the most dangerous of criminals are protected, the Israeli authorities have adopted strict rules for the handling of interrogations. These guidelines are designed to enable investigators to obtain crucial information on terrorist activities or organizations from suspects who, for obvious reasons, would not volunteer information on their activities, while ensuring that the suspects are not maltreated.[88]

Israel cited foiled terrorist attacks to justify its policy:

---

it Ever OK? A Human Rights Perspective (New York: New Press), pp. 29, 39. See note 89 below.

86 Concluding observations of the Committee against Torture: Israel. 12 June 1994. A/49/44, paras. 159–71 (Concluding Observations/Comments), para 168.

87 Ibid.

88 Special report submitted by Israel on 6 December 1997 in accordance with a request made by the Committee against Torture on 22 November 1996, CAT/C/33/Add.2/Rev. 1, 18 February 1997. Accessible at <www.unhchr.ch>. Precise details on the methods used remains secret so as to prevent Palestinian groups training their forces to withstand interrogation. However rules are in place to ensure 'disproportionate pressure is not used.' See paragraph 9 CAT/C/33/Add.2/Rev. 1.

GSS (General Security Service) investigations of terrorist organizations' activists during the last two years (reveal that) some 90 planned terrorist attacks have been foiled. Among these planned attacks are some 10 suicide bombings; 7 car-bombings; 15 kidnappings of soldiers and civilians; and some 60 attacks of different types including shootings of soldiers and civilians, hijacking of buses, stabbing and murder of Israelis, placing of explosives, etc.[89]

Other justifications for the use of coercive interrogation methods included the fact that persons subject to these methods have the right to seek an injunction against the GSS.[90] This is a curious justification. Did interrogators advise detainees of this right before the 'torture lite' commenced?

In 1999 the Israeli Supreme Court put an end to legal argument that coercive interrogation was permissible. President Barak of the Israeli Supreme Court stated that 'Physical force must not be used in these interrogations; specifically, the persons being interrogated must not be tortured.'[91] Luban has highlighted the reason why the Israeli Supreme Court 'backpedaled from an earlier permission to engage in "torture lite" in emergencies':

the interrogators were torturing two-thirds of their Palestinian captives.[92]

These statistics give credence to the 'slippery slope' argument: once torture is permitted, a culture can easily emerge where the use of torture becomes routine. This is illustrated by events during the Argentinian Dirty War. Luban has noted that by war's end, young officers hardened to the business of torture 'were placing bets on who could kidnap the prettiest girl to rape and torture.' The same writer notes by reference to Abu Ghraib reports and studies that '[e]scalation is the rule, not the aberration' (Luban 2007).

In 2001 the Committee against Torture[93] responded by welcoming the 1999 decision of the Israeli Supreme Court. The court had held that the use by the Israel Security Agency (ISA) of 'moderate physical pressure' through certain interrogation methods was illegal as it violated the constitutionally protected right to dignity. It also commended the Israeli Government's decision not to initiate legislation to authorize

---

89 Special Report Submitted by Israel on its Interrogation Policies and Practices. Consideration of Reports Submitted by States Parties under Article 19 of the Convention. Second periodic reports of states parties due in 1996. Addendum Israel CAT/C/33/Add.2/Rev. 1, 18 February 1997.

90 For relevant Israeli jurisprudence see: *Abd al-Halim Belbayi* (HCJ 336/96), *Muhammed Abdel Aziz Hamdan* (HCJ 8049/96).

91 *Judgments of the Israel Supreme Court: Fighting Terrorism Within the Law* (Israel Supreme Court, 2005). See Judgment of Aharon Barak President of the Israeli Supreme Court HC 5100/94, *Pub. Comm. Against Torture in Isr. v Gov't of Israel*, 53(4) PD 817, 835.

92 David Luban (2007), 'Liberalism, Torture, and the Ticking Bomb', in Stephen P. Lee, *Intervention, Terrorism and Torture: Contemporary Challenges to Just War Theory*, pp. 249, 256 (citations omitted).

93 Conclusions and Recommendations of the Committee against Torture: Israel, 23 November 2001. CAT/C/XXVII/Concl.5. (Concluding Observations/Comments) Convention Abbreviation: CAT Committee Against Torture, 27th session 12–23 November 2001.

the use of physical means during police or ISA interrogations. Whilst acknowledging the security difficulties facing Israel, the committee regretted that the 1999 court decision did not contain a definite prohibition of torture. It also highlighted with regret the detention and alleged torture of juveniles, numerous allegations of torture by law enforcement officials, and 'the judicial practice of admitting objective evidence derived from an inadmissible confession.' It called upon Israel to 'take all necessary effective steps to prevent the crime of torture and other acts of cruel, inhuman or degrading treatment or punishment', and institute effective complaint, investigative and prosecution mechanisms relating thereto.[94] It recommended, *inter alia*, that 'Necessity as a possible justification to the crime of torture should be removed from the domestic law.' Moreover, legislative measures should be taken to ensure 'the exclusion of not merely a confession extorted by torture but also any evidence derived from such confession.'[95]

Israel has been reluctant to pass a law removing the necessity defence (in torture cases or otherwise). Its position is that the defence is not an absolute one and only arises where there is an evidentiary foundation supporting the claim of necessity. Moreover Israeli law recognizes that torture is never lawful, but may be excused in circumstances of necessity. It is arguable that the Israeli approach is not at odds with the *jus cogens* prohibition on torture because Israeli interrogators who commit torture must be prosecuted. (They are not above the rule of law.) On the other hand, the mere use of torture is contrary to *jus cogens*.

There is another dimension to the Israeli approach that warrants mention. Where the necessity defence is available there is no need to adopt Dershowitz's proposal for judicial torture warrants. The legal shortcomings of the Dershowitz model make avoidance of the proposal highly desirable. By making judges complicit in a system of judicially sanctioned torture the Dershowitz model triggers a normative conflict between (a) the *jus cogens* prohibition on torture and (b) the municipal law which would need to be passed by states adopting this model.

Israeli practice (including its refusal to abolish the necessity defence) suggests that states (including democracies with a strong commitment to the rule of law) may be willing to use coercive methods of interrogation where the perceived security benefits outweigh any detriments such as 'naming and shaming' by the Committee Against Torture, states or NGOs. If the terrorist threat increases other states may adopt the Israeli model.

Torture and the 'War on Terror': Analysis of US Law and Practice

Torture has long been prohibited under US law. In 1944 the US Supreme Court held that:

> The Constitution stands as a bar against the conviction in an American court by a coerced confession. There have been, and are foreign nations with governments dedicated to an

---

94 Ibid.

95 Ibid. See also 'Observations of the Committee against Torture: Israel. 18 May 1998. A/53/44, paras.232–42 (Concluding Observations/Comments).

opposite policy: governments which convict individuals with testimony obtained by police organizations possessed of an unrestrained power to seize persons suspected of crimes against the state, hold them in secret custody, and wring from them confessions by physical or mental torture. So long as the Constitution remains the basic law of our Republic, America will not have that kind of government. (*Ashcroft v. Tennessee*)

A number of relevant prohibitions under US civil and military law are noted here. Almost all pre-date the terrorist attacks of 11 September 2001.

US military law

The Military Extraterritorial Jurisdiction Act of 2000 (Public Law 106–778) enables US civilians to be prosecuted in federal courts for certain crimes committed outside US sovereign territory while employed by or accompanying US forces. The *transporting of persons for torture* is also prohibited under US law (United States Code, Title 18, Section 242). US nationals or anyone present in the United States who, while outside the US, commit or attempt to commit torture can also be prosecuted: 18 USC § 2340A (Human Rights Watch 2004). The Uniform Code of Military Justice makes it an offense for military personnel to mistreat prisoners (UCMJ, Articles 77–134).[96] Specific crimes include cruelty and mistreatment (Article 93), murder (Article 118) and maiming (Article 124) and assault (Article 128). Interrogation methods involving torture would violate one or more of these articles (The Torture Papers 1241). War crimes by US soldiers are punishable under the federal War Crimes Act 1996 (18 USC § 2441). War crimes include violations of the Geneva Conventions, such as breaches of Common Article 3 to the Geneva Conventions which prohibits torture.

Civil law

As a ratifying party to the Torture Convention, the US has given a solemn undertaking to do all it can to bring an end to torture *and* other acts of cruel, inhuman or degrading treatment or punishment at home and abroad (Article 16). Acts committed within the US which fall within the treaty definition of torture, are, depending upon the nature of the abuse, punishable as crimes including assault, threatening conduct, grievous bodily harm and so on under US federal and state penal law. The US Constitution also contains indirect protections against the use of torture. It bans cruel and unusual punishment (8th Amendment) and unreasonable search or seizure,[97]

---

96 For criticisms of these laws in regard to providing inadequate protection from torture see: Human Rights Watch (2006).

97 The 4th Amendment (Search and Seizure, 12/15/1791) to the US Constitution protects:

The right of the people to be secure in their persons, houses, papers, and effects, against unreasonable searches and seizures, shall not be violated, and no Warrants shall issue, but upon probable cause, supported by Oath or affirmation, and particularly describing the place to be searched, and the persons or things to be seized.

while guaranteeing due process[98] and the right against self-incrimination.[99] Torture committed outside the US is also prohibited. It is a criminal offense for any person 'outside the United States (to) commit or attempt to commit torture' (US Torture Statute, 18 USC § 2340A).

US jurisprudence

Decisions of the US Supreme Court underscore the illegality of torture and coercion during interrogation. In *Ashcroft v Tennessee* that court declared: 'The Constitution of the United States stands as a bar against the conviction of any individual in an American court by means of a coerced confession.'[100] In *Bram v United States*[101] it ruled that an involuntary confession – even one procured abroad by officers of another state – could *not* be used in a federal prosecution in the USA. The present US administration does not regard these decisions as applicable to those detained in the 'war on terror' and held offshore (for example, at Cuba and in secret detention camps in Eastern Europe).

US practice post-9/11

In the aftermath of the 2001 terrorist attacks on the USA, the Bush administration sought legal advice on whether coercive interrogation of terror suspects held outside the US were lawful, and if so, what were the legal limits. The pivotal document is a memorandum dated 1 August 2002 from Assistant Attorney-General Jay S. Bybee (of the US Department of Justice's Office of Legal Counsel) to Alberto R. Gonzales (Legal Counsel to President Bush).[102] Bybee opined that coercive methods were permissible because torture as defined under US law covers only extreme

---

98 5th Amendment (Trial and Punishment, Compensation for Takings, 12/15/1791) US Constitution:

> No person shall be held to answer for a capital, or otherwise infamous crime, unless on a presentment or indictment of a Grand Jury, except in cases arising in the land or naval forces, or in the Militia, when in actual service in time of War or public danger; nor shall any person *be subject for the same offense to be twice put in jeopardy of life or limb*; nor shall be compelled in any criminal case to be a witness against himself, nor be *deprived* of life, liberty, or property, without *due process* of law; nor shall private property be taken for public use, without just compensation.

99 5th Amendment (Trial and Punishment, Compensation for Takings, 12/15/1791) US Constitution.
100 322 US 143, at 155.
101 168 US 532.
102 Memorandum for Alberto R. Gonzales Counsel to the President, Assistant Attorney-General Jay S. Bybee in the US Department of Justice's Office of Legal Counsel, 1 August 2002, RE: Standards of Conduct for Interrogation under 18 USC §§2340–2340A, in (2005) *The Torture Papers* (Cambridge University Press), p. 172.

acts.[103] Bybee's opinion was underpinned by his interpretation of the decision of the European Court of Human Rights in *Ireland v the United Kingdom* (1978).[104]

In that case the court held that practices including wall standing, hooding, subjection to noise, sleep deprivation and deprivation of food and drink, used in combination for hours on end, *were inhuman and degrading but did not amount to torture*.[105] Bybee construed *Ireland* as offering a legal basis for the use of such methods to soften up detainees for interrogation.[106] He also noted that the Israeli Supreme Court had adopted a similar approach in *Public Committee Against Torture in Israel v Israel*.[107] While that court had found that a range of interrogation techniques used by the GSS were illegal, Bybee seized upon the fact that while the Court had found that use of these methods amounted to cruel and inhumane treatment, it was silent on whether they amounted to torture.[108] The methods in question included sleep deprivation, shaking the person in a violent manner, forcing the person to crouch on the tips of their toes, excessive tightening of handcuffs, and a collection of methods used at the same time (known as the Shabach). The Shabach involved covering the person's head with a hood, playing loud music, and tying them to a seat in a stress position. Sleep deprivation and the Shabach were used together during 'intense non-stop interrogations.'[109]

Bybee opined that 'torture ... covers only extreme acts.'[110] Physical pain would only be torture if 'accompanied by 'serious physical injury such as death or organ failure.' Severe mental pain would only be torture if it resulted in 'lasting psychological harm such as seen in mental disorders like post-traumatic stress disorder.'[111] The interrogation methods described above would be unlikely to fall into this category because the two decisions discussed above 'appear to permit, under international law, an aggressive interpretation of what amounts to torture, leaving that label to be applied only where extreme circumstances exist.'[112] Yet interrogators who overstepped the mark and committed torture could still be exonerated, because 'necessity or self-defense could provide justifications that would eliminate any criminal liability.'[113] This rationale was ultimately adopted by the Bush Administration when Secretary of Defense Donald Rumsfeld authorized a range of counter-resistance methods including some of those described above.

---

103 See §§ 2340–2340A of title 18 of the USC.

104 *Ireland v the United Kingdom* (1978) 2 EHRR 25, Paragraph 104.

105 See Ibid.

106 'Memorandum for Alberto R. Gonzales Counsel to the President', Assistant Attorney-General Jay S. Bybee in the US Department of Justice's Office of Legal Counsel, 1 August 2002, in *The Torture Papers*, p. 172, at p.198.

107 *Public Committee Against Torture in Israel v Israel*, 38 ILM 1471 (1999), Para 9.

108 *The Torture Papers*, pp. 198–9.

109 *Public Committee Against Torture in Israel v Israel*, 38 ILM 1471 (1999), Para 13.

110 See *The Torture Papers*, p. 213.

111 Ibid., p. 214.

112 Ibid., p.199.

113 Memorandum for Alberto R. Gonzales Counsel to the President 1 August 2002 Re: Standards of Conduct for Interrogation under 18 USC §§2340–2340A, *The Torture Papers*, pp. 198 and 214.

In a 'Working Group Report on Detainee Interrogations in the Global War on Terrorism', dated 2 March 2003, from government lawyers to Donald Rumsfeld, further legal justifications for the use of brutal interrogation methods were offered. The report stated:

> Congress may no more regulate the President's ability to detain and interrogate enemy combatants than it may regulate his ability to direct troop movements on the battlefield.[114]

On this view presidential power overrode not only treaty obligations but also Congressional statute law enforcing the convention.[115]

The danger of this approach has been proven with the deaths of detainees during interrogations conducted in Iraq and Israel. In 1995 a Palestinian detainee in Israeli custody who was violently shaken 12 times in 24 hours fell into a coma and died without regaining consciousness.[116] Iraqi General Abed Hamed Mowhoush died during interrogation whilst in Coalition custody. An autopsy report stated that he died of 'asphyxia due to smothering and chest compression.'[117] While the second death may have involved methods that went beyond what was authorized by US authorities, both cases highlight the danger that once coercive interrogation has been authorized, it may be taken too far. Moreover some authorized methods may prove lethal even though they don't fit the US definition of torture. The other factor is of course that where physical and mental abuse involving cruel, inhuman or degrading treatment is permitted during interrogation, there is a real danger that interrogation 'specialists' may 'overstep the mark.'

In any event, the rationale for coercive interrogation offered by Bush administration lawyers appears weak when subjected to legal analysis. Put simply, both torture and cruel, inhuman or degrading treatment are prohibited in all circumstances under the Torture Convention. The US is bound by this treaty. The preamble to this treaty recognizes the desire of states parties to 'make more effective the struggle against torture and other cruel inhuman or degrading treatment or punishment throughout the world.'[118] US conduct is in direct violation of Article 2 and also offends other operative provisions of the Torture Convention.[119] The Vienna Convention on the Law of Treaties,[120] an instrument the US helped to draft and has now ratified, requires

---

114 Working Group Report on Detainee Interrogations in the Global War on Terrorism, 2 March 2003, in Greenberg and Dratel, *The Torture Papers*, pp. 241–85, 256–7. (Note: the entire report is yet to be released.)

115 Anthony Lewis, Introduction, *The Torture Papers*, p. xv.

116 Eitan Felner, 'Torture and Terrorism: Painful Lessons from Israel' in Kenneth Roth, Minky Worden, Amy D. Bernstein (eds), *Torture: Does it Make Us Safer? Is it Ever OK?*, pp. 29, 37.

117 See Anthony Lewis, Introduction, *The Torture Papers*, p. xv; See also Seymour M. Hersh (2004), *Chain of Command: The Road from 9/11 to Abu Ghraib* (HarperCollins), pp. 44–5.

118 Paragraph 6 of the preamble to the Torture Convention.

119 Ibid., see Articles 18 and 19.

120 United Nations, *Treaty Series*, vol. 1155, p.331.

that states refrain from acts which would defeat the object or purpose of a treaty they have signed (Article 18). US interrogation practices during the 'war on terror' violated this rule. Moreover, cruel and inhuman treatment of detainees offends the US Constitution.

In response to the mistreatment of detainees in Abu Ghraib, a number of US legal commentators have highlighting the profound legal and ethical obligations of government lawyers (Bilder and Vagts 2004). Such obligations extend to legal counsel embedded in the White House, Pentagon and State Department. Bilder and Vagts note that the places where the Nazis executed lawyers who advised the German High Command that Hitler's orders to execute allied commandos were illegal, are now national memorials. By contrast no one visits the graves of those who acted contrary to this legal advice and were later hanged at Nuremberg (Bilder and Vagts 2004).

The Military Commissions

One of the most striking US laws passed since 9/11 is the Detainee Treatment Act (2005). It regulates the detention of persons captured during the 'war on terror.' While it bans inhumane and degrading treatment of detainees, Human Rights Watch has observed that this law prevents those detained at Guantánamo Bay from 'raising claims in an independent court alleging torture or other abuse *even after they are released from custody*' (Human Rights Watch 2006, emphasis in original). It also prohibits aliens at Guantánamo Bay from applying for *habeus corpus* (see Section 1005(e)). The Bush administration's ambivalence towards the mistreatment of detainees during interrogation was further underlined by Military Commission Instruction No. 10 (US Department of Defense 2006). The military commissions were established in order to try terror suspects detained at Guantánamo Bay. Instruction No. 10 bars the admission of evidence at military commissions if obtained by torture. However the instruction does not prohibit the admission of 'evidence acquired by abusive interrogation that falls short of torture but nonetheless violate the prohibitions against cruel, inhuman or degrading treatment' (Human Rights Watch 2006).

The military commission instructions are open to question for other reasons. Prosecutors are not obliged to ascertain or disclose in military commission hearings whether confessions or other evidence against detainees was obtained by torture or coercion. Nor must these disclosures be made in proceedings before Combatant Status Review Tribunals or Annual Review Boards. These US military bodies, which evaluate the status of detainees at Guantánamo Bay, may admit evidence that they regard as being of 'probative value' – *even if obtained by coercion*.[121] The incompatibility of the Bush administration's post-9/11 law and practice with fundamental constitutional rights has been demonstrated in a number of US court cases. In June 2006 the US Supreme Court ruled in *Hamdan v Rumsfeld* that original military commission established by the Bush administration lacked the power to proceed because its structure and procedures violated both the Uniform Code of

---

121 Federal Judiciary Emergency Special Sessions Act of 2005, Pub. L. No. 109-163, §100(3)(b). Stat. 1993, 119 (2005).

Military Justice and the four Geneva Conventions signed in 1949.[122] The revised military commission[123] established after the decision in *Hamdan* has also been criticized. It may, like its predecessor, ultimately be rendered unconstitutional by the US Supreme Court.

The Geneva Conventions

The first military commissions at Guantánamo Bay were declared unconstitutional because they failed to afford detainees their rights under the Geneva Conventions (*Hamdan v Rumsfeld*). It is not only detainees whose rights were breached. States parties to the Geneva Conventions – including the US – have a binding obligation to grant representatives of the International Committee of the Red Cross (ICRC) access to detainees held during armed conflict and subsequent military occupation. As custodians of the Geneva Conventions, ICRC representatives have the right under the Geneva Convention III (1949) to visit persons detained during the conflicts in Afghanistan and Iraq. US officials continue to deny the ICRC access to detainees in secret CIA camps in Europe and have refused to confirm the identity of such detainees. It is therefore impossible for the ICRC to ascertain whether these detainees are being afforded their rights under Geneva law (including the right to humane treatment and to not be tortured or mistreated during interrogation).

Abu Ghraib and its Legacy

The abuse of detainees at Abu Ghraib during the occupation triggered an avalanche of international criticism. Moreover torture by US personnel breached orders imposed by US administrator Paul Bremer in an attempt to stabilize Iraq.[124] Publication of images of prisoner abuse triggered a drop in support for the US mission in Iraq. Some Coalition member states withdrew their troops and personnel from the multinational force. Doubts were raised about the ability of the US to restore security throughout the country and win the hearts and minds of the Iraqi population. This is to say nothing of the loss of US prestige among the community of nations. These wider consequences underscore the potential 'ripple effect' of state-sponsored torture or cruel and degrading treatment.[125]

The mistreatment of detainees at Abu Ghraib occurred at a time when Coalition forces in Iraq were under considerable pressure to get results in their counter-insurgency efforts. US Defense Secretary Donald Rumsfeld authorized the use of

---

122 *Hamdan v Rumsfeld, Secretary of Defense, et al.* (No. 05-184) 415 F. 3d 33, pp. 49–72 (Justice Stephens).

123 See Military Commissions Act of 2006, Pub. L. No. 109-366, 120 Stat. 2600 (17 October 2006).

124 Torture, cruel, inhuman and degrading treatment or punishment, and discrimination were all prohibited under CPA Order 7 of June 2003.

125 See William Pfaff, 'What We've Lost: George Bush and the Price of Torture', *Harper's Magazine* November 2005, 51.

counter-resistance methods that were heavily criticized. Authorization for their use was later revoked. These interrogation methods, together with inadequate training and supervision of US personnel, contributed to an environment where serious prisoner abuse was committed with impunity (Luban 2007).

Bybee's analysis of torture has Orwellian overtones. The advice that cruel and degrading treatment of detainees is lawful notwithstanding the clear prohibition on such conduct under the Torture Convention and *jus cogens*, is from a legal perspective, difficult to fathom. It reflects a willingness to side-step binding international norms that stand in the way of domestic policy. 'Counter-resistance' techniques that breached the Geneva Conventions, US law, and international human rights law, were acceptable to US Secretary of Defense Rumsfeld (and presumably other senior White House officials) before the Abu Ghraib scandal broke. Thereafter the more brutal interrogation methods were quickly revoked. By then it was clear to most observers that these techniques were fuelling the insurgency in Iraq as well as anti-US sentiment worldwide.[126] The point is underscored by the decision of the US State Department to postpone the release of its 2003–2004 annual report on human rights around the world.[127] The report summarizes actions in foreign countries to end abuses including torture. The torture and unlawful killing of detainees at Abu Ghraib and elsewhere in Iraq were not mentioned. The irony of these omissions was not lost on the international media.

The US government was also reluctant to acknowledge that the incidence of international terrorism had increased since the Iraq war and the prisoner abuse scandals (Glasser 2005). By contrast, Islamist terror organizations were quick to cite US human rights violations against Muslims in Iraq, Afghanistan and Guantánamo Bay as a justification for militant jihad. The use of torture by US agents proved a propaganda weapon for al Qaeda and other international terrorist organizations. While Al Qaeda's training manual encourages its members to make complaints of abuse by their captors,[128] independent corroboration of such abuse represents an unfortunate victory for al Qaeda.[129] In the minds of potential al Qaeda recruits, US abuse of Muslim detainees demonstrates the evils of the US and the legitimacy of recourse to violent jihad against US interests. Several Guantánamo Bay detainees have claimed that US interrogators tortured them, and sent them to foreign countries to be tortured.[130] While photographic proof of mistreatment of detainees at Guantánamo

126 For a detailed criticism of the Bush administration interrogation practices, see ibid.,50–56.

127 *Supporting Human Rights and Democracy: The US Record 2003–2004*

128 Al Qaeda Training Manual <http://www.usdoj.gov/ag/trainingmanual.htm> accessed 28 November 2005.

129 See for example: Human Rights Watch (2005), 'Leadership Failure: Firsthand Accounts of Torture of Iraqi Detainees by the U.S. Army's 82nd Airborne Division', September, Vol. 17, No. 3(G) <http://hrw.org/reports/2005/us0905/> accessed 27 January 2008.

130 One victim of the US policy of rendition was Australian citizen Mamdouh Habib. Pfaff notes that 'Habib (was) sent to Egypt for interrogation, said after release that during his six months in Egypt he had been hung from hooks, repeatedly shocked, beaten and nearly drowned. When he eventually arrived at Guantánamo Bay most of his fingernails were missing', p. 52 (Note 125 above).

Bay has not been publicly revealed, US soldiers who worked at the Cuban gaol have confirmed that torture and prisoner abuse took place (Davis 2005; Saar and Novak 2005). An FBI email (released after a federal court ordered government agencies to comply with a Freedom of Information Act request) also refers to torture having occurred during interrogations at Guantánamo Bay.[131] Meanwhile the American Council Liberties Union obtained autopsy reports that reveal homicides of detainees in US custody.[132] It has also been reported that a leaked UN document says the treatment of detainees at Guantánamo Bay meets the definition of torture under the Torture Convention. ('Guantanamo Inmates Tortured' 2006).

Such evidence of torture in US detention facilities (Lewis 2004) heightens concerns that detainees in secret CIA camps are suffering similar abuses. It also allows credence to be given to unfounded allegations made against US interrogators. This point reinforces concerns that any intelligence benefits gained from recourse to torture and other forms of abuse during interrogation may be outweighed by the adverse publicity and loss of 'hearts and minds.' When the rule of law and human rights are denigrated by a state, the integrity of its government is undermined. Such governments are less likely to be believed when they seek to refute mischievous allegations of mistreatment of detainees. Most detainees in the US-led 'war on terror' are Muslim. Most victims of these humiliations have been Muslim. Some of the abuses have involved deliberate measures to insult the religious beliefs of detainees. Such behavior has been widely reported. Inevitably the task of persuading critics that the 'war on terrorism' is not 'war on Islam' is now more difficult.[133] The mistreatment of Muslim members of the US military has done nothing to overcome this misconception. The story of Muslim military chaplain James Yee is striking (Yee 2005). Yee was posted to Guantánamo Bay as a chaplain in 2002. While there, Yee became increasingly concerned about the mistreatment of detainees. He and other Muslim military personnel were treated with suspicion by colleagues on account of their Islamic faith and religious practices. Yee was himself detained and held incommunicado for a month and remained in a maximum security facility for a further two months. Charges of mishandling classified materials, adultery, storing pornography on his Army laptop and lying to investigators were laid against Yee. All were dropped. Threatened espionage charges never eventuated. Yee's experience has

---

131 'FBI E-Mail Refers to Presidential Order Authorizing Inhumane Interrogation Techniques' (12/20/2004). The FBI email can be found at: <http://news.bbc.co.uk/1/shared/bsp/hi/pdfs/09_05_05_fbi_email.pdf> accessed 11 January 2006. For a comprehensive collection of US government documents demonstrating that detainees were tortured go to American Council Liberties Union website. Direct link to torture documents <http://www.aclu.org/torturefoia/> accessed 27 January 2008.

132 See American Council Liberties Union website: <http://www.aclu.org/> Direct link to autopsy reports: <http://action.aclu.org/torturefoia/released/102405/> accessed 27 January 2008.

133 In this writer's view the so-called 'war on terror' is not a war on Islam but a struggle to defeat extremist ideologies that have emerged within the Islamic world. The involvement of Muslim states such as Jordon, Afghanistan, Pakistan and Saudi Arabia and other Arab states in US-led counter-terrorism initiatives indicate that the struggle waged by these governments is against Islamists who have chosen the path of terrorism rather a war against the Islamic faith itself.

done little to assist the reputation of the US military among Muslims. Allegations that US soldiers urinated on the Koran and flushed copies down toilets sparked open demonstrations of anti-US sentiment in Afghanistan. Four people died in such riots in Jalalabad. Whether allegations of mistreatment of the Koran are accurate or not became a secondary issue. The perception that US officials are capable of such abuses is the inevitable product of confirmed cases of prisoner abuse. Once abuses of this nature are confirmed, allegations of a similar nature may be difficult to counter in the mass media. In order to prevent extremist ideologies that feed off and encourages such stories, states involved in counter-terrorism must ensure that their personnel fastidiously respect the international rule of law by upholding the Geneva Convention and basic human rights norms. Compliance must be exemplary. Soldiers must maintain discipline in their remarks, behavior and attitudes. In the context of US troops of Middle Eastern nations, compliance with human rights norms requires awareness of Islamic principles and practices. Failure to adhere to them may lead to the perception (if not the reality) of violations of the right of the local population to freedom of religion.[134]

Does Terrorism Justify Torture?

US President George Bush has asserted that everything changed after 9/11[135] and by implication the existing international legal order must adapt if the threat posed by terror organizations is to be met. The aggressive 'counter-resistance' techniques authorized by Rumsfeld appears to be a direct result of this thinking.[136] So does

---

134 Images of US soldiers posing beside the corpses of detainees demonstrate either a lack of awareness of humanitarian law and Islamic norms or a reckless indifference to them. Some members of the US military may have believed that humiliation and abuse of prisoners would aid interrogation, and provide important intelligence. Whether torture of detainees does in fact yields useful intelligence is a matter of ongoing conjecture. However there is no doubt that from a public relations ('hearts and minds') point of view, it is clearly counter- productive. News of abuse of detainees can fuel resistance to occupation and heighten terrorist activity. Abuse of detainees in Iraq united otherwise disparate forces in a common purpose – the desire to expel an occupation force that was denigrating Islam and mistreating Muslims. Torture and abuse at Abu Ghraib clearly worked against US interests in Iraq – it inspired an escalation in insurgent attacks on Coalition forces and did nothing to thwart the escalation of terrorist violence.

135 'After 9/11, the world changed for me, and I think changed for the country. It changed for me because, like many, we assumed oceans would protect us from harm, and that's not the case, it's not the reality of the 21st century. Oceans don't protect us. They don't protect us from killers. We're an open country, and we're a country that values our openness. And we're a hard country to defend. And, therefore, when we see threats overseas, we've got to take them – look at them in a new light.' US President G. Bush, 'President Addresses the Nation in Prime Time Press Conference', 13 April 2004 <http://www.whitehouse.gov/news/releases/2004/04/20040413-20.html> accessed 12 April 2007.

136 Note: The US continues to deny that President Bush has 'authorized, ordered or directed in any way any activity that would transgress the standards of the torture conventions or the torture statute, or other applicable laws' in order to extract confessions from prisoners

Vice-President Dick Cheney's efforts in 2005 to exclude the CIA from the ban on cruel and degrading treatment of detainees (Smith and White 2005). This effort failed. However it demonstrated that – at the highest levels of the US government – some officials believe that terror suspects should be subjected to treatment that is prohibited under international law.

States that persist with coercive interrogation techniques leave themselves open to other criticisms including disingenuousness when it comes to adherence to human rights and democratic norms. In the end torture is not justified, not simply because it is morally and legally wrong but, as McCoy has noted, the price a society pays for abiding the use of torture is far too high: 'Torture will not and cannot serve as a bargain-price shortcut to security' (McCoy 2006).

Defining 'Terrorism'

The coercion of 'terror suspects' during their interrogation gives rise to the need to define the term 'terrorism.' So too does the use of the phrase 'war on terror.' While it is generally accepted that terrorism is 'violence deliberately inflicted upon civilians in order to instil fear in the general population', agreement on the precise scope of the term terrorism has proved elusive for a range of reasons (see Chapter 1.2). In 2000, an *ad hoc* committee established by the General Assembly pursuant to resolution 51/210 (1996) began work on a draft comprehensive convention on international terrorism. To date no agreement has been reached on a definition of terrorism. Additional to the factors canvassed in Chapter 1.2, many others may be added including: the age-old problem of where to draw the line between combatants and unprivileged fighters; controversy over whether war or peace time legal regimes apply to international terrorism or whether there is a *lacuna*; the unwillingness of some countries to include state terrorism within the definition of terrorism; and questions about whether terrorists should be treated in the same manner as common criminals.

Terrorism as defined by the occupier

Can combatants be charged as terrorists or only as unprivileged fighters? Are attacks on civilians during peace time acts of terrorism or common crimes? Should the perpetrators be prosecuted as common criminals? What about irregular fighters captured on the battlefield? The question of how to classify captured enemy fighters is addressed under Geneva law. This legal regime was not followed by the

---

taken in Iraq or Afghanistan. See: 'White House Releases Documents on Torture in War on Terror', available at <http://www.globalsecurity.org/security/library/news/2004/06/sec-040623-usia04.htm> accessed 29 January 2008. While this may be so, evidence that Rumsfeld authorized torture of detainees is mounting: Julian Coman (2004), 'Interrogation abuses were "approved at highest levels", *Sunday Telegraph* (London), 13 June, p. 26. Claims by former detainees, the Red Cross reports, and confessions by Abu Graib staff, and leaked US government memorandums all point toward official authorization of torture during interrogation.

US in the 'war on terror' until the US Supreme Court ruled that compliance with the Geneva Conventions was mandatory. The Geneva Conventions recognize the belligerent status of a range of actors including 'organized resistance movements'. Such movements may for example launch attacks upon occupying forces in a bid to expel them from occupied territory. Whether members of a resistance force are 'organized' and meet the other requirements necessary to qualify as 'combatants' (and thereby enjoy immunity from punishment for participating in hostilities) are questions of fact. Those who do not are unprivileged fighters, and have no such immunity. A further complication is determining whether attacks upon civilians who are collaborating with the occupying army are permissible or punishable acts. (For example, were members of the French resistance who targeted local citizens for collaborating with the Nazis 'terrorists' or 'freedom fighters'?)

US military spokesmen in Iraq routinely classified all who engage in attacks on Coalition and Iraqi forces during the occupation as 'terrorists.' This approach appears to be context based (the US were occupiers and under attack from resistance fighters) rather than an attempt to objectively apply Geneva Conventions to those involved in armed resistance. By contrast the US described the Mujahideen who struggled against Soviet occupying forces in the 1980s as brave and noble patriots. They were freedom fighters engaged in legitimate resistance to foreign occupation. This is unsurprising. Resistance to Russian forces benefited the US in its Cold War against the Soviet Union.

In 2003–04 'the shoe was on the other foot.' Coalition forces faced with stiff resistance to their occupation of Iraq. Iraqi resistance forces were not brave Mujahideen but 'terrorists.' The US responded with 'counter-resistance techniques' in a bid to coerce intelligence out of captured enemy fighters. US Department of Defense memorandums, and documents signed by the commander of US forces in Iraq, General Ricardo Sanchez, gave US personnel a mandate to engage in violations of the Geneva Conventions.[137] This is difficult to reconcile with US condemnation of Soviet mistreatment of captured Afghan fighters in the 1980s. It suggests that adherence to international law is not usually the principal concern of occupying forces as they battle resistance movements.

Terrorism as defined by resistance movements

Arab states have consistently maintained that the concept of terrorism must accommodate the right to struggle against foreign occupation.[138] There is historical support for their position. The Allies assisted and encouraged French resistance forces operating in German-occupied territory during World War II (Clarke 2005). Members of the French resistance sometimes resorted to acts of terror. Bombs were thrown into restaurants where French citizens and German soldiers fraternized.

---

137 US memo shows Iraq jail methods 30 March 2005, <http://news.bbc.co.uk/2/hi/americas/4392519.stm>.

138 Challiss McDonough, 'Iraqi Conference Separates 'Resistance' from Terrorism', Cairo, 21 November 2005 <http://www.globalsecurity.org/wmd/library/news/iraq/2005/11/iraq-051121-voa05.htm>

(French citizens who collaborated with the Nazis were regarded by the resistance as traitors.) These attacks were generally viewed by the Allies not as terrorist crimes but wartime acts of necessity – nasty but inevitable acts of violence in a vicious struggle against German aggression. Indeed in the face of genocide by an occupying force, such conduct may be justified today.[139] While international law does not prohibit resistance to occupation, nor does it squarely address the issue of whether collaborators are (a) lawful military targets or (b) civilians entitled to protection. Clearly collaboration with a belligerent occupying army can place the collaborator 'in harm's way.' If collaborators assist the war effort of the occupier, they become a military target of the resistance. If the opposite were true, the capacity of those subjected to brutal occupation to resist would be severely curtailed. Attacks upon those who engage in this type of collaboration are not expressly prohibited under the law of armed conflict. (Spying and espionage have long been recognized as punishable acts under international law.) On this view civilians who assist an occupying army that is waging a war of aggression make themselves military targets, however, upon capture they are entitled to a trial before a competent tribunal. Where information provided by collaborators aids the occupier in the commission of crimes against the occupied population, attacks on the former may, depending on the particular circumstances, be justified as acts of self-defence and self preservation. The critical question is the circumstances in which such acts are carried out. The summary execution of unarmed persons who are under the power of their adversary (including collaborators) is punishable under domestic criminal law (murder) and international law (war crime).

Consequently, from a resistance perspective, not all those who target occupying forces (or those who collaborate with them) are terrorists. However unprivileged fighters and those who commit war crimes or other crimes against international law may be punished.

The search for a meaningful definition of terrorism

While the precise scope of the definition of terrorism is yet to be agreed, it clearly includes the deliberate or indiscriminate targeting of civilians who have not taken part in armed conflict and have not provided military assistance or intelligence to the enemy. As the vast majority of casualities of war are now civilians rather than combatants, the importance of a comprehensive treaty banning terrorism has never been greater. The summary execution of civilians is condemned under international law during both peace and war time. The challenge for states is to ensure that this understanding is reflected in a comprehensive treaty on terrorism that governs both state and non-state actors. Irrespective of how terrorism is defined, the torture of those involved in terrorism is – and should remain – prohibited in all circumstances. In the present battle against radical Islamists, both Muslim and non-Muslim states have been tempted to try to extract intelligence through torture. However as has

---

139 While extra judicial killing of unarmed persons during wartime is prohibited under Geneva Law, the right of personal self-defence is a general principle of international law and a right under the municipal law of states (see Chapter 1.2).

been demonstrated above, this approach is both a violation of international law and a counter-productive strategy during a struggle against radical Islamists. Their ideology encourages militant jihad where fellow Muslims are living under oppression and humiliation. Torture involves both.

Torture by Occupiers: A Catalyst for Resistance

Not even super-powers are immune from the laws of physics. While it is often said that the US has violated international norms with impunity during the 'war on terror', this is not entirely correct. A fundamental law of physics is that 'for every action there is an equal and opposite reaction.' This law applies, by analogy, to extra-legal responses by terrorists and others to US violations of international law. The torture, humiliation and sexual abuse of detainees at Abu Ghraib certainly caused a reaction. It proved to be a propaganda coup for terrorist organizations intent on recruiting and radicalizing Islamic youth. So too did the release of a Red Cross report which estimated that 70 to 90 per cent of those imprisoned in Iraq 'had been arrested by mistake', often by soldiers who used excessive force in the process (Dratel and Greenberg 2005). There is little doubt that such practices contributed to an escalation in terrorist and insurgent violence in Iraq, and in international terrorism in general. When the rule of law is violated in occupied territory through torture of detainees, legal methods of redress may be minimal. Where high level perpetrators are shielded from prosecution by virtue of their status as occupiers, and international tribunals such as the ICJ and the ICC are prevented from dealing with such matters, international legal mechanisms offer little or no assistance to victims of torture. Those outraged by the abuses of an occupying power have throughout history engaged in violent resistance, and in some instances terrorism. Harsh occupation breeds resistance. The use of torture by an occupier fuels terrorism. The growth in terrorism in Iraq during (and beyond) the occupation suggests that coercive interrogation of detainees heightened armed resistance and terrorism.

In an increasingly lawless environment, international terrorist groups in Iraq were able to carry out attacks with relative impunity. A number of attacks were launched on Abu Ghraib itself (Knickmeyer 2006). In such a climate the torture and execution of captured occupying troops is not surprising. Iraq has a population of 25 million people. Many Iraqis have easy access to weapons. After the US Secretary of Defense ignored the advice of US generals on the number of ground troops needed to pacify Iraq and Paul Bremer disbanded the Iraqi army, Coalition forces were left exposed and undermanned. The emergence of an array of well armed insurgent forces was not entirely surprising. In turning to aggressive interrogation methods the US began to make many enemies and to lose friends. Like terrorism, torture is a sign of weakness. It undermines efforts to appeal to the 'hearts and minds' of the local population. It alienates an occupying army from the occupied population and renders its mission more dangerous. Torture by the occupier gives terrorist groups a sense of legitimacy. It swells their ranks.

Evidence Obtained by Torture

Pre-trial torture during interrogation has long been regarded as a breach of fundamental rights. It demonstrates the abandonment by the state of due process, natural justice and the right of the individual not to be subject to arbitrary punishment, or cruel and unusual punishment. The judicial torture warrant proposal, while compatible with the rule of law in a narrow sense, is ultimately a corruption of it.[140] The reasons are obvious: reliance upon evidence extracted under torture is fraught with dangers. The information obtained may be false or incomplete. Some people will agree to false allegations in order to end the pain. Innocent people may be named. While a prisoner of war in Vietnam, Senator McCain was physically coerced into providing the names of members of his flight squad. Instead, McCain provided the names of members of an American football team. This information proved sufficient to end the abuse. Decades later McCain asserts that torture of terror suspects is both unreliable and counterproductive:

> It seems probable to me that terrorists we interrogate under less than humane standards of treatment are also likely to resort to deceptive answers that are perhaps less provably false than that which I once offered ... Mistreatment of enemy prisoners endangers our own troops who might someday be held captive.[141]

Moreover information extracted through torture may end up before military commissions. Under the rules of the US military commissions the prosecution may tender evidence without calling the person who provided the information. When the witness is available but is not called the accused is deprived of a fair trial. If the witness is not present the veracity of his or her testimony cannot be examined by counsel. As John North, the President of the Law Council of Australia has noted in his rebuke of the military commission process at Guantánamo Bay, 'You can't cross examine a piece of paper.'[142]

Torture and Liberal Democracy

The use of confessions extracted under torture is not dissimilar to the legal process employed during the Spanish Inquisition or by the Star Chamber in 17th-century England. 'Torture according to law' is an anathema to international human rights

---

140 Dershowitz canvassed the prospect of judicial approval of the torture of a detainee who knows of the location of a ticking bomb but refuses to divulge the information (see note 23 above at p. 156). McCain notes that in such a rare situation, where extreme measures are taken to extract information that saves the lives of innocent people, these factors would be taken into account when judging the actions of interrogator. However this does not require an exception to be written into law, as this would 'risk opening the door to abuse as a matter of course, rather than a standard violated truly *in extremis*.' (See note 141 below at p. 36.)

141 Senator John McCain, 'Torture's Terrible Toll', *Newsweek*, 22 November 2005 (*The Bulletin* with *Newsweek*, p. 34).

142 Latest Law Council Report Highlights More Hurdles for Hicks <http://www.lawcouncil.asn.au/read/2005/2414078345.html> 21 July 2005 accessed 4 January 2006.

law. However international outrage at the use of torture and rendition during the 'war on terror' appears to have strengthened the human rights movement. As noted above, the US Supreme Court and other US courts have ruled on a number of occasions that denial of terror suspects their Geneva Convention rights, and efforts to legitimize the same by executive decree is unconstitutional and exceeds the war time powers of a US president. While laws of this kind enacted by elected representatives are accepted by some courts, it is difficult to see how such laws could be reconciled with the prohibition on cruel and unusual punishment. They clearly offend the spirit, and in this writer's view the letter, of various amendments to the US Constitution which guarantee fundamental rights. They also undermine the democratic project by eroding confidence in this mode of governance, and providing propaganda for terrorist organizations seeking to topple democratically elected governments in Afghanistan and Iraq. They also undermine tentative steps towards greater democracy in a number of other Arab states. Put crudely, if the 'war on terror' is a war to win the hearts and minds of Muslims, torture of Muslims is hurting rather than helping the war effort.

Terrorists captured during armed conflict should be prosecuted before competent tribunals. Those arrested during peace time should be dealt with by civil courts or international tribunals. Torture of terror suspects and use of such evidence in military commissions undermines efforts to deal with terrorists in accordance with the international rule of law and human rights. It also undermines the prospect of securing a conviction – evidence extracted through torture is inadmissible in proceedings before a properly constituted court.

Torture and Efforts to Promote Human Rights

The prohibition on torture is one of the cornerstones of the human rights movement. Its importance is reflected in numerous judicial decisions, treaties, protocols and other instruments. Recourse to torture as a method of counter-terrorism is a significant set back to the human rights movement. The US has been at the forefront of efforts to promote compliance with basic human rights. The submission of the US Department of State, *Country Reports on Human Rights Practices*, to the US Congress has become a significant annual event in the human rights calendar. Most states that sanction torture attract strident criticism from the US in these reports. (Close allies are usually spared such treatment.) Having defined itself as a global watchdog on state compliance with human rights, the US record is now under intense scrutiny. US involvement in the abuse and torture of detainees, and the transfer of detainees to states that routinely use torture as an interrogation method (Campbell 2002) have damaged the reputation of the USA. Such practices suggest a lack of commitment to the universality of the human rights, democracy and the international rule of law.

In its defence, the Bush administration has asserted that pre-9/11 international norms may not apply post-9/11. In 2005, it sought to exempt the CIA from a US bill on torture.[143] During negotiations on the text of a resolution on the General Assembly's Global Summit in 2005 the US insisted on the deletion of all reference to the principle that use of force should be used as a last resort.[144] These developments reflect a belief that the protection of US citizens from the threat of terrorism may require occasional departures from international law, perhaps even fundamental human rights. However, as has been demonstrated, this approach appears to have done more harm than good.

Effective Counter-Terrorism Requires Measures that Work in the Long Term

For some interrogators, torture is regarded as an essential tool for extracting information from uncooperative terror suspects. Such information may lead to the arrest of other members of a terror network and prevent terrorist attacks. However, as has been demonstrated, such methods are impermissible under international law. Nor are they likely to be endorsed by lawmakers in democratic states. By contrast dictatorial regimes are less constrained. Torture can be authorized at the highest levels of government with few if any legal constraints. Short of a foreign invasion or military coup, there is little prospect of accountability for the use of force. Saddam Hussein held onto power in Iraq for three decades by employing Stalinesque methods of oppression. Torture was employed as a *modus operandi* by Iraqi's secret police and intelligence services. While brutally effective in quelling resistance to his rule, Saddam was deeply unpopular. He was the target of a number of assassination attempts and uprisings. Torture did not bring security to Iraq or its president. Saddam was a prisoner within his own state, unable to visit his properties on the French Riviera. Nor could he move freely and publicly among his own people without a small army of Special Republican Guard and other security personnel to protect him. The same is true of autocratic rulers in a variety of Arab states. Brutal methods of suppressing dissent, such as torture, breed hatred, resentment, and a desire for justice and revenge.

Torture by occupying forces also breeds resentment. It may accentuate rather than ameliorate security problems. A population that regards occupation as oppression is likely to resist. Events in Iraq suggest that coercive interrogation failed to stem a sustained campaign of resistance. Radical Islamist groups were able to exploit the use of torture by their enemies in the propaganda war for the hearts and minds of the *umma*. Photographic images of prisoner abuse at Abu Ghraib will circulate

---

143 *The Washington Post* reported in October 2005 that: 'The CIA is holding an unknown number of prisoners in secret detention centers abroad. In violation of the Geneva Conventions, it has refused to register those detainees with the International Red Cross or to allow visits by its inspectors. CIA personnel have been implicated in the deaths during interrogation of at least four Afghan and Iraqi detainees. Official investigations have indicated that some aberrant practices by Army personnel in Iraq originated with the CIA.' Editorial, 'Vice President for Torture', *The Washington Post*, 26 October 2005, p. A18.

144 UN General Assembly, Revised Draft Outcome Document of the High-Level Plenary Meeting of the General Assembly of September 2005, submitted by the President of the General Assembly, A/59/HLPM/CRP.1/Rev.2, advanced unedited version, 5 August 2005.

throughout the Middle East (and the world) on Arab and Islamic websites, CDs, and email for years if not decades to come.

Terrorism, Torture and the Slippery Slope

Once an exception to the prohibition on torture is made in terrorism cases, the door is opened for police investigators to enter the 'slippery slope' that leads to the routine use of torture. They may soon be tempted to resort to torture in non-terrorism cases, such as serial murder investigations. They may be willing to justify the use of torture on spurious grounds. Common criminal conspiracies may be branded terrorist plots to provide a trigger for the use of coercive powers. If police believe that time and resources can be saved by coercive interrogation, they are likely to cut corners in this way. Hence the downward slide towards the routine use of torture. Effective counter-terrorism has always been about intelligence gathering and addressing the root causes of political and religious violence. It requires competent and properly resourced police investigators and intelligence agents. Arrests of terrorists is usually the end result of careful and patient investigative work rather than torture. Covert surveillance and the clandestine infiltration of terror networks and organizations can yield significant counter-terrorism benefits without the costs of resorting to torture. While intelligence gathering is a necessary strategy it is not sufficient. Other strategies must also be used. Efforts must be made to persuade potential recruits and existing members of terror groups that violence is not an effective way of promoting their goals. The ideological fallacies of radical Islamists must be respectfully but thoroughly exposed. States must also work towards ending rather than fueling injustices. They must demonstrate compassion to populations vulnerable to terrorism by guaranteeing their human security. Unlike torture – which serves to aggravate a sense of injustice – methods that build trust, tolerance and cooperation must be employed.

If the torture of detainees was an effective means in eliciting reliable intelligence, and one that could be used to destroy terrorist organizations without fueling further terrorism, there should have been a steady decline in terrorism in Iraq and other fronts in the 'war of terror' after Donald Rumsfeld authorized the use of aggressive counter-resistance techniques on terrorists and terror suspects. Moreover, Israel would have brought an end to attacks upon its territory. Other states would have publicly condoned the use of such torture. None of these things have happened. Violence in Iraq and Afghanistan did not abate when prisoners were abused. It escalated. Even if some detainees have given up the names of other members of terror organizations when subjected to torture, this has not halted terrorism. The US government has conceded that 'At least 12 of those who have been released have been found again in the battlefield – some of them killed in battle, others captured again, and at least one was found to have ordered some very significant terrorist activities after being released from Guantánamo' (Mintz 2004). While this story doesn't reveal how many, if any, of those who returned to the battlefield detainees were mistreated in custody, many of them would have been aware of the prisoner abuse that was prevalent from mid 2003. This is likely to have triggered feelings of anger and humiliation.

For these and the other reasons expounded above, legalizing torture cannot be the answer to terrorism. If it was, there would be little if any terrorism in the Middle East. Moreover, many states with internal security problems would have passed laws to authorize it. No democratic state is likely to pass pro-torture laws (even those with serious terrorism problems). Torture is the antithesis of the modern democratic state. It is the end of any pretence at a 'civilized' legal system.

Judicial Torture Warrants – A Theory That Should Never Be Put Into Practice

Dershowitz's contention that torture can and should be regulated by law and then sanctioned by judges has been greeted with general distain by human rights lawyers. (And rightly so.) The theory is a moral, philosophical and legal disgrace. Dershowitz implies that what is 'lawful' is also right and just. He also presupposes that where torture is authorized under domestic law, it trumps conflicting international human rights norms. The theory implies that the rule of law can accommodate any law including one that sanctions torture. I will deal with the last criticism first as it is the weakest of the three mentioned above. In theory, a law enabling torture warrants to be issued could, in some states, be consistent with the rule of law. It assumes that: (1) the torture law was validly enacted and is constitutionally sound, and (2) the state is not party to a regional human rights convention under which a regional court may strike down the law for offending the prohibition on torture. From there, torture warrants issued under the law would be valid if: (a) the statutory requirements for issuing a torture warrant are met; and (b) the judge issuing the torture warrant does so in accordance with the law. Such warrants could then be executed (the person named in the warrant could be tortured) and this would be within the rule of law.

The argument collapses when an attempt is made to reconcile the practice of torture with the *jus cogens* character of the prohibition on torture. Even if such legislation passed constitutional muster it would still violate international law. The prohibition on torture is non-derogable. Its character is derived from the collective view of states that such conduct is never acceptable. Conduct that offends these absolute prohibitions cannot be right or just. States that pass laws that contravene peremptory norms violate international law and undermine democratic principles. In doing so they undermine the integrity of the rule of law, which is itself a cornerstone of democratic polity. To promote democracy, human rights and the rule of law on the one hand, whilst condoning torture in counter-terrorism investigations on the other, is therefore untenable. States that adopt such an approach undermine their integrity and reputation. To pay lip service to basic human rights whilst simultaneously justifying the breach of international obligations amounts to legal trickery and deception. States that adopt such an approach may pay a heavy price in the long term. Double standards are remembered long after commendable behavior is forgotten. In 15 years time will the world remember:

(a)   The details of multi-million dollar re-construction
       projects for Iraq funded by the US government? or
(b)   The details of prisoner abuse at Abu Ghraib or Guantánamo Bay?

Rightly or wrongly, international condemnation of torture by US agents is often more strident than criticism of the terrorist attacks that inspired this policy in the first place. Ultimately, judicial approval of acts of torture is open to the same criticism as judicial executions. Innocent people will be tortured, just as innocent people have been executed. Thirty-eight states in the USA have now imposed a moratorium on executions. This follows the release of 13 death row inmates who had been wrongly convicted in the State of Illinois ('Spotlight on US death penalty' 2002). Judicially sanctioned torture may undermine confidence in the rule of law in a similar way. The torture of persons named in a torture warrant who are later found to be innocent would be a serious blow to the justice system.

Conclusion

Torture has long been a tool of statecraft. Its use remains widespread. However such is the power of the prohibition on torture that most states that engage in the practice deny doing so. It cannot be denied that intelligence that could prevent a terrorist attack could be extracted from some terror suspects during their torturous interrogation. However this possibility has not proved a sufficient incentive for states to legalize the practice. This reflects: (1) ongoing support for the absolute prohibition on torture under international law (at least publicly); and (2) recognition that the possibility of success at the micro level (stopping specific terrorist plots) is outweighed by macro level concerns (the danger of inspiring further terrorism). Ongoing support for the prohibition on torture – notwithstanding the rise in terrorism in Iraq and elsewhere – is event from the following recent developments. In 2005 the House of Lords reaffirming the international law prohibition on torture and unanimously ruled that evidence obtained by torture is inadmissible in British courts of law.[145] In February 2006 a report by four UN Special Rapporteurs and the Chairperson of the UN Working Group on Arbitrary Detention concluded that US interrogation practices at Guantánamo Bay violated the prohibition on torture.[146] In the same year the Bush administration changed its position on the torture of detainees by reversing its earlier opposition to legislation banning 'cruel, inhuman or degrading treatment or punishment' of anyone in US government custody, regardless of where they are held. In October 2005, the US Senate passed the bill (which had been put forward by Republican Senator John McCain) by a margin

---

145 *A (FC) and others (FC) (Appellants) v Secretary of State for the Home Department (Respondent) (2004) A and others (Appellants) (FC) and others v Secretary of State for the Home Department (Respondent) (Conjoined Appeals)* [2005] UKHL 71: Philippe Naughton, 'Law Lords rule against use of torture evidence', 8 December 2005, Times Online.

146 Report of the Chairperson of the Working Group on Arbitrary Detention, Ms. Leila Zerrougui; the Special Rapporteur on the independence of judges and lawyers, Mr. Leandro Despouy; the Special Rapporteur on torture and other cruel, inhuman or degrading treatment or punishment, Mr. Manfred Nowak; the Special Rapporteur on freedom of religion or belief, Ms Asma Jahangir and the Special Rapporteur on the right of everyone to the enjoyment of the highest attainable standard of physical and mental health, Mr Paul Hunt. UN Commission on Human Rights 62nd Session, 15 February 2006. E/CN.4/2006/120, 37.

of 90 votes to 9 (Thomas and Hirch 2005, 28). Whether this law is being followed or breached in secret CIA detention camps is yet to be confirmed by independent sources such as the ICRC.

References

Al Qaeda Training Manual, Available at US Department of Justice <www.usdoj. gov/ag/manualpart1_1.pdf> accessed 27 January 2008.
Amnesty International Report (2006) Available at <http://www.amnesty.org/en/ research> accessed 27 January 2008.
Amnesty International (2006), 'United States of America: Below the radar: Secret flights to torture and "disappearance"', 5 April 2006 <http://www.amnestyusa.org/ document.php?lang=e&id=ENGAMR510512006>, accessed 28 January 2008.
Amnesty International (2003), <web.amnesty.org/report2003/irn-summary-eng>.
Amnesty International Report (2007), Egypt – Systematic abuses in the name of security 11 April <http://www.amnesty.org/en/news-and-updates/feature-stories/ egypt-planned-anti-terror-law-could-intensify-abuses-20070411>, accessed 27 January 2008.
Amnesty International Report (2005), 'USA: Guantánamo and beyond: The continuing pursuit of unchecked executive power', 51/063/2005, 13 May <http:// web.amnesty.org/library/Index/ENGAMR510632005>.
Amnesty International Report (2001), 'The crackdown on Falun Gong and other so-called "heretical organizations"', AI Index: ASA 17/011/2000.
Applebaum, A. (2005, January 12), 'The Torture Myth', *The Washington Post*, p. A21.
Athey, S. (2007), 'The Terrorist We Torture: The Tale of Abdul Hakim Murad', *South Central Review* 24:1, 73–90.
Babington, C. and White J. (2005), 'House Supports Ban on Torture: Measure Would Limit Interrogation Tactic', *The Washington Post*, December 15, p. A01.
Bilder, R.B. and Vagts, D.F. (2004), 'Speaking Law to Power: Lawyers and Torture', Editorial Comment, 98 *American Journal of International Law*, 689, 695.
Bugnion, F. (2002, September), 'Just wars, wars of aggression and international humanitarian law', *International Review of the Red Cross* (originally published in French), Vol. 84, No. 847, pp. 523–46.
Burke, Jason (2004), 'Al-Qaeda launches online terrorist manual', *The Observer*, 18 January <http://observer.guardian.co.uk/international/story/0,6903,1125877,00. html> accessed 28 January 2008.
'Bush: Terror suspects not tortured' (8 November 2005) Available at:<http:// mwcnews.net/content/view/2150/51/> accessed 28 January 2008. (No longer available).
Campbell, D. (2002), 'US sends suspects to face torture', *The Guardian*, 12 March (website), <http://www.guardian.co.uk/afghanistan/story/0,1284,665939,00. html>, accessed 28 January 2008.

Clarke, B. (2005), 'The juridical status of civilian resistance to foreign occupation under the law of nations and contemporary international law', 7 *University of Notre Dame Australia Law Review*, 1.

Charter on Human and People's Rights OAU Doc. CAB/LEG/67/3 rev. 5, 21 *ILM* 58 (1982), entered into force 21 October 1986.

Coman, Julian (2004), 'Interrogation abuses were "approved at highest levels"', *Sunday Telegraph* (London), 13 June, p. 26.

Compilation of General Comments and General Recommendations Adopted by Human Rights Treaty Bodies, UN Doc. HRI/GEN/1/Rev.1 at 30 (1994).

Convention Against Torture and Other Cruel, Inhuman or Degrading Treatment or Punishment General Assembly Resolution 39/46, UN Doc A/39/51 (1984), entered into force 26 June 1987.

Crozier, B. (1975), *A Theory of Conflict* (New York: Charles Scribner's Sons).

Davis, M. (9 May 2005), 'Soldier lifts lid on Guantanamo "abuse" ', BBC News, Washington, <http://news.bbc.co.uk/2/hi/americas/4523825.stm>, accessed 28 January 2008.

Dicey, Albert V. (1914), *Law of the Constitution* (8th edition) (London, Macmillan).

Dershowitz, A.M. (2002), *Why Terrorism Works: Understanding the threat, responding to the challenge* (New Haven: Yale University Press), pp. 156–60.

—— (2004), 'Opinion: Torture Warrants', *The Spectator* (1 May).

Draft articles on Responsibility of States for internationally wrongful acts, adopted by the International Law Commission at its fifty-third session (2001), Article 2.

Dratel, J.L. and Greenberg, K.J. (2005), 'Report of the International Committee of the Red Cross (ICRC) on the Treatment by the Coalition Forces of Prisoners of War and Other Protected Persons by the Geneva Conventions in Iraq During Arrest, Internment and Interrogation (February 2004)', in *The Torture Papers: The Road to Abu Ghraib* (Cambridge: Cambridge University Press, 2005), p. 388.

duBois, P. (1991), *Torture and Truth* (London: Routledge).

Editorial, 'Vice President for Torture', *The Washington Post*, 26 October 2005, p. A18.

Felner, E. (2005), 'Torture and Terrorism: Painful Lessons from Israel', in Roth, Kenneth, Worden, Minky and Bernstein, Amy D. (eds.), *Torture: Does it Make Us Safer? Is it Ever OK? A Human Rights Perspective* (New York: New Press), pp. 29, 32–5.

Fox, G.H. and Roth, B.R. (eds) (2000), *Democratic Governance and International Law* (Cambridge: Cambridge University Press).

Glasser S.B. (2005), 'U.S. Figures Show Sharp Global Rise In Terrorism: State Dept. Will Not Put Data in Report', *The Washington Post*, Staff Writer, 27 April, p. A01.

Greenberg, K. (2005), *The Torture Papers: The Road to Abu Ghraib* (Cambridge: Cambridge University Press).

—— (ed.) (2006), *The Torture Debate In America* (New York: Cambridge University Press).

Grier, P. and Chaddock, G.R. (2005), 'Leaks about CIA prisons overseas spark fury', *The Christian Science Monitor*, 10 November.

'Guantánamo Bay inmates "tortured"' (13 February 2006), <http://news.bbc.co.uk/go/rss/-/2/hi/americas/4710966.stm>, accessed 28 January 2008.

Heath, J. (1982), *Torture and English Law: an Administrative and Legal History from the Plantagenets to the Stuarts* (London: Greenwood).

Henckaerts, J.M. and Doswald-Beck, L. (2005), *Customary International Humanitarian Law*, Volume I, xxx (Cambridge: Cambridge University Press).

Henckaerts, J.M. and Doswald-Beck, L. et al. (2005), International Committee of the Red Cross (Cambridge: Cambridge University Press).

Hersh, S.M. (2004), *Chain of Command: The Road from 9/11 to Abu Ghraib* (New York: HarperCollins).

Human Rights Committee (1994), General Comment 20, Article 7 (44th session, 1992), Compilation of General Comments and General Recommendations. Adopted by Human Rights Treaty Bodies, UN Doc. HRI/GEN/1/Rev.1 at 30.

Human Rights Watch (2006), Human Rights Watch's Submission to the Committee Against Torture in Response to United States Positions Expressed During the Committee's Consideration of the Second Periodic Report of the United States on 5 May and 8 May, 2006, <http://hrw.org/us/hrw_response_051706.pdf>, accessed 28 January 2008.

Human Rights Watch, 'Renditions and Diplomatic Assurances: "Outsourcing" Torture', <http://www.hrw.org/campaigns/torture/renditions.htm>, accessed 28 January 2008.

Human Rights Watch (2006),'No Sanctuary: Ongoing Threats to Indigenous Montagnards in Vietnam's Central Highlands', June, Vol. 18, No. 4 (C).

Human Rights Watch (2005), 'CIA Whitewashing Torture: Statements by Goss Contradict US Law and Practice', <http://www.hrw.org/english/docs/2005/11/21/usdom12069.htm> accessed 28 January 2008

Human Rights Watch (2005), 'Leadership Failure: Firsthand Accounts of Torture of Iraqi Detainees by the US Army's 82nd Airborne Division', Vol. 17, No. 3(G), <http://hrw.org/reports/2005/us0905/>, accessed 28 January 2008.

Human Rights Watch (2005), 'The New Iraq? Torture and ill-treatment of detainees in Iraqi custody', <http://hrw.org/reports/2005/iraq0105/> accessed 17 April 2007.

Human Rights Watch, 'Torture Worldwide' <http://hrw.org/english/docs/2005/04/27/china10549.htm>, accessed 24 November 2005.

Human Rights Watch (2004), 'Summary of International and U.S. Law Prohibiting Torture and Other Ill-treatment of Persons in Custody' (updated 24 May 2004), <http://hrw.org/english/docs/2004/05/24/usint8614.htm>, accessed 28 November 2005.

Human Rights Watch (2004), 'Vietnam: Independent Investigation of Easter Week Atrocities Needed Now', A Human Rights Watch Briefing Paper, 28 May.

Human Rights Watch (2004), ' "Like the Dead in Their Coffins" Torture, Detention, and the Crushing of Dissent in Iran', June, Vol. 16, No. 2(E).

Human Rights Watch (2001), '"Stifling Dissent", A Human Rights Watch Report', May, Vol. 13, No. 4(E).

ICJ Reports (2004), Legal Consequences of the Construction of A Wall in the Occupied Palestinian Territory, 9 July 2004, Para 106–114.

Ignatieff, M. (2006), 'To ask the tough questions', *The Weekend Australian*, 1 February.

International Commission of Jurists (2000), Report by the Western Australian Branch of the International Commission of Jurists concerning Sterilisations of Ethnic Montagnards in the Central Highlands of Vietnam (Copy on file).

International Covenant on Civil and Political Rights, adopted and opened for signature, ratification and accession by General Assembly resolution 2200A (XXI) of 16 December 1966, entry into force 23 March 1976.

International Covenant on Social and Economic Rights, adopted and opened for signature, ratification and accession by General Assembly resolution 2200A (XXI) of 16 December 1966, entry into force 3 January 1976.

'Iran Hangs Bahai In Religion Case', New York Times, 24 July 1998, p. A-4.

Israel Supreme Court (2005), Judgments of The Israel Supreme Court: Fighting Terrorism Within the Law.

Kamen, H. (1965), *The Spanish Inquisition* (London: Weidenfeld & Nicolson), pp. 61, 172–6.

Klein, N. (2005), 'Torture's Dirty Secret: It Works', The Nation, 30 May.

Knickmeyer, E. (2006), 'Inspectors Find More Torture at Iraqi Jails: Top General's Pledge To Protect Prisoners "Not Being Followed"' *The Washington Post*, Foreign Service, 24 April 24, p. A01.

Lane, C. (2006), 'High Court Rejects Detainee Tribunals: 5 to 3 Ruling Curbs President's Claim Of Wartime Power', *The Washington Post*, Staff Writer, 30 June, p. A01.

Lewis, N.A. (2004), 'Red Cross Finds Detainee Abuse in Guantánamo', New York Times, 29 November. <http://www.nytimes.com/2004/11/30/politics/30gitmo. html> accessed 28 January 2008.

Luban, D. (2007), 'Liberalism, Torture, and the Ticking Bomb', in Lee, S.P., *Intervention, Terrorism and Torture: Contemporary Challenges to Just War Theory* (Dordrecht: Springer), pp. 249, 254.

McCain, J. (2005), 'Torture's Terrible Toll', *Newsweek*, 22 November.

McCoy, A. (2006), *A Question of Torture: CIA Interrogation, From the Cold War to the War on Terror* (New York: Metropolitan).

McDonough, C. (21 November 2005), 'Iraqi Conference Separates "Resistance" from Terrorism', Cairo, <http://www.globalsecurity.org/wmd/library/news/iraq/2005/11/iraq-051121-voa05.htm>.

Mackay, D. (2003), 'Torture of Iraq's athletes', *The Observer*, 2 February <http://sport.guardian.co.uk/athletics/theobserver/story/0,10541,887103,00.html> accessed 28 January 2008.

Metz, H.C. (ed.) (1987), *Iran: A Country Study* (Washington: GPO for the Library of Congress).

Mintz, J. (2004), 'Released Detainees Rejoining The Fight', *The Washington Post*, 22 October, Staff Writer, p. A01.

Nowak, M. (the Special Rapporteur of the Commission on Human Rights on the question of torture) and Louise Arbour (United Nations High Commissioner for Human Rights) in a Joint Statement on the Occasion of The United Nations International Day in Support of Victims of Torture.

Nowak, M. (10 March 2006), UN Commission on Human Rights: Report of the Special Rapporteur on torture and other cruel, inhuman or degrading treatment or punishment, Manfred Nowak, on his mission to China from 20 November to 2 December 2005, E/CN/.4/2006/6Add.6, Para 301.

Optional Protocol to the Convention against Torture and other Cruel, Inhuman or Degrading Treatment or Punishment, adopted on 18 December 2002, 37th session of the UN General Assembly under resolution A/RES/57/199.

Otterman, M. (2007), *American Torture: From the Cold War to Abu Ghraib and Beyond* (Melbourne University Press).

Pfaff, W. (2005), 'What We've Lost: George Bush and the Price of Torture', *Harper's Magazine*, November, p. 51.

Priest, D. (2005), 'CIA Holds Terror Suspects in Secret Prisons: Debate is Growing Within Agency About Legality and Morality of Overseas System Set Up After 9/11', *The Washington Post*, Staff Writer, 2 November, p. A01.

Protocol No. 11 (ETS No. 155).

Saar, E. and Novak, V. (2005), *Inside the Wire: A Military Intelligence Soldier's Eyewitness Account of Life at Guantánamo* (New York: Penguin).

Shamir, Y. (1994), *Summing Up: An Autobiography* (Little Brown and Company).

Smith, R.J. and White J. 'Cheney Plan Exempts CIA From Bill Barring Abuse of Detainees', *The Washington Post*, Staff Writers, 25 October 2005, p. A01.

Smith, T. (2005), 'Torture: The slippery slope to surrender to terror', *Australian Review of Public Affairs*, 8 August <http://www.econ.usyd.edu.au/drawingboard/digest/0508/smith.html>.

'Spotlight on US death penalty' (6 June 2001), <http://news.bbc.co.uk/2/hi/americas/1492746.stm>, accessed 27 January 2008.

Stover, E. and Nightingale, E. (eds) (1985), *The Breaking of Bodies and Minds: Torture, Psychiatric Abuse, and the Health Professions* (Freeman: New York).

Suedfeld, P. (ed.) (1990), *Psychology and Torture* (New York: Hemisphere).

The Falun Gong Human Rights Working Group (2004), United Nations Reports on China's Persecution of Falun Gong.

Thomas, E. and Hirch, M. (2005), 'The Debate over Torture', *Newsweek*, The Bulletin, 22 November, pp.25–33.

'Trial of Wilhelm von Leeb and Thirteen Others' (The High Command Case) (1949) 12 Law Reports of Trials of War Criminals 1, Nuremberg Tribunal.

UN General Assembly (2005), Revised Draft Outcome Document of the High-Level Plenary Meeting of the General Assembly of September 2005, submitted by the President of the General Assembly, A/59/HLPM/CRP.1/Rev.2, advanced unedited version, 5 August.

United Nations (November 2001), Conclusions and Recommendations of the Committee against Torture: Israel.

United Nations (1969), 'Vienna Convention on the Law of Treaties', Treaty Series, vol. 1155, p.331. (entered into force 27 January 1980).

United Nations (1998), 'Rome Statute of the International Criminal Court', Treaty Series, vol. 2187 p. 90 (entered into force 1 July 2002).

United States Code.

Universal Declaration of Human Rights, UN General Assembly Resolution 217A (III), UN Doc A/810 (1948).

US Congress House Concurrent Resolution 188, 24 July 2002.

US Department of Defense (24 March 2006), 'Military Commission Instruction No. 10. Certain Evidentiary Requirements', <http://www.defenselink.mil/news/Mar2006/d20060327MCI10.pdf> accessed 28 January 2008.

Walzer M. (1992), *Just and Unjust Wars* (2nd edition) (New York: Basic Books).

de Wet, E. (2004), 'The prohibition of Torture as an International Norm of jus cogens and Its Implications for National and Customary Law', 15 *European Journal of International Law*, 97–121.

'White House backs torture ban law' (15 December 2005), <http://news.bbc.co.uk/2/hi/americas/4533342.stm>. Accessed 28 January 2008.

Yee, J. (2005), *For God and Country: Faith and Patriotism Under Fire* (New York: Public Affairs).

Cases

Al-Adsani v United Kingdom (2002) 23 HRLJ 39.

Barcelona Traction, Light and Power Co. Ltd. (Belg. v Spain) [1970] 3 ICJ 32 (5 February).

Filartiga v Pena-Irala, 630 F.2d 876 (2nd Cir., No. 79-6090, 30 June 1980).

Hamdan v Rumsfeld, 126 S.Ct. 2749 (2006).

Nicaragua v United States of America, ICJ Reports (1986), Judgment of 27 June 1986 – Merits.

Rasul v Bush, 124 S.Ct. 2686 (2004).

Prosecutor v Anto Furundzija, Case No. IT-95-17/1-T10, Trial Chamber Judgment, 10 December 1998.

Pub. Comm. Against Torture in Isr. v Gov't of Israel, 53(4) PD 817, 835.

Regina v Evans and Another and the Commissioner of Police for the Metropolis and Others Ex Parte Pinochet (On Appeal from a Divisional Court of the Queen's Bench Division) House of Lords (24 March 1999).

Chapter 3

Is International Terrorism an Inevitable Consequence of Globalization?

3.1   Legal Aspects of Globalization

Ben Clarke

Introduction

This part of the chapter explores the relationship between globalization and the escalation of international terrorism. It does so by highlighting the tendency for some ethnic and religious conflicts to be exported beyond their traditional realms. These issues are explored through the framework of the rule of law and human rights. It will be argued that ethnic and religious warfare and related terrorist activity is often the product of long-standing grievances involving serious violations of fundamental rights. Implicit in this analysis is the liberal theory of rights and justice.[1] A series of case studies demonstrate that suppression of fundamental rights by autocratic regimes can trigger social and political disorder. The denial of what the liberal project would term *justice* and respect for basic *rights* often leads to anarchy and terror. This is illustrated across a variety of contexts including colonialism, foreign invasion, military occupation and regime change. Their role in fanning and sometimes creating ethic and religious tensions is explored in some detail. At a more basic level it is noted that where power vacuums exist in 'post-conflict' processes, the door to large-scale sectarian violence may be opened. Moreover such vacuums create opportunities for international terrorist organizations to fill the void. Contemporary Iraq is an example *par excellence*. It forms the central case study and is discussed at length.

In exploring ethnic, cultural and religious dimensions to modern terrorism, a number of factors are considered. They include:

---

1 20th-century Anglo-American jurisprudence examined the way rule of law, rights and liberal polity interact: See H.L.A. Hart (1961), *The Concept of Law* (Oxford University Press); Joseph Raz (1979), *The Authority of Law* (Oxford University Press); Ronald Dworkin (1977), *Taking Rights Seriously* (Cambridge, MA: Harvard University Press); Lon L. Fuller (1965), *The Morality of Law* (New Haven, CT: Yale University Press); John Rawls (1971), *A Theory of Justice* (Cambridge, MA: Belknap Press of Harvard University Press) and (1993) *Political Liberalism* (*The John Dewey Essays in Philosophy, 4.* New York: Columbia University Press). *Contra* see: Thomas Hobbes (1650), *The Elements of Law, Natural and Political*, written in 1640 and the writings of German jurist Carl Schmitt (numerous). (Their writings project the 'illiberal story' about sovereignty and the necessity of violence to maintain order.)

- the impact of globalization on ethnic and religious conflict and terrorism,
- the role played by diaspora communities in the internationalization of ethnic and religious conflict,
- the right of self-determination and indeed the introduction of European conceptions of 'law', 'rights', 'justice' and 'the rule of law' into non-European societies,
- the problem of colonial frontiers and post-colonial ethnic and religious tumult,
- the emergence of ideologies and organizations that promote terrorism, and
- the role al Qaeda and affiliate organizations have played in fueling ethnic and religious tumult to further their ideological goals.

Iraq is now an epicenter of contemporary ethnic and religious terror (including but not exclusively Islamist terror). It provides the quintessential example of the way external and internal forces can destabilise a nation and facilitate ethnic and religious tumult and terror on a large scale. This part of the chapter concludes by canvassing responses to ethnic and religious tumult. A range of legal and political strategies are proposed.

Ethnic and Religious Violence: Origins and Trends

Ethnic and religious violence has been part of the human condition since antiquity. It is well documented in literature from ancient Greece, Rome and India as well as the sacred texts of a number of world religions. Acts of terror against civilian populations occurs in dozens of states every year. Such events have been played out in innumerable ethnic and religious conflicts over the last millennium.

Until recent times such violence has usually been localized (most commonly intra-state but sometimes regional). Twentieth-century advances in transportation, technology and weaponry have facilitated the rapid spread of ethnic and religious conflicts. Geo-political changes after the collapse of the Soviet Union have also influenced this process. Political vacuums in post-Soviet societies have sometimes been filled by those seeking to re-ignite long suppressed ethnic and religious conflict. Another factor is the growth of radical Islamist ideologies. In the case of al Qaeda in Iraq, it has attempted to impose its ideology by waging a campaign of sectarian violence. Like others before them, they have demonstrated a capacity to deliver low cost, high impact, death and destruction. The usual targets of Islamist terror are rival sects, 'apostate' Arab governments and the Western nations that support them. Over the last decade the US has responded to this threat by destroying actual or suspected terrorist training camps, and attempting to kill or capture terrorist leaders and their followers. There has been mixed success in these efforts. Sometimes these methods have contributed to ethnic and religious divisions and related violence. This theme is discussed in detail below in the context of Iraq.

Globalization and the export of ethnic and religious violence

Globalization has been defined as 'the integration of capital, technology, and information across national borders, in a way that is creating a single global market and, to some degree, a global village' (Friedman). It has brought continents, peoples and cultures closer together. In removing obstacles to communication, trade and travel, globalization has led to the 'shrinking of the world.' A globalized world is one in which 'political, economic, cultural and social events become more and more interconnected ... [and] societies are affected more and more extensively ... by events in other societies' (Baylis and Smith 2001). Since the collapse of the Soviet Union, globalization has been dominated by Western (predominantly US) norms. Capitalism, privatization, corporatization, 'free trade', and freedom of religion have emerged as global yet controversial norms of the post-Cold War era. Underlying globalization has been the technology innovations of Silicon Valley, California (the internet, Microsoft, Google).

Globalization has provided a vehicle for the export of all manner of things, both good and bad. Among the bad things are religious and ethnic conflict. People, ideas and commodities can cross international borders at a frightening pace. Like other actors in the international arena, terrorist organizations have exploited the benefits of globalization. They have also been shaped by it. As one commentator has recently observed, 'terrorists act across borders but ... terrorism itself is facilitated by the processes of globalization' (Khan 2004).

Globalization, terrorism and technology

Globalization and modern technology allows funds to be sent across the world instantaneously by electronic transfer. Documents, video recordings and texts messages can be sent via high speed communication devices in laptops and mobile phones. Messages can be encoded and encrypted. These technologies enhance the capacity of state and non-state actors to provide education, training, intelligence, and funds to military and para-military organizations in distant war zones. A range of radical Islamist groups have used advanced communication technologies during the planning, coordination and execution of terrorist operations. Localized disputes that would hitherto have received little or no media attention can now gain international exposure. Marginalised communities can disseminate their message to a global audience instantaneously via the internet. Terrorist organizations regularly air their grievances in this manner via messages telecast before, during or after terrorist acts. In this way extremists can publicise their cause and perhaps even influence opinion in ways that were previously the exclusive domain of powerful states.[2]

---

2 The flow of thousands of jihadis into Iraq to join armed resistance to Coalition forces was brought about through a call to arms by Mujahideen both within and outside Iraq. The call by these non-state actors was disseminated on satellite channels, internet sites, radio, in newspapers and at mosques.

The role of diasporas in the spread of ethnic and religious violence

In the era of globalization, diaspora communities, many exiled by war, have emerged throughout the world. They carry with them ethnic and religious world views that reflect their history and culture. Their world view may include age-old ethnic and religious hatreds. If transmitted from one generation to the next, such hatreds may be perpetuated in the new country. In some cases members of a diaspora have provided the finance, weapons and fighters needed to carry on age-old struggles. Irish ex-patriots in various parts of the world (including North America) gave significant assistance to the IRA during its struggle to restore Irish sovereignty over Northern Ireland. Some ex-patriot Tamils, South Africans, and Palestinians have also funneled aid to compatriots in the homeland, to further struggles waged to reclaim ancestral lands.[3]

Denial of Self-Determination as a Trigger for Ethnic and Religious Conflict

Attempts to exercise the right of self-determination have often triggered ethnic and religious tumult. Indeed terrorist violence is an all too common feature of self-determination struggles. The term self-determination is not defined in either the Charter of the United Nations or the principal human rights treaties that recognize this right. Nonetheless, as the Charter makes clear, states have an obligation to 'promote the realization of the right of self-determination ... in conformity with the provisions of the Charter of the United Nations.' This collective right was invoked by peoples across the world during the de-colonization era. Peoples of territories that were subjected to colonial rule and alien occupation have now, in most instances, exercised this right. However in some cases the right was forcibly denied. This occurred in South Africa under Apartheid, the former Southern Rhodesia during the period of white minority rule under Ian Smith, and in East Timor following Indonesia's invasion and purported annexation of the territory in 1975. The right is still being denied to the peoples of: West Papua, which was absorbed into Indonesia with UN consent but without a local referendum; Tibet, which was invaded by China and annexed without UN consent or a referendum; and occupied Palestine (the West Bank remains under Israeli occupation, while Israeli forces enter Gaza at will in order to carry out military operations again those suspected of firing missiles into Israel or planning attacks upon Israel). The denial of self-determination to the peoples of East Timor and Palestine triggered sustained ethnic and religious conflict. In the course of these struggles, civilians were at various times deliberately targeted by rival factions. This highlights the propensity for terrorist violence where a people are forcibly denied their collective right of self-determination by an occupying power.

In the case of Tibet, China has suppressed political opinion and religious practice through tight state control of life in Tibet and the resettlement of Han Chinese into

---

3 Whether one considers this to be 'aid to terrorist networks' depends upon where one stands. This is the reason why the UN General Assembly was unable to agree upon a definition of terrorism at the UN Global Summit in 2005. Many states refused to agree to a definition which on its face seemed entirely acceptable – their reasoning: it would undermine the right to resist foreign occupation.

Tibet 'province.' This policy has rendered ethnic Tibetans a minority in their own country: a calculated strategy to prevent them from exercising their right to self-determination. Indonesian authorities are pursuing the same policy in West Papua. In this case the ethnic, religious and cultural differences between the occupiers and occupied in West Papua are just as profound. Indonesia is mostly Muslim while the vast majority of West Papuans are Christian, some still follow traditional customs which Muslims may find offensive. The ethnic differences are also significant. Indonesians are predominantly Javanese, Sundanese, Madurese and Malay. By contrast West Papuans are tribal people who share a common ethnic heritage (and island) with their Papua New Guinea neighbors.

Since 1969, Indonesia has attempted to impose its norms on West Papua. In doing so it has suppressed the cultural and political aspirations of the people of West Papua. These measures have been resisted. Unlike China's experience in Tibet, armed resistance to Indonesian rule in West Papua have never been entirely crushed. Notwithstanding its strong military presence in West Papua, Indonesian authorities have, over the decades, encountered mass demonstrations, political protests of various kinds, and occasional guerrilla attacks. While most West Papuans have preferred the path of non-violence in their pursuit of self-determination, their efforts have been unsuccessful. Brutal repression of the separatist movement culminated in the assassination of Chief Theys Eluay in November 2001. Eluay had consistently advocated a non-violent path to independence and enjoyed tremendous support across West Papua. The circumstances of his death suggest the involvement of the Indonesian Army's Special Operations Command (Kopassus). Kopassus has been involved in the suppression of separatist movements in other parts of Indonesia. State-sponsored terrorism is an all too common method employed by authoritarian regimes to quell self-determination struggles waged by ethnic or religious minorities.

Internal and external self-determination

Self-determination can be divided into two categories: internal and external. External self-determination is achieved where an occupied or colonized people gain sovereignty, separate statehood and independence. Internal self-determination 'is concerned mainly with "collective rights" of a group of people(s) within the boundary of a modern "nation-state"' (Sakhong 2004). In democratic states, including democratic former colonial territories that have achieved statehood, the right of self-determination is exercisable by the people of the state *as a whole*. If a region wants to break away and form its own sovereign state, this must occur through democratic and constitutional processes. Under most democratic constitutions this would require either an amendment to the constitution or for a majority of citizens to approve the separation in a nation-wide constitutionally valid referendum.[4] These requirements make it very difficult for minority groups to achieve external self-determination. They are more likely to achieve a limited measure of self-determination (such as the

---

4 See *Reference re Secession of Quebec* [1998] 2 SCR 217.

protection of language and cultural rights).[5] In some instances, they have managed to gain a degree of regional autonomy.[6] These are manifestations of *internal* self-determination.

Use of force to win self-determination

If independence-minded minorities within stable democracies have no right under international law to unilaterally secede, what is the position in autocratic or totalitarian states? Where minorities are subject to brutal oppression by a tyrannical government, recourse to armed struggle may be viewed as the only viable option for the protection of basic rights and the survival of a people (Gardam 1993, 66). The right to struggle for self-determination enjoyed strong support during the era of de-colonization. The General Assembly repeatedly reaffirmed the right of self-determination for peoples living under colonial rule, racist regimes and alien occupation to struggle against these conditions. In 1977, at the twilight of the de-colonization era, most states ratified a Protocol which recognized the legitimacy of struggles against these forms of oppression.[7] For states party to this instrument, resistance struggles against colonialism, racist regimes and alien occupation do not constitute terrorist campaigns *per se*. However this Protocol does not address *jus ad bellum* (the right to wage war). Whether such struggles are inherently lawful remains a matter of controversy. Importantly, while Arab states have for many decades defended the right of Palestinians to resist the Israeli occupation, international institutions are now moving towards outlawing all forms of armed struggle by any group against a state (Khan 2004, 188).

Colonialism and its Legacy

Much of the ethnic and religious tumult in the developing world can be traced back to the legacy of colonization. The European scramble for Africa, the triangular slave trade, and wars over mineral wealth have left a bitter legacy in many developing states. Divide and rule tactics were often used by colonial powers to maintain control over the colonized and facilitate the extraction of tradeable commodities. Such strategies often triggered ethnic and religious conflict. So too did colonial

---

5 See, for example, *UN Declaration on the Rights of Indigenous Peoples*, UN Doc. A/HRC/1/L.10, 30 June 2006.

6 A recent example is the Kurdistan Regional Government in Kurdish provinces of northern Iraq. This essentially autonomous government exercises constitutionally recognized authority over the provinces of Erbil, Dohuk, and Suleimaniya and *de facto* authority over areas in Diyala and Ninawa and Kirkuk.

7 Protocol Additional to the Geneva Conventions of 12 August 1949, and relating to the Protection of Victims of International Armed Conflicts (Protocol 1) (adopted on 8 June 1977 by the Diplomatic Conference on the Reaffirmation and Development of International Humanitarian Law applicable in Armed Conflicts). See Article 1(4). As at 10 June 2007 there were 167 states party to Protocol I. Source: states party to the main treaties <http://www.icrc.org/Web/eng/siteeng0.nsf/html/party_main_treaties>, accessed 5 December 2005.

boundaries inherited by many newly independent states. Pre-existing ethnic and tribal boundaries were often ignored by colonial powers as they carved up 'the new world' between themselves. As former colonies gained independence, differences over territorial boundaries became a source of conflict within and between a number of emergent states.

In Africa, the Middle East and South East Asia, Western powers colonized innumerable local communities, and in doing so, disrupted local customs, norms and equilibriums. In the process, ethnic and religious divisions were often unleashed or exploited. Colonial rule had cataclysmic effects upon the social, cultural, economic and political fabric of many local communities. Local kingdoms were often dismantled – never to be revived. The political order imposed upon castes, tribes, clans, and ethnic and religious groups in colonized territory was eventually overthrown by liberation movements or displaced upon the transfer of power to local governments. Newly independent territories faced the task of deciding how they would construct their new states. This process often involved ethnic and religious violence. A classic example is post-colonial India which is discussed below.

Ethnic and religious violence has also been fuelled by foreign domination or military intervention in post-colonial states. The Congo and Angola have seen decades of ethnic conflict triggered by foreign demand for natural resources. The 'diamond wars' have involved a range of state and non-state actors. Private militias, government forces and mercenary units have engaged in conventional battles, guerrilla warfare, terrorism, and political assassinations in their quest to gain access to or defend mineral rich territory. Local populations, denied the right to determine their political future free from foreign interference, have struggled to form stable national governments in these states.

Ethnic and Religious Violence in Post-Colonial States and Societies

The majority of contemporary armed conflicts are internal rather than international in character. Many occur within states that are still coming to grips with the legacy of their colonial past. Traditional societies in the Middle East, Africa, Asia, South America, Australia and North America experienced catastrophic change during colonial times. Indeed few non-European nations escaped the imprint of European colonial rule. Japan (until 1945), Thailand and Bhutan are among the few nations to have done so.

Border wars

In 1986 the International Court of Justice resolved a frontier dispute between two post-colonial states[8] by applying the doctrine of *uti posseditis* (the notion that former colonial frontiers prevail in the event of a dispute over national borders). In doing so, the Court declined to recognize pre-colonial ethnic and tribal boundaries. This approach has been embraced by states for one simple reason – acceptance of this

---

8 ICJ Reports (1986) 554, *Burkina Faso/Mali case.*

doctrine has averted border wars. Had the principle not been embraced, some emerging nations would have been left with the difficult question of whether to designate borders on the basis of pre-colonial frontiers. The difficulty with the latter approach is that such borders were often contested, having shifted over time as rival kingdoms, tribes and sectarian groups conquered, ceded or surrendered territory. However, not all post-colonial states have been willing to accept boundaries designated by others. In some cases the borders were never properly defined. Those unwilling or unable to resolve frontier disputes through peaceful means (such as binding arbitral or judicial resolution) have embarked on often protracted border wars. The prolonged border conflict between India and Pakistan, the related dispute over Kashmir, and the border wars between Ethiopia and Eritrea are quintessential examples.

Post-colonial ethnic and religious tumult

In some cases colonialism, or struggles to end it, broke down barriers between tribal and religious communities. Diverse population groups developed a strong sense of nationalism, a common desire for independence, and a willingness to struggle together to bring an end to colonial rule (Tanzania). In other cases the colonial experience fermented ethnic and religious divisions (Kenya).

The latter result was sometimes the product of the colonizer favoring one group against another. In some cases rival groups had been pitted against one another on the battlefield (India).[9] The bitterness arising from such conflicts was rarely forgotten when the colonial powers departed. In some cases civil war broke out shortly after independence, with rival ethnic and religious groups – who in some cases shared little in common other than their colonial heritage – fighting for power. This was often the result of rival groups being bundled together into unitary states after little or no consultation (Iraq). In such cases some degree of post-colonial conflict was perhaps inevitable[10] – particularly in states such as the Congo, where education, development and nation building had not taken place during the colonial era.

Biafra   There are many examples of post-independence ethnic and religious conflict. Only a few are discussed here. In the years after independence, civil war has broken out in dozens of states including the Congo, Nigeria, Ethiopia, Pakistan, the Sudan and Somalia. The Biafran conflict in Nigeria deserves special mention. Shortly after Nigeria secured independence the Igbo people of the resource rich Eastern Region of

---

9 In others, local groups were enlisted to fight for the colonizer in conflicts waged against other powers.

10 It is important to note that armed conflict has not always broken out in post-colonial states. Colonialism and the struggle to end it have often inspired diverse peoples to work together against the colonial power. Some societies gained independence without a shot being fired and remain united and peaceful nations. Botswana is a good example. (Although this can be attributed to the fact that almost all of its citizens are Batswana and therefore share the Sotho-Tswana culture.) Mainland Tanzania has also enjoyed peace and unity (with a few minor hiccups along the way). It is comprised of more than 120 ethnic groups. (The Tanzanian island of Zanzibar is however a different story. It has experienced sporadic ethnic and religious tumult.)

Nigeria attempted to secede. Civil war broke out between the Nigerian army and the Igbo people of Biafra when the sovereign nation of Biafra was proclaimed in 1967. Almost three years after the declaration of statehood, the Biafrans were defeated. The war and famine triggered by this secession struggle cost the lives of over a million people.

Rwanda and Burundi   Rwanda and Burundi are archetypal examples of states that have suffered catastrophic ethnic violence in the post-colonial era. This outcome can be traced back to colonial frontiers which cut through tribal communities and their lands. Rather than each having their own ethnically homogeneous state, the Hutu and Tutsi peoples ended up on both sides of the border. Both states have experienced serious ethnic conflict since independence. The Rwandan genocide reveals the speed at which ethnic hatred can be whipped up and transformed into a policy of mass killing. While the warning signs were present, few would have foreseen that one million Tutsis and moderate Hutus would be slaughtered by Hutu extremists in just 90 days (Carroll 2004).

Sri Lanka   In contrast to the speed of the Rwandan terror, Sri Lanka has experienced a long and torturous history of ethnic violence. Sporadic ethnic and religious conflict between the Sinhalese (predominantly Buddhists) and the Tamil minority (predominantly Hindus) has endured for three decades. Theirs is an archetypal post-colonial struggle involving ethnic and religious rivals. Once again the impact of colonialism in generating this conflict is significant.[11] The twin conflicts in Sri Lanka (the Tamil struggle for a separate homeland and the militant struggle of the Sinhala community) have ethnic and economic foundations. Fighting has been characterized by regular use of terror tactics by Tamil Tigers in attacks on Sinhalese and Muslim communities (as well as rival Tamil groups). Sinhalese terror attacks on Tamils have also occurred (Abeyratne 2002). Persistent efforts to bring this post-colonial struggle to an end have been unsuccessful.

India   India has experienced sporadic ethnic and religious violence since gaining independence from Britain in 1947. The European legacy in India dates back 500 years. Prior to the British gaining control over all of India, the subcontinent had experienced Dutch, Danish, Portuguese, British and French influence. Britain in particular took advantage of sectarian divisions to consolidate its hold on India. It exploited and sometimes created discord between rival Indian ethnic and religious groups. In the process it was able to dismantle powerful kingdoms.

---

11 See: Pradeep Jeganathan, 'Authorising History, Ordering Land: The Conquest of Anuradhapuraâ', in Jeganathan, P and Q. Ismail (eds) (1995), *Unmaking the Nation: The Politics of Identity and History in Modern Sri Lanka* (Colombo: Social Scientists Association); International Crisis Group, *Sri Lanka: The Failure of the Peace Process*, Asia Report No. 124, 28 November 2006, pp. 1–17; Bruce Kapferer (1988), *Legends of People, Myths of State: Violence, Intolerance and Political Culture in Sri Lanka and Australia* (London and Washington: Smithsonian Institution Press), pp. 29–48, 72–84; Steven Kemper (1991), *The Presence of the Past: Chronicles, Politics and Culture in Sinhala Life* (Ithaca and London: Cornell University Press), pp. 53–69.

British colonization brought with it new systems of education, governance, administration and bureaucracy. In the process, many customs, traditional laws and practises were extinguished. When India eventually won its independence on 15 August 1947 – the day after the partition of India and Pakistan – the restoration of pre-colonial kingdoms, legal systems, frontiers and power relations (a return to the pre-colonial *status quo*) was impossible. The intervening centuries of change could not be wiped away. 'Muslim Pakistan' and predominantly 'Hindu India' emerged from colonialism to immediately embark upon a bitter border conflict. More than a million Hindus, Sikhs and Muslims were killed in violence fueled by the partition of British India. Many more were left homeless:

> Twelve million people were forced to move – Hindus to India, and Muslims to Pakistan. Both groups moved because they feared being ruled by leaders of the other faith. If a Hindu, Muslim or Sikh was caught on the wrong side of the dividing lines, they were driven out of their homes. (Gupta 2000)

Prior to partition, many participants in the violence had lived side by side in relative peace. Since independence, occasional ethnic and religious violence (including acts of terror) has been a characteristic of the Indian political landscape. Bombings, insurgencies and riots have seen thousands killed every year. Such terrorism is often the product of ethnic and religious tensions, which are fueled by other factors such as competition among rival groups for political power and scarce resources. Mahatma Ghandi, the symbol of India's struggle for independence, was himself a victim of ethnic and religious hatred. He was assassinated by a Hindu extremist not long after independence. Ghandi had recently called for tolerance towards Muslims living in India. (It is important to note that a number of theorists contend that post-colonial Hindu/Muslim tensions are a complex product of colonization, and that contemporary Hindu identity is itself a product of colonialism.[12])

Notwithstanding the tremendous challenges that India faces, it has emerged as a united and vibrant liberal democracy. The economic benefits of India's embrace of globalization have been substantial. While ethnic and religious tensions still exist, alongside chronic poverty and a vast array of other human security problems, in recent decades many sections of the population have enjoyed significant improvements in living standards. Over the same period there has been a decline in terrorist violence.

---

12 See: Nicholas B. Dirks (2001), *Castes of Mind: Colonialism and the Making of Modern India* (Princeton, NJ: Princeton University Press), pp. 19–42, 107–23 and 173–97; Lorenzen, David N., 'Who Invented Hinduism?' in (1999) 10 *Comparative Studies in Society and History*, 630–59; Werner Menski, 'Hindu Law as a Religious System' in Andrew Huxley (ed.) (2002), *Religion, Law and Tradition: Comparative Studies in Religious Law* (London: Routledge Curzon).

Regional Ethnic and Religious Violence in the Middle East

Ethnic and religious conflict in the Middle East has spawned decades of international terrorism involving a range of actors. They include Jewish, Kurdish, Christian, Druze, and Muslim militants. The epicenter of ethnic and religious conflict in the Middle East has, for many decades, been Palestine. For this reason the origins of this particular conflict, and its contemporary implications, are critiqued in some detail.

Palestine

The Palestinian conflict has deep roots which were briefly sketched in Chapter 1.2. Animosity between Arabs and Jews peaked in the 1940s when Zionist forces seized Palestinian lands and unilaterally created a Jewish state (Israel). Arab territory under Israeli control increased over subsequent decades after Israel won a series of wars against its neighbors. Most were triggered by Arab attempts to reclaim Palestinian territory lost in the 1948 war. The loss of Palestinian territory to Israeli control has generated anger, humiliation and a thirst for justice among the dispossessed. It has also been a key source of terrorism in the region. Anti-Israeli sentiment has been compounded by a range of factors including: the illegal annexation of territory by Israel (including Jerusalem); the construction of concrete barriers that divide (and in some cases encircle) Palestinian communities; and Western diplomatic, economic, financial and military support for Israel. The plight of Palestinian refugees has led many Arabs and Persians to support the Palestinian struggle against Israeli occupation. Ideologies that celebrate terror attacks upon Israeli citizens have gained widespread popularity. Such actions are regarded by many on the 'Arab street' as heroic acts of resistance to Israeli aggression rather than terrorist acts worthy of condemnation and punishment.

Terrorism by Zionist forces   The first large scale Middle Eastern terrorist bombing in the UN era, was the bombing of the King David Hotel in Jerusalem by Irgun militants in 1946. Irgun was a Zionist militia then engaged in hostilities with Palestinian Arabs and the British. This calamity precipitated an escalation of the conflict and the eventual withdrawal of the British from Palestine.[13] A 1947 UN Partition Plan for Palestine proposed that: a large proportion of Palestine be handed over to the Jews for the creation of a Jewish homeland; a significant proportion remain under British control; Jerusalem should have the status of an international city; and the remainder of Palestine be under Arab control. This plan was unacceptable to both the Arabs and the Jews. The Palestinians were required to give up sovereignty to large areas of their territory which had been illegally seized by Zionist extremists (this included dozens of towns and villages). Key Jewish figures also rejected the plan. They had

---

13 The King David Hotel in Jerusalem was the base for the British Secretariat, the military command and a branch of the Criminal Investigation Division (police). Ninety-one people were killed, most of them civilians: 28 British, 41 Arab, 17 Jewish, and five others. Nicholas Bethell (1979), *The Palestine Triangle: The Struggle between the British, the Jews, and the Arabs, 1935–48* (London: Andre Deutsch).

no faith in the British or the UN to deliver the promised Jewish homeland, and doubted that their security would be guaranteed under the plan.

The emergence of the Jewish state   In a climate of growing sectarian violence and potential civil war, British forces withdrew from Palestine on 14 May 1948. On the same day Zionist leader Ben Gurion read the unilateral declaration of statehood.[14] That act triggered an attempted invasion of Israel by the armies of Egypt, Iraq, Jordan, Lebanon and Syria. The Arab forces were decisively defeated. During the fighting, thousands of Palestinian Arabs fled or were expelled from their homes and have not yet been allowed to return. These events laid the foundations for decades of ethnic, religious and political conflict in the Middle East.

The Six Day War/an-Naksah   The next seismic event in the region was the Six Day War of 1967. Triggered by a range of factors which go beyond the scope of this discussion,[15] this conflict – known to Arabs as *an-Naksah* (The Setback) – resulted in a stunning victory for Israel, which almost quadrupled the territory under its control.[16] It also led to a close alliance between the US and Israel which guaranteed the latter military and technological superiority over its adversaries. With US and European prodding, Israel eventually signed peace treaties with Egypt and later Jordan. However it refused to relinquish control of occupied Palestinian territories on the West Bank of the River Jordan and in the Gaza Strip. This provided the impetus for a sustained Palestinian resistance struggle. A David and Goliath struggle ensued, the Arab fighters resorting to clandestine methods of warfare, including terrorism, against their militarily superior foe.

Post-1967 resistance and the escalation of regional terrorism   Backed by a number of Arab states (often covertly) as well as private individuals, the PLO emerged as the symbol of Palestinian resistance. However after Israel was admitted to the UN as member state in 1949, it enjoyed all the rights of a sovereign including the right to defend its territory from armed attack. Guerrilla attacks upon Israel's sovereign territory were *prima facie* a violation of the UN Charter. As a sovereign state Israel had the right of self-defence against such attacks, and has exercised this right on many occasions. Meanwhile, most Arab states refused to recognize the existence of the State of Israel, and were willing (either directly or indirectly) to support armed resistance to the occupation of Palestinian territory. Some states went so far as to call for Israel to be destroyed. Numerous Arab resistance groups have emerged since 1967. They include Fatah, Hamas, Al-Aqsa Martyrs' Brigades, and Palestinian Islamic Jihad and Hezbollah. All have conducted military operations against Israeli

---

14 Gurion had links with the Irgun movement and had agreed to the bombing on the King David Hotel.

15 See: Michael Oren (2002), *Six Days of War: June 1967 and the Making of the Modern Middle East* (Oxford University Press).

16 Israel occupied the Sinai in Egypt, the Golan Heights in Syria, and the West Bank and the old city of Jerusalem which had been under Jordanian control. The Sinai was returned to Egypt in 1982.

targets and interests. Civilians have been deliberately targeted in many of these operations. Hamas and Islamic Jihad have conducted numerous suicide bombings inside Israel. Israel has responded by conducting military operations in Palestinian towns and villages and launching attacks on the homes, vehicles and offices of suspected terrorists/liberation fighters. They have also targeted metal work shops and other buildings suspected of being used for the storage or manufacture of weapons. Israel has blocked roads, cleared olive farms, altered terrain, and locked down Arab communities as part of efforts to maintain security. The cycle of violence has reached a number of peaks. They include the 1982 Israeli occupation of southern Lebanon, the first *intafada* (1987–90), the *Al Aqsa intifada* (2000), and the 2006 Hezbollah/Israel war. The ethnic and religious hatred that fuels this cycle of violence is likely to persist until a comprehensive peace is forged which guarantees security for Israel, the right of return for exiled Palestinians and their descendants (or appropriate land compensation), and a viable Palestinian state.

Religious Violence on a Global Scale: The Emergence of al Qaeda

While the PLO and its prodigy have carried out acts of terror around the world, the nature and scale of their terrorist activities has been dwarfed by those of Al Qaeda and its affiliates. Al Qaeda is the birth child of Mujahideen resistance to Soviet occupation of Afghanistan. The founders of this terrorist phenomenon have successfully exploited ethnic and religious hatreds *and* the opportunities presented by globalization and modern technology to further their ideological struggle. They have inspired thousands of Muslims in various regions to organize themselves and engage in violent jihad. Al Qaeda's motivations are partly religious (the desire to foster an Islamic religious revival), and partly political (the quest to bring down the Saudi government and other 'apostate' regimes). The recent invasions of Iraq and Afghanistan triggered a significant rise in support for the organization and an expansion of its operations. Its international character was confirmed by the emergence of pro-al Qaeda terror cells in a number of states including Spain, Germany, France, Britain, the USA, Afghanistan, Pakistan and Saudi Arabia. The organization also established links with and/or inspired a range of terror networks in South East Asia including Abu Saif (a separatist movement based in and around the southern islands of the Philippines)[17] and Jamaah Islamia.

Al Qaeda and it affiliates have used modern technology to export their ideology into the laptops and televisions of a global audience. Young Muslims throughout the world can view stirring al Qaeda messages on Arabic websites, satellite TV channels, and local news broadcasts. Al Qaeda training manuals have been widely

---

17 Abu Saif's aims are to promote an independent Islamic state in western Mindanao and the Sulu Archipelago, and create an atmosphere conducive to the creation of a pan-Islamic super state in the Malay portions of South East Asia. It hopes to create an Islamic caliphate, stretching across South East Asia, incorporating Indonesia, Malaysia, Singapore, Thailand, Cambodia, Brunei, the Philippines and parts of northern Australia. Abu Saif seeks to restore and expand upon the political influence Islam exercised in the region between the 13th and 17th centuries.

disseminated through a number of mediums including internet web sites, DVDs and email.[18] The organization's propaganda messages are designed to fuel Muslim anger at the West. They highlight: the occupation of holy lands by non-Muslims; injustices towards the Palestinians; the abuse of Muslim detainees captured by foreign armies; corrupt Arab regimes; and a range of other actual or perceived injustices towards Muslims (Murphy 2005)

Al Qaeda offers its recruits a path to religious fulfillment. Suicide bombers who kill Westerners and other infidels are not terrorists but Mujahideen (holy warriors) who are guaranteed a place in heaven if they die in the cause of jihad. Live or die, this ideology offers its followers a path to glory: either temporal victory or eternal martyrdom.

Al Qaeda's "success" on '9/11' created a ripple effect. It has inspired Muslims from Egypt to Indonesia to engage in similar struggles in their own neighborhoods.[19] Al Qaeda's focus upon broad themes – such as the hypocrisy of the West in advocating human rights while at the same time supporting oppressive regimes in a range of Muslim countries – have resonated with Muslims from diverse backgrounds. It has also given non-Muslims cause to question the foreign policy of their governments. On the other hand, al Qaeda condemned the invasion of Iraq which ousted a tyrannical Arab regime *par excellence*. It seems that al Qaeda is not immune to the charge of hypocrisy. Another example is the willingness of al Qaeda to target civilians in Iraq on the basis of their sectarian affiliations. The fact that most victims of al Qaeda terrorism are Muslim has curbed support for its ideology – an ideology which promises that a lot more Muslim blood must be shed before all the 'apostate' Arab regimes are toppled and the dream of a pan-Islamic caliphate is realized.

The Spartan and pious lifestyle of al Qaeda's leadership (bin Laden renounced a life of opulent wealth) and their willingness to do what few others have (stand up against 'corrupt' and 'oppressive' Arab regimes and 'exploitative' foreign governments) has won them the admiration of a significant number of Muslims. Moreover, the recitation of poignant verses of the Koran by Ayman al-Zawahiri and others, reinforces the Muslim belief in the sacred duty of all believers to wage jihad against oppression and injustice (L. Khan 2004, Koran).

While some of al Qaeda's concerns may be valid, its methods are not. Recourse to suicide bombings at mosques, markets, hotels and other places where civilians gather, violate fundamental principles of international law. It is therefore unsurprising that spokesmen such as Osama bin Laden and Ayman al-Zawahiri generally invoke theological rather than legal arguments to justify their actions. This is illustrated by al Qaeda's preference for the selective quotation of the Koran. These verses

---

18 Al Qaeda Training Manual, <www.usdoj.gov/ag/trainingmanual.htm>, accessed 4 December 2005.

19 'The phenomenon of Muslim national liberation movements among minorities seeking freedom from harsh non-Muslim rule is especially important at the local level: Bosnians, Palestinians, Kosovars, Chechens, Kasmiris, Uighurs, Moros and others have all turned to struggles that eventually internationalise': Fuller, Graham E. (2004), 'Terrorism Sources and Cures', in Garfinkle, Adam (ed.), *A Practical Guide to Winning the War on Terrorism* (Stanford, CA: Hoover Press), p. 20.

are offered up as irrefutable proof that violent attacks on non-military targets (for example, 'apostates') are authorized by God. The absolute prohibition on the deliberate targeting of civilians during times of war or peace cannot be reconciled with al Qaeda's *modus operandi*. Unsurprisingly, binding norms of international humanitarian and human rights law (many of which were shaped, in part, by the input of Islamic nations at international diplomatic conferences) are ignored by al Qaeda. So too is the fact that most of al Qaeda's victims to date have been Muslims. Unsurprisingly, the list of Islamic leaders and scholars from across the sectarian divide who have lined up to condemn al Qaeda and its methods continues to grow.

Can al Qaeda operations to expel occupying forces or end the oppression of Muslim populations ever be justified under international law?

An issue that requires analysis is whether armed struggles waged by al Qaeda forces to protect oppressed minorities or expel occupying forces could ever be justified under international law. Protocol I Additional to the 1949 Geneva Conventions recognizes the right to struggle against alien occupation, colonial rule and racist regimes.[20] This triggers an interesting question: could an al Qaeda-led armed struggle to liberate territory from foreign occupation be lawful? The answer is nuanced. In short a struggle to end occupation may in some circumstances be justified. However al Qaeda's involvement in such a campaign could not be legitimized (for reasons set out below).

First, al Qaeda has been designated a terrorist organization since the Security Council established the Al-Qaeda and Taliban Sanctions Committee in 1999 (UN Security Council Resolution 1267). This resolution has been reinforced by the practice of states. The international community has repeatedly condemned the activities of al Qaeda, and a significant number of states have supported the use of force against the Taliban and al Qaeda in Afghanistan. Moreover, as the organization has been outlawed, its members are *hostis humani generis* ('enemies of mankind') and al Qaeda's involvement in armed conflict is a breach of binding resolutions of the Security Council. Therefore states have an obligation *erga omnes* to prosecute members of al Qaeda – along with all other *hostis humani generis* including pirates, slave traders, torturers, and members of other internationally outlawed terrorist organizations.

Secondly, al Qaeda's *modus operandi* (deliberate attacks on civilians) is prohibited under both the laws of war and general international law.[21] For both reasons al Qaeda forces are unlikely to get recognition from states (other than Taliban-style regimes) as lawful belligerent forces. Moreover, as non-state actors, al Qaeda fighters lack combatant immunity. Al Qaeda attacks are therefore punishable as crimes against

---

20 Article 1(4) Protocol I Additional to the 1949 Geneva Conventions , <www.unhchr. ch/html/menu3/b/93.htm>, accessed 4 December 2005.

21 The United Nations has repeatedly condemned international terrorism as a violation of international law. For relevant resolutions of the UN General Assembly and Security Council see: 'UN Action to Counter-terrorism' <http://www.un.org/terrorism/> accessed 10 June 2007.

domestic law. Since the collapse of the Taliban regime in Afghanistan, al Qaeda has had no state ally and therefore no state recognition. While 'independent forces' and possibly 'organized resistance movements' can qualify as lawful belligerents under the international law of armed conflict,[22] it is doubtful that any state would be willing to recognize al Qaeda forces as lawful belligerents. (If any state does currently recognize al Qaeda, they are not saying so.) In any case, such recognition should only be afforded to those that purport to comply with the laws of war. This means, *inter alia*, that soldiers must be under responsible command and adhere to the laws of armed conflict. Captured enemy fighters must be afforded all the rights and privileges outlined in Geneva Convention III (1949). Summary executions are banned, and ICRC access to captives is mandatory. The targeting of civilians is also banned. Al Qaeda forces do not comply with these fundamental norms and cannot therefore expect to qualify as lawful belligerents under the laws of armed conflict. Consequently the participation of al Qaeda members in armed conflict should render these individuals liable to punishment *per se*, as unprivileged fighters. Where civilians have been deliberately or indiscriminately targeted, the perpetrators of such attacks are war criminals and may be punished for these crimes against international law.

Thirdly, as the targeting of civilians is a crime against international law, al Qaeda's terror tactics cannot possibly be a valid mode of pursuing the right of self-determination. The United Nations Security Council and General Assembly have repeatedly condemned international terrorism as a violation of international law.[23]

Fourthly, al Qaeda's campaigns are designed to, *inter alia,* destabilize countries and topple 'apostate' governments. While international law recognizes the right to self-determination, it has not recognized the right of states or non-state actors to intervene in the internal political affairs of states. Sovereign states are entitled to suppress internal uprisings and treat those involved as common criminals. Al Qaeda is attempting to topple democratically elected governments in Iraq and Afghanistan as well as a range of other regimes. Efforts to overthrow elected governments and impose non-democratic Islamist regimes cannot be reconciled with the emerging right of democratic governance. Most states now have some form of democracy, and all have repeatedly reaffirmed the UDHR which recognizes the right of citizens to elect their political representatives. The right of people to democratic governance may now have crystallized into a norm of customary international law, due to overwhelming state practice and *opinio juris* in favor of this practice.

Fifthly, even if a government that al Qaeda seeks to oust could be construed as 'racist' and therefore one that the people of the territory are entitled to struggle against, the International Court of Justice is yet to explicitly endorse the notion that self-determination may be won by force. There is also no widespread practice among states that lends support for the idea that such a rule exists. In any event, al Qaeda forces are unlikely to enjoy the support of the majority of the local population in states where they wage terrorist campaigns. It is doubtful that most Afghans

---

22 See Article 4(2) Geneva Convention III 1949.

23 See: 'UN Against Terrorism: Action by the Security Council' <http://www.un.org/terrorism/sc.htm> accessed 5 December 2005

or Iraqis would support the overthrow of their elected government by a terrorist organization. In Afghanistan, al Qaeda enjoyed a close relationship with the Taliban which ruled that country with extreme brutality. In Iraq, al Qaeda has targeted the political majority (Shi'ite and Kurds and their Sunni partners). Its recourse to suicide bombings in civilian areas would disgust most people.

Sixthly, terrorist activity offends the criminal law of all states. The killing of civilians is murder. Members of al Qaeda may therefore be prosecuted under municipal criminal law or before international tribunals for crimes against international law.

For these reasons, al Qaeda's activities cannot be regarded as lawful. Their military operations in Iraq, Afghanistan and elsewhere offend *jus in bello* and cannot be justified under *jus ad bellum*. While it is arguable that al Qaeda military units that fought Coalition forces in Afghanistan in 2001 were combatants who fought with the approval of the Taliban government (and were therefore entitled to POW status), the six factors noted above overwhelm such considerations. Today military operations by al Qaeda forces against state actors would not be permissible under international law, and could not be justified by reference to *jus ad bellum*.

Iraq as the Epicenter of Contemporary Religious Terror

Mesopotamia has been fertile ground for ethnic and religious conflict since antiquity. In modern times, its borders have been shaped by Ottoman rule and subsequent British occupation. After World War I the three Ottoman provinces of Mosul, Baghdad, and Basra were merged into a unitary state. Iraq encompasses a range of peoples. Its demography is characterized by a complex mix of ethnic, religious, and tribal groupings. Ethnics groups include the Arabs, Kurds, Iraqi Turkmen, Assyrians, Armenians, Persians, Shabaks and Lurs. Religious groups are more difficult to describe. Some 95–7 per cent of the population are Muslim, while the remaining 2–5 per cent of the population are either Christian or members of one of the other minority religions (Sabaean–Mandeans, Yarzidis, Bahais, and Hebrew Jews). There are no official figures of the proportion of Shi'ite and Sunni – this remains an intensely political issue. Available statistics fluctuate wildly. Western sources indicate that the Shi'ite constitute between 55 and 65 per cent of the population, and the Sunni (Sunni Arabs and Sunni Kurds) between 32 and 40 per cent.[24] However a recent Arab source suggests that Sunnis (Sunni Arabs and Sunni Kurds) constitute 60 per cent of the population and the Shi'ite 40 per cent.[25] Of the Sunni component of the population, 42–4 per cent are Sunni Arabs and 16–18 per cent Sunni Turks and Sunni Kurds. Attempts by this diverse collection of peoples to build a peaceful and unified state have met with mixed success. There have been periods of relative

---

24 CIA World Factbook, Iraq, available at <www.cia.gov> accessed 1 May 2007; See also *Encyclopaedia Britannica* accessible at <www.britannica.com>; Federal Research Division Library of Congress (November 2005), *A Country Study: Iraq*. Retrieved 2 May 2007. Accessed at <www.lcweb2.loc.gov>.

25 See Faruq Ziada, 'Iraqis by the Numbers: Is there a Sunni Majority in Iraq?', 27 December 2006, available at <www.counterpunch.org> accessed 1 May 2007; and (2006), *The Iraq Study Group Report* (First Vintage Books Edition), p. 102.

stability. However by the time Saddam gained a stranglehold on power in the 1970s, Iraq had experienced half a dozen military coups, significant ethnic and religious violence, and decades of political repression. This laid the foundations for a brutal three decades of state-sponsored terrorism.

Saddam's reign of terror

After a successful CIA-backed *coup d'etat* in 1968 (Morgan 2003), the Ba'ath Party set about consolidating its hold on power by resorting to terror. State-sponsored violence was inflicted by Saddam Fedayeen, the Special Republican Guard, the Iraqi secret police and other branches of Iraq's military, security and intelligence services. This was how Saddam, a Sunni Arab, and his close knit Revolutionary Command Council (comprised for the most part of fellow members of Saddam's Al-Tikriti tribe), were able to maintain control over a state whose population was predominantly Shi'ite and Kurdish. While both of those communities mounted a number of uprisings, they were never able to topple Saddam's regime.

Saddam's recourse to terrorism was both domestic and international in scope. Through his support for Palestinian militants in their struggle against Israeli occupation, Saddam built an international reputation as a defender of Arab nationalism.[26] His financial assistance to the families of suicide bombers was not forgotten. When Iraq was overrun by Coalition forces in 2003, many Arabs (including Palestinians) answered Saddam's call for jihad against the occupation. Some, including Zaqawi, were already in Iraq before the invasion. Their motives were varied. For Zaqawi the objective was to ignite a sectarian war. For some other jihadists the aim was to target Coalition forces and those who collaborated with the occupation.

Occupation, resistance and the slide towards sectarian terror

Upon the collapse of the Soviet Union the US was left without an opposing superpower. As a consequence, its capacity to impose its will on others was enhanced.[27] It did so in 2003 when it ousted the Ba'ath regime and occupied Iraq. The US then proceeded to pursue foreign policy objectives that were neither authorized by the Security Council nor permitted under the law of occupation.[28] This strategy triggered a significant rise in anti-US sentiment worldwide and considerable

---

26 Unlike Jordan and Egypt, Saddam never entered into a peace treaty with Israel but instead promoted a belligerent form of Arab nationalism and exploited anti-Israel sentiment in the region. By appealing to like-minded Arabs across the Middle East, Saddam was able to garner support for the Palestinian cause and win the admiration of many in the Palestinian Diaspora.

27 This point should not be overstated. The notion of US 'hegemony' is questionable. The US has had its share of foreign policy failures including the Iran hostage crisis, Lebanon, Cuba (the Bay of Pigs) and most recently Iraq. However their hegemony within these spheres was limited as the Vietnam War (US) and the war in Afghanistan (Russia) attest.

28 The Coalition Provisional Authority in Iraq radically overhauled a number of Iraqi institutions during the occupation. Dozens of state-run enterprises and industries were shut down during the transformation of Iraqi's economy. Thousands of Iraqis lost their jobs. In

hostility within Iraq for a host of reasons. For some Iraqis, their national identity, culture and/or religion was under threat. For others their political ideology was being dismantled.

The ouster of the Ba'ath regime in 2003 lifted the lid on underlying ethnic, religious and tribal divisions between segments of Iraq society. This eventuality had been predicted by opponents of the war. On 6 September 2002, Amr Moussa, the Secretary General of the Arab League, warned the US-led coalition that war to oust Saddam would 'open the gates of Hell.'[29] These comments were indeed prescient. Years after the ouster of the Ba'ath regime, the ethnic and religious tumult this event unleashed continues to reverberate throughout Iraq and across the region.

A bungled occupation and a rise in terrorism   The failure of the occupying powers during the crucial first few months of the occupation to secure Iraq and its borders, restore basic services, set a time timetable for elections, and win the confidence and trust of the Iraqi people, allowed radical Islamists the time and space to organize and conduct a sustained campaign of terrorist violence. The bombings at the Red Cross headquarters, the Jordanian Embassy, the UN headquarters (all in Baghdad), as well as the bombing outside the Imam Ali Mosque in Najaf (which killed Ayatollah Mohammed Baqr al-Hakim and at least 84 others) were pivotal events during this period. These successful attacks emboldened Sunni radicals whose campaign of armed resistance grew into a sustained insurgency. They also undermined the confidence the Shi'ite had placed in the occupiers and the Iraqi Governing Council to protect them, and fueled the growth of Shi'ite militias such as al-Sadr's Madhi Army.

Ba'ath sponsored terror during the occupation   The Ba'ath regime also bears some of the responsibility for sectarian violence that has spread through the country since 2003. Well aware that he couldn't prevail on the battlefield or prevent Iraq being occupied, Saddam laid the foundations for a sustained campaign of guerrilla resistance. If Ba'ath loyalists and other anti-occupation elements (including foreign jihadis) were able to render Iraq ungovernable, the occupiers would eventually withdraw. Saddam could then return to power. A number of factors suggest that this was Saddam's strategy. First, the Iraqi intelligence services, secret police and miscellaneous other state actors were heavily armed and generously funding in preparation for a long struggle. Weapons and ammunition caches were hidden throughout the country in the lead up to the war, a sign that preparations had been made for a sustained guerrilla war. Secondly, audio and video tapes released by Saddam during the occupation called for resistance to the occupation. Thirdly, many senior personnel within the Ba'ath apparatus remained at large throughout the occupation and participated in the insurgency. Fourthly, known terrorists such as Abu Musab al-Zarqawi were allowed to enter and remain in Iraq prior to the 2003 invasion. No attempts appear to have been made by Ba'ath loyalists to prevent

---

seeking to impose its will in this manner, the Coalition created significant opposition from many of those who had welcomed the overthrow of the Ba'ath regime.

29 'Iraqi air defence site attacked', 6 September, 2002 <http://news.bbc.co.uk/2/hi/middle_east/2238568.stm> accessed 5 December 2005.

radical Islamists from engaging in terrorist activities during the occupation. Fifthly, Saddam was a ruthless politician who had shown no compunction in the past about authorizing violence against Iraqis.[30] He would therefore have been unlikely to object to similar tactics being used by members of the resistance if they might result in his return to power. Saddam would have been well aware that Sunni extremists were likely to target the Shi'ite population. While generally regarded as secular in outlook, for the reason noted above Saddam would have been unlikely to object to a campaign of Sunni terror against the Shi'ite. He had no interest in the Shi'ite gaining power. In summary, Saddam's preparations for guerrilla war[31] – together with policy failures by the occupiers in the critical first few months[32] of the occupation – set the stage for the ethnic and religious tumult that has engulfed Iraq since March 2003.

Sectarian terror   Sectarian divisions in Iraq were exploited by a range of actors during the occupation. They included Ba'ath loyalists, Shi'ite militias, foreign jihadis and numerous local resistance groups that sprang up to oppose the occupation. As the multinational force failed to exercise effective control over Iraq, terrorism became an epidemic. Sunnis, Shia, Kurds and others were all targeted for abduction, execution and bomb attacks. After a period of Shi'ite restraint at the behest of Ayatollah Sistani and others,[33] Shi'ite retaliation could no longer be held back. With the Coalition and the Iraqi Governing Council failing to provide effective security, Shi'ite militias took matters into their own hands. Meanwhile tribal leaders in Sunni areas and other Sunni strongmen were doing the same. In this way the vacuum left by the collapse of the Ba'ath security apparatus was filled. With no shortage of weapons and porous borders, the conditions were ripe for a sectarian war.[34]

The end of the occupation and the beginning of civil war   By the time the Coalition Provisional Authority transferred power to an Interim Iraqi government in June 2004, the multinational force and Iraqi forces were dealing with a number of simultaneous

---

30 Saddam has previously committed crimes against humanity against Iraqi Shi'ite. After US forces withdrew from Iraq at the end of the 1990–91 Gulf War, thousands of Shi'ites were massacred in southern and central Iraq.

31 See 'Saddam Prepares for Guerrilla War with 40,000 Fighters' (Free Arab Voice), 22 May 2003 <www.globalresearch.ca> accessed 1 May 2007; 'Saddam's New War', *Newsweek*, 29 October 2003 available at <www.msnbc.msn.com> accessed 1 May 2007.

32 Fundamental mistakes made by Coalition forces following the invasion included their failure to: (1) plan for occupation and deploy enough troops to guarantee law and order throughout Iraq; (2) secure weapons caches and stock piles and prevent them being looted; (3) immediately announce support for free and fair elections in Iraq; (4) maintain but reform Iraq's armed forces; and (5) provide basic training for US soldiers in the Arabic language, Arab culture and the Islamic faith.

33 Scott Peterson, 'Iraq's religious factions make calls for restraint', *Christian Science Monitor*, 23 May 2005 <www.csmonitor.com> accessed 1 May 2007.

34 Sunni and Shi'ite militias and insurgent groups that have targeted Coalition forces, collaborators and sometimes each other, have received significant outside help. High-tech Iranian produced 'shaped explosives' have been used with devastating effect in roadside bomb attacks on Coalition vehicles.

conflicts. They included: a sustained Sunni insurgency; sporadic Shi'ite militia activity; and an orchestrated campaign of terror by radical Islamists. National elections in 2005 and the subsequent formation of a democratic government did not halt the carnage. Divided along sectarian lines, the Iraqi parliament was unable to act in a unified and decisive manner. In the absence of political solutions armed conflict and terrorist activity continued.

Musab al-Zarqawi and the terror campaigns of Sunni radicals   In April 2005 US military officials announced that they had recovered documents from a laptop that belonged to Abu Musab al-Zarqawi.[35] These documents suggested that al Qaeda operatives were waging an organized campaign of terror in Iraq, with the objective of sparking a sectarian war between the Shi'ite and Sunni and thereby rendering Iraq ungovernable.[36] The scale and intensity of terror attacks on Shi'ite communities from mid-2003 onwards has been catastrophic. The professionalism and planning involved in many of these attacks suggests that they are the work of well organized and funded Sunni extremists. Whether these efforts to prevent the emergence of a viable unified and democratic state (which will be dominated by the Shi'ite and Kurds rather than the Sunni) remains to be seen. Meanwhile attacks on mosques, market places, police stations, government buildings and bus stations continue.

Shi'ite death squads   By 2005 Shi'ite death squads had begun a campaign of abductions and executions of Sunnis. In the same year, routine abuse of detainees in the custody of the Iraqi Ministry of the Interior was uncovered.[37] This campaign of state-sponsored terror did not however prevent elections. Shi'ite parties dominate the Iraqi parliament after Iraqis voted along sectarian lines. In 2006 Iraq's Interior Minister acknowledged that unauthorized death squads were carrying out sectarian killings.[38] Human Rights Watch called for Ministry of Interior personnel responsible for the abduction, murder and torture of Sunnis to be prosecuted.[39] The confirmation of state-sponsored sectarian killings hampered efforts to restore the rule of law

---

35 Laptop from Iraq leads to arrest of Zarqawi men <http://www.iht.com/articles/2005/04/27/news/laptop.php>.

36 Text from Abu Mus'ab al-Zarqawi Letter <http://www.globalsecurity.org/wmd/library/news/iraq/2004/02/040212-al-zarqawi.htm> accessed 5 December 2005: 'Shi'ism is the looming danger and the true challenge. The solution that we see, and God the Exalted knows better, is for us to drag the Shi'a into the battle because this is the only way to prolong the fighting between us and the infidels… They are the proximate, dangerous enemy of the Sunnis, even if the Americans are also an archenemy. The danger from the Shi'a, however, is greater and their damage is worse and more destructive to the [Islamic] nation than the Americans. … the only solution is for us to strike the religious, military, and other cadres among the Shi'a with blow after blow until they bend to the Sunnis.'

37 Human Rights Watch (2006), 'Iraq: End Interior Ministry Death Squads', 29 October, accessible at <www.hrw.org> accessed 1 May 2007.

38 'Iraqi death squads not police', 12 April 2006 <www.news.bbc.co.uk> accessed 1 May 2007.

39 Human Rights Watch (2006), 'Iraq: End Interior Ministry Death Squads', 29 October, accessible at <www.hrw.org> accessed 1 May 2007.

in many Sunni cities and towns. To this extent al Qaeda in Iraq achieved a stated objective.

Democracy without stability: ethnic and religious terror in contemporary Iraq

At the time of writing Iraq is the epicenter of global terrorism. Radical Islamists are targeting a range of religious minorities including, Sabaean–Mandeans, Sunnis, Shi'ite and Kurds.[40] Iraq provides the most tragic and poignant example of ethnic and religious tumult in today's world. It remains a nation beset by sectarian, criminal and terrorist violence. The absence of stable government after the collapse of the Ba'ath regime left a power vacuum that has been partially filled by radical Islamists and insurgent groups. After the transfer of power to an Iraqi government in June 2004, three rounds of elections in 2005, and the formation of democratic government in 2006, Iraqi politicians remain dependent upon Coalition forces for the survival of their government. Divided on ethnic, tribal, religious and ideological grounds, the government lacks the unity needed to exert its authority over a range of non-state actors. Many jihadists, members of sectarian militias and others continue to engage in ethnic, religious and political violence with impunity.

'al Qaeda in Iraq'   Terrorist organizations operating in Iraq, such as al Qaeda in Iraq, have taken international terrorism to new 'heights.' They have successfully exploited aspects of globalization to pursue their ideological objectives. They have deployed modern technology (IEDs, laptop computers, mobile phones, video recording devices), modern weaponry (surface-to-air missiles, automatic firearms, grenade launchers, and shoulder-fired missiles), and guerrilla methods of warfare (in some cases learnt from other theaters of war such as Afghanistan). These tools have been used in conjunction with highly effective intelligence systems. Zarqawi's terror network and others besides have exploited and fueled Muslim outrage at the US-led invasion and occupation of Iraq. Flawed US counter-resistance strategies (including the bombing of civilian areas and the abuse of detainees) allowed Zarqawi's terrorist campaign to gain support and traction. Jihadi volunteers from more than 20 states answered al Qaeda in Iraq's call, with most coming from Saudi Arabia, Egypt, Iran, Jordan, Lebanon, the Palestinian territories, Sudan, Syria, Tunisia and Yemen (Myers 2005).[41]

Unable to go after the bulk of the Coalition forces, which remain protected in heavily fortified bases, jihadists went after soft targets. Their purpose was to undermine the Coalition's objectives and its will to remain in Iraq. They have done so by targeting vital infrastructure (as well as schools, hospitals and universities). They have also targeted private contractors, police and army recruits and others deemed to be collaborators. For al Qaeda in Iraq and other radical Sunni jihadists, the Shi'ite

---

40 United Nations Mission for Iraq, *Human Rights Report 1 January – 31 March 2007,* paragraphs 39–42. and *Human Rights Report 1 July–31 August 2006*, paragraph 53, available at <www.uniraq.org> accessed 1 May 2007.

41 An NBC news analysis of website postings found that 55 per cent of foreign insurgents came from Saudi Arabia, 13 per cent from Syria, 9 per cent from North Africa and 3 per cent from Europe.

are apostates (*kafr*) and may be killed. This goes some way to explain the willingness of radical Sunni Islamists to undertake a campaign of terrorism that is unprecedented in its intensity and ferocity. The scale of terrorist bombings in Baghdad, Najaf and elsewhere in Iraq, upon protected sites (for example, the UN building, mosques, Red Cross Headquarters and so on) is to the best of this writer's knowledge, unparalleled for a terrorist campaign waged by non-state actors in recent times.

Why did they go to such lengths? For al Qaeda, a democratic Shi'ite-dominated Iraq would represent a decisive rejection of al Qaeda's dream of a Sunni pan-Islamic caliphate. For Ba'athists, it would confirm the end of Ba'ath power in Iraq.

As unpopular as the presence of non-Muslim armies in Iraq is to many Iraqis and Muslims around the world, there is an implicit acknowledgment that a US withdrawal before al Qaeda in Iraq and other radical Islamist forces are defeated would be a disaster for the Shi'ite and many other Iraqis. Until Iraq is strong enough to maintain internal security and prevent foreign fighters entering the country at will, a US withdrawal could trigger an internecine struggle between Sunni and Shi'ite in a battle to determine who will exercise power in Iraq. Such a sectarian war could draw in neighboring states and last for years.

Unilateral invasion of Arab states by Western powers as a trigger for ethnic and religious terror

The US strategy of invading Arab states in order to end tyranny and impose democracy has not been a happy one. If the loss of civilian lives is the measure of success, then the bid to bring about 'transformative occupation' in Iraq has been a disaster. Equally catastrophic has been the US strategy of maintaining a presence in Iraq in order to draw foreign and local militant jihadists into a 'honey pot.' Opening up Iraq as a new front in the 'war on terror' ('President Addresses Nation, Discusses Iraq, War on Terror' 2005) has simply fueled sectarian divisions and opened the door to widespread terrorism by radical Sunnis and Shi'ites. Events in Iraq have clearly demonstrated that the occupation and domination of Muslim lands will inevitably trigger militant jihad. Resistance to foreign occupation, injustice and oppression are fundamental tenants of Islam. Unilateral use of military force by non-Muslim armies in Muslim states may remove a dictator but is unlikely to deliver long-term security. Instead it is a recipe for militant jihad, and in situations like Iraq, sectarian terrorism. Coalition attempts to keep the Iraqi city of Fallujah free from insurgent during 2004 and 2005 illustrates the difficulty. Coalition and Iraqi forces twice purged the city of terrorists/insurgents. Within months of conducting these military operations, Fallujah was repopulated with local insurgents and foreign jihads ('Iraq insurgents' defiant show' 2005). In situations like Iraq in the aftermath of the collapse of the Ba'ath regime ongoing terrorist violence is to be expected: the local population was heavily armed, foreign terrorist organizations had infiltrated the country, ethnic and religious tensions were high, the occupation was regarded as illegitimate by many Iraqis, there was insufficient police or security forces to maintain law and order throughout the entire state, foreign fighters were continuing to pour into the country, and international commitment to efforts to re-build and secure the nation was patchy. While the use of military force by foreign troops may be necessary in the short term to restore order and security, it is not a viable long-term solution. Political solutions are required if terrorism is to be halted. Failing this, security measures, including some adopted by Israel may be needed. They include: a highly capable intelligence agency (that is able to identify and infiltrate terrorist organizations), permanent and well resourced military and security forces, and the construction of security barriers similar to those erected by Israel to keep Palestinians terrorist/liberation fighters out.[42] This approach has reduced the number of terror attacks against Israelis but not undermined the resolve of Palestinian resistance movements or addressed the underlying causes of the violence. Nor does it halt 'war zone' terrorism. Physical barriers in Israel have quelled terrorism but not the anger, hatred, frustration and humiliation that inspires it. Such hatred may be instilled from childhood. War zone terrorists are unlikely to be deterred by heightened security measures. Volunteers motivated by despair and a desire for revenge at the loss of loved ones may be deeply traumatized. They may be easily drawn to the ideology of martyrdom. They may regard themselves as 'already dead.' Such people are likely recruits for suicide bombing operations at border checkpoints and upon soft targets such as buses and tourist sites. Martyrdom videos indicate that the motive for such attacks is often revenge for actual or perceived injustices against Muslims and a desire to go to paradise. (The Al Arabiya satellite television station devotes a TV program to this phenomena and related matters: *Sinaat al-Mawt* (The Death Industry)).

The Inculcation of Ethnic and Religious Hatred

Extremism in Pakistani maddrasses

There has been much discussion about the extent to which the education offered in some maddrasses in states such as Pakistan, Indonesia (Harvey 2003) and Saudi Arabia is contributing to ethnic and religious strife and ultimately terrorism. Some maddrasses offer a narrow curriculum which excludes English and the sciences and emphasizes rote learning of the Koran. Complaints have been raised that students have developed an 'intolerant, prejudiced and narrow-minded view of the world' and are susceptible to recruitment by terror organizations (Lawson 2005). Some Indonesian students who have attending such schools have gone on to commit terrorist bombings in Bali,[43] while others call for Indonesian Muslims to sacrifice their lives for their religion (Harvey 2003). However maddrasses with a narrow curriculum and an ideological focus on militant jihad do not account for all Islamist terrorism against non-Muslims. Many Muslims who embrace extremist Islamic ideologies have received tertiary levels of education. The July 2007 UK 'terror doctors' are a case in point. Ayman al-Zawahiri is also a medical doctor. Lack of education is therefore not an adequate explanation for the phenomena of Islamist extremism. Nevertheless it is important to emphasize the role that a balanced education can play in helping

---

42 Such security measures would not be a viable option for most of the world's states. The ongoing cost of providing security measures of this type would be prohibitive.

43 Bali is an island of Indonesia that derives its main income from non-Muslim Western tourists. More than 90 per cent of the population adheres to Balinese Hinduism.

students form a world view built on tolerance, rational enquiry, reason and humanity, rather than narrow ideologies that promotes intolerance and religious hatred. States must be prepared to invest in balanced education across the world in order to ensure that present and future generations of students have the chance to gain a rational and reason-based world view that can be reconciled with modernity. This strategy must be accompanied by systematic and comprehensive measures to tackle pressing issues in Muslim societies such as dispossession, poverty, illiteracy, health issues, corruption, lack of human security and poor governance. These measures are more likely to reduce ethnic and religious conflict than the unilateral use of force.

Conclusion

The rapid pace of globalization over the last decade has seen the export of extreme religious ideologies from the Middle East to other parts of the world. Such ideologies have been adopted in Eastern Europe, Western Europe, South East Asia, Central Asia, Russia, East Africa, North Africa and North America. In all of these places, and more besides, terrorist crimes have been committed by persons who have embraced these radical beliefs. These ideologies owe their existence, in part, to ethnic and religious divisions dating back centuries. Some were generated by colonialism, neo-colonialism and foreign occupation. Others pre-dated such calamities, but were fermented by them.

Terrorist violence is not the inevitable product of ethnic and religious discord. Nor is it a necessary element of post-colonial transition. There are many multi-ethnic and multi-faith societies (including post-colonial states) that are not plagued by terrorist violence. Many African, Asian and South American countries fall into this category. However some post-colonial nations have experienced large scale ethnic and religious violence. Radical Islamism represents a significant threat to social harmony in many multi-ethnic and multi-religious states. It has become the main source of sectarian strife and terrorism in the contemporary world. Its exponents reject the international human rights movement as an imposition of Western values on non-Western people and cultures. Their rejection of human rights and democracy is at odds with the aspirations of the majority of people throughout the world. By waging a campaign of terrorism to pursue their goals, radical Islamists have violated but not destroyed the international rule of law. They have violated the human right of their victims while at the same time strengthening the resolve of the human rights movement. (A movement that continues to gain ground throughout the Islamic world.)

Globalization has provided tools for the dissemination of radical Islamist ideas and methods.[44] Modern communication systems such as the internet enable their instantaneous transmission. Islamist terror cannot be eradicated by blocking access to these technologies. We cannot wind back the clock. Globalization is here with all its benefits and costs. Ethnic and religious conflict and associated violence

---

44 Global protests in February 2006 by Muslims offended by Danish cartoons featuring the Islamic prophet Mohammed are a reminder of the power of the internet as a tool for dissemination of material that may spark ethnic or religious unrest.

within Islamic communities and societies must be addressed through ideological transformation. Islamic leaders and clerics must persuade all sections of the *umma* that notions of 'Political Islam' that call for or tolerate the use of violence to: (a) bring down existing governments; (b) impose a pan-Islamic caliphate, or (c) punish perceived offenses against Islam, are neither an acceptable nor accurate reflection of Islam. Many Muslim leaders have already done so. This message also needs to be conveyed in schools and mosques. Again this has happened, although not universally. A similar approach needs to be adopted with respect to other religious traditions and political ideologies that tolerate or sanction the use of violence.

Where ethnic and religious groups are competing for scarce land and resources (a common source of conflict) the human security needs of these peoples needs to be protected. This may require a range of measures, some of which are mentioned below and others are outlined in Chapter 4.2. Key measures include education, dialogue, exposure to other cultures ideas and perspectives, promotion of cooperation, respect for religious differences (including the right to hold different beliefs and views), development, and resolution of outstanding injustices such as the Palestinian question. In this way young lives and minds can be shaped not by violence and hatred but universally accepted values such as mercy, compassion, tolerance and justice. Ethnic and religious conflicts cannot all be resolved by acceding to the (often overlapping) demands of the disputants. A range of short- and long-term strategies must be adopted. In the short term peaceful dispute resolutions must be energetically pursued.

Terrorism born of ethnic and religious hatred is clearly reversible. This has been demonstrated a number of times over the past century. In Northern Ireland, South Africa and Sierre Leone, ethnic and religious terror has been transformed into national reconciliation, disarmament and peaceful co-existence through negotiation. None of these processes have been easy or perfect. However globalization offers numerous opportunities for the resolution of ethnic and religious conflict. International forums such as the 2005 UN General Assembly Global Summit are an example. They provide a forum for regional and international dialogue, and an environment for the planning and development of strategies to address the sources of ethnic and religious violence. Chapter VI of the UN Charter sets out the peaceful dispute resolution methods under international law. It encourages states to resolve disputes through dialogue, mediation, conciliation, use of the good offices of statesmen such as the Secretary General of the UN, as well as arbitration or judicial settlement of disputes. Use of these mechanisms at the national, regional and international level can be an effective way of addressing ethnic, religious and political tensions before they spiral into conflict and terrorism.[45]

When injustices are resolved, the desire for revenge through terrorism can be abated, if not defused entirely. Sometimes concerted pressure may need to be applied to states to persuade them to change their practices. (A 'carrot and the stick' approach may be needed.) Where ethnic and religious tumult emerges, international pressure can be brought to bear on the relevant sovereign states to halt the abuses and begin the processes of restorative justice. If the relevant state is unwilling or unable to take effective measures to halt such abuses, then as a last resort, international intervention may be required (for example, to halt massive human rights violations).[46] One positive development in this field has been international agreement upon the legitimacy of humanitarian intervention by UN-authorized forces in order to avert or halt genocide.[47] If such action is to be taken with UN approval, the Security Council must authorize firm measures against states that have sponsored terrorism and failed to halt its growth. Failure to do so leaves the door open for further unilateral use of force by 'great powers' against 'outlaw states' (Simpson 2004). The catastrophic effects of such interventions have been highlighted above. Rather than halt human rights abuses within Iraq, Coalition forces ended up committing them. They also triggered religious violence and terrorism on a scale not seen since the Rwandan genocide.

---

45 Proactive measures to prevent or quell terrorist violence may require commitment at a number of levels. At the local level it may require protection of the rights of minorities, delivery of health care, education, and access to employment and other basic rights. At an international level, assistance by states and international organizations may be required so that vulnerable states can realize social, economic, cultural, education and developmental goals and resolve local or regional disputes. These efforts may help avert ethnic and religious conflict. It is through alleviation of the causes of ethnic and religious violence (such as internal or external oppression of minorities, or competing claims to territory), that terrorist violence can be averted.

46 The recent genocide in the Darfur region of the Sudan reflects the ongoing reluctance of the UN and regional organizations to intervene in the internal affairs of states, even when massive human rights violations are in progress. The Security Council and African Union are yet to put the kind of pressure on the Sudanese government (or take sufficiently robust action themselves) that is needed to halt terror attacks by Arab militias on African Sudanese.

47 This occurred at the 2005 General Assembly Global Summit. It is a welcome and necessary exception to the doctrine non-intervention into the internal affairs of sovereign states. Such interventions are needed where governments commit or sponsor massive human rights violations (including terror campaigns against ethnic and religious minorities). This principle complements the 'responsibility to protect' doctrine. See *The Responsibility to Protect* (Report of the International Commission on Intervention and State Sovereignty 2001).

References

Abeyratne, S., 'Economic Roots of Political Conflict: The Case of Sri Lanka', Department of Economics, University of Colombo Visiting Fellow Division of Economics, Australian National University, <http://rspas.anu.edu.au/economics/publish/papers/wp2002/2002_01%20Sirimal&20Aberatna%20ANU&20WP.pdf>, accessed 6 January 2006.

al Qaeda Training Manual, <www.usdoj.gov/ag/trainingmanual.htm>, accessed 4 December 2005.

Baylis, J. and Smith, S. (2001), *The Globalization of World Politics: An Introduction to International Relations* (2nd edition) (Oxford University Press).

Bethell, N. (1979), *The Palestine Triangle: The Struggle between the British, the Jews, and the Arabs, 1935–48* (London: Andre Deutsch).

Carroll, R. (2004), 'US chose to ignore Rwandan genocide: Classified papers show Clinton was aware of "final solution" to eliminate Tutsis', *The Guardian*, 31 March (website), <http://www.guardian.co.uk/rwanda/story/0,14451,1183889,00.html>.

Dirks, N.B. (2001), *Castes of Mind: Colonialism and the Making of Modern India* (Princeton, NJ: Princeton University Press), pp. 19–42, 107–23 and 173–97.

Dworkin, R. (1977), *Taking Rights Seriously* (Cambridge, MA: Harvard University Press).

Friedman, T., *The Lexus and the Olive Tree*, <http://www.thomaslfriedman.com/lexusolivetree.htm>, accessed 6 January 2006.

Fuller, Lon L. (1965), *The Morality of Law* (New Haven, CT: Yale University Press).

Fuller, G., 'Terrorism: Sources and Cures', pp. 15–25, in Adam Garfinkle (ed.) *A Practical Guide to Winning the War on Terrorism* (2004).

Gardam, J.G. (1993), *Non-combatant Immunity as a Norm of International Humanitarian Law* (Kluwer Academic Publishers).

Garfinkle, A. (ed.) (2004), *A Practical Guide to Winning the War on Terrorism* (Stanford, CA: Hoover Press).

Geneva Convention III (1949) Article 4(2).

'Gunmen kill Iraqi tribal chief', <http://news.bbc.co.uk/2/hi/middle_east/4462436.stm>, accessed 5 December 2005.

Gupta, A. (5 October 2000), *Opinion Partition of India* <http://www.boloji.com/opinion/0022.htm>, accessed 5 December 2005.

Hart, H.L.A. (1961), *The Concept of Law* (Oxford University Press).

Harvey, R. (3 September 2003), 'Spotlight on Indonesia's Islamic schools', <http://news.bbc.co.uk/1/hi/world/asia-pacific/3198537.stm>.

Hobbes, T. (1650), *The Elements of Law, Natural and Political* (London).

ICJ Reports (1986) 554, *Burkina Faso/Mali case*.

ICJ Reports (2004), *Legal Consequences of the Construction of a Wall in the Occupied Palestinian Territory*.

International Crisis Group (2006), *Sri Lanka: The Failure of the Peace Process*, Asia Report No. 124, 28 November, pp. 1–17.

'Iraqi air defence site attacked' (6 September 2002), <http://news.bbc.co.uk/2/hi/middle_east/2238568.stm>, accessed 5 December 2005.

'Iraq insurgents' defiant show' (2005), *West Australian*, 2 December, p. 27.

Jeganathan, P. (1995), 'Authorising History, Ordering Land: The Conquest of Anuradhapuraâ', in Jeganathan, P and Q. Ismail (eds), *Unmaking the Nation: The Politics of Identity and History in Modern Sri Lanka* (Colombo: Social Scientists Association).

Kapferer, B. (1988), *Legends of People, Myths of State: Violence, Intolerance and Political Culture in Sri Lanka and Australia* (London and Washington: Smithsonian Institution Press), pp. 29–48, 72–84.

Kemper, S. (1991), *The Presence of the Past: Chronicles, Politics and Culture in Sinhala Life* (Ithaca and London: Cornell University Press), pp. 53–69.

Khan, M.A. Muqtedar (2 February 2004), 'Teaching Globalization in the Era of Terrorism'. Lecture given at University of Richmond, <http://www.ijtihad.org/globalterror.htm>, accessed 6 January 2005.

Khan, L. Ali (2004), *Theory of International Terrorism: Understanding Islamic Militancy* (Leiden: Martinus Nijhoff Publishers).

Lawson, A. (14 July 2005), 'Pakistan's Islamic schools in the spotlight', <http://news.bbc.co.uk/2/hi/south_asia/4683073.stm>, accessed 5 December 2005.

'Laptop from Iraq leads to arrest of Zarqawi men' <http://www.iht.com/articles/2005/04/27/news/laptop.php> accessed 10 June 2007.

Lorenzen, D.N. (1999), 'Who Invented Hinduism?', 10 *Comparative Studies in Society and History*, 630–59.

Menski, W. (2002), 'Hindu Law as a Religious System' in Andrew Huxley (ed.), *Religion, Law and Tradition: Comparative Studies in Religious Law* (London: Routledge Curzon).

Morgan, D. (20 April 2003), 'Ex-U.S. Official Says CIA Aided Baathists CIA offers no comment on Iraq coup allegations', <http://www.commondreams.org/headlines03/0420-05.htm>.

Murphy, D. (5 August 2005), 'Al Qaeda to West: It's about policies', <http://www.csmonitor.com/2005/0805/p01s02-woiq.html>.

Myers, L. (20 June 2005), 'Who are the foreign fighters in Iraq? An NBC News analysis finds 55 percent hail from Saudi Arabia', <http://msnbc.msn.com/id/8293410/>, accessed 5 December 2005.

Oren, M. (2002), *Six Days of War: June 1967 and the Making of the Modern Middle East* (Oxford University Press).

'President Addresses Nation, Discusses Iraq, War on Terror', Fort Bragg, North Carolina (28 June 2005), <http://www.whitehouse.gov/news/releases/2005/06/20050628-7.html>.

Protocol Additional to the Geneva Conventions of 12 August 1949, and relating to the Protection of Victims of International Armed Conflicts (Protocol I). Adopted on 8 June 1977 by the Diplomatic Conference on the Reaffirmation and Development of International Humanitarian Law applicable in Armed Conflicts. <www.unhchr.ch/html/menu3/b/93.htm>, accessed 4 December 2005.

Rawls, J. (1993), *Political Liberalism* (*The John Dewey Essays in Philosophy, 4*) (New York: Columbia University Press).

—— (1971), *A Theory of Justice* (Cambridge, MA: Belknap Press of Harvard University Press).

Raz, J. (1979), *The Authority of Law* (Oxford University Press).

Reference re Secession of Quebec (1998) 2 SCR 217.

Sakhong, Lian H., 'A Struggle For Self-Determination In Burma: Ethnic Nationalities Perspective'. A speech delivered at Conference on Indo–Burma Relations, India International Centre on 16–17 September 2004, <http://www.ibiblio.org/obl/docs/ Struggle_for_S-D.htm>, accessed 6 January 2006.

Simpson, G. (2004), *Great Powers and Outlaw States* (Cambridge: Cambridge University Press).

Text from Abu Mus'ab al-Zarqawi Letter, <http://www.globalsecurity.org/wmd/ library/news/iraq/2004/02/040212-al-zarqawi.htm>, accessed 5 December 2005.

'The "Clash of Civilizations": Perception and Reality in the Context of Globalization and International Power Politics' (2004), 7. Lecture delivered at the International Forum on Globalization and a Dialogue between Civilizations.

UN Doc. A/HRC/1/L.10 (30 June 2006), UN Declaration on the Rights of Indigenous Peoples.

'UN Action to Counter-terrorism' <http://www.un.org/terrorism/> accessed 10 June 2007. A website listing states party to the main treaties <http://www.icrc.org/Web/ eng/siteeng0.nsf/html/party_main_treaties), accessed 5 December 2005.

UN Against Terrorism: Action by the Security Council, <http://www.un.org/terrorism/ sc.htm>, accessed 5 December 2005.

3.2   Terrorism, Story-Telling and Existential Communication

T. Brian Mooney

Understanding the nature and causes of terrorism has occupied a very prominent position in both the practical and theoretical spheres with great urgency particularly since the tragic events of 11 September 2001. Nevertheless, terrorism is a very old phenomenon when defined from a position of power. Definitions abound. One could look for the examples provided in the *US Code and Army Manuals* of the early 1980s or the formulation of the British government which is substantially similar declaring as terrorism '… the use, or threat, of action which is violent, damaging or disrupting, and is intended to influence the government or intimidate the public and is for the purpose of advancing a political, religious, or ideological cause' (Chomsky N., 2005, 18). Noam Chomsky in a devastating, passionate and caustic critique of foreign and domestic policies of 'enlightened' states, together with the intellectual orthodoxies which prevail in 'enlightened' societies, has persuasively demonstrated that such definitions will not do. And the reason is simple because the definition applies both historically and contemporaneously to the policies not just of 'them' – the terrorists, but also to the policies and activities of the governments of 'enlightened' societies – 'us.' Chomsky highlights numerous examples, here I will mention just a few to bring home the force of the point.

The official definitions are unusable, because of their immediate consequences. One difficulty is that the definition of terrorism is virtually the same as the definition of the official policy of the US, and other states, called 'counter-terrorism' or 'low-intensity' warfare or some other euphemism .... Japanese imperialists in Manchuria and North China, for example, were not aggressors or terrorists, but were protecting the population and the legitimate governments from the terrorism of 'Chinese bandits'.... When the UN General Assembly, in response to Reaganite pressures, passed its strongest condemnation of terrorism in 1987, with a call on all states to destroy the plague of the modern age. The resolution passed 153 to 2, with only Honduras abstaining. The two states that opposed the resolution explained their reasons in the UN debate. They objected to a passage recognizing 'the right to self-determination, freedom, and independence, as derived from the Charter of the United Nations, of people forcibly deprived of that right ... particularly peoples under colonial and racist regimes and foreign occupation.' The term 'colonial and racist regimes' was understood to refer to South Africa, a US ally, resisting the attacks of Nelson Mandela's ANC, one of the world's 'more notorious terrorist groups,' as Washington determined at the same time. And 'foreign occupation' was understood to refer to Washington's Israeli client. So, not surprisingly, the US and Israel voted against the resolution, which was thereby effectively vetoed – in fact, subjected to the usual double veto: inapplicable, and vetoed from reporting and history as well, though it was the strongest and most important UN resolution on terrorism. (Chomsky N., 2005, 18–19)

Chomsky catalogues a disturbing history of double standards in respect to terrorism in relation to Syria, Israel, Iraq, Afghanistan, the Balkans and in several South American countries, all conceived of in terms of the definitions of terrorism being plastic enough only to apply to 'them' and never 'us.' Opponents of the 'might is right' political and moral thesis gaze back with horror at the island of Melos.

So what can a philosopher hope to contribute to a debate on terrorism? Definitions are especially difficult since 'one man's terrorist is another man's freedom fighter.' I suspect that issues such as terrorism need to be viewed in a broader context in philosophy and especially moral philosophy. If we can place in 'brackets' for a moment an 'us/them' mentality we can situate the debate within the context of deeply contested and incommensurable discourses over the very nature of rationality and moral dispute.

The range of fundamental disagreements in respect to issues of deeply held beliefs in both philosophy and everyday life is extraordinary. Clearly, the domain of the religious is one central arena of deeply cherished but fundamental beliefs, which radically diverge. Here we may think of the disputes that often violently divide the Muslim from the Jew, the Hindu from the Buddhist and all of the religious traditions from the atheist. This is true not just between religions but within religious traditions as is so painfully witnessed in the internecine conflict between various Christian denominations as too the tensions between the Sunni and Shia factions of Islam. Such religious disagreements are often enough supervened by political dimensions. In philosophy too whole departments in the academies have fallen apart on deeply held beliefs.[48] The sheer amount and intensity of contested beliefs surely forces us to

---

48 I have in mind here, by way of example, the splitting of the philosophy department at Sydney University into two separate departments divided on ideological (and no doubt

ask whether there is a position or positions (beliefs) that are incontestably true. The battlefield of warring beliefs apparently suggests a negative response.

The late philosopher David Lewis wrote that:

> Whether or not it would be nice to knock disagreeing philosophers down by sheer force of argument, it cannot be done ... . Once the menu of well-worked out theories is before us, philosophy is a matter of opinion. (Lewis D., 1983, x–xi.)

As I have mentioned fundamental disagreement among philosophers is standard and often venomous as the disputes between 'analytic' and 'continental European' philosophy attests. But it is perhaps worthwhile to point out what may be likely sources of such disagreement and dispute among rational discussants as this may prove helpful in identifying underlying structures of disagreement and fundamental belief that can issue in terrorism.[49] First of all people have deeply embedded beliefs of a religious, moral, political or scientific dimension that are acquired independently of studying philosophy. Secondly, there are the crucial formative influences of the student entering into philosophy, including the importance of teachers, fellow interlocutors, and the manner in which philosophy is first broached. Thirdly, there is the particular academic setting or context, the institutional allegiances and dominant forms of discourse and enquiry and the temperaments of the individuals involved. Finally, one can point to the underlying psychological or social causes that predispose individuals to adopt or favor certain viewpoints or attitudes.

Now the importance of this very brief analysis of the causes of fundamental disagreements in philosophical circles lies (not in the failure of reason *per se*) in the commitments that we fatefully 'grow' into. Some, if not all, of our most deeply held positions are not at all the result of reasoned enquiry but belong to the realm of habituation and affect. It is my contention that this is the arena in which we must look for the causes and cures for terrorism. In the rest of this part of the chapter, I would like to concentrate on the existential dimensions of such profound disagreement seeking out the dimensions of affect that enculturate our beliefs, in doing so I will appeal to the importance of narrative and story telling as a strategy to overcome radical disagreement. At an existential level, the problems appear quite clearly. The radical subjectivism and relativism of so many students is but one indication of the malaise. Contemporary society and more pointedly the contemporary university have elevated the virtue of tolerance to the center stage. If we have no way to bring to closure the interminability of ethical debate, if we have agreed that there are no satisfactory rational resolutions to moral dilemmas and if we cannot agree on a substantive account of rationality that could settle debates, then, we ought to be subjectivists or relativists (or perhaps sceptics). Justice, once conceived of as the cornerstone of the virtues, with its ordering power of temperance, no doubt historically embedded, but nonetheless a fundamental power of the human soul, has

---

personal) grounds, as well as the political disputes that affected the University of Louvain (Leuven).

    49 In the following discussion I am deeply grateful to discussions held in June, 2005 with Alasdair MacIntyre at The Erasmus Institute Summer Faculty Seminar held at the University of Notre Dame du Lac, South Bend, Indiana.

given way to a pluralism which rejects any unity of the virtues, any objective account of the nature of human reason (and of the human person who exercises such reason). Incommensurability is ensconced at the very heart of debate and incommensurability names the contemporary zeitgeist.[50] Students and their teachers burdened with the deadening impact of the zeitgeist or what Plato refers to as the Great Sophist (Plato, *Republic*, 492–3) – the embodiment of the zeitgeist in pedagogy and politics – are ineluctably enmeshed in the system. The political and the pedagogical rehearse together the myopic pursuit of economic *tele*, reducing even the desire to understand and devaluing the pursuit of reflectiveness, and since tolerance above all must be respected, we will become politically correct.

It is quite clear that this rather dramatic and stark cameo of contemporary reality is deeply contestable but I think that enough of us can recognize our own parts in the tragedy to allow it to stand for the sake of my argument. Because I only need this to represent one aspect of the nature of our daily lives for the argument to proceed, I am interested in the 'attitudes' that derive from the characteristics I have highlighted above and how they inform debate. At a strategic level, in debate, several phenomena attest to these 'attitudes.' No doubt the strategies I will soon adumbrate are old but nevertheless they have achieved a kind of apotheosis in the contemporary world.

The central strategy in debate I would like to highlight is often in colloquial terms referred to as 'pigeon-holing.' The phenomenon itself is ordinary and in itself not as interesting as what it yields at the level of existential and intellectual communication. Pigeon-holing is a typical approach to intellectual understanding. One seeks to understand the other and his/her views by categorizing the other in a wider context. Thus, one knows better what strategy of debate to adopt once an initial categorization strategy has already been adopted, that is, once one knows whether one's interlocutor is, by way of examples, conservative or radical, Liberal or Labor, a feminist, an economic rationalist, a Marxist, a deconstructionist, an atheist, agnostic or Christian.

Indeed, there is nothing disingenuous about such strategies. They are central to debate and are ensconced in metaphysics and logic, 'not p' is defined or grasped in contradistinction to 'p', non-being as the contrary of being. When we seek to understand the positions of a difficult philosopher it is often enough useful to see who that philosopher's intellectual opponents would be, and this will provide occasion for further reflection and understanding.[51]

Nevertheless, such a strategy has in existential terms important and unfortunate, but perhaps not necessary, consequences. Let us say, for example, I am considering in a dialectical interchange a topic of deep contention and moral relevance. One could choose among a great variety of morally contentious issues but let us focus on the issue of artificial contraception. Let us suppose further that one's interlocutor identifies one as a traditional Catholic. As soon as this strategy is adopted, a perceptible shift occurs at the level of existential communication. Because our

---

50 Here I am concerned with 'rational' incommensurability not 'value' incommensurability.

51 Professor J.J. McEvoy used this methodology as one pedagogical tool, and I have found it invaluable.

Catholic is emotionally and intellectually attached to the Catholic tradition, the debate quickly places him in an awkward position. Instead of reasonably dealing with the issue at hand he becomes a representative of a tradition and partly because he is seen as such by his interlocutor. Perhaps he feels constrained, for example, to defend the cogency of the Catholic Church's prohibition on artificial conception if one accepts their premises.

Existentially dialectical communication has moved away from the arena of genuine interchange between persons and the debate has entered the realm of ideology. Our Catholic has become the representative of a tradition and a whole universe of thought and belief. Moreover, since his interlocutor is committed to a very different viewpoint, let us say she is a secular feminist, he imposes his own form of pigeon-holing on her as well. Here we are confronted with all the intellectually hardened and encrusted views, reasons and arguments that embody the discourses from within which our interlocutors are identified. In a very important sense, the Catholic has lost sight of the other as person just as the secular feminist has done. Both are no doubt still communicating but at a different level and on a platform that will rarely yield understanding or advance debate. Such strategies as pigeon-holing can lead to the interminability of contemporary ethical debates.

There is a kind of tiresome inevitability to such strategies. Clearly, however, they are neither odd nor even deliberatively obstructive, we abandon ourselves to the strategies because they are so commonplace, so ordinary. Our identities are forged in very complex ways with overlapping and sometimes contradictory arenas of care and concern. It is partly because we are affectively bound up in communities of identity that we tend towards such strategies. The deeper one's affective commitments the more readily we rise to meet challenges to such affective commitment. These are not matters peripheral to us but rather they are partially constitutive of who we are. So on the one hand the phenomenon of pigeon-holing often lends to identification with intellectual positions beyond the scope of the dialogue, and on the other, the other and myself are no longer communicating in the real sense of participative dialogue.

Alasdair MacIntyre's philosophical analysis of the bankruptcy of contemporary moral debate provides an especially powerful analysis of the dynamics of incommensurable rationalizations (MacIntyre A., 1990; 1988; 1981). The shrill clamor of assertion and counter-assertion is deeply dependent on his provocative and somewhat depressing analysis of incommensurable rational discourses, and the practices, traditions and narrative histories within which they evolve and are played out. Concepts such as reason and ethics are diverse and diverge because, according to MacIntyre, they are tradition dependent. And even if some form of Thomistic Aristotelianism is adopted as a superior mode of rational inquiry because it in principle can deal with lacunae and epistemological crises in other modes of rationality, it too, falls prey to the specter of having no epistemological foundational account, outside of that particular tradition, which secures once and for all, the truth claims within that tradition. Once again we are haunted by Lewis's dictum that 'Once the menu of well-worked out theories is before us, philosophy is a matter of opinion' (Lewis D., 1983).

Existentially we are left with little more than the intellectually encrusted rationalizations that mark the contours and perspectives of our own traditions, and debate, aside from the epistemic crises that effect the internal coherence of particular traditions, is nothing but the ineffectual rattling of intellectual sabres. It is in this context that the full force of existential narratives seems to cut through intellectual debates and opens the real possibility of dialectic. In Australia, despite the political polemics on broader questions of asylum seekers, the stories, once they are allowed to emerge, of suffering, can create new ways of approaching the issues. The life stories of those who have suffered the circumstances and conditions of injustice can create a community of affective concern. The same may be said of the narrative histories emerging from our fractured relationship with indigenous Australians. We are moved by the harrowing brutality (even if well-intentioned) meted out to the 'stolen generations.' While the average Australian may still be nervous about having an Aboriginal family or Afghan family as our next door neighbors, partly because we find it difficult to move beyond cultural stereotypes, and perhaps because we have certain viewpoints of an intellectually inchoate sort about the value of autonomy. Nevertheless, the stories embed themselves in the psyche and we find it increasingly difficult to accept the common forms of pigeon-holing, such as 'queue-jumpers' or 'dole bludgers.'

Perhaps then, the problem lies with our broader commitments (our *paideia*) as well as the manner in which we engage in debate. The hardened positions that are built up as rationalizations – political, social, economic, cultural, philosophical – amount to a failure, a failure that stories sometimes tear apart. Behind the intellectual positions, the rationalizations that foster both commitment and indifference, we are, from time to time brought into the domain of the fateful – 'there but for the grace of God, go I.' We affectively participate in the lives of others, and this intelligence of the heart cries and rails against injustice. It is this logic of the heart that identifies and affectively participates in the life of the other, that rekindles the bonds of broken humanity, and deepens our understanding of existential predicaments.

If I may be permitted I would like to recount a short personal story that I will call 'The Day that Santa Claus Died.' I tell this story to indicate just how deeply the problems of intellectual and affective identity shape the contours of a life, and how bigotry and myopia can be deeply engrained in a psyche, as a result of what befalls us and which only later take the shape of an intellectual position.

I grew up in a city – Belfast – and a country – the North of Ireland – that was from my earliest youth riven by factional dispute. My own movement towards philosophy is partially explained by the attempt to understand the conditions that framed my responses to this world.

First of all I grew up in an impoverished background. I lived in a small Catholic and Nationalist enclave of some 1,000 families completely surrounded by Protestant and Loyalist districts. Our family lived in a modest home with two rooms upstairs and two rooms with a scullery downstairs with an outside toilet in the back yard. We had no garden and the front door looked directly on the pavement of the tenement street. The old linen mills that had provided employment for my grandparents' generation were long closed by the time I was a lad, and the major source of employment in East Belfast was in ship-building. The great cranes of Harland and Wolff provided the daily backdrop towards the sea, while the Black Mountain loomed gloomily to the north. In Ballymacarrat, my area, there had been for sometime an effective rate of 80 per cent unemployment among Catholics. Protestant families living only a stone's throw away were employed for the most part in the docks and among the other attendant industries built on the back of sea trade.

My father is a large man of almost six feet two inches – a traditional Catholic and family man – a man who under the most difficult circumstances lived out his religious beliefs with a very old fashioned morality. A man who learned to do house work, due to long periods of unemployment, when few men of his generation would have done so. A man who never went to the pub and although overtly emotionally restrained lived for his family.

One Christmas Eve, I must have been about 12 years old (and this may give you some idea of the naivety of the times or at least my own naivety) I told my Mum and Dad around 8.00 p.m. on a typically dark and wet Belfast winter night, that I was going for a walk to see if there were any signs of Santa Claus's imminent arrival. I even remember on returning home that I told my parents that I had thought I'd heard the tinkling of bells from Santa's sleigh. No doubt smiling to each other my Mum and Dad told me that Santa doesn't come to children unless they are asleep. So after laying out a glass of milk on the unlit hearth, I went up to bed where my sisters were already sleeping.

Nevertheless, I was far too excited to sleep and some time later I crept to the stairs and since the parlour door was open I peered in. It was the first time in my life that I had ever seen my father crying. He was very upset and I gathered from the tearful conversation he was having with my mother that he had just been laid off from a job in a large bakery because they had found out he was a Catholic. As a result, he was unable to buy us the Christmas presents he had hoped to. At the time this was deeply confusing and even frightening for me, not only had I seen a side of this normally emotionally restrained man I had not seen before, but I had also learnt that Santa Claus was not real.

As a young person, the effect of this double revelation was traumatic. It marked the beginnings of an initiation into a sense of bigotry, of identifying with an economically, politically, educationally and socially deprived tribe. The intellectually hardened positions adopted as a young adult – anti-British, anti-Loyalist, pro-Republican – were to a large extent *post facto* rationalizations that occurred as a result of this incident and many others to follow. As years went by and one is struck by the monstrous inequities that plagued the political situation in the North of Ireland, it became all too easy to render the world into pigeon-hole us/them scenarios, and to excuse a culture of murder.

Perhaps the greatest irony in my story of living in such a milieu is that while I, like most Catholics would appeal to considerations of justice and injustice as ways of explicating our predicament, so too did Protestants. The fact that many Protestants lived in arguably only marginally better economic situations did not effect, until much later, my inability to identify with their identity and have concern for justice for them, and to an even greater extent, my antipathy towards, as I saw it, the source of the injustices in the historical duplicity of the British government.

My own experience bolstered by the violent deaths of family members, the bombings of our home, internment without trial and daily harassment from Loyalist gangs and the British forces are mere cameos in a situation that must be writ large.

There are very few people in the North of Ireland, including the hundreds of British soldiers and those killed in the bombing campaigns in England who are untouched by events. Each has a story and a different set of evaluative criteria within which identity is forged. Each has their own conception of justice and injustice.

Philosophers, of course, have long ago identified these problems and some have attempted to provide strategies for overcoming them. Alasdair MacIntyre advocates Thomistic Aristotelianism on the basis that it has greater explanatory power than rival versions of moral inquiry such as Geneology or Encyclopaedia (MacIntyre A., 1990). Habermas has taken a very different view embedded as he is in the values of the Enlightenment project and has proposed a communicative mode of moral deliberation (Habermas J., 1984; 1987). In Jurisprudence the positivist tradition has sought to deal with irresolvable conflict in procedural ways (Boukema H.J.M., 1980;. Hart H.L.A., 1961; Rawls J., 1972; 1996). Yet others have sought insight in the various methods of conflict resolution (Attig T., *et al.* (eds), 1984; Avruch K., *et al.* (eds), 1991; Tidwell A., 1998). What these and other strategies have in common is the idea that that there must be some reasonable basis for accommodating radical difference, that radical difference need not ineluctably lead to conflict, that the conversation ought not to stop. And indeed, at least to this point I agree. Nevertheless, my suspicion is that we will not find the solution at the level of discussion about reasonableness. At this level everything remains contentious and a longer and harder road needs to be pursued.

So what if it turns out in the maelstrom of competing views about what is rational that it is something less susceptible to modern accounts of rationality that wins the day and keeps the conversation flowing. Feelings and emotions such as those we have when we affectively participate in stories and narratives I suspect are often enough more important than reason and indeed often enough reason follows in their wake. It is important to make it very clear here that I am not in any way advocating a wholesale rejection of rationality. I am making two interrelated points: (1) that in situations of stark philosophical disagreement Lewis's idea that all is opinion closes off the possibility of discussion, and this need not occur; and (2) that in cases of stark philosophical disagreement appeals to considerations based upon conflicting accounts of rationality offer no way forward. Indeed, the argument I will presently put forward will have the conclusion that emotions and feelings are constitutive elements in what counts as reasonable and that without a thorough exploration of the existential grounds for beliefs, together with a *paideia* of desire, no possibility of agreement is achievable. However, while I will not pursue these latter points in detail I want to reiterate the key idea that this discussion is offering a method to continue conversation.

This is the position, I believe, that Plato adopts, at least in the *Gorgias*.[52] The theme of the *Gorgias* is that of existential and not merely intellectual communication and the theme is developed within the context of war and battle (*polemou kai maches*) presaged by the opening line of the dialogue. Socrates sets himself up against what he conceives of as the corrupt and decadent state of Athenian society – the battle

---

52 In what follows I am deeply indebted to the reading of the *Gorgias* presented by Voegelin, E. (1957).

to be waged is over the soul of the youth (Voegelin E., 1957, 24). Gorgias, the Sophist and teacher of rhetoric will bring his formidable skills of oratory to the service of *Realpolitik*, while Socrates will point to the fundamental aspects of human connectedness which unite both individuals and communities. Gorgias will threaten violence, Socrates will seek to persuade by attempting to touch the existential core of his opponents and to keep conversation alive by opening up to the vista of the *pathemata*.

It is Socrates who introduces the fundamental question when he suggests to Chaerophon that he should ask of Gorgias 'Who he is?' (447d). As Voegelin so eloquently puts it this question cuts '... through the network of opinions, social ideas and ideologies. It is the question that appeals to the nobility of the soul.' It is a question that ultimately reveals a more sympathetic picture of Gorgias because despite his clever words Gorgias clearly feels uncomfortable that the 'unscrupulous and vulgar' Polus (Voegelin E., 1957, 25) is the direct product of his sophistical education.[53] The crucial outcome of the dialectical sparring between Polus and Socrates occurs when Polus is forced to the conclusion that a person who does evil acts contrary to his own interests and will. On the basis of this admission Polus's espousal of the virtues of the tyrant is proven to indicate the powerlessness of the tyrant. At this point Socrates presents the Platonic version of the Sermon on the Mount – doing injustice is worse than suffering injustice and doing injustice without undergoing restorative punishment is worse again (Plato, *Gorgias* 479d–e). Polus however is deeply reluctant to accept the conclusions of the dialectical sparring, as Voegelin points out:

> Polus is forced into admission, but the admission is sulky. He cannot deny that the conclusions follow from the premises, but the results are absurd (*atopa*) (480e).

> He is embarrassed, like Gorgias, but with a difference. For Gorgias still has some sense of decency; he is aware of the existential conflict underlying the intellectual clash, and his conscience worries him. Polus is too hardened to be worried by a conscience; he is intellectually beaten, but his defeat cannot touch off a spark of decency in him ... . The violent reaction comes from the activist, from Callicles, the enlightened politician. (Voegelin E., 1957, 28)

The key to understanding the depth of the problem adumbrated by Plato is that intellectual agreement does not bring in its wake existential understanding. The breaches in communication run far too deep. When Callicles threatens violence against Socrates (a threat that historically becomes realized since Callicles is one of the politicians who is involved in the prosecution of Socrates ultimately leading to the death penalty) the complete rupture of dialogue has been effected. The reasoned positions are upheld by commitments that go deeper than what can be understood to be rationally justifiable. Tragedy and violence are the consequences. It is at this point

---

53 In what follows I assume a familiarity with Plato's *Gorgias*. It is not my intention to provide here a reading of the *Gorgias* but to present the denouement of Plato's characterization of the problems of incommensurable beliefs and discourse in order to bring out his 'solution' to the problems.

under the threat of violence that Socrates opens the possibility of moving beyond the intellectual positions and rebuilding the bonds of communication. Plato does this through Socrates's elaboration of the notion of the *pathemata*.[54]

> Pathos is what men have in common, however variable it may be in its aspects and intensities. Pathos designates a passive experience, not an action; it is what happens to man, what he suffers, what befalls him fatefully and what touches him in his existential core – as for instance the experiences of *Eros* (481c–d). In their exposure to pathos all men are equal, though they may differ widely in the manner in which they come to grips with it and build the experience into their lives … . The community of pathos is the basis of communication. Behind the hardened, intellectually supported attitudes which separate men, lie the *pathemata* which bind them together. However false and grotesque the intellectual position may be, the pathos at the core has the truth of an immediate experience. If one can penetrate to this core and reawaken in a man the awareness of his *conditio humana*, communication in the existential sense becomes possible. (Voegelin E., 1957, 29–30)

There is, of course, no guarantee that the strategy of appealing to the pathemata will work. Indeed, Plato with the knowledge of Socrates's trial and death seeks a transcendental judgement of the dead in the *Gorgias*. Nevertheless, the vista of the *pathemata* leaves open further sources for communication and beyond the shrill clamor of rational assertion and counter-assertion.

In this part of the chapter I have attempted to show that there are grounds for deeply held and cherished positions that are not founded on reason, that our rationalizations are often enough reactive to experiences, and that these formative experiences can be so deeply embedded in our psyche and thus constitutive in fundamental ways to our identity that reason in the most fundamental sense is positively debarred from its appropriate role. I have argued that story-telling and appeals to the *pathemata* can rekindle existential communicative bonds and that some strategy of this sort is required if we are to deal seriously with moral and philosophical disagreements and thus to understand and effectively deal with terrorism.

Lying further behind this discussion is the beginnings of a sketch of what needs to be taken into account in a theory of rationality. The affective bonds and experiences we undergo are crucial to a theory of rationality so to engage at the intellectual level we need a pedagogy of emotion and most particularly desire. Perhaps the last word should be left to Plato's rehearsal of the issues:

> Only if the soul is well-ordered can it be called lawful (*nominos*) (504d); and only if it has the right order (*nomos*) is it capable of entering into communion (*koinonia*) (507e). The pathos is no more than a precondition for community; in order to actualise it, the *Eros* must be oriented towards the Good (*agathon*) and the disturbing passions must be restrained by *Sophrosyne*. If the lusts are unrestrained, man will live the life of a robber (*lestes*). Such a man cannot be the friend of God or other men, for he is incapable of communion, and who is incapable of communion is incapable of friendship (*philia*) (507e). *Philia* is the existential bond among men; and it is the bond between Heaven and Earth. Because *philia*

---

54 *Pathemata* is the plural form of the singular *pathos*. I explore the meanings below.

and order pervade everything, the universe is called *kosmos* (order) and not disorder or licence (*akosmia, akolasia*) (508a).

References

Attig T., *et al.* (eds) (1984), *Social Policy and Conflict Resolution* (Bowling Green: Bowling Green State University).

Avruch K., *et al.* (eds) (1991), *Conflict Resolution: Cross Cultural Perspectives* (New York: Greenwood Press).

Boukema H.J.M. (1980), *Judging: Towards a Rational Judicial Process* (Zwolle: W.E.J. Tjeenk).

Coady C.A.J. (2004), 'Terrorism and Innocence', *The Journal of Ethics*, 8, 37–58.

Chomsky N. (2005), 'Simple Truths, Hard Problems: thoughts on terror, justice and self-defense', *Philosophy*, 80, 18.

Habermas J. (1984 & 1987), *The Theory of Communicative Action*, Two Volumes (Beacon Press).

Hart H.L.A. (1961), *The Concept of Law* (Oxford: Clarendon Press).

Held V. (2004), 'Terrorism and War', *The Journal of Ethics*, 8, 59–75.

Lewis D. (1983), *Philosophical Papers,* Vol. 1 (Oxford: Oxford University Press), x and xi.

Lukes S. (2005), 'Liberal Democratic Torture', *British Journal of Political Science*, 36, 1–16.

MacIntyre A. (1981), *After Virtue* (London: Duckworth).

—— (1988), *Whose Justice? Which Rationality?* (Notre Dame: University of Notre Dame Press).

—— (1990), *Three Rival Versions of Moral Enquiry: Encyclopaedia, Genealogy, Tradition* (Notre Dame: University of Notre Dame Press).

Plato, *Gorgias.*

—— *Republic.*

Rawls J. (1972), *A Theory of Justice* (Oxford: Clarendon Press).

—— (1996), *Political Liberalism* (New York: Columbia University Press).

Tidwell A. (1998), *Conflict Resolved? A Critical Assessment of Conflict Resolution* (New York: Pinter).

Voegelin E. (1957), *Order and History*, Vol. III (Baton Rouge: Louisiana State University Press).

Waldron J. (2004), 'Terrorism and the Uses of Terror', *The Journal of Ethics*, 8, 5–35.

3.3   The Politics of Religious Violence

Rob Imre

In this part of the chapter I will analyze some specific aspects of the relationship between politics and religious violence and ask two overarching questions. First, is religious violence different from terrorism in general? Secondly, is religious violence, and by implication, political violence under the general rubric of 'terrorism', anathema to liberal democracy? Here I claim that all kinds of political violence are intimately linked to democracy and democratic change. Religious symbols and religious organizations have always been linked to change towards and away from democracies in the modern period. Witness the shifts in political legitimation in Poland from the 1950s to the 1980s and the cooptation of Orthodox Christian symbols in Russia by the Bolsheviks. I also claim that there is, and will continue to be in the near future, a clear *modus operandi* for groups seeking, and eventually gaining political and social change, by the use of force, in all kinds of societies. I also claim that we are probably witnessing the change of said violence into a generalized kind of religious violence. This means that the danger of the 'new' version of religious terrorist is that they are performing for God and not for the international media. Thus, by the time we have realized that all we need to do to shut down the 1970s version of the PLO is to not publicise anything they do, the world has passed us all by. Today, it is immaterial whether or not the global media sees bin Laden, or other similar manifestations, the terrorism will continue in the eyes of God and the internet. If religious terrorism becomes the dominant mode of violent political change, then there is no real way to stop the phenomenon, except by divine intervention or an extremely controlled technological environment that would alter our societies in the developed world so that they are unrecognizable.

Much has been made of the organizing force of religion in the contemporary world. There are those that argue that in the post-Cold War era, religion has replaced the certainties of the past and has become the predominant active force in organizing people in opposition to each other. Indeed, in some cases, the clash of civilizations thesis has replaced ideas about grand conflict in that empires no longer compete, but rather civilizations, in the guise of religions and with a totalizing force of 'culture', operate to draw lines of opposition and as such demarcate conflicts around the world. Thus Islam and the 'Islamic world' becomes the main opposition to 'the West' and Judeo-Christian values secularized in the contemporary world. But this is a gross over-simplification of conflicts that have their roots in historical grievances, instrumental politics and history, and deeply ingrained social inequalities. I argue here that at least two things are present that demonstrate the false assumptions about the relationships between civil society and religion: first, that civil society as it develops historically in any part of the world is not anathema to violence and violent expression in the so-called 'East', 'West', or any other distinction we choose to divide the world; secondly, that religion and religious beliefs, ideas and practices, may or may not act in conjunction with civil society's development, regression, or acceptance. As a result, I argue that it is a false claim to suggest that civil society and religion are in opposition, just as it is a false claim to suggest that there are 'Western' and 'Asian' dichotomies of dealing with the prevalence of religion as a social force operating with/against civil society. Religion can become an intimate part of national identity, such as Poland and Malaysia, or it can form a part of a shared religious and sometimes conflictual national identity as in India and the United States.

Mixing the Terms: Battling for Symbols

When we talk about civil society, we can also use a number of revolutions to demonstrate the development and change of how a variety of societies around the world have brought about the construction of a particular form of civil society. If we discuss the Russian Revolution of 1917, we can see that there is a case in which the notion of positing civil society against religion and/or a combination of those against the 'bourgeoisie', is a simplification of the complex reality. As Figes and Kolonitskii demonstrate in their work *Interpreting the Russian Revolution: the language and Symbols of 1917*, we see that the ideological shifts are predicated on the use of a particular set of symbols, and that these symbols can operate to replace each other quite neatly. It is not difficult to 'supersede' an Orthodox Russian cross with a hammer and sickle, nor is it difficult to demonstrate that the move to attempt to incorporate the peasantry as against the landowners and the bourgeoisie was done through the use of symbols that began with the iconography of Russian Orthodoxy and then moved into the hagiography of the Russian communists.

The Soviets subsumed into their march of history earlier revolutions, most particularly the French Revolution. Unlike the Soviets, who implicitly created a new Soviet religion that was a partial 'transubstantiation' of Russian Orthodoxism, the Jacobins explicitly created a new religion in their attempt to replace Catholicism in France. Although both groups attempted to purge their revolutionary civil societies of the old religion the French Revolutionary and Soviet models were not secular even when they argued they were. If anything the French model is janus-faced one where religion is thought to lie outside of schools and public institutions but where a civic and nationalist religion inhabits the place of Old Catholicism. The concept of civil society as cut off from religion, then, has serious limitations, even when the most extreme models are considered.

Another so-called secular state is the United States of America. Like France, the separation of church and state is meant to be present at the inception of the modern state. And yet the religiosity of American political culture is often remarked upon by commentators and critics from inside the US political system as well as those outside of its participatory sphere. The American Revolution, like the French and Russian Revolutions was as much a religious dispute as a political one and religion has been a key factor in American politics to this day. Scholars influenced by Marxist secularism in the 20th century wrote religion out of these events (or contained it in discussions on the confiscation of church property in the case of France). What these Western secular models do is pretend that religion is not a force in their institutions and political culture even when it has been historically a shaping force and continues to exist as such. One example of this flaw is found in the most extreme interpretation of the Western secular model – as interpreted in France – and the dispute over hijab wearing by Muslim girls in French schools. Because it is seen as an overtly religious expression, French officials claim to be personally 'offended' by those who choose to don the hijab. Further, the claim is that this is a direct threat to French civil society, when Catholic nuns and Catholic and Buddhist monks are not required to adhere to the same rules. There are many more issues here but we are not looking at the hijab specifically and a comparative analysis on the reception of a resurgence of Islam in 'Western' and/or 'secular' society might shed more light on this. The point here is that secular/civil societies are at odds with a select few 'symbols' that threaten the monopoly of power.

There are a number of other considerations when discussing the issue of the relationship between civil society and religion. For example, we could discuss liberation theologists in Latin America who were decidedly 'religious' and in many cases quite doctrinaire, Catholics, who sought to promote a kind of 'civil democracy' by advocating the overthrow of military dictatorships and bringing peasants out of their dire poverty. Many were assassinated, the most famous being Bishop Romero, nuns were abducted and raped, and all in very Catholic and quite religious countries. We could argue here that a semi-orthodox religion was operating to develop civil society and democracy, and to reject the control successfully instituted by dictatorships in the region. It is a good contrast to questions about the rise of Islam and it allows us to ask the question: what is the problem with Islam? Is it the Imams, is it Islam as a religion, is it Islam as a social force? Further, does it make a difference if it is a 'right and good' challenge to civil society? For example, the challenge of American Islam in the 1960s led mainly by African Americans who lived their lives as second-class citizens, or the liberation theologist activists, or anti-Soviet Muslims, or Albanian Muslims challenging the Yugoslav civil order and so on. Once we begin to peel back the layers we see that in the modern period we have a series of conflicting examples of civil society and religious forces. It is not such a clear positing of a dichotomy between the two.

In Sri Lanka, it has become increasingly more obvious that Buddhism as a religion, and Sri Lankan Sinhalese Buddhism as a cultural force, are operating to (re)create Sri Lanka as a mono-faith, mono-cultural nation-state. In this case, religion freed from the constraints of the doctrine, freed from the constraints of the doctrinaire Buddhists, have placed the faithful in a position in which they must choose between either their faith, or a civil society as defined by multi-lingual, multicultural, multi-theistic contemporary society. The Bhikku doctrine has shifted from the rest of Buddhism's teachings in order to involve themselves directly in the politics of the day in Sri Lanka. In the Sri Lankan case, we see that religion as a cultural force is in fact operating as a complex social force. That is, unlike liberation theology, Sinhalese Buddhism seeks to provide a doctrine for those who hold the reins of power and develop a spiritual justification for that hold on power. Our problem here in the contemporary world is that the intractable conflict in Sri Lanka does not seem to be getting any closer to reducing the violence and is the largest case of terrorist activity apart from the 'insurgency' in Iraq in recent years. Indeed, without the Iraqi 'insurgency', Sri Lanka would have continued to experience the high levels of violence, despite attempts to broker peace (by Norwegian representatives for example), and without being directly affected, the world could easily turn a blind eye.[55]

K.M. de Silva (1981) completed his work, *A History of Sri Lanka* just before the main parts of the ethnic conflict began. This book is an important publication because it demonstrates the understanding of the development of Sri Lankan history as understood by the intellectual elite during the 1970s and 1980s. The work provides a foreground to the ethnic conflicts which erupted in 1983. After de Silva's work, a number of books were published which questioned the development of the modern nation-state in the region. For example, Homi Bhabha (1990) has contributed a number of works including his pivotal study *The Nation and Narration*. Bhabha provides a framework to understand the way in which histories of nations, coupled with various myths of peoples, combine to point to a particular view that can be contested. Further, Partha Chatterjee (1993) in *The Nation and its Fragments* provides a critique of the attempt at simplistic unities of peoples under one religion and/or one ethnic group. Chatterjee's claim is that a de-centering of the idea of the nation-state can begin by looking at some specific regional histories. This de-centering can possibly lead to alternative ways of looking at the nation-state; one that need not be the homogenizing worldview offered by the 19th-century understanding of the nation-state. So if we are examining the current role of religion in this process, we see that Sri Lanka is attempting to create this homogeneity through Sinhalese Buddhism.

The roots of the current ethnic violence can be easily traced back to the Bandaranaike regime in the late 1950s. Bandaranaike's socialist policies as well as the National Language Act of 1956 can be described as the first attempt to consolidate power and bring the newly formed Sri Lanka together under the umbrella of a 'modern' nation-state. It was here, in the years between 1956 and 1959, that Bandaranaike sought to make manifest the notion that is so basic in Sinhalese, that the words for 'nation', 'race' and 'people' were synonymous. However, this is not unique to Sinhalese, neither in terms of the problem of original definitions nor in the problems of the unwillingness or incapacity of political leaders to take this argument further. There are examples of political leaders stuck in similar problems around the world in which differing political groups, sometimes emerging political groups, have significantly different concepts of what it means to have a political idea of group belonging. In our opinion, the most remarkable failure of Bandaranaike's regime is his inability to promote a set of culturally responsive policies to address the idea of ethnic cohesiveness of Sri Lanka. Yugoslavia provides a similar case. Here, we are referring to the concept of the unity of a people and how that is brought together or separated by notions of linguistic nationalism or by notions of separated or unified cultural continuity. For example, during particular time periods in the South Balkans, Croatian political leaders saw the Bosnian Muslims as *de facto* Croatians. The argument was that since most Bosnian Muslims were people who had voluntary chosen Islam as a religion under more 'liberal' policies during the Ottoman period, they were ethnically Croatian, certainly Slav, and probably not Serb. This history

---

55 This is precisely my point about statecraft in an earlier chapter. Without having direct interests, and/or threats from, Sri Lanka, most of the world ignores the conflict.

can be written a number of different ways and if we choose to emphasize periods of conflict, then the contemporary manifestation of national culture can thus be one of conflict, and vice versa. Homi Bhabha also touches upon this issue in his *The Nation and Narration* but he does so from a slightly different perspective. Bhabha's view is that the old nation-states of the West have now found themselves reliant upon some version of 'Othering' and this has been reproduced the world over. In Sri Lanka's case, we see this in the development of the 'other' in what Bhabha would call the foundationalist fiction that all modern nation-states must perform and reproduce. In performing this, religion may or may not play a role as a social force. Religion might operate as a useful force for creating this homogeneity, or it might resist the domination of elites, or any number of things.

As such, one can claim that without the inception of the Sinhala-only Act, we would not have seen the cohesion of the Tamil minority concerns that erupted as a particular form of ethnic violence. Bandaranaike seemingly did not realize that post-colonial Sri Lanka was a plural society, that is to say a society with multiple languages, religions, and ways of life, and that to impose a 'single identity' would entrench conflict, regardless of historical claims by various groups. In all cases where pluralism was recognized in some manner during the development of the modern nation-state, we see the mitigation of conflict, including violent conflict. We can also claim that non-recognition of self-identified minority groups within a pluralist society will lead to a number of possibly quite serious problems such as disgruntled intellectuals and elites who might eventually lay claim to the legitimacy of violence such as the case in Yugoslavia in the 1980s, the masses riding a wave of cultural renaissance engaging in protest that eventually legitimates the use of violence such as was the case in Quebec in Canada, a contracting labor market such as was the case in Australia in which a hostile environment in the 1950s and 1960s led to migrants from Southern Europe returning to the European continent during post-World War II reconstructions and causing labor shortages in Australia.

The political problem here is one that modern nation-states have grappled with all over the world. The argument goes something like this: we have an 'other' among us. This group of people has representatives of their larger community externally, that is external to the borders of our nation-state, and they are in contact with this larger group to the detriment of the local group. So it was not simply the case that Tamil and Sinhalese were now self-defining along linguistic lines that were meant to separate people in the modern version of Sri Lanka, nor was it simply the case that there was a minority and majority. It was also factored in that the Tamils had greater numbers in India, who by definition, not necessarily political reality, were meant to be members of the same group. We also see this in the Hungarian case in Romania for example, as well as in Turkey with both Kurds and Armenians. In the Hungarian case, this has been a problem throughout the modern period, at least since the mid-1800s, and in the recent referendum, Hungarians have voted to deny special rights to Romanian citizens of ethnic Hungarian origin, dispelling the idea that ethnic ties are always stronger than civic ties. In the Armenian case, Ataturk, and the brigade of Young Turks before him, successfully used the Armenian history as a case of manufactured political dissent. False collaborations with the Russians, and various enemies of the state, coupled with a special version of 'secular' Islam, brought about a genocide in which several hundreds of thousands of innocent Armenian villagers were slaughtered and attempts at erasing their presence from the modern Turkey were acted upon.

The problems encountered by the Bandaranaike regime is similar to the classic problem encountered by the decolonizing and post-colonial regimes of number of nation-states in the post-World War II period. Power, interests, competing political parties and individuals were wrapped up in the necessity to join the new world order in a situation in which the Westphalian nation-state was the only perceived way in which to successfully do so. As Matossian (1962) points out in the emblematic examination of this problem in that the intellectuals and political leaders of these decolonizing nation-states were faced with three questions: '(1) What is to be borrowed from the West? (2) What is to be retained from the nation's past? (3) What characteristics, habits, and products of the masses are to be encouraged?' In this context, we are left with all of the classical dilemmas of the modern nation-state. For example, who are the 'true' people? Are they the peasants as so many European nation-states have self-defined? Are they the great men (as men are usually written in as the 'founders' in most historical approaches to the development of the nation-state), the achievers who are the epitomes of the people? Are they the partially Westernized intellectuals? And how do we organize all of these people through the development of the foundational myth and common understanding of what the nation-state means in the modern terms of the concept?

In the case of Sri Lanka, the idea that Tamils as a people have a separate history or the converse idea that the Sinhalese have some form of separate history, directly implying, from both parties, that there is an ancient development of this separation, is not a pre-modern concept. In fact, we see very similar things in the attempts to develop singular identities in a number of nation-states in the modern period both in South Asia as well as outside of the region. Just as Partha Chatterjee claims in *The Nation and Its Fragments,* 'the idea that "Indian nationalism" is synonymous with "Hindu nationalism" is not the vestige of some pre-modern religious conception. It is an entirely modern, rationalist, and historicist idea. Like other modern ideologies, it allows for the central role of state in the modernisation of society and strongly defends the state's unity and sovereignty.' And like Chatterjee's claims about India, Sri Lanka has similar problems in terms of its development of linguistic nationalism supported by the Buddhist Sinhala revival and the overall renaissance of Sri Lankan culture in the 1950s and 1960s. As such, the religious force is not only an afterthought, but becomes a force that seeks to disentangle a group of people that have been entangled for centuries, again, much like Yugoslavia, and so this is neither a clash of civilizations nor a situation in which religion is operating against civil society. Sinhalese Buddhism, led by the Bhikku's, is a social force that is looking to reorganize civil society, not rejecting democracy, but instead creating a French style 'secularized' state with a mono-faith view, which is ultimately a failure, as witnessed by the ongoing violence.

Transnationalism and Diasporic Terror

Finally, I discuss here the effects of transnational forces and diasporic communities on religion and changing religious social forces. An interesting South Asian diaspora is the Sikh diaspora, especially the one in Canada. I suggest here that it is interesting because Sikhs are a very visible minority with cultural and religious practices that must necessarily set them apart from the majority of Canadians. Sikhs will have all of the classical 'problematic' features of a migrant community in that they will seek to maintain a separate language, in some cases schools for their children, a separate and closed religion, a number of exceptions to their diet and dress, and being visibly South Asian with long beards on many of the men, will immediately identify them as a minority group. Further, many Sikhs carry with them the myth of being a 'militant race' of people and have kept this idea as a key component of their identity. Combined with a number of legitimate grievances against the Indian nation-state, this has combined for a potent mix of simmering conflict and social upheaval. However, I argue here that despite all of this, Sikhs in Canada (and elsewhere, but I am discussing Canada for a particular reason that will become clear below) represent a successful non-integrationalist, non-assimilationist, diaspora community capable of self-sustaining its religion and language while *not* opposing or being detrimental to civil society in Canada (as well as other migrant nations such as Australia, Britain, and the United States).

In the early 1980s some of the unresolved political tensions of partition in India resurfaced in that Sikhs were becoming more interested in separate communities from the Hindu majority. Communal violence began to flare up again and various domestic political factions in India were calling for Khalistan to be created as a separate state within India with the possibility of independence later. The Hindu-dominated armed forces in India razed the Golden Temple, the Sikh holy shrine, with the suspicion that militants were using the temple as a cover for smuggling arms. Sikh communities around the world were understandably upset by this turn of events and many began to advocate a hard-line stance against the Indian government. This eventually led to the assassination of the Prime Minister by her own Sikh bodyguards. The violence spilled out onto the streets in India and there was a great fear that this would also ripple through the diaspora. Then in 1985, Sikh extremists placed a bomb on an Air India flight leaving Canada, bound for London, and the plane exploded over the Atlantic Ocean before it had a chance to land at Heathrow airport. All of the 329 passengers and crew died aboard the plane. The bombings were meant to be a response to the increasing levels of violence in India against Sikhs and the planes themselves were said to have undergone the most sophisticated of checks available at that time. Nothing was detected in the usual x-raying of baggage in either Toronto or Montreal where the plane was flying from and it simply disintegrated in the air above the Atlantic Ocean.

Sikhs have followed Khalsa in various parts of the world and have done so in opposition to, as well as in conjunction with, the prevailing ideology, disposition, and/or religious orientation of the nation-state in which they find themselves. The question here is whether or not transnationalism and the current state of diaspora and diasporic politics will posit religion as a social force that operates against democratic civil society, or alternatively will bolster the development of democratic civil society, or perhaps something else. The Sikh case, particularly in Canada, and to some extent the UK and the USA, demonstrates that religion and civil society can work in conjunction to produce free and inclusive public polities even in the face of terrorism. The Sikh case also demonstrates that we do indeed have choices to make and can stand up to terror of all kinds, principally through an open-society approach.

In India in particular, and in South Asia in general, there have been problems with Sikh militants, especially those making the claim that the Sikh homeland in the Punjab, Khalistan, should be regarded as a goal for true Sikhs. We know about the assassination of Indira Gandhi by her Sikh bodyguards as well as the role that Sikh militants played in the Air India bombing that took place in Canada in June of 1985. All 329 people on board the plane were killed and the usual sorts of bungling was uncovered by investigative journalists well after the tragedy. Aside from the particulars of the actual investigation of the terrorist activities, I claim here that the reaction by the Canadian public, by policy-makers, and by the Sikh community itself, demonstrates that there is a capacity for 'Western' secular (civil) societies to accommodate orthodoxy in religion and vice versa. Orthodoxy, it seems, can still be orthodox in the middle of a multi-religious, multi-ethnic, and multicultural society. While these are difficult choices of accommodation, especially when such a terrible tragedy has occurred, it can still happen that groups that have radical elements can be accommodated in a multicultural society.

In the context of Canadian multiculturalism, the quest is to make cultures visible. In contrast to French responses to the hijab in school for example, Ontario had students and teachers demonstrating for the right to enjoy diversity and policy makers and administrators stating clearly that religion could also be a public celebration. Further, after the Air India bombing, there had been some internecine strife in the Sikh community throughout Canada. An editor of a Sikh newspaper was murdered in 1992 and there had been links to militants who were smuggling arms into Canada and making various threats about terrorist activity. The responses of civil society, that is the public response and the response of policy makers included making exceptions for the wearing of the turban in all sorts of functions, increasing Sikh police presence in areas where Sikhs had migrated, opening up political organizations to include South Asians and make South Asians visible in prominent political positions, demonstrate to the Canadian public that Sikhs were not a threat to society, and even to ensure that the RCMP had Sikh candidates. The Sikh community responded by engaging in school exchange programs, opening up religious holidays and various activities to the public, and ensuring that life was made difficult for extremists threatening peace and prosperity in Canada. The various Sikh communities sought to protect themselves, not by closing in on themselves, as this would have delivered secrecy in to the hands of possible extremists and militants, but rather chose to open up to the Canadian society at large and thus made it quite difficult to house an extremist set of views within their own communities since the 'outside world' of Canadian civil society got to know them a lot better.

The case of the Sikh diaspora, and the position of Sikh individuals and communities within India itself, offers us a clear demonstration of the capacity for contemporary nation-states of all kinds to adapt to demands of particular groups as well as the capacity for these groups to work in cooperation with the nation-state in which they find themselves. In this case we see that the Canadian government at various levels has managed to make exceptions for Sikh communities and individuals and has provided a flexibility unseen in many other liberal democracies. This has operated to bolster civil society in the Canadian case in that diversity is made public, diversity is shown to be possible even when citizens need to be given special rights according to their religion, and civil society is even bolstered in the face of terrorist attacks. I often wonder what would have happened in the current climate of fear. Would the Canadian and UK governments, and then perhaps the US and Australian, have taken more drastic measures and developed internment programs for Sikhs? Would we have seen assets seized, pointed house searches, arbitrary arrests, and detentions without trial? It is quite interesting that this did not occur and that, in general, a more open and tolerant policy, with both sides initiating dialogues of all kinds has ensured the avoidance of further tragedy.

Conclusion

The relationship between religion and civil society is a complex one. Religious violence may be a manifestation of a conflict between social forces that oppose each other, religious leaders and political leaders for example, or religious violence may be supported by nation-states with the purpose of re-ordering civil society as in the case of Sri Lanka. Civil society in its broadest definition may benefit from religion and even from religious violence in a number of ways and there need not be an antagonistic relationship, as is the case in India. Further, it is clear that the notion of a 'Western' civil society opposed to an 'Asian' religious force is not very helpful in explaining how these social forces act upon or in conjunction with each other. Religious violence is not confined to a particular part of the world nor is it confined to a particular type of operation within nation-states. The assumption that the 'secularization' of religion, that is the move from doctrine to culture, will somehow benefit civil society may or may not be the case depending on where an individual or a group may situate themselves politically. We have seen in Sri Lanka that the global religion of Buddhism has become a version of cultural chauvinism and as such the move from the 'doctrine' to society at large (or a proto-civil society) in Sri Lanka has in fact provided the majority with the ability to extract and/or reject a minority.

The assumption that maintaining the doctrine, keeping religious and cultural practices separate, must necessarily lead to a kind of civil disorder is clearly not the case as we have seen with Sikhs in Canada. Here we see that even in the case of extreme violence there is still the capacity for contemporary multicultural nation-states to be flexible enough to accommodate difference and allow for exceptions of all sorts. It must be said that the Sikh communities have also worked hard to accommodate themselves to a new environment and that this is not in this case, nor can it be in general, a one-way relationship of singular accommodation. The general conclusion here is that there is a great diversity in this relationship between civil society and religion and that the complexities must be drawn out in order for us to come to a better understanding of them. It is clear that a retreat into some version of singular, uniform, identity in a nation-state is not helpful to cooperation, and religion and religious cultural forces as well as individuals can choose to cooperate with those around them or choose to engage in conflictual relationships. It is here that multiculturalism still has great relevance as a general approach to the development of civil society.

References

Abeyratne, S. 'Economic Roots of Political Conflict: The Case of Sri Lanka,' *The World Economy*, Vol. 27, No. 8.

Asian Development Bank, *Country Economic Review: Sri Lanka: II. Short- and Medium-Term Economic Prospects and Policy Issues* <http://www.adb.org/ Documents/CERs/SRI/2001/cer_sri203.asp>.

Bartholomeusz, T.J. and de Silva, C.R. (eds) (1998), *Buddhist Fundamentalism and Minority Identities in Sri Lanka* (Albany, NY; State University of New York Press).

Bhabha, K. Homi (ed.) (1990), *Nation and Narration* (London: Routledge).

Bloom, M. (2005), *Dying to Kill: The Allure of Suicide Terror* (New York: Columbia University of Princeton).

Brown, Judith (1994), *Modern India: The Origins of an Asian Democracy* (Oxford: Oxford University Press).

Chandra, Bipan, *et al.* (eds) (2000), *India after Independence: 1947–2000* (Delhi: Penguin India).

Chatterjee, Partha (1997), *State and Politics in India* (Delhi: Oxford University Press).

—— (1993), *The Nation and its Fragments: Colonial and postcolonial histories* (Princeton, NJ: Princeton University Press).

Combs, Cindy (2006), *Terrorism in the Twenty-First Century* (New Jersey: Pearson).

Crenshaw, Martha. (1998) 'The Logic of Terrorism: Terrorist Behaviour as a Product of Strategic Choice' in Walter Reich (ed.), *Origins of Terrorism* (Woodrow Wilson Center Press).

De Silva, K.M. (1981), *A History of Sri Lanka* (Delhi: Oxford University Press).

Dirks, Nicholas B. (2001), *Castes of Mind: Colonialism and the Making of Modern India* (Princeton, NJ: Princeton University Press).

Edirisinha, R. (2005) 'Multination Federalism and Minority Rights in Sri Lanka' in Kymlicka, W. and Baogang, H. (eds), *Multiculturalism in Asia* (Oxford University Press).

Feroz, A. (2000), *Ethnicity and Politics in Pakistan* (Karachi: Oxford University Press).

Gambetta, D. (2005), *Making Sense of Suicide Missions* (Oxford: Oxford University Press).

Gurr, T.D. (1993), *Minorities at Risk: A Global View of Ethnopolitical Conflicts* (Washington DC, Institute of Peace Press).

Hasan, M. (ed.) (1993), *India's Partition: Process, Strategy and Mobilization* (Delhi: Oxford University Press).

Imre, Robert (2006) 'Diaspora and Security Dilemmas: The War on Terror and the "Other" in Australia', in Vanden Driesen, C. and Crane, R. (eds), *Diaspora: The Australasian Experience* (New Delhi: Prestige), pp. 317–30.

International Crisis Group, *Sri Lanka: The Failure of the Peace Process*, Asia Report No. 124, 28 November 2006.

Jaffrelot, C. (2003), *India's Silent Revolution: The Rise of the Lower Castes in North India* (London: Hurst & Company).

Jalal, A. (1995), *Democracy and Authoritarianism in South Asia* (Cambridge: Cambridge University Press).

Jeganathan, P. (1995), 'Authorising History, Ordering Land: The Conquest of Anuradhapuraâ', in Jeganathan, P and Q. Ismail (eds), *Unmaking the Nation: The Politics of Identity and History in Modern Sri Lanka* (Colombo: Social Scientists Association).

Jones, O.B. (2003), *Pakistan: Eye of the Storm* (New Haven: Yale University Press).

Kapferer, B. (2002), 'Ethnic Nationalism and the Discourses of Violence in Sri Lanka,' *Journal of Transnational and Crosscultural Studies*, Vol 9, Issue 1, April.

—— (1989), 'Nationalist ideology and a comparative anthropology,' *Ethnos*, Vol. 54.

—— (1988), *Legends of People, Myths of State: Violence, Intolerance and Political Culture in Sri Lanka and Australia* (London and Washington: Smithsonian Institution Press).

Kemper, S. (1991), *The Presence of the Past: Chronicles, Politics and Culture in Sinhala Life* (Ithaca and London: Cornell University Press).

Kymlicka, W., *Culturally Responsive Policies*, paper prepared for 2004 UNHDR, online <http://hdr.undp.org/docs/events/global_forum/2005/papers/Will_Kymlicka.pdf>.

Lorenzen, D.N. (1999), 'Who Invented Hinduism?' in 10 *Comparative Studies in Society and History*.

Malcolm, N. (1994), *Bosnia: A Short History* (New York: New York University Press).

Matossian, M. (1962), in Kautsky, J.H. (ed.), *Political Change in Underdeveloped Countries* (New York: John Wiley).

Menski, W. (2002), 'Hindu Law as a Religious System' in Andrew Huxley (ed.), *Religion, Law and Tradition: Comparative Studies in Religious Law* (London: Routledge Curzon).

Oren, M. (2002), *Six Days of War: June 1967 and the Making of the Modern Middle East* (Oxford University Press).

Sen, A. (2005), *The Argumentative Indian: Writings on Indian History, Culture and Identity* (London: Allen Lane).

Smith, J. (2004), *Federalism* (Vancouver: UBC Press).

Wilson, J. (1988), *The Break-up of Sri Lanka: The Sinhalese–Tamil Conflict* (Honolulu, USA: University of Hawaii Press).

Ziring, L. (1997), *Pakistan in the Twentieth Century: A Political History* (Karachi: Oxford University Press).

Chapter 4

Counter-Terrorism:
Public/Social Policy, Social
Engineering and Just War

4.1 Bungle in, Bungle out, Muddle through

Rob Imre

In this part of the chapter I provide an assessment of some administrative, public policy, and social policy approaches that are designed to deal with terrorists and terror organizations. I use some key examples such as the FLQ and Sikh terrorist organizations in Canada, the RAF in West Germany, the Red Brigades in Italy, the Weather Underground in the USA and a number of others. I claim here that modern and post-modern bureaucracies are very limited in their capacity to deal with the terrorist phenomenon. But the reason for this, as I have demonstrated elsewhere, is not that there is a lack of 'security' or capacity for 'clamping down' on various groups. I claim here that the move from the banalization of human experience (characterized by the post-World War II period) to the 'governmentality' of the late modern period (characterized by the post-Cold War era), has provided us with both limitations and opportunities in how we deal with terrorism. Underlying this part of the chapter is at least one central claim that modern bureaucracies have the capacity to bungle these major problems, and that muddling through will be democracy's saving grace.

In this discussion, I examine the possibility of effective counter-terrorism measures. I claim at the outset that most counter-terrorism laws are ineffective and relying on a legal position to challenge a socio-political problem will result in possible *post facto* punishments of groups or individuals engaged in violent conduct, but will act as a deterrent measure for these groups in only a very limited manner. It is akin to the illegality of the act of suicide, and in this case suicide bombing. Here, I am not arguing about the civil liberties aspects of the new anti-terrorist legislation that so many nation-states have adopted, nor am I discussing whether we should support these new laws or if we should be concerned with abuses of power in this context. These are questions answered in another part of this book. Instead, I should like to analyze some of the contextual problems that arise when we seek to stop terrorist organizations and I should like to ask questions about what might work against terrorism as a socio-political phenomenon. Here I examine three specific aspects of new legislation that most nation-states find in common. In examining these aspects, I am doing so not as a legal scholar but rather as a social scientist examining the phenomenon of the procedure surrounding the legislation. I shall go on to look at three specific 'solutions' that I claim need to be discussed in response to the legal changes in order to question the future direction of global society.

Judges Decisions

In the new legislations we are relying on a particular legal solution that is placed in the hands of justices (judges) in Australia, the United States and the United Kingdom. We are seeing the claim that judges will decide upon various aspects of the new anti-terror laws. One of the problems with these kinds of legal solutions is that there is an assumption that there is a kind of Rawlsian right procedure. Once that right procedure is in place, the judge can follow it and all will be well. But we know that right procedure does not ensure justice. Will there be judges who in turn stand up and say, after following the right procedure, that we have not achieved justice? Right procedure also takes away individual responsibility. If justice is not served, who will do more than claim 'I was following the procedure'? Here, it seems clear that political leaders are relying on the conservative voting currents of the public in some of these nation-states to help justify this position in that there is an underlying assumption that people in positions of authority must necessarily know what they are doing. In both Australia and the United States for example, the post-September 11th climate has allowed both Prime Minister Howard and the Attorney-General Ruddock to claim that placing writs in the hands of experienced justices will mean that the correct decisions will be made.

Interestingly, given the trends in post-World War II liberal democracies, it is easy to conceive of a situation in which short-term political campaigning is opposed to the long-term deliberative tasks of the respective judiciaries. This is interesting because it will change the dynamic of politics in a number of liberal democratic states by making the politics of the day quite conservative as has been the case in a number of nation-states such as Australia and the United States, and the various justices placed in a situation in which they are the defenders of democracy and liberal values even if they have been appointed based on their 'tendency to vote conservative' on given social issues. What I mean by this is to say that it appears that justices have learned a number of lessons from dealing with terrorists and organized crime syndicates in the UK (the IRA), Italy (Cosa Nostra 'Mafia' as well as the Red Brigades), the United States (a number of crime syndicates) to show that it is always better for democratic institutions to preserve their liberal heritage than to provide extra-judicial authority to judges. It is interesting that politicians have made attempts to justify their own attacks on civil liberties by appealing to socially conservative judges and judiciaries, who have overwhelmingly rejected these claims and have said they intend to oppose this kind of poorly thought out legislation that has come about in response to recent terrorist campaigns. So bungling in to create laws to crack down on terrorist individuals and organizations in liberal democracies has seen a backlash from the judges involved in possibly judging these decisions. Rather than a 'power grab' by judiciaries in liberal democracies, we have seen the opposite. This is quite similar to the 'judicial activism' exhibited in the case of land claims and resource access claims by Aboriginal and Indigenous groups in Australia and the United States. Judges decisions have gone in favor of the weak and not the strong. Aboriginal groups in Australia have long had the sympathy of the judiciary. Early indications are that justices in liberal democracies around the world are not in favor of their own new powers. The Haneef case in Australia is yet another example of this in which the justices involved continually opposed the claims made by the Australian federal government and sought to dilute both the judicial powers as well as the powers of the minister for immigration to detain as well as deport Dr Mohammed Haneef.

Preventative Detention

Prisons and various modes of human incarceration have also been used by a number of human societies through the ages. We inherit a specific kind of detention in the modern period and that specific kind of incarceration developed into full blown 'concentration camps' in which we take human populations, label them as problematic for modern society, and separate them from the general population. This began in two historical conflicts, the Boer War and the Cuban prisons in the wars of liberation in the early part of the 1900s. This developed further throughout the colonial world as the Great Powers of Europe saw the need to incarcerate parts of their populations. The problem here is not a legal one, in terms of civil and human rights, but rather a structural problem in examining the socio-politics of the problems surrounding the inceptions of various kinds of detentions. In this case, we will most certainly see the misapplication of detention measures that will lead to abuses of various kinds, and we will also see the general neglect of the people being detained.

The history of detention of all kinds is also a history of the abuse of the intention of that said detention. For example, during the World War II, we see a vast majority of cases of detained peoples experiencing a kind of benign neglect. That is to say, they become the forgotten, the reasons for their detention are not catalogued, they are shifted around from location to location, they have their lives so disrupted that they can never recover, they are people who have the stigma of potential terrorist attached to them for the rest of their lives and so on. It is not the case that we will see a humane treatment of people, it is the case that preventative temporary detention does not work to stop terrorist organizations from spreading violence but it certainly disrupts the lives of many ordinary citizens. 'Detention', that is to say legal incarceration, of any kind immediately presupposes that there is a power relationship between a subordinate group and a superordinate group of people. The idea that we can claim a 'temporary super/sub-ordination' is a tenuous one.

Paranoid nation-states are looking to justify detention measures rather than justify methods to stop violence. Detention of potential 'violent offenders' has a number of obvious problems associated with it that has been commented upon by civil rights organizations, but my focus here is to ask questions about where this might take us in a socio-political direction. That is to say, how will this effect politics and societies that adopt this process as a regular way of dealing with potential problems with terrorism. Preventative detention is a good way to enhance paranoia and social disruption. It is a poor way to ensure that violence is stopped. Political violence can also occur if specific people are in prison and organizations can commit terrorist acts even if their members have been incarcerated. Political terrorism and religious violence cannot be stopped by systems of detention and must instead be rooted out by destroying the very organizations from below. In the case of the Italian Cosa Nostra and the Canadian problem with the Quebec Liberation Front in the 1970s, the organizations were successfully countered not through detention of large groups of people, nor through 'preventative detention' measures in which justices were given greater scope to incarcerate – the activities of these organizations were already illegal, just as plotting to explode bombs is an illegal activity – rather it is through infiltration and investigation, not incarceration, that terrorist organizations such as these can be countered.

Sunset Clauses

Taxes of various kinds used by modern-nation states are filled with 'sunset clauses.' In fact one might go so far as to say that the very idea of taxation is one giant 'sunset clause' in which modern governments of all stripes are prepared to vary in the slightest possible way but are completely unwilling to make major changes about. If we situate the discussion in historical terms, most of the time taxes were designed to finance wars. The new Commonwealth of the Thirteen Colonies immediately following the rebellion against the British because of taxation, 'no taxation without representation' being the slogan of the day, kept the taxes in place in order to fight the British, and to start building and buying naval warships. The British, in turn, used taxes as temporary measures to finance various wars with the French and so on. The point is that all nation-states had the same rhetoric surrounding taxation in the pre-Keynesian period. Taxes were meant to be temporary measures to fund specific initiatives. I am not arguing that taxes are a bad idea, a good idea, or anything in between. My argument here is that taxation is a famous, gigantic sunset clause.

And there are other problems with sunset clauses beyond their unreliability. For example, we should at least ask if it is a just law now, why was it not a just law previously, nor a possible just law in the future? The assertion that we can use these set laws now while there is a problem to address is quite problematic. If there is a socio-political problem now, then we should focus on trying to provide a solution to that problem. What we do by bringing in 'draconian measures' (as Premier Peter Beatty of Queensland affectionately called them) is to justify a current fear climate, rather than demand of our political leaders that they fix this given problem. Providing more powers to the police, and then saying they will be taken away at a particular time in the near future will also develop a reticence among the police forces to use these powers. It has been shown in many historical circumstances that temporary powers granted to the authorities sends confused messages to everyone involved: we say we are giving the authorities more powers, powers that are somewhat debatable in the first place, then we say those powers will be rescinded at a later date since the powers are undemocratic. So can the authorities act or not? Will they face retribution now, during the enactment of these new powers or later when the powers have been rescinded? Police unions in a number of nation-states, Australia, Canada, the UK, have spoken out against any 'extra' powers granted them by various anti-terror legislation for fear that if the legislation changes again, people who are the victims of the extra use of these powers will launch lawsuits against the police themselves. And getting policing authorities involved in socio-political problems have never provided solutions to these socio-political problems in democratic countries.

Proffered Solution 1: Targeting Muslims

There has been some significant debate about this and some have seen a kind of 'profiling' as a solution to the socio-political problem of terrorism. This raises a number of questions and I am going to deal with some of the non-legal aspects of this here. For example, if we have a terrorist organization with key members in Australia are we going to go after them if they are non-Muslim or are we going to be going after only Muslim terrorists? Are PLO operatives terrorists and what if other groups, who might be Muslim, have a just cause? Do they operate in Australia or do we not allow them to do so? There is a lot of talk about ethnic and/or racial profiling without considering the ramifications of using a static identification model to attempt to identify a constantly changing, very dynamic, type of organization and reorganization. This is a big mistake and it has been borne out by similar kinds of profiling, mainly at borders of nation-states around the world, that it is not effective and only aggravates the situation you are trying to address. First, as any good social scientist will tell you, we don't have clear definitions of what ethnicities and races actually are, and we certainly don't know where the boundaries are, that is to say, where these races and ethnicities begin and end. We can only have effective profiling if the populations remain relatively static: if we want to shut down ethnic Chinese businesses in Indonesia, we can do it with some effectiveness as we know where the communities are and where they live, if we want to shut down particular religious organizations in Australia, we can probably do so for similar reasons in that there are groups affiliated with places of worship (rather than some kind of phenotype) and in both cases we can use military means to do so. We could employ (or deploy as the case may be) a kind of historical discourse in which we construct a timeline detailing the developing present condition with clear roots in our own past, make them enemies through this, and then disperse the populations and create an alternative cultural memory. These are effective means to destroy communities that have been used in the past, not necessarily effective in terms of stopping terrorism in the long term, and there have been many attempts to do this historically. Ethnic/racial profiling is the same tactic and is merely a rationalist gloss-over of the same approach. The attempt to develop a phenotypical standard by which to measure behavior is wholly inaccurate. There is no evidence to support the idea that human phenotype links with set behavioral characteristics.

A number of serious analyses of this particular issue have claimed that human beings are currently, and will be in the conceivable future, the best able to recognize anomalies in the movement of people. This means that implementing a system that relies on technology rather than human experience will have far too high a failure rate. Face recognition technology is the prime example of this. Computers can catalog huge numbers of facial nuances but have a clear incapacity to develop a high level of recognition rates. Human beings can do this innately and those people who have long years of experience dealing with people crossing borders have a finely tuned sense of potential problems or anomalies.

But as soon as the real terrorist organization, not the Chinese business people and not the religious group mentioned above, discover that there is a kind of profiling going on, they will change their profile. This is the modern 'racialist' mistake, that phenotypical categories are immutable and that they are inextricably linked with specific kinds of behavior. They will also hire mercenaries, people who do not appear as the authorities think they should appear, and will then make it easier to commit the crimes they seek to commit. It will be easier because in this dynamic, the authorities and the public will assume that profiling is working and there need not be a more sophisticated approach and there need not be any checks in place. The point here is at least twofold. First, reliance on particular systems of recognition must be flexible rather than based on static recognition categories. Secondly, the rate of error in most of the security measures in use today is simply too high to provide reliable methods to stop terrorists.

It has long been the case that profiling does not work at border checks and usually reifies existing problems and prejudices. Security profiling is the equivalent of having border guards in Europe *always* checking baggage moved around by Roma people (a scenario that most backpackers using trains in Europe have seen time and again). If a person looks or acts 'Gypsy-like' in some way, this is a guarantee that border guards will check their baggage. Logically one would then assume that once this practice has become regular, real criminal groups will be able to avoid detection by simply hiring people to do this another way. So the effect of the baggage checks is to harass individuals and families that have a certain set of phenotypical characteristics, and will not necessarily do anything about large-scale smuggling or illicit activity of any kind. It is even more complicated with terrorism since we are talking about some potential violent act. From a purely practical view then, targeting various groups, and using security measures to stop people who have a particular appearance is highly inadequate in limiting organized terror groups as they will simply shift tactics. The solution is to be found in the two other avenues I discuss below.

Proffered Solution 2: Disaster Management

If we were serious about the possible social disruption caused by terrorism, we would see a completely different approach from governments in the 'West'. Fridge magnets and telephone hotlines are not the equivalent of a disaster management policy. What do we do in the event of a real disaster? What do we do in the event of a real terrorist attack in which transport lines, economies, public services, food supplies and so have been affected? This should cause some serious suspicion that governments are not serious about terrorism in 'Western' countries like Australia, Canada, and the United States, as they have refused to implement preparedness training and response for citizens in these nation-states. It is interesting that there is so much discussion about 'security' and that public events are filled with 'security personnel' of one kind or another but the citizenry has had almost no preparation for these sorts of possible attacks. Will the added capacity of various policing agencies (especially things about arbitrary arrests, holding without trial, seizing assets, and so on) do anything about disasters once they have begun? Will this distribute food quicker, will it ensure transportation continues (rail, road, sea, air) so that businesses and workplaces are not stalled, will it ensure that medical teams are delivering the kind of regular day-to-day care our societies need, or that emergency teams of all kinds (medical, fire, general police, trauma counseling teams, and so on) are facilitated in their work? This is the discussion we need to be having about terrorism and the main question is: what do we do in the event of a major disruption of our lives through mass violence? We need to make sure that there are a set of commonly held procedures in place so that we know how to respond. If we are assuming that terrorism is a reality, and that it is possible here (wherever 'here' might be) then why are we not being informed and coached as to the best ways to cooperate with authorities and facilitate their disaster relief efforts? What do we actually do if the 'radical (Islamist)' groups around the world begin to increase their access to parts of the 'West'? Who are we going to call?

We are still being fed the divisive and practically useless things about terrorist hotlines so my neighbors can look at me through their blinds while I am writing my books in the early hours of the morning. I know this of course since I am trying to see what they are looking at. I might know what their favorite Tuesday night television program is but what do I do if the power stations, train stations, major highways, or some large public events are targeted by terrorist groups? Even basic things like a common radio frequency, a set website to go to for information in case of such an attack has never been discussed. Either governments of these nation-states are too stupid to figure out some of these basic disaster preparedness procedures, or they are not serious about terrorism as a real danger. In this case we have been doubly fooled. On the one hand we have voted people in public office who cannot organize some of our crucial public institutions to respond to a crisis, or on the other hand, there is no real danger and we have been fed the same manipulative lies that we were fed about WMD in the lead up to the Iraq invasion. This might be a false dichotomy or a straw person argument but at the very least we must realize that if there is a serious threat, we should do something about it by organizing citizens to respond. Imagine if we were able to gather good evidence to tell us that the likelihood of regular natural disasters were to occur in some of our cities. Then we proceeded to ignore all of it and periodically engaged in a kind of panic about what needs to be done about it. Rather than build earthquake-proof buildings, dams and dykes for flood areas, not bother to install hurricane warning systems, we simply leave it all in the hands of fate and when the disaster does occur, we respond with whatever basic means are available at the time. Most governments in liberal democracies seem to approach a potential catastrophe with the now iconic views of the schoolchildren ducking under desks and shutting their eyes to the impending atomic attack in the 1950s and 1960s.

Proffered Solution 3: Diasporic Communication and Multiculturalism

Political pluralism has long been one of the greatest mitigations of social and political conflict that 'Western' societies have in their political cultures. This pluralism in the United States, Canada, Australia, and New Zealand, for example, has had us witness an incredible amount of diversity in these nation-states with comparatively little social and political conflict. In comparison to the state of war that existed between Pakistan and India for several decades following partition, there is no outright expression of a war, cultural or armed, going on between the various South Asian groups in the United States, Canada, Australia, and New Zealand. It would appear that multiculturalism, as a result of a kind of diasporic communication between diasporas of different kinds as well as with their various 'places of origin', have contributed to this.

In spite of claims that multiculturalism as a lived idea is no longer viable, we still see the capacity of groups all around the world to live side by side and prosper. I have treated some of these issues in detail elsewhere (Imre 2005a; 2005b; 2006) and will summarize some of my arguments. There are a great number of different kinds of multiculturalism all of which are situated in particular national-cultural conflagrations. There are at least, multicultural policies, multicultural polities, multicultural ideologies, multicultural ideas, driven by individuals, governments, political actors and corporate entities of all kinds. Indeed, the best treatment of this diversity centers around Will Kymlicka's many books. There remains to be written a single book-length work that deals with the variety of approaches to a flexible and contested concept of multiculturalism and multicultural ideas that compares the various approaches in their national contexts. The notion that there is a 'failure' as I argue (Imre 2005a, 2005b) is factually incorrect as we do not see the dismantling of nations such as Canada, Australia, New Zealand, Great Britain, and so on due to the fact that people are expressing identities superseding their 'national' identity, or that people are expressing multi-layered identities that include a kind of ethnicity, religion, and civic affiliation. In fact most of the policies surrounding multiculturalism are thriving and people are making genuine attempts to live together in peace. The fact that there is debate about issues and terminology, such as assimilation, integration, radical pluralism, and so on, simply means that groups and individuals in diverse societies are looking to debate the terms of their cooperation rather than groups and individuals struggling for power.

In Chapter 3.3 on religious violence I discussed the Canadian Sikh case in some detail and this is a good example of multiculturalism at work. We see similar things happening in the United States where despite great suspicion and anti-Muslim feelings globally due to terrorist organizations claiming Islamic justification for their violence, there remains great cooperation in the United States between and among the various religious organizations. A clear policy solution to terrorist activity is to support multicultural policies and move away from the demands of homogenization by the failed project of the 19th-century version of the nation-state. Communication between and among diasporic groups needs to be supported and the 'failure' of multiculturalism is a manufactured product of a neo-conservative political agenda rather than the lived reality of most citizens of diverse societies.

Conclusion: Idiocy, Fear and Trembling in the West

Another aspect of the public policy debate about responding to terrorism that has not been treated with any kind of seriousness is the fact that the vast majority of attempts at terrorist acts in the developed world are run by groups of fools. People who are clearly not very clever at all will be able to obtain a media focus based on thwarted or attempted plans of terrorist acts. Examples abound. And in these cases we are left pondering why the global media will focus on this activity and why political leaders will be so ready to emphasize the 'danger' that we face from local terrorists. If we look at terrorist activity through this lens, then we are back to a number of the claims I make in Chapter 1.1 of this book. There is no clear set of linkages among the groups, al Qaeda as a sponsor, a specific religion as a foundation ideology, hatred for the same sets of people, and so on. The only real set of linkages is that people have grouped together to lash out at the societies in which they live.

After examining these cases, we can only conclude that too many of these 'terrorist' incidents are in fact part of another phenomenon. Perhaps it is the case that bored, isolated, not-so-clever individuals have managed to somehow find others of their ilk, find an incidental connection, rather than an essential commonality, and as such develop a 'plan' that will ensure they achieve their aim. The salve for their resentment appears to be an ultra-violent act that will somehow provide them with the kind of recognition they feel they deserve. We could even go so far as to argue that the terrorism phenomenon will save a number of lives. Instead of taking up arms and randomly attacking innocent individuals, these disgruntled 'groups' will develop a 'plan of action' such as the plan to blow up parts of JFK airport in New York which upon further examination could not possibly have worked (jet fuel pipelines were to be crashed and set on fire).

Another good example is the group that sought to kidnap the Canadian Prime Minister Harper, behead him, kidnap a number of other Federal members of parliament, and explode a large portion of the Federal Parliament building in Ottawa. The reaction to the news that such a group existed and had plotted such dramatic acts were diligently reported in the Canadian media and obviously the paranoia escalated but anyone who has been to the Canadian Federal Government Parliament building in Ottawa would know how difficult it would be to drive a truck into the lobby and execute this plan. These individuals were foiled by Muslim groups cooperating with the authorities in Toronto. The simple conclusion here is that these Muslim groups and individuals saw the capacity for their own safety to be threatened if people committed acts of violence in their own names and as such had been cooperating with federal authorities for some time to root out extremists. This is another case of old-fashioned human interaction rather than reliance on technology for security.

So the question for us is: what does all this mean? Is there a crisis of multiculturalism? Are there second and third generation Muslims radicalizing and forming groups ready to take up extreme violence? Do we have situations in which the cause and effect linkages exist, as was discussed in Chapter 1.1, and we are able to stop the cause and thus the effect, of this kind of social disruption and extreme violence? Then answers to these questions are both yes and no. Thinking Muslims will no more radicalize than other religious, ethnic, or groups forming around various identities. Our panic at fools attempting to engage in violence they see on television, movie plots, and various websites, is detrimental to understanding how to stop these phenomena. In all cases, normal 'police work' that is to say, cooperative interaction, is the way forward.

References

Arendt, H. (1964), *Eichmann in Jerusalem* (New York: Viking Penguin).

Bauman, Z. (2004), *Wasted Lives* (Polity Press: London).

Bloom, M. (2005), *Dying to Kill: The Allure of Suicide Terror* (New York: Columbia University of Princeton).

Brubaker, R. (2004), *Ethnicity Without Groups* (Cambridge: Massachusetts: Harvard University Press).

Combs, C. (2006), *Terrorism in the Twenty-First Century* (New Jersey: Pearson).

Crenshaw, Martha (1998), 'The Logic of Terrorism: Terrorist Behaviour as a Product of Strategic Choice', in Walter Reich (ed.), *Origins of Terrorism* (Woodrow Wilson Center Press).

Dalby, S. (2002), *Environmental Security* (Minneapolis: University of Minnesota Press).

Gambetta, D. (2005), *Making Sense of Suicide Missions* (Oxford: Oxford University Press).

Goodin, R. (2006), *What's Wrong With Terrorism?* (Cambridge: Polity Press).

Gunning, J. (2007), 'A Case for Critical Terrorism Studies', *Government and Opposition*, Vol. 42, No. 3, pp. 363–93.

Haugaard, M. (2002), *Power: A Reader* (Manchester: Manchester University Press).

Hoffman, B. (2006), *Inside Terrorism* (New York: Columbia University Press).

Imre, R. (2005a), 'Transnationalism and Migrations: Re-ascribing Meanings'. <http://www.inter-disciplinary.net/ci/interculturalism/ic2/s8.htm.

—— (2005b), 'Political Pluralism in Diverse Societies: Citizenship and Migration in Australia, Canada and Aotearoa/New Zealand'. <http://www.interdisciplinary. net/ci/interculturalism/ic2/s1.htm>.

—— (2006), 'Diaspora and Security Dilemmas: The War on Terror and the "Other" in Australia', in Cynthia van den Driesen and Ralph Crane (eds), *Diaspora: The Australasian Experience* (New Delhi: Prestige), pp. 317–30.

Jurgensmeyer, M. (2000), *Terror in the Mind of God* (Berkeley: University of California Press).

Laquer, W. (2004), *No End To War: Terrorism in the Twenty-First Century* (New York: Continuum).

Roy, O. (2004), *Globalised Islam* (London: Hurst).

Sagemen, M. (2004), *Understanding Terror Networks* (University of Pennsylvania Press).

Simms, M. and Warhurst, J. (eds) (2005), *Mortgage Nation: The 2004 Australian Election* (Bentley: API Network).

Terriff, T., Croft, S., James, L. and Morgan, P. (2003), *Security Studies Today* (Cambridge: Polity Press).

Thomas, C. (2000), *Global Governance, Development and Human Security* (London: Pluto Press).

4.2   Effective Counter-Terrorism: Sound Foreign Policy, Intelligence Gathering, Policing, Social Engineering and Necessary Use of Force

Ben Clarke

The UN Charter was founded upon the bold vision of the attainment of a world without violence. It is only by addressing the conditions that give rise to terrorism that such violence can be quelled. These conditions may be complex. So it is with terrorism waged by radical Islamists. The Islamic faith as understood by the majority of the world's Muslims is not a source of terrorism. However Islamist ideologies that promote violence are. Islamist ideologies often focus upon past and present injustice against Muslims, and actual or perceived oppression of Muslim communities and societies. Human rights violations against Muslims in Palestine and Iraq provide fertile ground for the expression of such ideas. The danger arises where religious instruction draws upon these conditions to instill doctrines of hatred, violence, and ethnic or religious intolerance. Where Muslims are taught that they have a religious duty to fight oppression, injustice and humiliation by killing civilians living under the pagan or apostate governments blamed for these humiliations, Islamist terror is virtually inevitable. In this sense the 'war on terror' will be decided as much by curriculum content in the maddrasses of Pakistan and the Islamic schools in the West, as it will by diplomatic negotiation in Jerusalem and Geneva. It will certainly not be won or lost on a conventional military battlefield.

History has proved that specific terrorist organizations can and have been dismantled.[1] While total victory in an ideological 'war on terrorism' is unattainable, specific ideologies can be defeated over the medium to long term (for example, Nazism). In order to achieve this outcome in the present struggle, states need to know which strategies are effective (and which are counter-productive or inconsequential) in the quest to bring Islamist terror to a halt. This part of the chapter offers suggestions as to how states, regional organizations and international bodies may identify and pursue effective counter-terrorism strategies. It expounds a multi-dimensional counter-terrorism strategy to deal with the organization and ideology of al Qaeda (and similar terrorist groups). It draws upon lessons learned by states and international organizations in their current struggle to halt international terrorism by radical Islamists. The discussion begins with an obvious caveat: terrorism cannot be completely eradicated.

---

1 Examples include the Baader-Meinhoff Gangs in Germany, and the Red Brigades in Italy.

Even if terrorism in eliminated in the present era, one cannot rule out the prospect of future terrorist campaigns. Terrorism is a method of warfare which has been employed by clandestine resistance movements against great powers for thousands of years. The contemporary struggle against Islamist terrorism is no different.

States are engaged in a multi-level struggle against organizations and networks whose ideology and methods offend the prevailing international legal order. Radical Islamists seek what the UN Charter forbids: the violent overthrow of 'apostate' regimes and the imposition of their vision of Islam. There will be no decisive military victory in a battle between standing armies controlled by sovereign states. The community of states are united in their opposition to terrorism, at least in principle. All states have sought to distance themselves from radical Islamists. Only a handful of governments continue to finance Islamic resistance movements or tolerate their activities within their sovereign territory. Al Qaeda does not enjoy official support or recognition from any state. Radical Islamists look to Muslims themselves and not their governments for support. Theirs is a battle for the allegiance of the ordinary Muslim on 'the Arab street', in the local British mosque or Islamic youth organization, in the mountains of Pakistan and Afghanistan, and throughout the Indonesian archipelago.

There are two aspects to the struggle: (a) identifying and dismantling operational terrorist organizations and infrastructure, and (b) challenging the ideologies that underpin them. Radicalized cells of Islamist fighters who are committed to militant jihad and have the capacity to launch terrorist attacks pose the immediate threat. However in a number of cases militant Islamists have been willing to reassess their strategy where a dialogue has been opened with learned Islamic scholars who set out the orthodox view that the taking of innocent life is not permitted in Islam. For those unwilling to engage in dialogue, states and international organizations may have no option but to use force to suppress their activities.

The outcome of the 'war on terror' ultimately depends upon whether the proponents of radical Islamist ideologies are able to persuade the *umma* that their vision of Islam is worth fighting for and that terrorism is an acceptable path to attaining that vision. Either the ideologies that promote and facilitate terrorism will be discredited and marginalised (and thereby lose or reduce their power to attract and radicalize Muslim youth), or they will continue to win support until Islamists gain political power in one or more Arab and Muslim states (through elections, mass uprisings or the *coup d'état*). For the reasons outlined in this part of the chapter, marginalization is the most likely outcome in most, if not all, Arab and Muslim states.

Counter-Terrorism, the Rule of Law and Human Rights

Before canvassing the options available to states and other international actors in formulating counter-terrorism policies, a number of observations need to be made. First, states must address the threat of terrorism within the framework of the rule of law and human rights. The reasons why this approach is necessary are outlined in my previous contributions to this book. In essence this strategy is in the interests of states themselves. It provides the framework within which to balance competing societal demands. An example is the need to take firm measures to protect the population from terrorist attacks while at the same time not engaging in methods that may create a backlash and fuel terrorist ideologies. Without a human rights and rule of law based framework for counter- terrorism, states will appear hypocritical in their denial of basic rights to Muslim terror suspects but not to other crime suspects. There is also the danger of a drift towards autocratic rule, as basic rights and freedoms give way to sometimes spurious or ill-defined national security interests.

Counter-terrorism checks and balances: the important questions

In developing national counter-terrorism policies a number of questions need to be addressed:

- What is the actual or perceived terrorist threat?
- How is it assessed and by whom?
- Are current or proposed anti-terrorism laws proportionate to the threat?
- Are they flexible enough to deal with diverse threats?
- What basic rights need to be protected under such laws?
- What role do intelligence agencies play in assessing terrorist risks and threats?
- Can they simply rely upon foreign intelligence or are local sources needed?
- How reliable is local and foreign intelligence?
- Are the intelligence agencies sufficiently independent of government to provide objective and robust advice?
- Can governments be prevented from manipulating intelligence for political purposes?
- Should whistle blowers be afforded legal protection when they highlight the distortion of intelligence by government?
- Should legislators or bipartisan parliamentary committees have access to intelligence during debates on whether to deploy troops on international counter-terrorism operations?

These questions have gained prominence post-9/11, reaching their zenith in 2003 when a Coalition of states invaded Iraq on the basis of flawed intelligence. This part of the chapter critiques a number of aspects of Australian foreign military policy since 2001. It asks whether specific deployments have heightened or reduced terrorism and its ideologies, and underscores the dangers of departing from a rule of law based response to terrorism. It also proposes a range of measures to tackle terrorist threats. These measures take into account lessons learned in recent years.

The Integrity of Government and the Manipulation of Intelligence

The war in Iraq triggered an escalation of terrorist violence. Members of the 'Coalition of the Willing' no longer deny this fact. US President George Bush has characterized Iraq as 'a central front in the war on terror.'[2] Proponents of global militant jihad agree. The ongoing presence of US troops in Iraq has been a pillar of al Qaeda's recruitment strategy for years. How did this rapid rise in Islamist terror come about? What lessons can be learnt so as to avoid a similar escalation in terrorism in the future?

Australian Prime Minister John Howard justified his nation's involvement in the 2003 invasion of Iraq on the basis of US intelligence estimates. So did other members of the Coalition of the Willing. These were estimates about the military threat posed by Iraq.[3] The intelligence upon which they were based was put to the test in the aftermath of the invasion. UN and US inspectors scoured Iraq in their search for weapons of mass destruction.[4] When neither weapons of mass destruction nor evidence of their recent disposal could be found, and Colin Powell acknowledged that claims made in his speech to the UNSC in February 2003 were based on flawed intelligence, the media spotlight fell upon the role of intelligence agencies and their relationship with the governments that went to war.

In Australia, the 'Office of National Assessments' (ONA) and the 'Australian Security Intelligence Organisation' (ASIO) are the agencies responsible for obtaining and providing intelligence to the federal government. The role of these intelligence agencies is central to any detailed analysis of Australian counter-terrorism policy.[5]

In the wake of the Iraq war, a range of issues need to be explored including: methods used to obtain intelligence; the quality of intelligence received; the wisdom of reliance upon intelligence provided by foreign governments (particularly where those governments may have an interest in exaggerating intelligence); the manipulation or 'massaging' of intelligence by government to suit its foreign policy objectives; and the independence and integrity of agencies that assess intelligence, such as the ONA (Kingston M., 2004).[6] These matters came to a head after Andrew Wilkie, an analyst at the Office of National Assessments, resigned in March 2003. He did so in protest at the disparity between intelligence assessments he was privy to, and the Howard government's exaggerations of both the threat posted by Saddam Hussein's regime and its links to al Qaeda (Wilkie 2004). Wilkie argued publicly

---

2 Speech by President George Bush to the convention of the Veterans of Foreign Wars in Salt Lake City, 22 August 2005 <http://www.whitehouse.gov/news/releases/2005/08/200508 22-1.html> accessed 19 April 2007.

3 'Howard commits troops to war', 18 March 2003, *Sydney Morning Herald* (website) (updated 20 April 2007) <http://www.smh.com.au/articles/2003/03/18/1047749732511.html> accessed 20 April 2007.

4 See *Report of the US Intelligence Community's Pre-war Intelligence Assessments on Iraq*, US Senate Select Committee on Intelligence (Report ordered 7 July 2004) <www. globalsecurity.org> accessed 29 April 2007. The report confirms that flawed intelligence on Iraq was one of the most damaging intelligence failures of recent US history.

5 For a recent review of these agencies and their failures on Iraq see Philip Flood (2004), *Report of the Inquiry into Australian Intelligence Agencies,* Chapter 3 'Recent Intelligence Lessons' <http://www.dpmc.gov.au/publications/intelligence_inquiry/index.htm> accessed 20 April 2007.

6 Andrew Wilkie, a former intelligence officer at the ONA has claimed that the ONA told the federal government what it wanted to hear. See also: Wilkie A., 2004.

that the Australian government's case for going to war was premised on manipulated intelligence. The Howard government's willingness to misrepresent the truth for political ends had already been demonstrated during the children overboard affair and on other occasions (Woolford 2004). In light of these events scepticism about whether the government could be trusted to not mislead the public about terror threat levels is understandable (Gordon 2005). One would imagine that a consequence of these developments would be a diminished capacity of government to persuade the public that the threat of terror attacks justifies restrictions on civil liberties. Yet public concern about security and terrorism was sufficient to enable the government to persuade the parliament to enact tougher anti-terrorism laws while at the same time maintaining that Australia's involvement in the war on Iraq has not increased the threat of terrorist attacks against Australians or Australian interests. The latter claim has been rejected by terrorism experts and the Australian public alike (Nicholson 2004 a, b). Warnings issued by known Islamist terrorist organizations of attacks against Australian interests have to be taken seriously. Terrorist attacks against Australians and Western interests in Bali and Jakarta graphically demonstrated that the threat posed by some of these organizations is real.

Even so, concern that government is manipulating intelligence and exploiting 'fear of terrorism' for political gain places the public in a difficult position. We rely upon the government, its intelligence agencies and security apparatus to protect us from terrorist threats within our borders, and to a lesser extent, overseas. On the other hand we are aware that it is in the political interests of government to play up the risk of terrorism and pass ever tougher laws. Ultimately the public has little choice but to trust government. Some degree of trust in politicians is an unavoidable part of the 'social contract' between the government and the governed. If this trust is misplaced, and the public believe that fear of terrorism has been manipulated by government to peruse policies that have harmed the national interest, the government can be removed at the ballot box. Hope and trust must then be placed in the successor regime that it will enact laws and pursue policies (domestic and foreign) that better serve the public interest.

The Nature of the Threat to Australia

Government-endorsed intelligence estimates are not the only source of information on terrorist threats. Counter-terrorism experts, police agencies, security firms, NGOs, UN agencies, investigative journalists, and think tanks offer alternative sources of information that are readily accessible on the internet. An analysis of these sources reveals a widely held belief that radical Islamist terror networks are seeking to conduct terror attacks inside Australia. Jemaah Islamiyah and al Qaeda have indicated their intention to target Australia and Australian interests ('Al-Qaeda bomb threat to Australia', 2003; 'US, Australia warn of Indonesia terror attacks: Militants may be planning to kidnap foreigners over Christmas', 2005). Islamist terror attacks in London, Madrid and Bali and elsewhere have targeted the citizens of states that have been involved in military operations in Iraq and Afghanistan. Australian forces have been deployed in both states for several years. The Bali bombings of 2002 and 2005, while not exclusively aimed at Australians, killed and maimed dozens of Australian citizens. In November 2005, more than a dozen Islamists were arrested in Sydney and Melbourne on terrorism charges. Material presented by the prosecution at their bail applications suggested that terror attacks within Australia had been planned.[7] Australia's nuclear reactor at Lucas Heights was the alleged target. Police seized 165 railway detonators and videos entitled *Are you Ready to Die?* and *Sheikh Osama's Training Course.* They also found recorded statements of some of the accused who said that they wanted to die for jihad and cause maximum damage to buildings and lives.[8] If the *modus operandi* of Islamist terrorists in London, Madrid and Indonesia had been followed, attacks would likely have been against soft targets including airports arrival and departure halls, buses, trains, shopping malls, schools, public sports facilities, restaurants, night clubs, and other places where people gather in significant numbers and there are few if any security checks. However, it needs to be emphasized that Muslims represent as little as 1.5 per cent of the Australian population (approximately 200,000 people in 2001 and possible 300,000 in 2007).[9] If opinion polls conducted in Islamic nations on support for terrorist organizations are anything to go by, only a small percentage of Australian Muslims could be expected to endorse organizations like al Qaeda and fewer still would be willing to provide active support[10] (Cooke D. and Lopez E., 2005).

Responsible Government and Counter-Terrorism Policy

The general measures proposed in this part of this chapter are, in this writer's view, a necessary response to the threat of terror attacks by radical Islamists. These proposals are not directed at any particular state. Specific counter-terrorism policies will depend on a range of factors including the threat level, budgetary limits and other capacity constraints. While the effectiveness of these proposals cannot be guaranteed into the future, robust adherence to them is likely to enhance security and reduce the threat of terrorist attacks.

---

7 Elisabeth Lopez, Dewi Cooke (2005) 'Raids disrupt "imminent" attack', 8 November <http://www.theage.com.au/articles/2005/11/08/1131212027799.html?from=top5> accessed 5 January 2006.

8 Michael Vincent (2005) 'Lucas Heights potential target for alleged terrorist attack', 14 November <http://www.abc.net.au/worldtoday/content/2005/s1506095.htm> accessed 24 April 2007.

9 *Year Book Australia* (2007), 24 January 2007 <http://www.abs.gov.au> accessed 24 April 2007.

10 See 'Muslim Public Opinion on US Policy, Attacks on Civilians and al Qaeda', 24 April 2007, *The Program on International Policy Attitudes at the University of Maryland*, pp. 10–14, accessible at <www.worldpublicopinion.org> accessed 28 April 2007.

Responsible Government and Necessary Responses to Terrorism

States have a responsibility to protect their citizens from terrorism. Determining what, if any, counter-terrorism measures should be taken is a matter for government. This issue can trigger intense political debate. Important questions include:

- What is the nature of the threat?
- Are the proposed measures necessary?
- Would they actually prevent terror attacks?

Where states face a serious threat of an attack, a multifaceted approach is usually adopted. The precise response depends upon the nature and severity of the terror threat. The starting point is an assessment of existing law and policy to ensure that, *inter alia,* law enforcement and prosecution authorities have adequate powers of investigation, interrogation, detention, prosecution and extradition. Other matters to be considered are: intelligence gathering systems; training of police, defence force and security personnel; and inter-agency counter-terrorism coordination. States must also evaluate whether involvement in overseas military deployments is based on sound counter-terrorism policy. In this regard a critical appraisal of the policies and practices of allies may be necessary. Lessons learned from counter-terrorism operations by Coalition forces in Iraq and Afghanistan are numerous.[11] One is that the abuse of detainees by interrogators and others is counter-productive where a sizable proportion of the local population supports the resistance. Another is that where terrorist campaigns are committed as part of a national liberation struggle, such violence may not be brought under control until a political settlement is reached. This may require 'negotiations with terrorists' – something that governments are generally reluctant to do. A third is that 'transformative occupation' requires troop numbers, resources and international support that was lacking during the occupation of Iraq. Occupation 'on the cheap' in a country as volatile, heavily armed, and fractious as Iraq is a recipe for social disorder and terror.

When adopting counter-terrorism measures states must adhere to the rule of law and fundamental human rights norms. Counter-terrorism law and policy that encroaches upon civil liberties must not go so far as to violate *jus cogens* or non-derogable ICCPR norms. Moreover such laws must only remain on the statute books for so long as there is a demonstrable terrorist threat to the State. Under the International Covenant on Civil and Political Rights, states parties may only resort to indefinite detention without charge or trial where a state of emergency has been declared by the government.[12]

---

11 Chairman's Report, 'Lessons learned from recent terrorist attacks: Building national capabilities and institutions', NATO–Russia Council Conference, Ljubljana, Slovenia 2005 <http://www.nato.int/docu/conf/2005/050727/index.html> accessed 21 April 2007; United States Institute of Peace (2002), *The Diplomacy of Counterterrorism: Lessons Learned, Ignored, and Disputed* <http://www.usip.org/pubs/specialreports/sr80.pdf> accessed 20 April 2007.

12 International Covenant on Civil and Political Rights, GA res. 2200A (XXI), 21 UN GAOR Supp. (No. 16) at 52, UN Doc. A/6316 (1966), 999 UNTS 171, *entered into force* 23

A number of states have been reluctant to take robust measures to minimize terrorism. Some have concerns about undermining strategic alliances, disrupting trade partnerships, or jeopardizing delicate internal political balances. Others have little or no Islamist influences within their territory, and do not consider themselves part of the 'war on terror' (for example, Southern African states such as Zambia and Namibia). They have other pressing issues. Islamist terror is viewed as a problem for states that caused or fueled this phenomenon. There is also a growing belief that the 'war on terror' is radicalizing young Muslims. Iraq is seen as evidence of confused and misguided US policy which is exacerbating terrorism. Then there are the Muslim states where a strong Islamists presence has been left to fester. Their failure to rein-in radical Islamists has resulted in a demonstrable increase in the threat level. Pakistan is an obvious example. While it has handed over many of the senior al Qaeda members, presently in US custody, it has failed to halt the proliferation of maddrasses that teach hatred, intolerance and violence (the so called 'terrorist factories'). It has also been complicit in the resurgence of the Taliban by signing a peace agreement in September 2006 with the pro-Taliban militants that control a semi-autonomous tribal area on the Afghan border. Meanwhile al Qaeda and Taliban fighters have launched attacks inside Afghanistan from bases in Pakistan. For its part the US has created a terrorist breeding ground in Iraq through its flawed policies in that country. It has also failed to devote enough troops and resources to help suppress the Taliban and al Qaeda threat in Afghanistan and Pakistan.

Defining Terrorism

Before we look at various tools that may be employed to counter the threat of terrorism, it is necessary to identity precisely what conduct states are obliged to prohibit and prevent (or failing this, to punish). As noted in Chapter 1.2, terrorism involves the deliberate targeting of civilians in attacks designed to cause fear among a population.[13] This definition reflects the one adopted by the General Assembly in its 1994 definition of terrorism.[14] Terrorism violates both domestic and international law. However it is not only those who detonate explosives that are culpable. All those who facilitate, encourage, aid, promote or finance terrorist violence are also

---

March 1976. Article 4(1). There are at least 160 states parties. For the current list see <www. ohchr.org> (homepage).

13 Under Australian federal law, terrorism is defined as an action or threat of action intended to advance a political, ideological or religious cause and to coerce or influence by intimidation an Australian or foreign government or intimidate the public or a section of the public, that causes serious physical harm or death to a person, or endangers a person's life or involves serious risk to public health or safety, serious damage to property or serious interference with essential electronic systems: Section 100.1 of the Commonwealth Criminal Code Act 1995.

14 'Measures to eliminate international terrorism', A/RES/49/60, 9 December 1994. Paragraph 3 defines terrorism as: 'Criminal acts intended or calculated to provoke a state of terror in the general public, a group of persons or particular persons for political purposes are in any circumstance unjustifiable, whatever the considerations of a political, philosophical, ideological, racial, ethnic, religious or any other nature that may be invoked to justify them.'

criminally liable.[15] States are required under binding resolutions of the Security Council to prohibit such conduct, and punish those who engage in the same.[16]

Proscribing Terrorist Organizations

One method of tackling terrorism is to ban and isolate organizations that engage in violence against civilians. The United Nations Security Council maintains a list of proscribed terrorist organizations and individuals.[17] More than 400 individuals and entities have been banned. Most belong to, or affiliated with, the Taliban and/ or al Qaeda. As with many decisions of the Security Council, the banning of an organization can be intensely political. Hamas (the dominant Islamist movement in the Occupied Territories) has been banned by the European Union, Australia, Canada, the United States, and Israel, but not the Security Council.[18] Some Islamist organizations in South East Asia including Jemaah Islamiyah and Abu Saef have been condemned by both the Security Council[19] and the General Assembly.[20]

While UN resolutions provide a general framework for tackling terrorism, the fulfillment of responsibilities under these resolutions is usually left to states. Australia has been active in this regard. It has passed a raft of counter-terrorism laws over the past five years, and has (with mixed success) tried to assist its neighbors in adopting counter-terrorism strategies. Under these laws, the federal Attorney-General has been granted the power to proscribe, by regulation, any organization that is directly or indirectly engaged in or preparing, planning, assisting in or fostering the doing of a terrorist act. In recent years at least 17 terrorist organizations including al Qaeda, Jemaah Islamiyah, Hamas, and the Hizballah External Security Organization have been proscribed.[21] The act of proscribing these organizations precludes them from operating legally inside Australia, and puts the public on notice that membership of

---

15 Ibid., under paragraph 5(a), which deals with state sponsored terrorism, states have an obligation to 'refrain from organizing, instigating, facilitating, financing, encouraging or tolerating terrorist activities and to take appropriate practical measures to ensure that their respective territories are not used for terrorist installations or training camps, or for the preparation or organization of terrorist acts intended to be committed against other states or their citizens'.

16 See discussion of SC Res. 1373 (2001) below.

17 The list is maintained by the Sanctions Committee of the United Nations Security Council. See <http://www.un.org/Docs/sc/committees/1267/1267ListEng.htm> accessed 4 January 2006.

18 See 'List of proscribed terrorist organizations in Australia, the USA, the United Kingdom, Canada, European Union and United Nations' <http://www.ag.gov.au/www/agd/rwpattach.nsf/VAP/(153683DB7E984D23214BD871B2AC75E8)~Attachment+A+-+AG_s.PDF/$file/Attachment+A+-+AG_s.PDF> accessed 24 April 2007.

19 See for example Security Council Resolution 1566 (2004).

20 General Assembly Resolution, 12 September 2001 (First Resolution of the 56th UN General Assembly (2001).

21 'Protecting Australia against terrorism: Australia's national counter-terrorism policies and arrangements' <http://www.pmc.gov.au/publications/protecting_australia/preparedness/1_legislation.htm> accessed 4 January 2005.

these organizations is banned. These benefits must be balanced against the risk that banning such groups may simply drive extremists underground where their activities will be more difficult to monitor.

Reviewing Foreign Policy

(a) The Middle East: an overview

The impact of foreign involvement in the Middle East upon the rise of Islamist terror is a highly nuanced question. It would be impossible to quantify with any precision. 'Western' military and political involvement in the region predates the crusades of the 12th century AD. More recently, Ottoman rule, French and British colonial influence, the Cold War (Soviet and Western influence) and Arab nationalism have all influenced the politics of the region. Post-Cold War influences have also been significant. Some Arab regimes remain dependent for their survival on Western military and economic backing. Many Arab regimes have been overthrown in coups or proxy wars, some of which have been orchestrated by foreign powers. Humiliation and frustration at the plight of Muslims across the Middle East has been a major source of strength for Islamist terror organizations.

Al Qaeda justifies its attacks as holy war to expel Western crusaders, Zionists and others from the holy lands. Its message is not new. Nor are its methods. Religious extremism, sectarian divisions, tribal conflict and political and religious violence have been part of the political landscape of the Middle East for well over a millennium. While foreign involvement in the region has been constant, it has not always been imposed. Indeed it is sometimes actively requested by Arab states and Muslim societies. The government of Kuwait requested US help to expel Iraq from Kuwait in 1991. The Hashemite monarchy in Jordan, the Mubarak government in Egypt, and the Saudi monarchy in Saudi Arabia (to name but a few) all accept Western military and/or economic support to strengthen homeland security, suppress extremism and check the rise of new and violent forms of political Islam.[22]

Nonetheless, for radical Islamists in the Middle East, Western involvement in their region is a root cause of their struggle. It has been exploited by al Qaeda and their ilk in the propaganda war for the allegiance of Muslims. Terrorist organizations that invoke Islam are striving to win an ideological war within the Islamic world and beyond. The Middle East policy of Western states and international organizations is therefore of fundamental importance. Prudent foreign policy may help reduce

---

22 In November 2005 the US pledged $1.3 billion in military aid and $495 million in economic assistance to Egypt; Jordan was granted $250 million in economic assistance, taking total US aid to Jordan to more than $7 billion: 'US raises Jordan aid to over $500 m in 2006', 4 October 2006, Reuters <http://www.alertnet.org/thenews/newsdesk/L04457868.htm> accessed 27 April 2007; 'Bush Signs $20.9 Billion 2006 Foreign Aid Spending Measure', 15 November 2005 <http://usinfo.state.gov> accessed 27 April 2007. For counter-terrorism activity by North African and Middle Eastern states see: *Country Reports on Terrorism*, Chapter 5 (US Department of State, Office of the Coordinator for Counterterrorism) 28 April 2006 <http://www.state.gov/s/ct/rls/crt/2005/64344.htm> accessed 27 April 2007.

Islamist terror, imprudent policy has the potential to incite the same and increase the flow of funds and fighters to al Qaeda and similar organizations.[23]

There is room for debate as to whether Islamic extremism and global militant jihad would have arisen without the rising US influence in the region. US support for Israel – while most Palestinians remain dispossessed and exiled – has been the crucible of Middle Eastern politics since 1967. It has, in one way or another, fueled terrorism and violence in the region. While Western involvement in the Middle East has at times fueled terrorism, at others it has thwarted it. As al Qaeda and other such entities strive to depose 'apostate' regimes across the Muslim world, Arab regimes (including Iraq, Saudi Arabia, Egypt, Jordan, Afghanistan, and Pakistan) have received significant international assistance in their efforts to suppress al Qaeda. All have carried out successful operations to kill or capture members of radical Islamist terror networks. Nonetheless there have been numerous recent terrorist attacks across the region, reflecting a failure by these governments to halt the planning and execution of these crimes. However a number of key questions remain to be answered:

1. Have US policies (including counter-terrorism activities) in the Middle East triggered more extremism than it has thwarted?
2. Are Muslim countries firmly committed to the eradication of the types of religious extremism and hatred that inspire al Qaeda and its ilk?
3. Or are Arab and Muslim governments playing the US off against the extremists in a bid to hold onto power?

A detailed examination of these questions is beyond the scope of this chapter. Considered answers are perhaps best left to future generations of political scientists and historians who will have the benefit of hindsight. However the questions themselves are of great importance and deserved detailed study and discussion.

(b) Palestine/Israel

The crucible of Middle Eastern politics has, since 1948, been the conflict between Israel and the Palestinians. The emergence of a Jewish state in the heart of Palestine – and the wars that followed – are matters that have been politicized to the point where it is all but impossible to critique these developments without being accused of partiality. Yet if their impact upon the rise of Islamist terror is to be assessed, one must wade into the mire. A number of the seminal events in this conflict are noted in Chapter 2.3.

---

23 See Thomas L. Friedman (2005), 'No Mullah Left Behind', *The New York Times*, 13 February, p. 15:

> ... the Bush team is – as others have noted – financing both sides of the war on terrorism. We are financing the U.S. armed forces with our tax dollars, and, through our profligate use of energy, we are generating huge windfall profits for Saudi Arabia, Iran and Sudan, where the cash is used to insulate the regimes from any pressure to open up their economies, liberate their women or modernize their schools, and where it ends up instead financing madrassas, mosques and militants fundamentally opposed to the progressive, pluralistic agenda America is trying to promote.

A detailed historical review is beyond the scope of this study. Instead, aspects of the conflict that are directly connected to the rise of Islamist terror are noted.

The first point that needs to be underscored is that support for dispossessed Palestinians remains strong across the Middle East. This has translated into significant support on the 'Arab street' for militant groups that oppose Israel and back the right of return for exiled Palestinians. Secondly, Islamist terror networks born out of the Palestinian struggle are unlikely to diminish without a political resolution of the Palestine/Israel crisis. Thirdly, while US support for Israel appears to have fueled Islamist terror, most governments in the Middle East (and beyond) are strongly opposed to the terrorist activities of radical Islamists. The governments of Iraq, Saudi Arabia, Egypt, Jordon, Lebanon, Afghanistan and Pakistan are among the many non-Western regimes actively involved in the fight against al Qaeda and affiliate organizations. The security apparatus (*mukhabarat*) of Arab states monitor and curb the rise of groups that may pose a threat to the security of the nation and government. In the cases of Lebanon and Iraq their capacity to do so is limited by deep sectarian divisions and weak government. Fourthly, while Islamist terror attacks have been carried out in many Arab states since Osama bin Laden issued his 'Declaration of the World Islamic Front for Jihad against the Jews and the Crusaders' in 1998, neither al Qaeda nor any other Islamist terror organization has been able to topple a government in the Middle East (or beyond).

In concluding this discussion, a political resolution of the Palestinian/Israeli conflict may trigger a significant decline in Islamist terror in the region. However such an eventuality would not satisfy al Qaeda's principal demands (the removal of apostate regimes and US influence in the region). Peace agreements, while necessary for regional stability and economic and political development, will not end al Qaeda terror or the influence of its ideology.

(c) Iraq

The 2003 invasion of Iraq was, for most legal scholars, legally questionable to say the least.[24]

---

24 Ulf Bernitz *et al.* (2003), Letter to the Editor, 'War Would be Illegal' *The Guardian* (London) 7 March, p. 29 <http://www.guardian.co.uk/Iraq/Story/0,2763,909314,00.html> accessed 8 May 2004 (16 British academics declared that 'before military action can lawfully be undertaken against Iraq, the Security Council must have indicated its clearly expressed assent'); Jeff Sallot (2003), 'Attack illegal, experts say,' *Globe and Mail*, 20 March <http://www.globeandmail.com/servlet/story/RTGAM.20030320.ulaww0320/BNStory/International> accessed 8 May 2004. ('Dozens of Canadian law professors and experts in international law' asserted that the U.S.-led coalition's war against Iraq was illegal); Terry D. Gill (2003), 'The War in Iraq and the Contemporary *Jus ad Bellum*', 5 *International Law FORUM de droit international*, 241–6, 245; Carsten Stahn (2003), 'Enforcement of the Collective Will after Iraq', 97 *American Journal of International Law*, 804, 806 (citations omitted); Nigel D. White (2005), 'Self Defence, Security Council authority and Iraq', in Richard Burchill, Nigel D. White and Justin Morris (eds) *International Conflict and Security Law: Essays in Memory of Hilaire McCoubrey*, 235, 262; Paul Muggleton, The International Crime of Aggression (SJD Thesis, 2005) 155, 183; Peter Slevin (2003), 'U.S. Says War Has Legal Basis Reliance on Gulf War Resolutions Is Questioned by Others', *Washington Post* (Washington), 21 March, <http://www.washingtonpost.com/ac2/wp-dyn?pagename=article&node=&contentId=A1332-

Some have gone so far as to characterize it as a 'crime of aggression.'[25] The

---

2003Mar20&notFound=true> accessed 3 May 2006; Mahmoud Hmoud (2003–04), 'The Use of Force against Iraq: Occupation and Security Council Resolution 1483', 36 *Cornell Int'l LJ* 435; E. De Wet (2004), *The Chapter VII Powers of the United Nations Security Council*, 284–289; Mirko Bagaric and James McConvill (2003), 'The War in Iraq: The Illusion of International Law? Where to Now?', 8 *Deakin LRev*, 147, at 147 (footnote 2). See also Mohammad Taghi Karoubi (2004), *Just or Unjust War? International Law and Unilateral Use of Armed Force by States at the turn of the 20th Century* 195–212, 239 (citations omitted); John E Noyes (2003–04), 'American Hegemony, U.S. Political Leaders and General International Law', 19 *Conn J Int'l L*, 293 at 304; Anne Marie Slaughter (2004), 'The Use of Force in Iraq: Illegal and Illegitimate', 98 *Am Sac's Int'l L Proc*, 262, 262; Richard Falk (2004), 'The Iraq War and the Future of International law', 98 *Am Soc'y Int'l L Proc*, 262 at 263; Thomas M. Franck, 'The Role of International law and the UN after Iraq', 98 *Am Soc'y Int'l L Proc*, 262 2004 at 267; Patrick McLain (2002), 'Settling The Score With Saddam: Resolution 1441 And Parallel Justifications For The Use Of Force Against Iraq', *13 Duke J of Comp & Int'l L*, 233; John Yoo (2004), 'Using Force', 71 *U Chic L Rev*, 729 at 791; Professor Phillippe Sands QC, 'Lawless World: International Law After 9/11 and Iraq', University College London and Matrix Chambers University of Melbourne Law School Alumni Lecture 2005, 15 June 2005, 14–16; Nicole Deller and John Burroughs, '*Jus ad Bellum:* Law Regulating Resort to Force', Section of Individual Rights & Responsibilities, American Bar Association <http://www.abanet.org/irr/hr/winter03/lawregulatingresorttoforce. html> accessed 8 February 2006; Nicholous Shultz (2006), 'Case Note – Was the war on Iraq Illegal? – The Judgement of the German Federal Administrative Court of 21 June 2005', 7 *German Law Journal*, 1, 5 (no pagination) <www.germanlawjournal.com> accessed 10 June 2006. But see Yoram Dinstein (2005), *War Aggression and Self Defence*, pp. 297–300; John Yoo (2003), 'Agora: Future Implications of the Iraq Conflict: International Law and the War in Iraq', 97 *American Journal of International Law*, 563; Adam Tait (2005), 'The Legal War: A Justification for Military Action in Iraq', 9 *Gonz J Int'l Law*, 1; Michael Novak (2003–04), 'Just Peace and the Asymmetric Threat: National Self-Defense in Uncharted Waters', 27 *Harvard Journal of Law and Public Policy*, 817, 836; Joshua Rozenberg (2003), 'Why the Sword is Mightier than the Law', *Telegraph* (London), 13 March, 24; Ruth Wedgwood (2003), 'Legal Authority Exists for a Strike on Iraq', *Financial Times*, 14 March; Secret Memorandum from the Attorney General to the Prime Minister, 7 March 2003; Legal advice received by the Australian government: *Memorandum of Advice on the Use of Force Against Iraq* of 18 March 2003. See 'The government's legal advice on using force', *Sydney Morning Herald* (Sydney) <http://www. smh.com.au/articles/2003/03/19/1047749818043.html> accessed 3 November 2005.

25 Hans Koechler (ed.) (2004), *Iraq Crisis and the UN Power Politics vs. the International Rule of Law*, p. 65; 'PM may be targeted by criminal indictment: lawyer' ABC Television, *Lateline*, 16 June 2005 <http://www.abc.net.au/lateline/content/2005/s1394137.htm> accessed 14 February 2006. The crime of aggression was first recognized under the Nuremberg Charter. A number of Germans were convicted at Nuremberg of waging a war of aggression against states occupied by Germany: See Case No. 72 Trial of Wilhelm Von Leeb And Thirteen Others (*The German High Command Trial*) United States Military Tribunal, Nuremberg, 30 December. 1947–28 October 1948. This crime has been recognized by the international community by its inclusion in Article 5(1) of the Rome Statute of the International Criminal Court which states:

> The jurisdiction of the Court shall be limited to the most serious crimes of concern to the international community as a whole. The Court has jurisdiction in accordance with this Statute with respect to the following crimes: (a) The crime of genocide; (b) Crimes against humanity; (c) War crimes; *(d) The crime of aggression* (italics added).

consequences of the invasion have been catastrophic. Millions of Iraqis have fled the country. Hundreds of thousands of Iraqis have lost their lives or been seriously injured. Multiple terrorist attacks each day are not uncommon in post-Saddam Iraq. The ousting of the Ba'ath regime and the failure of the occupiers or the elected Iraqi government to secure the country, has enabled terrorist organizations to proliferate. In this environment terror attacks are often carried out with complete impunity. Moreover there is no real prospect that the conviction and punishment of those responsible for the war and its aftermath will end the violence.

Since 2003, several conflicts are being waged in Iraq, often simultaneously. They include: ongoing armed resistance to foreign troops by a cross section of the Iraqi population; sectarian conflict within and between tribal and religious communities in Iraq; organised campaigns of terrorist violence by al Qaeda in Iraq and other Islamist terror organizations, and military operations by Coalition and Iraqi forces against local militias as well as foreign elements. In addition to all of this is the wanton criminal violence of lone wolves and criminal gangs.

In the immediate aftermath of the 2003 invasion there was lawlessness and looting in many parts of Iraq. Much of the infrastructure of the country had been destroyed during the war or was in near collapse (after decades of Ba'ath neglect compounded by the impact of UN sanctions). The Security Council was asked by the occupying powers for assistance to address Iraq's many problems. Given the multiple needs of the Iraqi people, the Security Council had little choice but to recognize the occupation and work with Coalition members states in an attempt to rebuild and stabilize Iraq. Had it decided otherwise, Britain and the US could have exercised their powers of veto to defeat any resolution that condemned the invasion and called for the immediate withdrawal of the occupying forces.

The presence of an occupying army (comprised for the most part of US personnel) was a honey pot for radical Islamists bent on militant jihad. From 2003 volunteers entered the country through Iraq's largely un-patrolled borders. Islamist terror organizations recruited jihadis from around the region and the world. As the violence escalated some states withdrew their forces from the US-led Coalition in Iraq. Others decided the best way to thwart the rise of Islamist terror was to remain in Iraq and capture or kill its practitioners. They participated in a belated attempt at organized counter-insurgency. This involved reconstruction and nation building (the battle to win heart and minds) and military operations (destruction of terrorist cells, and attempts to disband militias and discourage other opponents of the international force) have regularly come under attack (often from roadside bombs). The regular sabotage of reconstruction projects, an ongoing campaign of suicide bombings against military and civilian targets, and the growth of sectarian killings, prevented the international force from achieving its objectives. These attacks also undermined

---

This provision was adopted by the 160 participating states at Rome in 1998, demonstrating that the crime of aggression is well established under international law. While the ICC is yet to define 'aggression', the United Nations General Assembly has done so. In Article 3 of Resolution 3314 (XXIX) Definition of Aggression (14 December 1974), aggression is defined to include 'The invasion or attack by the armed forces of a State of the territory of another State, or any military occupation, however temporary, resulting from such invasion or attack'.

the authority of the interim Iraqi government. The UN persisted. Having endorsed the transfer of power to an interim government in June 2004 it supported a series of elections in 2005 in an effort help deliver the rule of law and democracy to Iraq. Questions may be raised about the legitimacy of elections while 150,000 foreign troops that entered Iraq in violation of the UN Charter remained in the country. The answer is twofold: those forces were authorized by the Security Council to remain in Iraq *and* there was little alternative. There was no momentum for an Arab force to replace the predominantly American force. A withdrawal of foreign troops before the elections would have handed the streets to rival sectarian militias, terrorist organizations, and criminal gangs – a recipe for civil war. Moreover in the ensuing power vacuum, the Ba'ath regime – which had utilized terror as an instrument of domestic policy for decades – could have fought its way back to power. The UN therefore had little choice but to support the elections, albeit under imperfect conditions.

By 2007 the UN and the international force in Iraq found themselves between a rock and a hard place: damned if they stayed and damned if they left. Many states that regularly contribute troops and other personnel to UN peace operations stayed out of Iraq entirely. They include Canada, Pakistan, New Zealand and numerous African and Arab states. Security Council Resolutions 1483, 1500, 1511 and 1546 provided the mandate for the 'Coalition of the Willing' to remain in Iraq to engage in reconstitution, promote responsible government, help stabilize Iraq and, by implication, fight terrorist organizations such as al Qaeda in Iraq. However lack of international unity on post-invasion Iraq and strong opposition to the presence of US fostered an environment in which Islamist terror has flourished.

Justice, Development, Economic Growth and Religious Moderation

The UN's Global Counter-Terrorism Strategy sets out a range of measures that are designed to 'address the conditions conducive to the spread of terrorism' and 'build States' capacity to prevent and combat terrorism.'[26] A lot of work needs to be done if the measures are to be implemented successfully. States must cooperate in order to: resolve conflicts; end oppression; eradicate poverty; deliver sustained economic growth, sustainable development, global prosperity, good governance, human rights for all and rule of law; improve intercultural understanding and respect for all religions, religious values, beliefs or cultures.[27] As has been noted, al Qaeda's appeal rests in part upon its determination to end the oppression, injustice and poverty that many Arab Muslims endure (conditions al Qaeda blames on the West, Zionists and Arab regimes – with some justification). Radical Islamist ideology will continue to draw young Muslims into the 'terrorism conveyor belt' until states work together to improve the plight of Arabs. This requires a commitment by Arab and Muslim states and their partners to the diverse elements of the global 'counter-insurgency'

---

26 See United Nations General Assembly Global Counter-Terrorism Strategy 'Plan of Action' at <http://www.un.org/terrorism/strategy-counter-terrorism.html> accessed 27 April 2007.

27 Ibid.

strategy. They will not be able to dismantle the apparatus of terror until human rights are respected, repression is lifted, corruption is minimized or eliminated, poverty and ignorance are reduced, and children receive a balanced education that promotes moderation, tolerance, peaceful resolution of disputes and compassion. If the cycle of violence and terror is to be broken in the Middle East, Afghanistan and beyond states must work together to deliver justice, development and good governance. For the West's part there must be a re-think of foreign policy to ensure these goals are being promoted rather than undermined.

While the level of commitment by Arab states to these benchmarks varies, all have given their, in principle, support to the Global Counter-Terrorism Strategy. At the 2005 World Summit of the General Assembly, members of the Arab League and the Conference of Islamic States asked for assistance in their efforts to 'address the root causes of terrorism', through *inter alia*, 'diplomacy, financial and economic measures, and encouraging moderate trends.'[28] It remains to be seen how committed these states are to taking the hard decisions needed to resolve these problems. Without their active support the strategy cannot succeed.

Foreign Military Policy

Military operations designed to deal with the threat posed by terror organizations may be a necessary ingredient of national and regional counter-terrorism strategies. On their own they will never be a sufficient response. They should always be conducted in accordance with the UN Charter. States should only engage in external military operations where this use of force is justified in self-defence, authorized by the UN Security Council, or recommended by the UN General Assembly acting pursuant to the 1950 'Uniting for Peace' resolution.

Coalitions of states should only engage in international counter-terrorism operations that fall within this legal framework. If requested to engage in military operations that are in breach of international law, states should refuse to participate for the following reasons. First, action taken against terrorist organizations outside the Charter framework will provide a propaganda boost for the terrorists. Secondly, those who engage in the unlawful use of force may be complicit in the commission of crimes against peace, including the crime of aggression. Thirdly, if force is to be used against regimes in Muslim nations, the international legitimacy of the operation is paramount. One of the many lessons learned from the war in Iraq is that without the active support of all neighboring states, use of force inside Muslim lands is likely to be a magnet for radical Islamists from across the region. Even with the support

---

28 See Statement of his Excellency Prof. Ekmeleddin Ihsanoglu Secretary General of the Organization of the Islamic Conference at the High-Level Plenary Meeting of the United Nations General Assembly, United Nations headquarters – New York, 16 September 2005 <http://www.oic-oci.org/index.asp> accessed 24 November 2005. By contrast, both Islamist terrorists and critics of Islam point to the text of the Koran and Hadith as the legal authority for militant jihad: See 'Al Qaeda Fatwa: World Islamic Front against Jews and Crusaders', published in *al-Quds al-Arabi* (London UK), 23 February 1998, p. 3; and Ayaan Hirsi Ali (2007), *Infidel: My Life* (Free Press), pp. 169–92.

of neighboring states, the use of force by a predominantly non-Muslim Coalition of states (and perhaps even a predominantly Muslim force) is likely to incite radical Islamists to engage in what they characterize as necessary jihad to oppose the intervention and the 'apostate' regime installed in its wake.[29] Events in Iraq and Afghanistan have shown that the 'jihad' is likely to be waged through a sustained campaign of terrorist violence.

Policing

Policing (including forensic investigation, intelligence gathering, surveillance, and the interrogation of suspects) plays an important role in domestic and international counter-terrorism. At the domestic level, police and intelligence agencies need to be provided with the tools to engage in effective counter-terrorism. Intelligence agents must be recruited from within the sectarian communities from which terrorists emanate. Adequate resources must be provided for intelligence gathering.[30]

The Security Council has imposed significant policing obligations on states in the fight against terrorist groups.[31] They include international and regional cooperation in policing and intelligence gathering. States must also report to their counter-terrorism activities to the Security Council's Counter-Terrorism Committee. Its role is to monitor compliance by states with their international responsibilities in this area. Matters that must be reported to the Committee include:

1. the development of police and intelligence structures for the detection, monitoring and apprehension of those involved in terrorist activities and those supporting terrorist activities;
2. customs, immigration and border controls measures to prevent the movement of terrorists and the establishment of safe havens; and
3. controls to prevent terrorists gaining access to weapons and munitions.

However the Security Council has not issued a blank check for states to do as they please when conducting military and policing operations against terror suspects. States must adhere to the rule of law, human rights norms, judicial safeguards and

---

29 See Ayman Al Zawahiri (2001), *Knights Under the Prophet's Banner* (*Fursan Taht Rayah Al-Nabi*); Laura Mansfield (2006), *His Own Words: Translation and Analysis of the Writings of Dr Ayman Al Zawahiri*; Laura Mansfield (2007), *Al Qaeda 2006 Yearbook: The 2006 Messages from Al Qaeda*.

30 Close cooperation with neighboring states to enhance regional law enforcement capacities is an important means of combating terrorism. The development of a regional center for joint law enforcement operations between Indonesia and Australia in Semarang, Indonesia represents a significant development in this field: 'Australia-Indonesia law centre opens', 3 August 2005 <http://www.theage.com.au/news/national/australiaindonesia-law-centre-opens/2005/08/03/1122748693180.html> accessed 5 January 2006.

31 See SC Res. 1373 (2001) and SC Res. 1456 (2003).

humanitarian law.[32] As noted in Chapter 2.3, non-derogable norms such as the prohibition against torture must be adhered to at all times. This is both legally and strategically important. States that allow terror suspects to be tortured undermine efforts to counter the ideology of radical Islamists. The latter are more than willing to exploit the propaganda value of such abuses. Torture of Islamist terror suspects by agents of democratic states undermines the rule of law and the universality of human rights. Such practices also lend support to the anti-democratic ideology of terrorist networks such as al Qaeda.

The interrogation of terror suspects must be conducted within the bounds of international law. It must be subject to judicial oversight. Legislative reform to expand the powers of investigative agencies in terrorism cases must make adequate provision for judicial review of the length and conditions of confinement. Terror suspects must be afforded the right of appeal against detention orders, conviction and sentence. Remedies must also be available for police misconduct. Innocent parties held by police under expansive powers of arrest and detention must be compensated. This is of particularly important in the struggle by Western countries against Islamist terror cells operating within their own sovereign territory. In countries like Australia where Muslims are a small minority of the population, men of Middle Eastern appearance are likely to face greater police scrutiny than other men. At least one former ASIO official has called for an ethnicity/nationality-based approach.[33] This is short sighted and cannot be reconciled with the prohibition on racial discrimination under Australian law. Australian Federal Police Commissioner Mick Keelty has rightly pointed out that if new anti-terrorism laws are used in a heavy-handed fashion this may encourage support for terror groups.[34] It is therefore essential that proper operational procedures and judicial protections are in place to minimize the risk of detention and interrogation on the basis of appearance, ethnicity or religion alone.

Foreign Policy and Support for 'Modern Islam'

As has been noted, the foreign policy of states can play a powerful role in the promotion of moderate Islamic ideologies. The vast majority of Muslims live in developing states in conditions of poverty. Most lack the educational, health, social, economic and technological opportunities that Westerners often take for granted. They often live under autocratic and corrupt regimes. They are vulnerable to the seductions of extremism in their quest for solutions to life's basic challenges. Ignorance and poverty are the soil in which ideologies of hatred and intolerance

---

32 Security Council resolution 1456 (2003), states that 'States must ensure that any measure taken to combat terrorism comply with all their obligations under international law, and should adopt such measures in accordance with international law, in particular international human rights, refugee, and humanitarian law.'

33 Reporter: Margot O'Neill, 'Former ASIO officer claims Islamic extremists are living in Australia', Lateline 2 August 2005 <http://www.abc.net.au/lateline/content/2005/s1428699.htm> accessed 24 November 2005.

34 See Ian Munro (2005), 'Top cop warns: new terror laws could backfire if abused', *The Age*, 23–24 December, p. 3.

are planted. The 'terrorist conveyor belt' in Pakistan is driven by these conditions. Afghanistan's democratic government has responded to these challenges by building maddrasses of its own which offer a balanced education. The attainment of knowledge is an important aspect of Islam. With broad based curricula, school education can fill young minds with the tools to embrace the opportunities and challenges of the modern world.[35] This is part of the wider project to promote 'modern Islam.'[36]

There is much that wealthy states – both Muslim and non-Muslim – can do to break the cycle of radical Islam. Building and funding modern schools, universities and hospitals is one way. However helping some Muslim societies out of poverty requires political, economic as well as ideological reform. The 'transformative occupation' model (external intervention) can be a painful and costly process as the experiences in Afghanistan and Iraq have shown. This approach should not be undertaken without UN approval. The preferred path is internally driven transformation. While international assistance will often be necessary to bring about economic and political reform, this should be provided with the consent of the host state and UN endorsement. UN member states must work together to foster capacity building projects and human rights throughout the Muslim world (UN Charter, Article 1). The aim must be to promote international trade, cooperation and friendly relations with all states.

Efforts by Arab regimes and other Muslim governments to counter radical ideologies need to be supported by states. At the 2005 World Summit of the General Assembly, both the Arab League and the Conference of Islamic States asked all states to assist them in their efforts to thwart extremist Islamic ideologies.[37] This project is now a universal one. If moderate Islam is to prevail over violent extremism, states

---

35 In 2006 the Afghan government announced its plans to set up madrasses (religious schools) to counter the influence of extremist elements and foster 'modern Islam.' Students will devote 40 per cent of their time to religious education, 40 per cent to maths, science and other subjects and 20 per cent to foreign languages. 'Afghanistan to Take Back Madrassas in 2007', website <http://www.embassyofafghanistan.org> (homepage) accessed 12 June 2007. President Kazai has also called for the maddrasses in Pakistan that teach hatred to be closed:

> There is a 15-year-old boy, … extremely poor, extremely desperate, extremely unaware of the rest of the world, in a Pakistani madrassa. And in that madrassa, the teacher tells him, 'Go to Afghanistan. The country has become Christian. The country has become Jewish. There are Americans … there in Afghanistan. Go kill them, and you will be in heaven straightaway.' Now, does it solve the problem by killing this young, ignorant person, or by going and closing that madrassa in Pakistan?

Source: Fareed Zakaria, Interview: 'I Know the Problem: The beleaguered Afghan president takes aim at his critics', *Newsweek International* (website) (updated 2 October 2006) <http://www.msnbc.msn.com/id/14975915/site/newsweek/>.

36 This term is used by President Hamid Kazai to describe the Islamic ideology he seeks to promote in Afghanistan. While not ideal, this terminology highlights the contrast between Kazai's vision and the fundamentalist Islamic ideology of the Taliban.

37 See Statement of his Excellency Prof. Ekmeleddin Ihsanoglu (2005), Secretary General of the Organization of the Islamic Conference at the High-Level Plenary Meeting of the United Nations General Assembly, United Nations headquarters: '… the OIC rejects and condemns violence and terrorism …What is needed, we believe, is to address the root

need to act at a number of levels. Support should be given to education, health and economic development from Algeria to Indonesia. This must be done in conjunction with genuine reform to build the rule of law, human rights and democracy and end corruption, nepotism and autocracy.

Monitoring and Enforcement: Counter-Terrorism Obligations under Security Council Mandates

The al Qaeda/Taliban Sanctions Committee

The al Qaeda/Taliban Sanctions Committee was established by the Security Council in 2001 (pursuant to resolution 1267 (1999)). It continually updates a consolidated list of individuals and entities belonging to or associated with al Qaeda and the Taliban. States use this list to enforce and implement the arms embargo, the travel ban and the assets freeze against listed individuals and entities.

The Monitoring Team

An Analytical Support and Sanctions Monitoring Team established in 2001 under Security Council resolution 1361 examines progress by states in fulfilling their counter-terrorism obligations. It offers expertise on things that need to be addressed such as: the drafting of legislation; monitoring of the financing of terrorism and international financial transactions, technical banking expertise; alternative remittance systems, charities and use of couriers; border enforcement, port security; arms embargoes and export controls; and drug trafficking.[38]

The Monitoring Team has noted the constantly evolving structure of the al Qaeda network and its ability to beat the sanctions regime and weapons embargo. The systems established by the Security Council can break down where states are unprepared to respond effectively when listed individuals arriving at a port of entry use lost or stolen travel documents. Basic capacity building is needed in state border control systems (for example, by linking customs to criminal databases and Interpol) to thwart attempts to travel on forged, stolen or lost documents. The effectiveness of these and other UN measures to curb terrorism has been questioned (Bianchi 2006).

Regional Cooperation and Capacity Building

Capacity building of police at a regional level is also needed. This means international cooperation to improve policing and intelligence gathering. In South East Asia, the capture and prosecution of al Qaeda, Jemaah Islamiyah, and Abu Saef operatives is a regional concern. Improvements are needed in the areas of witness exchange

---

causes of terrorism, using the art of convincing through local approaches while resorting to diplomacy, financial and economic measures, and encouraging moderate trends.'

38 The Monitoring Group first established pursuant to resolution 1363 (2001) <http://www.un.org/Docs/sc/committees/1267/1267mg.htm>.

and intelligence sharing. The refusal of the US to make captured Jemaah Islamiyah terrorist Hambali (Ruduan Ismuddin) available to testify in Indonesian criminal trials in 2003 is a case in point. It undermined Indonesia's capacity to mount successful prosecutions in terrorism cases.[39] By contrast, close Australian and Indonesian cooperation in the field of counter-terrorism has borne fruit. The military commander of Jemaah Islamiyah and various other pivotal members of this terrorist organization are now under arrest or have already been convicted and sentenced.

Coordination between Domestic Police and Intelligence Agencies

A terrorism summit held in Canberra in September 2005 resulted in agreement on a range of measures to enhance the powers of ASIO and Australia's federal, state and territory police forces.[40] A communiqué issued at the summit contains important principles and safeguards to ensure that counter-terrorism laws are not abused. They include provision for parliamentary and judicial review. It was also agreed that the laws should be exercised in a way that is 'evidence-based, intelligence-led and proportionate.' Moreover the counter-terrorism laws will be reviewed after five years and will 'sunset' after 10 years.

The agreement follows ASIO and the Office of National Assessments (ONA) briefings of state and territory leaders on the threat of terrorist attacks. These leaders were satisfied that there was a sufficient threat of terror attacks to warrant the proposed measures. The subsequent arrest of 18 terror suspects in Sydney and Melbourne in November 2005 vindicated this position. State, territory and Commonwealth parliaments have an important and continuing role in ensuring that the safeguards agreed at COAG are included in the laws. In December 2005

---

39 Wilkinson, Marian (2003), 'US denies Indonesia access to Hambali', *Sydney Morning Herald*, 22 September, <http://www.smh.com.au/articles/2003/09/21/1064082867811.html> accessed 24 November 2005.

40 Council of Australian Government's Communiqué Special Meeting on Counter-Terrorism, 27 September 2005 <http://www.coag.gov.au/meetings/270905/coag270905.rtf> accessed 24 November 2005.

There was agreement that:

1. The Commonwealth Criminal Code be amended to enable Australia better to deter and prevent potential acts of terrorism and prosecute where these occur. This includes amendments to provide for control orders and preventative detention for up to 48 hours to restrict the movement of those who pose a terrorist risk to the community.
2. The Commonwealth's ability to proscribe terrorist organizations will be expanded to include organizations that advocate terrorism.
3. Other improvements will be made, including to the financing of terrorism offense.
4. The Commonwealth Criminal Code be amended to enable Australia better to deter and prevent potential acts of terrorism and prosecute where these occur. This includes amendments to provide for control orders and preventative detention for up to 48 hours to restrict the movement of those who pose a terrorist risk to the community.
5. The Commonwealth's ability to proscribe terrorist organizations will be expanded to include organizations that advocate terrorism. Other improvements will be made, including to the financing of terrorism offense.

the federal government passed the Commonwealth Anti-Terrorism Act 2005. This legislation was the federal government's response to the COAG agreement. The original Bill was criticised for going beyond the measures agreed at COAG. Public debate over the Bill demonstrated a high level of public scrutiny of the potential impact of the government's proposed counter-terrorism laws. A number of aspects of the Bill attracted particular attention. It remains to be seen whether the proposed Public Interest Monitor will have sufficient independence and authority to publicly highlight any potential abuse of the law. Nonetheless it has the potential to be an informed voice in debate on the merits of law reform when the laws come up for review. The provisions on judicial review remain controversial. John North, President of the Law Council of Australia, has noted that:

> The power to make control orders is to be given to federal courts and is clearly non-judicial. Judicial power requires a fair procedure, including notice of the proceedings and disclosure of the basis upon which orders are sought and made. None of this occurs in relation to control orders.[41]

It remains to be seen whether the constitutionality of these provisions of will be challenged, and if so, whether they will survive judicial scrutiny by the High Court of Australia.[42]

Social Engineering

The suicide bombings carried out by young British Muslims (or British passport holders) in London in 2005, focused national attention on what may be done to prevent the radicalization of Muslims in Britain. A range of matters were canvassed including:

1. the psychological impact on Muslims of the intense media scrutiny of Islam since 11 September 2001;
2. the perception of some Muslims that their religion was under attack from the West;
3. Muslim anger and humiliation at Britain's involvement in Iraq;
4. the role of extremists (including some Imams) in propagating radical Islamist ideas (including religious intolerance and hatred of the West); and
5. the threat of further political and religious violence by self-radicalized Muslim youth.

For some Muslims living in non-Muslim states (particularly those who experience racism and social isolation in Western countries), radical Islamist ideologies can provide a sense of community, identity and belonging. They can also foster a culture whereby young people may be vulnerable to radicalization to the point where they are

---

41 'Anti-Terror Bill Compromised', 25 October 2005 <http://www.lawcouncil.asn.au/read/2005/2418069228.html> accessed 5 January 2006.

42 See Criminal Code (Cth) (1995), Division 104.

willing to engage in terrorism. A number of strategies to address this problem have already been noted, including the promotion of moderate Islamic theology in Islamic schools, colleges and mosques.[43] Another is to challenge Islamist ideologies that promote hatred and intolerance, through dialogue and theological discussion. Here the Islamic doctrine of *itijihad* (reinterpretation of the Koran in the context of modernity) offers a useful path to moderate interpretations of the Koran. Another method is to review materials used in religious instruction. In 2007, a British government inquiry was ordered into texts used at an Islamic school.[44] The spotlight has also been cast on Saudi funded colleges and the books they use – not just in Britain but also in the US, Australia and beyond.[45] A report entitled *Saudi Arabia's Curriculum of Intolerance* analyzed Saudi Ministry of Education textbooks used during the 2006 academic year, in elementary and secondary school Islamic studies courses.[46] The report concluded that these teaching materials promoted an ideology of hatred of those who do not subscribe to the Wahhabi sect of Islam.[47] Prior to the report's release, the Saudi Ambassador to the US, Prince Turki al Faisal, stated that official Saudi textbooks have been reviewed to remove content that incites intolerance towards those of other faiths and worldviews.[48] However the Institute of Gulf Affairs has challenged this claim.[49] Saudi Arabia's moves to continue reform in this area, so as to exclude materials that may incite religious hatred, are welcome. Indeed all states have an obligation to take measures to ensure that school curriculum and pedagogy do not promote religious, ethnic or political violence or hatred.[50] They must also take effective measures to halt the export of extremist ideologies by their citizens.

---

43 Mustapha Kara-Ali, a member of Australian Prime Minister John Howard's Muslim Community Reference Group has prepared a guidebook entitled *The Way Forward for Australian Muslims: A Good Practice Guide for Building Identity and Resisting Radicalisation.* Kara-Ali's view is that immigrant Imams opposed to change are thwarting the integrating of Islamic youth into Australian society: See Richard Karaj (2006), 'Forcing identity crisis on youth', *The Australian*, 13 February,.

44 'Saudi school's regret over books', 20 February 2007 <www.news.bbc.co.uk> accessed 29 April 2007.

45 'Saudi textbooks leave students open to bin Laden's message', *USA Today*, 6 April 2006 available at <www.usatoday.com> accessed 28 August 2007.

46 The report is available on the Center's website <www.freedomhouse.org/religion> and IGA's website <www.gulfinstitute.org> accessed 29 August 2007.

47 Wahhabism is – by Western standards at least – an ultra conservative and anti-pluralist ideology. However this assessment may change if promised reforms are fully implemented. This Islamic sect was founded by Muhammad ibn Abd al Wahab (1703–92) and is the official ideology of the Kingdom of Saudi Arabia. For a Wahhabi account see: Abd Allah Al-Uthaymin, 'Muhammad Ibn Abd al-Wahhab's movement and some aspects of his doctrines' (Copy on file).

48 'Saudi Ambassador Addresses Town Hall Los Angeles', 21 March 3006 <www.saudiembassey.net> accessed 28 April 2007.

49 See Shea, Nina (2006), 'This is a Saudi Textbook (after the Intolerance was Removed)', *Washington Post*, 21 May, Page BO1. But see: Prince Turki al-Faisal, 'Educational Reforms in Saudi Arabia: We're Trying Hard to Change', 8 June 2006 at <www.saudi-us-relations.org> accessed 29 August 2007.

50 Both the Israeli government and Palestinian Authority have also been called upon to ensure that school books promote peace and not hatred of the other. See: Resolution 1245

Another strategy is to deny entry to radical Imams who preach intolerance and hatred of non-Muslims, and monitor them closely in their home states. A number of states have implemented such policies. In Europe for example, visiting Imams have been warned that their visas will be revoked if they violate racial and religious hatred laws. Some have been expelled on these grounds.[51] Proactive measures to ease tensions with non-Muslims and stave off radicalization have also been launched by Muslim organizations.[52]

Other measures have been more controversial. The French ban on the hijab in public schools is a case in point. It is perceived by many Muslims as a slight against Islam and a denial of their right to freedom of religion. Some schoolgirls have indicated that they started wearing the hijab as an act of protest rather than a demonstration of religious commitment. This raises the question: What did the French government expect teenage Muslim girls to do when it imposed such a ban? Welcome the ban? France is the birthplace of liberty, equality and fraternity. Protest is a national pastime. While integration is important so as to avoid economic and social marginalization, telling people what to wear or not wear is more in line with autocratic theocracy than liberal democracy.

In summary 'social engineering' has an important role to play in protecting Muslim youths from being radicalized to the point where they are willing to involve themselves in religious violence. However such policies must be carefully evaluated to ensure that they do not violate human rights. They must be non-discriminatory in nature and effect.

Military Force

Some terrorist organizations have shown a willingness to strike against civilian targets across the world, and a refusal to compromise on ideological objectives that are irreconcilable with the principles and purposes of the UN. Where this attitude prevails, diplomacy and negotiations in the search for political solutions to terrorism are all but impossible. With no means of deterring such groups from the path of suicidal terror, preventative measures may be necessary (Schonsheck 2007). However the use of force by states (against clearly identifiable military targets such as known al Qaeda training camps) must be conducted within the UN Charter framework. Military action by states is permissible under international law in the exercise of the right of self-defence (Article 51). This right was reaffirmed

---

(2001) Middle East Conflict, 26 April 2001, Council of Europe's Parliamentary Assembly.

51 Nathalie Malinarich, 'Europe moves against radical imams', BBC News Online, 6 May 2004; Alison Caldwell, 'Canadian Sheikh refused entry to Australia', ABC Radio, *PM* program, 4 April 2007 at <http://news.bbc.uk/2/hi/europe/3686617.stmwww.abc.net.au; Colin Randall, 'France ejects 12 Islamic "preachers of hate" ', 30 July 2005 <www.telegraph.co.uk> accessed 28 April 2007, 29 April 2007.

52 The Brussels-based Federation of Islamic Organizations in Europe claims that some 400 Muslim groups in 28 countries from Russia to Spain have signed a 26-point European Islamic Charter which urges Muslims to integrate positively into society: 'Islamic pact to stave off radicalisation', *The Western Australian*, p. 34.

by the Security Council in the context of terrorism in resolutions passed on 12 and 28 September 2001. Force may only be used to counter terrorist threats where the provisions of Article 51 are satisfied or a mandate for such action has been issued by the Council. Pre-emptive strikes against known al Qaeda training camps may be justified under resolution 1373 (2001) although the temporal limits of this resolution are unclear. Where strikes against terrorist organizations are carried out with the prior consent of the state within whose borders the terrorists are based, no Council approval is needed for such action.

As has been noted, international counter-terrorism measures that are not justified under the right of self-defence, and not authorized by the Council, will likely be in breach of UN Charter principles. The unilateral use of force against Iraq by Coalition forces in 2003 is a case in point. It was conduct in violation of the general prohibition on the use of force (Charter of the United Nations, Article 2(4)) and offered a propaganda boost for terrorist groups and their sympathizers. States that use force outside the international rule of law also expose themselves to the risk of international criminal litigation. Where such conduct amounts to a crime of aggression they may be prosecuted for committing crimes against peace. Military interventions of this type are not only legally but also morally questionable. As one commentator has recently observed 'the moral case for preventative intervention has not yet been made' (Lee 2007).

The struggle to rein-in non-state actors that engage in terrorism requires international unity – particularly when the 'host state' refuses to deal with international terrorist groups located within its borders. As the Iraq war demonstrates, the invasion of Arab states without international consensus is more likely to ferment terrorism than facilitate its defeat. This was one of many 'lessons learned' by Coalition forces in that conflict. States that have been infiltrated by terrorist organizations need to be supported in their efforts to tackle terrorism. Where a request is made by a state for armed assistance to deal with terrorists, the responding state may use force against the terrorists in the exercise of the collective right of self-defence.[53] If the victim state is unwilling or unable to call for such assistance, Security Council authorization will be needed before military action is launched by foreign powers.

Contextual Responses

In summary, states need to respond to the threat of Islamist terror at two levels: international and domestic. At the international level, states must participate in global efforts to prevent international terrorism. This requires measures to be taken in accordance with the obligations of states under binding resolutions of the Security Council. At the domestic level, states must take necessary steps to protect their citizens through counter-terrorism policies that reflect local conditions. The domestic response will necessarily differ from state to state. This is evident from a recent report

---

53 See *Nicaragua Case* (1986), International Court of Justice (Judgment) (Merits). See also Security Council Resolution 1373 (2001).

on counter-terrorism policies of Russia and a number of NATO member states.[54] It critiques the 'lessons learned' by the USA, Russia, Turkey and Spain, following Islamist terror attacks in each of these states. There were significant differences in the way these nations experienced and responded to terrorism. Contrasts were highlighted in the following areas: the level of preparedness for such attacks; the nature of the terrorist attack; the ongoing threat; the capacity to thwart future attacks; and the social, cultural, religious, economic and political context in which the attacks had occurred. What is evident from this report is that while there are some measures that all states should be taking to reduce the threat of terrorism, the specific action required will vary from state to state.

Conclusion

Effective counter-terrorism calls for a variety of strategies. In the context of terrorism carried out by radical Islamists these strategies include:

1. the development of policies aimed at reducing the appeal of extremist ideologies ('social engineering');
2. enhancement of intelligence gathering compatibilities;
3. policing measures that limit the capacity for terror attacks to be launched;
4. shifts in foreign policy to avoid policies that inspire terrorist activity;
5. development of interrogation methods that are affective but do not violate the prohibition on torture; and
6. where force must be used against terrorist organizations and governments that sponsor them, due respect for UN Charter norms as well as wider principles of international law (for example, *jus in bello*) (Weiner AS., 2007).

The importance of the last point cannot be overemphasized. The success of counter-terrorism operations often depends on local support and cooperation. Coercive and intrusive powers must be exercised with discernment. Compliance with human rights and humanitarian law principles is not only the law, it is a vital part of the 'hearts and minds' strategy inherent in any decent plan to undermine support for militant groups.

Negotiation with terrorist organizations is in some situations necessary – particularly where breaking off negotiations is precisely what the terrorists want (Macleod 2007). However states will usually deny that they have in the past, or will in the future, negotiate with terrorists. This is understandable. They do not want to encourage others to pursue their goals in this manner. However such negotiations do (and should) take place. A case in point is negotiations between US forces in Iraq and insurgents groups that the US had previously described as terrorists.

Terrorist activity can never be fully eradicated. However specific terror threats may be eliminated and ideologies that fuel terror undermined. The struggle against

---

54 Chairman's Report (2005), 'Lessons learned from recent terrorist attacks: Building national capabilities and institutions', NATO–Russian Council Conference <http://www.nato.int/docu/conf/2005/050727/index.html> accessed 22 April 2007.

international terrorism by religious extremists requires strategies aimed at achieving both objectives. However these efforts are unlikely to be completely successful without unity of purpose, firm commitment and resolve, careful planning, and adherence to human rights and the rule of international law by states. At the time of writing the international community continues to struggle to quell politico-religious violence by a range of actors. The prolonged nature of this struggle is a reflection of: the level of support for extreme religious ideologies; disenchantment at US mistakes in the 'war on terror'; unresolved questions concerning the compatibility of current Islamist ideologies with democratic polity; and related difficulties securing international cooperation to implement the UN counter-terrorism strategies. On the positive side, al Qaeda and its affiliates have been condemned by all states. Their ideology, activities, and indeed very existence represent an actual or potential threat to all governments. In an era where sovereign states remain the cornerstone of the international legal order, extremist ideologies that challenge this framework are unlikely to prevail in the long term.

References

'Afghanistan to Take Back Madrassas in 2007'. Accessible at <http://www.embassyofafghanistan.org> accessed 12 June 2007.

'Al-Qaeda bomb threat to Australia', 17 November 2003 <http://www.theage.com.au/articles/2003/11/17/1069004715713.html?from=storyrhs> accessed 5 January 2005.

'Anti-Terror Bill: Judiciary Compromised', 25 October 2005 <http://www.lawcouncil.asn.au/read/2005/2418069228.html> accessed 5 January 2006.

'Australia–Indonesia law centre opens', 3 August 2005 <http://www.theage.com.au/news/national/australiaindonesia-law-centre-opens/2005/08/03/1122748693180.html> accessed 5 January 2006.

Australian Security Intelligence Organisation Act 1979.

Aviation Transport Security Act 2004.

Bianchi, A. (2006), 'Security's Council's Anti-terror Resolutions and Their Implementation by Member States: an Overview', 4 *Journal of International Criminal Justice*, no. 5, pp. 1044–73.

Case No. 72: Trial of Wilhelm Von Leeb and Thirteen Others (*The German High Command Trial*), United States Military Tribunal, Nuremberg, 30 December 1947–28 October 1948.

Commonwealth Criminal Code Act.

Cooke, D. and Lopez, E., 'Raids disrupt "imminent" attack', 8 November 2005 <http://www.theage.com.au/articles/2005/11/08/1131212027799.html?from=top5> accessed 5 January 2006.

Council of Australian Governments (COAG) Communiqué Special Meeting on Counter-Terrorism, 27 September 2005 <http://www.coag.gov.au/meetings/270905/coag270905.rtf > accessed 24 November 2005.

Customs Act 1901.

Fareed Zakaria, Interview: "'I Know the Problem": The beleaguered Afghan president takes aim at his critics', *Newsweek International* (website) (updated 2 October 2006) <http://www.msnbc.msn.com/id/14975915/site/newsweek/> General Assembly Resolution 2200A (XXI), International Covenant on Civil and Political Rights, 21 UN GAOR Supp. (No. 16) at 52, UN Doc. A/6316 (1966), 999 UNTS 171, entered into force 23 March 1976. Article 4(1).

General Assembly Resolution, 12 September 2001 (First Resolution of the 56th UN General Assembly (2001)).

Gordon, M., 'Howard misled us, say voters', *The Age* <http://www.theage.com.au/articles/2004/08/17/1092508474760.html> accessed 23 November 2005.

His Excellency Prof. Ekmeleddin Ihsanoglu (2005) New York, 16 September <http://www.oic-oci.org/index.asp> accessed 24 November 2005.

Kearney, S. (2005), 'More terror cells forming', *The Australian*, 21 November.

Kingston, M., 'Few chances left to restore public service integrity'(published online 14 April 2004) <http://www.smh.com.au/articles/2004/04/14/1081838786370.html> accessed 24 November 2005.

Lee, S.P. (2007), 'Preventative Intervention', in Steven P. Lee (ed.) *Intervention, Terrorism and Torture: Contemporary Challenges to Just War Theory* (Springer), pp. 119, 131.

Macleod, A.M. (2007), 'The War against Terrorism and the "War" Against Terrorism', in Stephen P. Lee, *Intervention, Terrorism and Torture: Contemporary Challenges to Just War Theory*, pp. 187, 197–200.

Maritime Transport Security Act 2003 (Australia).

'Measures to eliminate international terrorism', A/RES/49/60, 9 December 1994 <http://www.un.org/Docs/sc/committees/1267/1267ListEng.htm> accessed 4 January 2006.

Migration Act 1958 (Australia).

Munro, I. (2005), 'Top cop warns: new terror laws could backfire if abused', *The Age*, 23–24 December, p. 3.

Nicholson, B. (2004a), 'Terrorist attack on Australia inevitable, warns FBI expert', *Sydney Morning Herald*, 16 March, <http://www.smh.com.au/articles/2004/03/16/1079199194943.html?from=storyrhs> accessed 24 November 2005.

—— (2004b), Iraq war increased risk, say experts', *Sydney Morning Herald* <http://www.theage.com.au/articles/2004/09/09/1094530767011.html?from=storylhs>

Pitts, W.G. (2003), 'Overview: field artillery in operation Iraqi freedom', *FA Journal*, September–October, <http://www.findarticles.com/p/articles/mi_m0IAU/is_5_8/ai_110732250> accessed 24 November 2005.

'Protecting Australia against terrorism: Australia's national counter-terrorism policies and arrangements', <http://www.pmc.gov.au/publications/protecting_australia/preparedness/1_legislation.htm> accessed 4 January 2005.

Reporter: Colvin, M. (2005), 'Govts should be sceptical of security intelligence: Evans', *PM*, 27 September <http://www.abc.net.au/pm/content/2005/s1469673.htm> accessed 24 November 2005.

Reporter: O'Neill, M. (2005), 'Former ASIO officer claims Islamic extremists are living in Australia', *Lateline*, 2 August, <http://www.abc.net.au/lateline/content/2005/s1428699.htm> accessed 24 November 2005.

Schonsheck, J. (2007), 'Determining Moral Rectitude in Thwarting Suicide Terrorist Attacks: Moral Terra Incognita', in Steven P. Lee (ed.), *Intervention, Terrorism and Torture: Contemporary Challenges to Just War Theory*, pp. 155, 158.

Security Council (SC) Res. 1566, 2004.

SC Res. 1456 (2003).

SC Res 1373 (2001).

SC Res. 1267 (1999) <http://www.un.org/Docs/sc/committees/1267Template.htm>

The Monitoring Group (2001) Resolution 1363 <http://www.un.org/Docs/sc/committees/1267/1267mg.htm>.

'US, Australia warn of Indonesia terror attacks: Militants may be planning to kidnap foreigners over Christmas', New Year, 22 December 2005. <http://www.msnbc.msn.com/id/10568382/> Accessed 5 January 2005.

Vincent, Michael (2005) 'Lucas Heights potential target for alleged terrorist attack', 14 November <http://www.abc.net.au/worldtoday/content/2005/s1506095.htm> accessed 24 April 2007.

Weiner, A.S. (2007), 'Law, Just War, and the International Fight against terrorism: Is it War?' in Steven P. Lee (ed.), *Intervention, Terrorism and Torture: Contemporary Challenges to Just War Theory*, pp. 137, 150.

Wilkie, A. (2004), *Axis of Deceit* (Melbourne: Black Inc. Agenda).

Wilkinson, M. (2003), 'US denies Indonesia access to Hambali', *Sydney Morning Herald*, 22 September.

Woolford, D. (2004), 'Senate inquiry finds PM misled public', *The Age*, 9 December <http://www.theage.com.au/news/Immigration/Senate-inquiry-finds-PM-misled-public/2004/12/09/1102182417469.html>.

4.3   Just War and Terrorism

T. Brian Mooney

In this part of the chapter I will argue that traditional just war theory provides the salient criteria for a polity's violent actions against groups that are not themselves, or at least, need not be polities. Traditional just war theory has its origins particularly in the writings of Aristotle, Cicero and St Augustine,[55] however was developed in the Scholastic and Neo-Scholastic periods by Aquinas, Grotius, Suarez, Vattel and Vitoria. Recently just war theory has received considerable pedigree as lying behind the codification of armed conflict in international law through the United Nations Charter and the Hague and Geneva Conventions. Contemporary apologists of just

---

55 See Aristotle, *Politics*, Book 1, chs. III & IV; *Nichomachaean Ethics*, Book VII; Cicero, *De Officiis*, *Philippics*; Augustine, *City of God*, Book XIX.

war theory are deeply influential in ethical and political debates and include writers such as Germain Grisez, John Finnis, Joseph Boyle, James Johnson and Michael Walzer (Boyle J., *et al*, 1987; Johnson J., 1984; 1999; Walzer M., 2004; 2000).

Although there have been attempts to deal with the relation between just war theory and terrorism[56] traditional just war theory was primarily concerned with rationally grounding the moral legitimacy of waging war between polities, states and nations. Nevertheless with the increasing prevalence of radical terrorist groups in the contemporary world that need have no official relation to a polity it is worth questioning again whether an extension of traditional just war theory to include waging of war against such groups is morally legitimate.[57] In this part of the chapter I will argue that some of the contemporary accounts of just war theory are inadequate because they fail to take traditional justifications for punishment in just war as central to justice.

Contemporary just war theorists have moved away from the notion of just war as including a punitive dimension and have focused on the central case of *jus ad bellum* as being defensive (Boyle J., 2003). In this they have been remarkably consistent with trends apparent in the international community. Justifications for war tend to be framed in terms of international agreements and international law, typically accompanied by a search for consensus usually thrashed out through the United Nations. Such approaches have lamentably met with limited success partly I suggest because many polities do not trust the motivations of powerful nations who attempt to build a consensus for war. It is in this context that I think traditional just war theory provides a set of meaningful normative guidelines on the justifiability of engaging in war (*jus ad bellum*), for conduct within wars (*jus in bello*) and for termination of hostilities at the end of war (*jus post bellum*).

As I argued in Chapter 2.2, 'Torture, Tragedy and Natural Law', St Thomas Aquinas thinks that there are salient moral features of action which trade on a distinction between the public and the private. War is one such arena in which public authority overrides personal authority:

> Just as the rulers of a city-state, kingdom or province rightly defend its public order (*res publicam*) against internal disturbance, by using the physical sword in punishing criminals... so too rulers have the right (*ad principes pertinet*) to safeguard that public order against external enemies, by using the sword of war (*Summa Theologica*, II-II, q. 40, a. 1c.)[58]

Moreover, just as a private individual must never intend to kill another person even in self-defence but proper public authority can intend to kill, so too it is only public

---

56 See Boyle J. (2003). Despite the fierce level of criticism I subject Boyle's arguments to I am deeply indebted to his article.

57 Of course, there are polities that do and have done terrorist acts. One could point clearly to some of the actions performed by North Korea and Afghanistan without in any way suggesting that certain actions of liberal democratic countries, such as the USA's involvements against the Sandinista regime in Nicaragua (to take but one case), should not be termed terrorist. In such cases the moral permissibility of engaging in war more closely aligns with traditional just war theory.

58 Henceforth *ST.*

authority that justifies the intention to kill in a just war: '... no private person has the right (*non pertinet ad personam privatam*) to initiate a war (*bellum movere*)' (Aquinas *ST*, q.40).[59]

Leaving aside difficulties that may arise in peripheral cases the waging of war requires three central conditions to be fulfilled in order to be morally justifiable:

1. legitimate public authority (*legitima auctoritas*),
2. just cause (*justa causa*), and,
3. proper intentions (*recta intentio*).

All three of these conditions together with a set of further specifications concerned with each must be met in order for a decision to wage war to be morally licit.[60] I will discuss each condition more fully below, however, it should be pointed out that even in the central cases of war in which all three conditions are fully met there are lacunae of a more practical nature. For example, proper public authority has limiting conditions over both the status of the authority and its moral rectitude and similarly just cause in and of itself is not sufficient since waging war against overwhelming odds which will cause severe suffering to innocents is deemed to be practically unreasonable, and right intentions may be defeasible through the use of certain illegitimate means.

Although my primary interest in this part of the chapter is with *jus ad bellum* there is nonetheless a requirement to briefly outline the foundational concepts of *jus in bello* and *jus post bellum* as there is a considerable degree of overlap between the three elements of traditional just war theory that are mutually enlightening. *Jus in bello* concerns the rules combating states must follow for the conduct of the war to be just. Such rules include prohibitions on the use of weapons of mass destruction such as nuclear weapons, biological or chemical agents and the like; requirements that no civilians (non-harmers) are to be deliberately attacked together with the infrastructure that supports non-combatants and correlatively that only those directly involved 'in harm' can be targeted; force may only be used proportionately to the end sought after; rules over the humane treatment of prisoners of war; no use of means *mala in se*, that is, that are evil in themselves such as lying, mass rape, genocide or treachery; and no willful reprisals or breaches of the rules of *jus in bello*.

Jus post bellum deals with the restoration of order, peace and justice after war. It includes principles of proportionality and publicity so that the settlement should be open and reasonable and not create the conditions for further injustice. Moreover, the settlement should secure the basic rights offended against but also promote the openness to fundamental human goods of the vanquished. Civilians are to receive

---

59 Nevertheless, Aquinas's account again admits of exceptions even to the notion of public authority. He entertains, but does not discuss in detail, peripheral cases in which a judge or 'even a private person' may legitimately defend the common good against 'bandits' when there is an incapacity to organize official resistance or when public authority is 'temporarily' absent. See *ST*. II-II, q. 123 a.

60 The other conditions are traditionally recognized as 'last resort', 'public declaration', 'probability of success' and 'proportionality.'

immunity from punishments and only those guilty of war crimes are to be punished. Punishment however must be proportionate and all war crimes must be punished on both sides. Compensation may be exacted but only on the condition that a polity's populace can still participate in fundamental human goods. Perhaps most importantly, there must be a concerted effort to rehabilitate the vanquished polity and its infrastructure.[61]

Proper Authority

Aquinas thinks that proper authority rests only with the head (*princeps*) of a polity. In the hierarchical world of the Middle Ages in Europe this would have been uncontroversial, however, there is nothing in the texts that require us to suppose that such authority need be individual, and therefore, the thrust of his discussion can cover constitutional and elected groups, such as is the case with contemporary democracies. Aquinas's concern with public authority addresses two concerns; first, that private individuals have no moral right to deliberately intend the deaths of others even in self-defence;[62] and secondly, that many disputes, conflicts and injustices can in principle be resolved by moving up the hierarchical chain, as it were, to courts of higher appeal. So the motivating factors are related to the requirement not to act in a private capacity with an intention to kill (only public authority can act on such an intention) and with procedural considerations related to peace so that only the ultimate public authority can legitimately draw the populace together for war. His justification for this approach is tied to Aquinas's definition of public authority and law which in the central case under discussion is:

> ... the rule (over) a free people ... the co-ordination of willing subjects by law which, by its fully public character (promulgation), its clarity, generality, stability and practicability, treats them as partners in public reason. (*ST*, I-II, q. 90; q. 95; q. 96 & 97)

The role then of public authority is one of trust invested in a 'sovereign' who has the care of the community, principally in respect to peace and justice, in their control.

It is worth noting that just as St Augustine was troubled by the notion of a private right to self-defence so too was Aquinas. Thus, it would be wrong to interpret Aquinas, as Rodin does (Rodin D., 2003 165–79) as thinking that the nature of a just war declared by proper public authority rests on an analogy between private self-defence and national self-defence. Indeed Aquinas at no point in his discussion of just war mentions a private right to self-defence; rather Aquinas's analogy is couched in terms of the legitimate authority exercised within a polity and extended to that authority exercised against outsiders (Boyle J., 2003, 156).

Leaving Aquinas for the moment it might well be speculated that given the nature of contemporary society proper public authority should be thought of in

---

61 For an excellent discussion of contemporary issues of *jus in bello* and *jus post bellum* see, Orend B. (2006).

62 See my fuller discussion in 'Torture, Tragedy and Natural Law', Chapter 2.2 in this volume.

terms of international bodies such as the United Nations and international law and conventions. Globalization and technology are two powerful factors in highlighting the international and transnational interdependence of contemporary states. In this context and despite ethnic, ideological, cultural and religious differences, when nations go to war the effects are often enough global and so it may well be thought that the prospect of investing proper public authority in a transnational body such as the United Nations is an ideal well worth pursuing. Clearly until such a body becomes effective particular states retain a *prima facie* duty to protect themselves from terrorism but the increasing interdependence of the contemporary world does seem to point in the direction just outlined and at some stage should be both procedurally and substantively central to the notion of public authority espoused in the just war tradition.

Just Cause

After proper public authority Aquinas settles on a second necessary condition for a just war – just cause. The motivating consideration here is drawn from his more general moral theory that any chosen action whatsoever must be done for a good reason and with a proper purpose. Unfortunately Aquinas provides us with no specific examples or reasons that justify a just war.[63] Nevertheless, beyond the elaboration of the moral principle just mentioned Aquinas points out that the nature of a just cause in respect to war is a *response* to the wrongdoing of outsiders and that the just war is essentially *punitive*, though punishment in Aquinas's account is deeply linked to justice. Here Aquinas refers approvingly to Augustine:

> We usually describe a just war as one that avenges wrongs, that is, when a nation or state has to be punished either for refusing to make amends for outrages done by its subjects or to restore what has been seized injuriously. (Quoted in Boyle J., 2003, 160)

This punitive dimension of Augustine and Aquinas's account of just war has come under immense criticism in recent times, particularly within the Catholic tradition. Thus, *The Catechism of the Catholic Church,* 2309, has *defined* just war as being solely defensive and not punitive, and this perspective is faithful to the Second Vatican Council's document *Gaudium et Spes* (itself a belated response to World War II) which declares:

> As long as the danger of war remains and there is no competent and sufficiently powerful authority at the international level, governments cannot be denied the right to legitimate self-defence, once every means of peaceful settlement has been exhausted. Therefore, government authorities and others who share public responsibility have the duty to protect the welfare of people entrusted to their care and to conduct such matters soberly … But it is one thing to undertake military action for the just defence of the people, and something else again to seek the subjugation of other nations. (*Gaudium et Spes*, para. 79)

---

63 For a later discussion with reasons and examples see Vitoria F. (1991).

Joseph Boyle has defended this innovation on traditional just war theory as being necessarily defensive and not punitive:

> The relationship between punishment, the common good of a polity, and the authority of the leaders who serve it are such that the punitive conception of just cause is not justifiable; in a word, leaders lack the authority to punish outsiders. The reasoning is as follows: political leaders have authority over their subjects and authority to punish malefactors. That authority is rooted in the common good of the polity and the special role of service which political leaders have to that good. The care for that good sometimes requires the use of force to stop and deter domestic criminals, those who share in the life of a political community but violate its just regulations. This reasonably includes the right to punish them as a means of restoring justice, which also enhances the fulfillment of the deterrent and defensive responsibilities of leaders. For the same reason, political leaders also have authority to lead and command defensive measures against externally based threats to the welfare of the polity. Defending subjects from injuries inflicted by outsiders plainly is a responsibility of those entrusted with the care of a polity's common good.
>
> What is needed at this point is a justification of the authority of the leaders of a polity not simply to command and organize defense from outside attack but precisely to punish those who are not its citizens or voluntary residents, namely, other polities and the subjects of other polities. For those who are resisted in defense do not thereby become subjects of the defending state. The condition of hostility does not make individual enemies participants in the common lives of the opposing communities, but only mutual external threats to those lives; similarly, the state of war does not collapse the common goods of the belligerents into one, or the authority of leaders into a kind of bloody election. A sign of the abiding political distinction among belligerent states and their citizens is the presumptive injustice of the victors lacking the impartiality of judges needed fairly to put the vanquished on trial.
>
> Yet that status of citizenship, that participation in the life of the community, is necessary if those who punish are to have the authority to do so. This is so because the authority to organize and command defense is not the stronger authority to punish, which involves imposing further burdens on those against whom defense is mounted than defense itself implies.
>
> Punishment can be a means to defense, insofar as it deters some from actions for which punishments are prescribed, and sometimes prevents the punished persons from continuing in their criminal activity. But it is possible to choose to defend without choosing to inflict any further harm on the attacker that might constitute punishment. The negative effects on those against whom one defends can perhaps be understood as punishment, but that sort of injury to the attacker is an unavoidable aspect of defense. Just as a private self-defender may ward off an attack with no punitive authority and no interest in punishing, so may a community.
>
> The stronger authority to punish is rooted in the leaders' coordination of the actions of community members for common action for the sake of a community's common good. That basis sets its limits. They may punish those over whom they have authority, not outsiders against whom they may authoritatively organize and defend. Consequently, the only ground for extending the authority beyond community members is instrumental. (Boyle 2003, 162–3)

I would like to address several issues raised by Boyle related to the innovation in traditional just war theory to exclude punishment. Boyle's argument that '… the defensive rather than punitive understanding of just cause which has developed in just war thinking in the 20th century is a proper development of traditional just war doctrine' (Boyle 2003, 163) is open to criticism on a number of fronts. His first point in defending the defensive model is that one cannot extend the right to justly punish internal acts of criminality to the punishment of external acts of terrorism because '… hostility does not make individual enemies participants in the common lives of the opposing communities, but only mutual external threats to those lives' (Boyle 2003, 163). This justification seriously underestimates the conditions of the contemporary world. It suffers from a rather old-fashioned notion of a polity or state as relatively homogeneous and separated (almost isolated) from other states and polities. It is precisely because the phenomenon of globalization, in particular in its economic form, itself embedded in a liberal democratic and hegemonic worldview, that renders this position untenable. We now inhabit a world that is so deeply inter-related that any appeal to the idea that there is no common good that is transnational, and so as Boyle thinks, that a polity is lacking in proper authority and just cause to punish terrorist action, is anachronistic. Economic (but not just economic) globalization has led to a very high degree of interdependence among sovereign nations and this can be readily discerned by the fact that a financial crisis, say, in South East Asia, has very serious consequences for the common good in much of the world.

Boyle also thinks that the punitive dimension of traditional just war theory is unjustified because the advocates of a just war involving punishment lack the 'impartiality of judges.' The legal analogy is a particularly weak one. If we have learned any lessons from critical legal theory in its manifold guises it is that the very notion of judicial impartiality is itself subject to social, economic, political and gender factors (Kelman 1987; Unger 1983; Brown and Halley (eds), 2003; Bauman 1996; 2002; Kennedy 2004). Certainly procedural and hopefully substantive objectivity among judges is an important idea but it is an ideal that everyday practices call into doubt. Moreover, once again internationalization and globalization have brought into sharp relief international bodies such as the United Nations and international courts, such as those for war crimes and human rights (a process stretching back to the Nuremberg trials) that even on a charitable reading of judicial impartiality would meet Boyle's criticism.[64]

Boyle believes further that the only ground for extending the just authority to punish from within a polity to terrorists from without (I leave aside the complex questions associated with internal terrorist activity for the purposes of this discussion) is instrumental. Here it would seem that he has in mind the coercive force of punishment which might deter future attacks. However this fails to capture a very significant dimension of the traditional Thomistic notion of retributive punishment, namely, the restoration of an order of justice that has been transgressed. The desire to punish when backed by proper authority is aimed at the good of redressing wrongs and is thus not primarily instrumental, although the deterrent aspect of just

---

64 Boyle also thinks that punishment 'can be a means to defense.' I will meet this objection directly in the next section on 'right intention.'

punishment, if it does in fact deter, is a side-effect of the restoration or recreation of a just equilibrium. Therefore, the traditional Thomistic conception of just punishment should not so readily be put aside, particularly in respect to just punishment of terrorists, which I discuss more fully later.

Right Intention

Even given that conditions (1) and (2) of a just war are fulfilled a war may still be unjust because it may be initiated with wrongful intentions, or during its course develop wrongful intentions. Thus wars engaged in out of hatred, a desire for revenge or for profit (oil) or some similar motive, or mixed motives, not fully consistent with justice will be unjust wars. Justice and peace are the central concerns and the ultimate rightful intentions guiding war and so a just cause does not excuse further mixed motivations. The key motivating condition here is related to the notion that a just war is in itself a 'last resort', that war is a 'bad' thing, and that the undoubted evils of war must serve the fundamental goods of justice and peace. Thus, the requirement of right intention is closely aligned with just cause and proper authority because the moral legitimacy of war, even in the context of a just cause and proper authority, leaves too much permissible without right intentions.

It is important to note that for Aquinas intention has a fully practical dimension. The fact that a person may desire and intend to flap their arm and fly is a matter of wishful thinking, of a volition that seeks to beat objective limitations.[65] This practical dimension to the notion of intention renders any action taken subject to practical requirements of reasonability. To engage in a war knowing, or having reasonable belief, that a polity will be soundly beaten with disastrous results for that polity is wrong, even when proper authority and just causes are present. The idea here is that it is practically unreasonable to have an intention that does not 'fit the facts' (Mooney 2000). It must be remembered that we are considering the case of a polity that goes to war with just cause and proper authority, in other words, a war proposed and engaged in by a public decision by those who are entrusted with the care of the community. The fact that individuals (soldiers) may engage in a war with motivations of hatred, revenge, and so on, is a different issue.

Right intention then is practically oriented towards specific and realizable goals which are reasonably believed to be achievable and which further the just cause by restoring or creating a more just peace. This, moreover, provides some of the reasons that shape the contours of *jus in bello*. The use of violence other than for the direct purposes of achieving justice and peace, of mixed motivations, of stratagems for ulterior purposes are all rejected by the close relationship between the three central conditions of just war. The fact that peace and justice are at the heart of right intention does not preclude concern or consideration for other goods associated with peace and justice (such as economic prosperity, safe travel, and so on) but these are, as it were, side-effects of the intention to create peace and justice. Just as it may legitimately be argued that certain benefits accrue from loving another person, it is

---

65 This notion is captured well in Plato's discussion of *pleonexia* in *Republic*, I.

nonetheless the case that what is loved *is* the other person, and the benefits supervene on such loving. One does not love the other person for the benefits that accrue, one's motivation to love is care for the other, the consequent benefits do not render the love of the person instrumental (see Mooney 2002). Similarly the benefits that accrue to the state of justice and peace should, in order for right intention to be fulfilled in just war, not be the motivating factors though they may be reasonably entertained as ancillary to the desire for justice and peace.

Nevertheless, to return to an earlier point, even a war fought with proper authority, just cause and right intention must be practically reasonable in a broader sense. I have in mind here that it will be an absolute requirement of just war in the sense I am elaborating that the goals of justice and peace are realizable. This requires of a polity engaging in a just war that the conditions for justice and peace cannot be 'one-sided' – the result cannot be justice and peace 'for us.' War, as a 'last resort', must, to be a just war, seek to engender the conditions of justice and peace (the goals that legitimate a just war) including the conditions that caused the original breach. These are unlikely to be capable of being achieved by war itself but nonetheless will be crucially tied to the notion of right intention and bolstered by the just war tradition of thinking on *jus post bellum*.

Proper Authority and the 'War on Terror'

It would seem that *prima facie* the leaders of a polity have the moral authority to respond to terrorist actions consonant with their responsibility of care for the community with which they are entrusted, just as they have authority to punish and deter criminal activity. Moreover this seems to be true at a broader level given that polities are increasingly not isolated but interdependent, and so the interests of justice and peace, will be concerned not just with a given polity's own 'subjects' but also its allies. Typically terrorist actions and threats not only cause deep wrongs in terms of the physical harms inflicted on innocents but also at a psychological level and thus represent severe attacks upon the public good. Thus, the moral legitimacy to respond to terrorism requires a holistic approach ranging through the education of the public to alert authorities to possible or actual sources of attack, through effective policing, surveillance, intelligence gathering up to and including military intervention.

Nevertheless, no polity exists, as I have repeatedly argued, as an independent entity and as a result the same constraints placed on just war, many of which have in the contemporary period led to the formation of international bodies and laws, must apply to the context of international operations. It thus seems to be important that restraints be placed on unilateral action. One reason for this is that in the practical realm 'mixed' motivations (or sometimes plain self-interest or the will-to-power) are prevalent and the necessary 'impersonality' required to fulfil the conditions of right intention and just cause will often enough be lacking. It does, therefore, seem to be both reasonable and prudent to consider the binding nature of international agreements and laws and thus to seek so far as possible a high level of international agreement. Once again the reason for this is plain – given the interdependent nature of the contemporary world unilateral military action is likely to suffer from sufficient bias, lack of information and insufficient impersonality so as to temper the central motivations required for a just war, namely, the realistic furthering of justice and peace. This however does not take away the right of an individual polity to wage a limited just war, rather it fosters a mentality of cooperation and consensus building and places checks on naked self-interest and wishful thinking. This consideration would appear to be wholly consonant with the application of traditional just war theory in the context of the contemporary world.

It must be admitted nonetheless that the context of the contemporary world creates a series of demanding questions that may not have been so clear cut in the Middle Ages when at least presumptively in Europe the social more of honor provided a backdrop to the exercise of war. Questions need to be addressed over preemptive military action and in particular against groups who are not themselves polities, but reside within the territory of a given polity (perhaps against the wishes of that polity's authorities) and whose territorial sovereignty may be transgressed in pursuit of terrorists. These sorts of complexities however are not the concern of this part of the chapter; suffice to say that difficulties of this kind provide further justification for requiring greater international cooperation and the fostering of such ties through more comprehensive and binding international agreements.

Just Cause and Terrorism

There are two central questions that need to be addressed in respect to the just war condition of just cause in relation to terrorism. Can a just cause against terrorism involve the punishment of terrorists? Or, on the other hand, must a just cause against terrorism be confined to defence? As I have already argued the notion of punishment delivered by public authority for the sake of justice and peace is central to the traditional just war theory espoused by Augustine and Aquinas. Nevertheless some contemporary just war theorists, particularly those closely associated with Catholic teachings have limited just war to defensive action (Boyle 2003).

I have already rehearsed the positions on this issue at a general level, here I merely apply these considerations to a just war on terrorism. Both positions hold in common the idea that military action taken against terrorism is justified, has a just cause, because of the wrong-doing of the terrorists both at the level of harm inflicted (or intended to be inflicted) on innocents and because of the climate of fear engendered by terrorist activity designed to alter a polity's structure, policies and order. Throughout this part of the chapter I have also worked with two assumptions (both controversial) that terrorists do not act in a just cause (because even on the assumption of some justice to the cause the means employed render the just cause redundant) as a 'last resort' and that terrorist organizations lack public authority (because they are putatively not entrusted with the care of the community as a common good). Both the punitive and defensive models of just cause thinking agree on this characterization of terrorism. So clearly there is relevant accounts of just cause against terrorism whether one works with the defensive or punitive models.

Problems however arise for the modern innovation of just war theory – the defensive model – in that a purely defensive conception has difficulties with the intrinsic nature of terrorist attacks. Once, for example, a terrorist act has already been committed any military action taken against the perpetrators of that act (though not perhaps the organization as such) would seem to be, at best, not a form of defence, and worse, purely instrumental. But perhaps it might be replied from the defensive model that terrorist activity is scarcely a 'one-off' action. Terrorist activity is coordinated, often long term and designed to break or alter the will of the polity and community under attack. Terrorists thus have a set of goals and often enough a relatively homogeneous set of intentions that unifies the terrorist group. It would then be argued that one can act defensively against such groups by preventing (further) terrorist activity, including against those who have already carried out terrorist actions, through the use of military force and by destroying the infrastructure that supports the on-going terrorist activity – seizing assets, destruction of safe-houses, and so on.

Nevertheless, this conception of defence does seem to stretch the notion a bit too much because it, on the same grounds, allows for preemptive and punitive actions against terrorists with a bit too much casuistical ingenuity. It can show why a defensive war against terrorism will allow for preemptive strikes and why a just war can be waged against an on-going terrorist group unified by a set of intentions that are socially consolidated within the group but what it fails to address is why this particular group of terrorists who have just bombed, murdered and maimed that group of innocents ought to be dealt with. In other words there is an important dimension of retributive justice as punishment that is left out of the picture. It is because there is a special kind of wrong-doing perpetrated by individuals X, Y and Z against the innocent individuals A, B and C (together with the effects on families, friends and the common good) that the purely defensive conception of just war is lacking. The intuition that undergirds this consideration is not purely instrumental in that it has deterrent or some similar value, nor is it narrowly retributive in the 'eye for an eye' sense; rather it is that the terrorist act constitutes an offense against the equilibrious order of justice. The restoration of a balance demands that just punishment be delivered to help restore or rebuild the equilibrium that has been so severely damaged by the terrorist act.

Right Intention and Terrorism

There are inherent practical difficulties associated with the final condition of right intention in order for a just war to be fought against terrorists. Such practical difficulties are the result of, or flow from, the complexity of the contemporary world. A just war will have a set of objectives that are constrained by practical or pragmatic features of the situation demanding military action, together with the constraints derived from *jus in bello* rules and deliberative constraints as to the likely consequences to the communities directly and indirectly effected *post bellum*.

Certainly there is considerable *de facto* reason to think that a just war with right intention can and should be waged against terrorists, and as I have argued, the set of right intentions need not be limited to purely defensive aims. But the matter is intractably complex. Just as a polity has the duty to protect the common good of people under its care from criminal activity so too it has the duty to protect the common good against terrorism. However the analogy with criminal activity can be pursued further. Are there limits to what a polity's leaders can justly do in defending (and propagating) the public good against criminals? While it is widely accepted that police services have a duty to protect and enhance the public good, should this include widespread and intrusive surveillance, draconian powers of detention and arrest, which for the public good may effect non-criminals? How should a polity act in situations in which criminal activity is largely located among socially (and economically) disadvantaged groups?

When one extends the analogy to contemporary terrorism the picture becomes even more complicated because terrorist groups are typically 'backed' by supporters and sympathizers who would never commit terrorist actions themselves, but who believe in the justice of terrorist causes, though they may well disapprove of the methods employed by the terrorist groups they sympathize with. How should such supporters and sympathizers be thought of and are they legitimately targets for defensive or punitive interventions? When considered from the perspective of the condition of right intention, it is the very 'mixed' nature of intentions that make it so difficult to assess whether or not right intentions are fulfilled in a manner suitable for a just war.

In other words it would seem that in order for there to be the requisite right intentions considerable deliberative and practical effort must be expended on the breaches of justice that breed the conditions under which malefactors resort to criminal activity, as too what breaches of justice create the conditions for terrorism. Clearly then the notion of right intention must be constrained, and deeply constrained, by *jus post bellum* thinking.

Moreover, the rightfully intended military response to terrorism must also be deeply constrained by *jus in bello* conditions. It would seem that right intentions can only be directed at those actually involved in the network of the terrorist groups. Sympathizers and supporters admit of very varying degrees and certainly just punishment or attacks on infrastructure of personal as opposed to logistic support would appear only to widen and deepen the conflict which the just war intends to correct. A central feature then of right intention must be the firm resolve to win over hearts and thus to fully address the causes that give rise to the terrorist threat.

It is for these reasons that a just war with right intention must never be anything but a last resort. Every political, social, economic, psychological and practical avenue must be exhausted. The world is a precarious and often dangerous place, we all live subject to tragedy and the possibility of loss. We cannot remove all risk from life and as a result perhaps a certain level of terrorism (contained as far as possible) needs to be accepted as another tragic dimension of ordinary life, as we prepare the conditions for addressing the causes of terrorism, and so to create, not just the absence of war, but the *amicitia* that fully grounds peace and justice. As Joseph Boyle notes: '... a just cause must serve peace and not simply protect an unjust status quo' (Boyle 2003, 170). It is my contention that just intention must have as a condition *sine qua non* an intention to rectify the causes that lead to terrorism if this is at all possible.

In this part of the chapter I have assumed that terrorist acts are wrong and on this assumption argued that a polity has a right to wage a just war on terrorism. I have further argued that the conditions for such a just war are settled by the three central conditions of traditional just war theory in respect to *jus ad bellum*, including a punitive dimension. Nevertheless, these conditions need to be supplemented with the other requirements of *jus in bello* and *jus post bellum*. The requirements of such a just war place severe restrictions on the right to engage, conduct and bring to a close a just war on terrorism to such an extent that much of what is now called the 'war on terror' fail to meet these requirements and thus render that war, in many respects, unjust.

References

Aristotle, *Nichomachaean Ethics*.

—— *Politics*, Book 1.

Augustine, *City of God*.

Bauman, R.W. (2002), *Ideology and Community in the First Wave of Critical Legal Studies* (University of Toronto Press).

—— (1996), *Critical Legal Studies: A Guide to the Literature* (Westview Press).

Boyle, J. (2003), 'Just War Doctrine and the Military Response to Terrorism,' *The Journal of Political Philosophy*, 11, 2, 153–70.

—— *et al.* (Finnis, J. and Grisez, G.) (1987), *Nuclear Deterrence, Morality and Realism* (Oxford: Clarendon Press).

Brown, W. and Halley J.E. (eds) (2003), *Left Legalism/Left Critique* (Duke University Press).

Gaudium et Spes.

Johnson, J. (1984), *Can Modern War Be Just?* (New Haven: Yale University Press).

—— (1999), *Morality and Contemporary Warfare* (New Haven: Yale University Press).

Kelman, M. (1987), *A Guide to Critical Legal Studies* (Harvard University Press).

Kennedy, D. (2004), *Legal Education and the Reproduction of Hierarchy: A Polemic Against the System* (New York University Press).

Mooney, B.T. (2000), 'Dennett on Ethics: Fitting the Facts against Greed for the Good' in Brook A., *et al.* (eds), *Dennett's Philosophy: A Comprehensive Assessment* (The MIT Press), pp. 309–27.

—— (2002), 'Plato on the love of individuals', *The Heythrop Journal*, Vol. 43, No. 3, pp. 311–27.

Orend, B. (2006), *The Morality of War* (Ontario: Broadview Press).

Rodin, D. (2003), *War and Self-Defense* (Oxford: Oxford University Press).

Unger, R.M. (1983), *The Critical Legal Studies Movement* (Harvard University Press).

Vitoria, F. (1991), *Political Writings* (Cambridge: Cambridge University Press).

Walzer, M. (2000), *Just and Unjust War* (New York: Basic Books).

—— (2004), *Arguing About War* (New Haven: Yale University Press).

Author Index

Subject Index